IRONS IN THE FIRE

REMINISCENCES OF A LIFETIME

by

Henry Michael Morley

*To Felicity,
all my love and
best wishes

Mike
March '06*

Hideaway Publications Ltd

© Henry Michael Morley 2005

The moral rights of the author have been asserted.

This book has been printed digitally for
Hideaway Publications Ltd
4 Erroll Road, Hove,
East Sussex, BN3 4QG
United Kingdom

Database right: Lightning Source UK Ltd (maker).

All rights reserved. No part of this publication may be reproduced, stored in a retrieval system, or transmitted, in any form or by any means, without the prior permission in writing of Hideaway Publications Ltd, or as expressly permitted by law, or under terms agreed with the appropriate reprographics rights organisation. Enquiries concerning reproduction outside the scope of the above should be sent to the Hideaway Publications Ltd, at the address above

You must not circulate this book in any other binding or cover and you must impose this same condition on any acquirer.

ISBN 0-9525477-2-4

Cover Design by Ashprint, Eastbourne
Photograph on Back Cover by Sarah Bourne

CONTENTS

Chapter 1: Childhood — Page 1

1. The Twenties - Preston
2. The Thirties - Ashwood Villas, Leeds
3. The Family
4. Grandparents: The Forsyth Line
5. Grandparents: The Morley Line
6. My Mother and Father
7. Cousins in the Thirties
8. Neighbours
9. Pastimes
10. Out and About Ashwood Villas
11. Schools in the Thirties
12. The Presbyterian Church
13. Holidays in the Thirties

Chapter 2: Adolescence — Page 53

1. Outbreak of War
2. Escape to the Farm
3. Brian Barton
4. The Grammar School Re-opens
5. Events at the Airfield
6. Aftermath
7. School in the Upper Sixth

Chapter 3: Pre-Adulthood — Page 95

1. First Bite of the Cherry
2. The Navy Lark
3. The Second Bite

Chapter 4: Apprenticeship — Page 147

1. Education and the Rugby Field
2. A Term at Stowe
3. Teaching at Sevenoaks School
4. Meeting Vera McKechnie
5. Wedding Bells

Chapter 5: Maturity in Eastbourne — Page 185

1. Moving to Eastbourne
2. Settling in
3. Seven years in Westcliff Mansion
4. Children at Home
5. Teaching at the Grammar School
6. The Uses of English
7. Changing Sites and Heads
8. Extra-Mural Activities
9. Family Relations
10. Marital Breakdown
11. The Sixth Form College emerges
12. Marriage à la Second Mode
13. Coming through Retirement
14. Conclusion

Appendix   A Plethora of Play Productions   Page 235

For Simon, Kate and Emma, my children,
the Morley-Forsyth families,
my loved ones
and my friends

Foreword

I have enjoyed writing these memoirs and make no apology for wanting to put them into book format. I have no ambitions to be 'published', being aware that there are always too many authors with far higher claims for attention than me, both in terms of achievement and skill. On the other hand, retrospectively from the resting point of my retirement years, there is a genuine personal fascination in recalling the past and trying to evaluate (no, simply record) the various stages of my development – a process which in my reckoning is divisible into five Ages: Childhood, Adolescence, Pre-Adulthood, Apprenticeship and Maturity. Of course, there are traditionally two more Ages, one of which I am in as I tap away at my PC, shrunk shank and all, though I hope my voice has not turned to childish treble. As for mere oblivion, well, I think I can accept that gladly, partly because I have measured out my life into a kind of order and become reconciled to whatever has happened. There is no moral message or didactic intention, except perhaps that 'the child is father to the man'.

I have tried not to libel or offend anyone. My reminiscences are based on truly held beliefs and memories. At times, I withhold full names but I have not disguised any of the 'characters'. If this leads to the bruising of sensitive egos or any sense of injustice, I apologise. Actually the biggest complaint will probably be the paucity of reference to friends and colleagues, but this is my story and there is a limit to the budget.

Thanks to the family, however far-flung, for being there. The last generation moves ever outwards; 'things fall apart, the centre cannot hold'. I hope this account of a lifetime provides a finger-hold for anyone spinning too fast out of range.

CHAPTER ONE

CHILDHOOD

1. The Twenties: Preston

Although bred in Yorkshire, I was born in Preston, a Lancastrian town. The birth date was 16th June 1926, and I am the third son of Noel (Doe) and Margaret (Cissie) Morley who were married in Chester in 1913. The family moved east of the Pennines at the end of the twenties and I have not been to Preston since leaving for Leeds in the West Riding. The rose was always white after that move. Memories of my birthplace are hazy; I was four years old when we left.

How far back can we remember? Some people say they recall being born, even the moment of delivery and the tying of the umbilical cord; under hypnosis they behave like babies. In my opinion autosuggestion and a lively imagination give rise to many a false memory. I reckon if you can remember anything before the age of three, you have done well.

One incident from early life in Preston makes me wonder. My mother told me more than once that I had narrowly escaped death or maiming as a toddler. Apparently I had trotted into the road whilst out for a family walk and bounced off the front mudguard of a passing motorcar. I affirm quite flatly that no memory of this remains. Apparently I was thrown back on to the pavement and my parents were amazed that I seemed to suffer no ill effects. Did the car stop? Was I entirely to blame? Were there floods of tears?

What I do remember is that for a period of time during those Preston days I was engaged in a curious terror of one particular car-driver. His car was not the one I bounced off (if any image remained it was of a black mudguard and this man's car was a light colour) but for some reason he played a little game with me. When I saw his car approaching on the main road, I scuttled to the wall for safety and he pretended to swing the wheel over as if heading for me. He grinned at me as he drove past. Eventually I told my mother – that's why I remember the experience. I have no memory of any action being taken but somehow I outgrew this terror. Or maybe we moved from Preston to Leeds. There is no doubt in my mind that the bouncing incident was at the root of my 'phobia', even though the memory was submerged.

I can date my earliest memory of Preston from May 10th 1929. I can be exact about this because that was when my youngest brother was born. I was a toddler of two and eleven-twelfths, and a nursemaid was looking after me while my mother was in labour and away from home. I missed my mother, without knowing what was going on. I suppose a new baby had been talked about but I was too busy toddling with the nurse-maid to care and then I remember being taken to the maternity home (not big enough to be a hospital) and there was my mother high up in a bed, lying back on pillows and smiling down at me as I stood at the foot of the bed holding the nurse-maid's hand, totally bewildered by this unexpected sight. My mother was there, she was obviously welcoming and I was pleased to see her, but what was the meaning of the little bundle she was holding, a bundle with some kind of screwed-up pink face at the top? Was this the start of sibling rivalry? I certainly became aware that somebody else belonged to my mother without necessarily belonging to me.

As for first memories of my father during these early years, I have one distinct image of him being helped out of rough waves that crashed on the beach where I stand helpless and uncomprehending. He staggers, doubled up with exhaustion; someone has thrown a towel over his bent shoulders and a man holds him from collapsing. Recently I asked brother John, three years older than me, if he remembers the occasion when Dad nearly got drowned. "Of course I do!" he replied, "It was his own fault!"

John was able to pinpoint the date to the summer of 1930 and the place too – Cleveleys, north of Blackpool, where the family was on holiday. Apparently my father had decided to ignore the red flag which signified dangerous swimming conditions. Obstinately, on a bleak grey day, he had taken us two boys with him to the beach – maybe to occupy us while Mum looked after the new baby. I imagine I pottered about building sand castles with brother John, unaware that Dad was out there trying to cope with rolling breakers and a treacherous undercurrent that pulled him further and further from the shore. He was capable of the breaststroke but little else in the way of powerful swimming.

As we pat the wet sand into buckets, there are shouts and cries; passers-by point to the dot in the water and watch as someone runs down to plunge to the rescue but I don't seem to realise what's going on. I suddenly look up to see Dad emerging from the crashing waves like a phantom castaway, haggard and shivering, his eyes staring blankly at us. He lies on the cold beach until an ambulance whisks him away. What do John and I do, two little orphans of the storm? Someone must have 'rescued' and taken us to our lodgings where no doubt Mum was having one fit or another. I remember being in the bedroom where Dad lay inert and watching as he suddenly leans over the side and retches into a jerry, brown water flowing out of his open mouth. And Mum hurries me out of the room, still bewildered.

But Dad recovered after a day or two and was well enough to meet the Lifesaver who pulled him from the salty jaws of death. I hope he bought him a pint of the best. Apparently it was reported in the local paper and the Lifesaver was commended for his brave action in saving my father who was correctly described as a visiting Inspector of Taxes on holiday. The outcome of that became a family joke for it seems the Lifesaver received an anonymous letter from someone who had read the report in the paper. The writer simply

CHILDHOOD

commented: "Dear Lifesaver, Next time you see a Tax Inspector in trouble, let the bugger drown."

Raking through the conduits of memory I discover nothing untoward or remotely spectacular about Preston. I have no recollection of family tiffs. I spent quite a lot of time astride my tricycle, pedalling up and down Hall Road which was flat and quite possibly a cul-de-sac. I possess an old sepia snap of myself and John sitting on our trikes, grinning at the camera in the back garden of our house probably. There is a more clearly defined memory of another tricycle incident, one of my favourites. It is a warm summer's evening and I am sitting on my trike near our house clutching a new penny. Because it glitters like gold, I can't stop looking at it in my hand. Some grown-up has given it to me and I treasure it. I show it to a friend and we both study it closely, me on my trike, the other little boy standing beside me. There are railings marking the border of the pavement and beyond these a small field full of summer grass. After looking at it for some time, my friend, whoever he is, tries to spin the coin or throw it up in the air. Why? I don't know, for the fun of it maybe. We watch it curve and drop over the railings into the long grass in the field. It disappears, no longer glinting but hidden from view. We peer through the railings in dismay, especially me for it is my penny. How can we look for it? The railings are too high to climb but there is a gate further along the road and so we run quickly to enter the field, deserting the trike, which marks the spot where the coin must have landed.

We search on hands and knees, parting the tufts of grass, looking for the buried treasure. I think I am close to tears, not a little resentful of my friend's rash action in spinning the coin. In the end we give up searching and I look angrily at him as he tries to explain what has happened. He tells me there are fairies living in the grassy field. They must have seen or felt the golden penny land near their hideouts and spirited it away. The fairies have taken my treasure and I won't get it back ever.

I believed him. I stared in wonder at the grass growing in the field. Useless to keep looking for the penny, it was no longer mine. I went back to my trike thoughtfully, but not at all angry and really quite pleased – even honoured except that I wouldn't have known that word. There was a bond between me and the little people who, every child knows, dwell in the underworld. If I had to part with my penny, I was glad the fairies claimed it. It made me feel just a bit special so I believed my little friend. It never occurred to me that he might be fibbing. He might have believed in fairies himself for all I remember.

It seems amazing that I have no recollections of Preston town, or even our family house, number 6 Hall Road, Fulwood. My father told me, years later, that he had kept ownership of the house (semi-detached or terrace?) and it proved a bad idea because there was a sitting tenant when 1939 froze all rents. Eventually the roof had to be replaced, costing a lot more than the rent, and Dad sold the house to the tenant cheaply in the fifties, glad to be shot of it. As for the town, probably I travelled no further than a few streets from home. I know what a Lancashire cotton-mill town looks like but I remember seeing nothing like that. Was I unusually ignorant of my surroundings or is this the normal response to an early environment?

2. The Early Thirties: Ashwood Villas, Leeds

Moving from Preston to Leeds was a step up from town to city though I don't know if Charles Dickens would have found much difference in mid-Victorian times. He visited Preston and based his iniquitous industrial Coketown in "Hard Times" on his experiences there. He might just as well have chosen Leeds, except the dark satanic mills were woollen not cotton and there was a vast proliferation of commercial activities in Leeds to match the manufacturing factories that belched foul fumes from tall chimneys in the Aire valley. By the time the Morley family moved in, Leeds was a conurbation that had expanded far beyond the rows of back-to-back houses where workers lived and toiled in expectation of a better life to come. Factory owners had built vast stone mansions on the industrial outskirts, nudging the landed gentry rather rudely, and the spaces in between were filled with housing developments of all sorts and sizes, mainly catering for the expanding layers of middle class citizens.

I lived for seventeen vitally formative years in number 9 Ashwood Villas, Headingley, Leeds during the thirties and forties. The Villas occupied a rectangle of land between two large mansions with extensive gardens. They consisted of about twenty granite-faced semi-detached houses each with modest front and back gardens, and a straight central lane, which like an aisle provided access to each property. This lane was cobbled and quite steep, with trees and bushes helping to give an air of privacy. It was certainly not built for cars. Few residents had garages or cars; we didn't, as no one knew how to drive. A vast, black-smutted Victorian Gothic Congregational Church marked the turning off the main road. At the top end of the Villas there was a T-junction road named Ashwood Terrace, which had a side entrance and a dead end. It provided a private play area for the Villa and Terrace boys (there were no girls). The compact limited development was without doubt secluded and somewhat exclusive.

I took it all for granted of course. The whole complex is a space-time continuum which needs sorting out, particularly in relation to 'my memoirs'. It's like a box with glass sides and having left it I can't get back in. I can only peer at it from the outside. Not that I have wanted to return. It took 30 years before I decided to pay a fleeting visit to my roots in the Villas. It was a moving experience and I wrote a poem afterwards:

CHILDHOOD

Ashwood Villas

I missed the turning at first.
Two squat pillars mark the entrance
but they have shrunk with age.
The trees overhanging garden walls
lean over silent cobblestones.
Where we played Across and Across
my arms outstretched can almost
touch the sides…almost –
the gap is still wide enough
to let the memories through.
But there is room for cricket
till you lose the ball in gardens
thick with laurel leaves.

The single lamp-post, base for
a thousand hide and seeks, still
keeps watch. Touch and Pass is like
a fleeting scamper through the past,
sending me running home again
to gulp Dandelion and Burdock.

The grey house bulks larger though,
as if absence has made it grow up.
The windows are inscrutably blank
And the front door impassive.

I remain outside, finding the garden
dwindles comfortingly.
The house is unentered
Dark corridors and rooms unexplored.

   I have entered the house since I wrote this poem but only in 'virtual reality'. Something quite extraordinary has occurred while I have been trying to put together these pages of early reminiscence and it's worth reversing direction to provide a 'flash forward' to 2001 which is the year I am starting to compile my Memoirs. What happened seems remarkable to me but maybe you will consider it is simple coincidence; on the other hand, maybe this is a case of 'synchronicity': disparate events seeming to inter-relate in time significantly.

IRONS IN THE FIRE

It is mid-2001. I take a break from tapping my early memories into the Amstrad and drive up to Scarborough to visit my brother John, who is not well. In the evening the family sit down to relax and Steve, John's son-in-law, asks if I have seen any of the TV programmes in the series entitled "The Middle Class". I knew of this documentary series which was broadcast only a month or so previously but I had ignored the programmes, feeling temperamentally unattracted to the bourgeoisie and preferring to think about my memoirs. So in answer to the question I say 'No' somewhat dismissively and Steve says the first episode is particularly interesting as it focuses on the rise of the middle class in Leeds during the nineteenth century. He has by chance actually made a video recording of this programme so would I like to see it?

Politely I settle on the sofa to while away an hour, vaguely interested in seeing black and white photographs of Leeds in its smoky Victorian days. There are long panning shots of the dark ribbons of terraced houses in narrow streets, prison-like factories with chimneys competing with church spires to rise above the pall that settles over Kirkstall and Hunslet; and lots of people in funny hats strutting jerkily all over the place. And then the camera colours the screen with views of a leafy sunny modern suburb where the Victorian middle-classes had established a salubrious headquarters through prospering times, in residential estates situated above the grey pall that drifted over valley dwellers. Although the ground level was on a par with the top of factory chimneys, the prevailing winds blew the industrial waste eastwards so Headingley had become a desirable area of the city to settle in. I am mildly excited to recognise local landmarks like the County Cricket Ground and St Michael's Church near the elementary school I attended before going to the Grammar School. This is my part of town all right.

Apparently, Headingley in mid-Victorian times was rapidly providing a variety of new properties catering for the newly emergent middle-class families, some lower middle, some middle middle, some upper middle and some unusually middle class. In search of the latter, the TV camera suddenly started to zoom into a particular Headingley locality and entered a narrow cobbled lane with two stone pillars marking the entrance. We were looking up an incline with greenery and houses with front gardens on both sides. It all seemed a trifle familiar but it wasn't until the commentator identified this as a typical mid-Victorian housing estate designed for 'professional' middle-class families that I realised this was MY street filmed in modern Technicolor glory. The man was saying, "This is Ashwood Villas" and there was no doubt about it, I was on home ground. I was able to recognise the houses and even recall the names of neighbours who had lived in the houses in my time. "Well!" I exclaimed, "What a coincidence!"

And then the camera lingered at a garden gate and we were looking at one of the houses head on. The narrator was explaining how we need to look more closely at the kind of property that was built for typical middle-class families of

CHILDHOOD

Victorian society so we walked up the path to the front door, all somehow rather familiar, and there it was, as plain as a pikestaff on the front door: number nine. We were entering number 9 Ashwood Villas: occupied by the Morley family sixty years after being built in mid-Victorian times. And yet it wasn't the same.

The same front door, though painted blue not green; the same front window through which we peered to see a girl tinkling on the piano but that wasn't quite right, the piano was out of position for our drawing room. The pokey passageway that led to the kitchen was too light and spacious but I remembered we had hung our outdoor coats from hooks along the dark, unlit side of this corridor. The hall, stairs and banisters were no longer a drab brown but brilliant white. Upstairs there was still the same staircase leading to the attic and maid's room but it was painted white. The damp dark cellars, used by us as washhouse, coal and coke store, now seemed like a garden flat, with a Victorian fireplace gleaming spick and span. The whole house was spotlessly clean; colours blazed, white gleamed and there were no dark corners. TV spotlights and a modern facelift made it seem as good as new and very nice too. Only it wasn't like my family home where four big boys bounced round the house during the thirties and forties, by which time no doubt the 'select middle-class image' was wearing thin. I reckon these TV documentary makers had led me up the garden path and though I could recognise corridors and rooms in the house I wasn't getting an authentic picture of my life in nine Ashwood Villas. I wondered if this make-over, probably inspired by Oscar Wilde's House Beautiful concepts, was any closer to the Victorian reality.

At least this 'coincidence' has led me to ponder my 'middle-class origins'. Steve recorded that programme upon a whim; by chance I visited Scarborough and saw the video. At that point of time I was trying to recall life in Ashwood Villas. Mere coincidence? Or a case of 'synchronicity'? Maybe psychic forces are at work. I await revelations as I remember a childish and somewhat petulant memory of life in the Villas...

I am standing at the front door of the house, looking at a big dark car which is slowly stopping beside the front gate. My mother, dressed to go out, stoops to kiss me and no doubt tells me to be a good boy. I hold someone's hand, probably the maid's, as Mum hurries down the path holding the familiar bundle and enters the car – she does not have to bend to sit comfortably, for this is an old-fashioned saloon car – and she waves to me happily before the car-door closes. But I have seen the bundle in her arms, the cradled new baby who claims her attention, and as the car starts to roll down the lane, I realise that I am being left behind, my brother is going for a ride in this magic chariot and I am not included. I don't cry; I just look reproachfully at my mother as she calls out "Bye bye" and the maid speaks comforting words. Mother smiles and looks at me. The car purrs as it drops out of sight. The front door closes. I carry on with my life, perhaps pushing a Dinky toy across the carpet. I don't think I resent my brother's privilege, nor do I think I am under-loved. The event has no undertones. Yet it has stayed with me for 70 years.

I remember rickets, spittle and pea-soupers from toddling along the streets of Leeds in the early thirties. There were matchstick men to place beside Lowry's Salford citizens. They were thin and wiry, big-booted and cloth-capped, with dark tight jackets and trousers but in Leeds they were bow-legged. I don't recall Lowry's figures being bandy; Leeds was noted for tykes suffering from rickets due to lack of calcium. Curiously, thinking of later years in Leeds, I recall no proliferation of deformed legs and I may have exaggerated the number; probably the civic health authority had cracked the problem with fortified water by the time I was staring at these urban cowboys who propelled themselves on curved legs. I hope I stared at them compassionately, aware that life had given them a raw deal, but I couldn't abide the globules of green and brown spittle they might leave on the pavement.

'Spitting is forbidden' or 'No Spitting' were common edicts in the trams of Leeds. To be fair, these round glittering galaxies were rare in the lower deck but often-evident upstairs (beyond the scrutiny of conductors). There were of course spit and sawdust bars in dark alleys in the city centre, and spittoons in the corners of pubs in those days ("ah, how I miss the spittoons..."/"You always did...").

Coughing up phlegm and catarrh was preferable to swallowing it, which really is a disgusting alternative, but only ladies and gentlemen of the middle classes kept handkerchiefs in their pockets or in handbags for the disposal of personal detritus. The pollution caused by industrial activity was obviously to blame. The atmosphere in Leeds was rarely clean and fresh, and people breathed air that was thick with particles of carbon and other chemicals. Who wouldn't want to dredge one's bronchial tubes, hawk and isolate a firm globule within the mouth, and then gently lob the foreign bodies as far as possible. Pea-soupers were the ultimate outcome of smoke and fog hanging in the atmosphere, producing a thick yellow blanket through which you almost literally felt your way blind-fold. Wrap a handkerchief over your mouth, breathe in sharply and then look at the dense yellow-brown stain. Every inhalation could rot your lungs.

Of course such pea-soupers (portmanteaued to 'smogs') were not limited to industrial towns and cities in the north of England, nor were they a new phenomenon, but they were certainly new to me. Leeds was cursed with one or two pea-soupers every winter. In one of them Uncle Les wrapped his Ford V8 round a lamppost in the City Centre and Auntie Glad, his passenger, broke her leg and sustained other injuries. As far as I know, it was post-war smokeless fuel that made the biggest difference after the war but, although everyone shared the pea-soupers in the thirties, I could always retreat into the secure self-contained

CHILDHOOD

world of the Villas where at least nobody spat on the cobbles and few bandy-legged visitors called.

Ashwood Villas was both a haven and a shell which no doubt was a good thing but, looking back, I think it must have contributed to my remaining somewhat detached from the 'real' world, and certainly far from being 'street-wise'. One early incident perhaps indicates a naive expectation of security and protection, though I don't really believe that because we had only recently moved into number 9 and damn it all, I was more or less at home. Maybe it was my first experience of nastiness.

I am aged perhaps five, stockily trudging up the cobbles towards my home, alone though I have no idea where I am coming from. Reaching the low hedge which fronts our garden I look up at the bedroom window where my mother is at her dressing table, probably brushing her hair. When she sees me she waves and smiles. I smile and wave back. I am sure our eyes meet. Suddenly two boys come running towards me from the top of the lane, laughing and shouting my name. I don't really know them, they are distant neighbours and I have not played with them since we moved in, yet here they are calling to me as if greeting a friend. I remember standing by the gate, shining with pleasure and glancing up at the window where my mother stands, as if to say, 'Look, Mummy, two boys coming to play with me, they're glad to see me, isn't it nice!'

Then they arrive, noisily bouncing round me, clutching my arms roughly, swinging me about and their voices take on a jeering note. I realise they are teasing, pretending to welcome me but actually taunting. I don't know why they did this. I look up at my mother, now staring down from her window with a frown, and self-control deserts me. I burst into tears and run up the path, leaving the two boys jeering and laughing. I remember running round the side of the house to the back door because the front door was shut, blubbing loudly though I wasn't physically hurt. Howling with self-pity, tears streaming down my cheeks, I ran up the stairs and burst into my mother's room, seeking her sympathy at this outrage, wanting her to embrace and soothe me with words of love. Unexpectedly my mother was angry and scolded me. "Stop crying at once!" she said. "That's not the way to behave. You have to stand up for yourself, not run away crying!"

I stopped blubbing at once. Suddenly my mother was not on my side, she had seen it all and chose to criticise me. I can still see her standing darkly in front of the window and little me standing in the doorway snuffling and sulking, trying to make sense of my mother's reaction. She was angry, yes, furious with those two boys' behaviour, but she was more upset by my response. Of course she eventually comforted me but the message got home. Dissolving into tears and running is no way for a brave little boy to behave, nor for a big one, but looking back, I wonder if either my mother or myself every really understood why I fled in tears that afternoon. Was it cowardice or indignation that I was made to look silly in front of her (though that did count) I think what really made me weep was the experience of deception and the betrayal of friendship; and the inadequacy of my innocence. I never played with those boys, in fact they must have left the Villas because there is no recollection of them in my memories of the thirties but then I recall very few friends outside the family in those early times. We were a self-contained family unit with Uncles and Aunts and Cousins living in the vicinity. There were of course neighbourly boys but surprisingly few lived in the Villas and Terrace and certainly there was always a dearth of girls, which was not considered a loss at the time.

3. The Family

It started in 1913 when my parents married. The wedding photograph shows clearly the six foot three height of Dad, wearing an unusually smart morning suit and a rather soppy smile, and sporting a somewhat bushy moustache that he shaved off eventually, prior to his going bald. He looks well pleased with the situation. My mother stands as tall as the best man and her brother Alec, and she is beautiful with floral veil and bouquet. Her dark hair is lustrous and thick. My father kept her dark locks when Mum cut her hair short (when?) and I still have this precious keepsake in my possession.

I don't know if my parents went in for family planning but certainly I suspect that after the birth of my eldest brother Fred in 1918 they were hoping for a baby-girl to join the family. Three more boys may have been a bit disappointing for them but it wasn't just ringing the changes that motivated Mum and Dad. Their first-born child had been a girl, christened Agnes Marcia, though she was always called simply Pat. She died in 1919, a victim of the 'flu' epidemic that swept through Europe in the wake of the Great War. She was six years old, a beautiful child who impressed everyone with her depth of personality. Her death must have been all the harder to bear because my mother was nursing a new born babe, a boy, while Pat was breathing her last. Mum and Dad never spoke much about Pat but they didn't have to; we boys apprehended what my parents had lost even though the details were vague.

I possess a soft-toned sepia studio photograph of this gently smiling, level-eyed child whom I never knew. I guess she was about five when it was taken. My parents chose not to display this during the Ashwood Villa years, possibly for the good reason that there were two oil paintings of Pat on regular show. These portraits were both painted by Frances Dodd R.A. who lived with her sister Phyllis in Chester near to my parents. They were good neighbours and the paintings were a tribute to family friendship. In the portraits Pat looks younger and more round-faced than in the photograph but with the same bobbed hair and

CHILDHOOD

straight fringe. In the larger painting she is sitting on a tea trolley with a basket of cherries by her side; this hung in the dining room, though never in a frame which is odd because it is a charming picture (now framed by me!) though thinly painted, as if the final touches were never applied. The other painting is a fine close-up of Pat's head and shoulders, a beautiful study of innocent freshness in an oval gold frame. This hung over the mantelpiece in the drawing room and really it became part of the furniture to us boys, taken for granted but nevertheless a presence like a fond memory.

When I was a teen-ager (and tall enough), I would approach the mantelpiece, perhaps stand on the fire-kerb and put my arms on the shelf so I could gaze long and closely into that child's face, particularly into her eyes, which shone and looked straight at me. She was brown-eyed like my mother. Pat was a beautiful image to grow up with, and I claim a special relationship on account of my silent communion with her portrait, though what my adolescent thoughts and feelings were I can't really say.

Brother Frederick James (named after both grandfathers) was eight years older than me, born in 1918. To begin with I don't think he impinged on my existence, and vice versa, for I have no recollection of any events that involved us both. But he was always there and gradually I became aware of the interesting things he was doing. I hero-worshipped him without realising it, my big brother who was so active and talented. Fred had a marvellous decade in the thirties, cut short when War broke out and he had to enlist. I expect he went straight to the Grammar School when we moved to Leeds and he fared well, though not academically. He was athletic and a good team player. In rugby and cricket he was awarded his colours, and was selected to attend the 1936 Duke of York's summer Camp, which attempted to mix socially upper and lower class adolescents. This may even have been the last such Camp, as the Duke of York had to become George VI. I remember Fred returning from the Camp, glowing with pride because his 'team' had won the first prize. No doubt he shook hands with royalty! And then Fred started to train as an architect at Leeds College of Art. This would be in 1937 and Fred proved a brilliant student, both in concepts and in model making.

Fred lived in the attic of number 9. It was quite a big room with windows jutting from the roof and walls angled interestingly, the only flaw being the water tank which bubbled and hissed, disturbing the isolated seclusion of the place. Here Fred would model wonderful modern housing estates or luxurious villas, which were part of his training. He seemed to work hard and enthusiastically but still found time to be one of the founders of a company of amateur entertainers called the Co-Optimists. Most of the players were Grammar and High School ex-pupils in love with the stage, but there was a very accomplished swing band called 'The Melodiensians' and the Players went round the Church Halls providing wholesome, pretty self-indulgent entertainment to packed audiences. We younger boys were thrilled to watch these spectacular (to us) productions and of course the influence on our own theatrical interests was immense.

Fred was always tolerant, good-humoured and robust with his brothers, but quite sensibly he didn't spend much time with us. His was an ideal influence, making us aware of outside interests but not hampering or pouring scorn on our own development. I think Mum and Dad were immensely proud of his successes, which seemed to keep at bay the usual worries about girl friends. As far as I remember, Fred didn't have a special 'girl-friend' at this time and certainly there was no local lass in the Villas to seduce him!

Brother John David was 5 years younger than Fred and 3 years older than me. Being in the middle can cause problems. I don't know whether little John had trouble accepting me as a new bundle getting in the way, but I guess there was no great contact with Fred, for five years is a long time between brothers and no doubt he worshipped Fred rather like me – from a distance. John was a sensitive boy and slightly nervous in disposition which may have been due to nature or nurture. He used to 'wet the bed' regularly and that caused a lot of lamentation. Dad once confided in me that there had been a visit to London with Mum while she was carrying John in her womb. Whilst there, she was scared out of her wits by an Italian who went berserk in the boarding house, running up and down the stairs with a knife and threatening everyone. John was always tall for his age but not strongly built and although he went to the Grammar School he never shone in the classroom. At home he was a bit of a loner, I think, though there were lots of occasions when he was part of a trio of brothers playing very happily together.

He left his mark on the family annals as a result of my mother inviting various ladies to partake of tea in the drawing room. Little John it seems was on his hands and knees pushing a toy between chairs and legs, when suddenly he let fly a fart – nothing too violent but enough to still conversation. One of the ladies leaned towards John and said reprovingly, "Excuse me!" John stopped playing and looked back at her accusingly. "It wasn't you, it was me," he said.

I haven't forgotten the time I fought John in the ring. Two older boys (nearer Fred's age) from neighbouring houses had been given two pairs of boxing gloves and seeing John and me in the garden they approached to persuade us to don them and take part in a boxing bout. Neither of us was really interested but partly as a result of flattering praise of our basic skills and the strange feel of padded gloves on our hands, we agreed to play their game. They were our seconds and backed us to win - John for his longer reach, me for my quicker reactions. So we fought a bit, more or less patting each other round the lawn, and then rested. Our seconds urged us to hit harder in round two. So I did and hit John on the nose. John looked at me reproachfully, tears welling and dropping his guard. My second egged me on to strike again but I was appalled. I suddenly

CHILDHOOD

realised we were a couple of dupes, being taken for a ride. I didn't want to hurt John nor he me. We refused to continue and chucked the boxing gloves back at them.

Of all of us, John was the only son to inherit an ear and a finger talent for music and the piano. My father was an accomplished classical pianist (he could 'vamp' but never play popular melodies) and keen choral singer. None of us, not even John, had any ability in sight reading or pitch, which no doubt disappointed Dad who wasn't very impressed by John's personal extemporising at the piano. He certainly wasn't willing to arrange piano lessons and that went for any of us. I remember once expressing an earnest desire to learn the piano and Dad started me off with a set of finger exercises which I had to practise regularly. Off I trotted to master the sequence of notes with stumpy fingers and after about ten minutes I had lost interest. That was the end of my aspiration. Like my sortie into gardening: I wanted to help so Dad set me to weed a pathway. I don't hold it against him; playing the piano (or gardening) was never going to be my forte. But for John? Maybe he should have been more encouraging.

And then, nearly three years after my arrival, the final son is born in Preston and the family is complete. The whole family was photographed shortly after our move to Leeds and a copy of the print is one of my most treasured possessions: a studio pose, carefully arranged to balance the positioning of father, mother and four children, all dressed unusually smartly in thirties clothes and actually, compared with many similar family groups, looking remarkably relaxed and unstuffy. At the centre of the composition is the new baby, held gently by Mum as if proudly presenting him to the camera as a final addition to the family with no further hopes of creating a second daughter. And the new baby chuckles broadly rather like Winston Churchill in a good mood, though he can't possibly know what is going on.

My younger brother was christened Neil Anderson. Cousin Ian Forsyth has researched the family genealogy in Scotland and informs me that Agnes Corson, who married James Forsyth in Kirkcudbrightshire in 1884 (our maternal grandparents), was the daughter of George Corson and his wife Margaret née Anderson. My mother was clearly named after Margaret Anderson, her grandmother, and kept the Scottish connection alive. It is certainly a lovely tongue-rolling moniker. My own names (Henry Michael, though I was always Harry at home) were ordinary enough to be solidly English, like my elder brothers' names: Frederick James and John David, but Neil Anderson has an exotic ring to it. And I bet Mum chose the name for the new baby despite Dad's grumblings!

I hope this doesn't sound like sibling envy. Of course there were moments in our upbringing when I felt rivalry as we competed for our parents' love and attention; there were times when I knew the baby was getting preferential treatment. But I don't think I had any cause to feel deprived and probably Neil could have claimed that on many occasions I pushed him out, for I was not backward in coming forward, and I never felt that Neil was anything less than my regular playmate. We tended to do things together and if I was the dominant one – well, I was 3 years older. However, I do remember that Neil in adult times indignantly claimed that I had broken his trike and also dropped a heavy stone on his foot thus causing his big toe nail to break off. Trivial now, but in their time cause for deep resentments.

Neil had a reputation for losing sulkily in family dice and card games, no doubt a natural reaction from the youngest competitor. Maybe I crowed over him when I won but not spitefully, I hope. Through these pre-teen years we squabbled and bickered but mostly adapted to each other well. On those occasions when Neil was invited to stay and play with his cousin Muir, who was the same age, I felt peeved and deprived. I cannot recall being friends with any 'outsider' of my own age during this period.

4. Grandparents: The Forsyth Line

All my grandparents died before I was five, probably one after the other though I don't know the order of their going, nor whether any of them died before I was born. Cancer seems to have struck them down, according to a vaguely recalled comment by my father. I have no memory of them except by means of photographic osmosis, for I have old snaps and sepia portraits that seep through my consciousness and provide evidence, if not living proof, of their existence. Perhaps I do remember them as a dark shadowy presence moving slowly (or not at all) in the background of occasional family gatherings but I can't differentiate between them and they remain just one blur or probably a re-constituted figment of my imagination.

Obviously there were four of them. Did they get on with each other, I mean as two pairs of parents brought together by the vagaries of their children's marriages? Or was there clear water between the family from Worcester and the family from Ashby de la Zouch? My guess is that they didn't find each other's company particularly conducive to friendship, and that's partly because I can't think of any grandparents in my experience who have cultivated close ties with 'the other side' of their children's marital union. One reason for this may be potential rivalry in their anxiety to claim loving contact with grandchildren, but more likely it is simply a sensitivity to basic differences between two pairs of personalities. Each couple wishes to preserve its privacy. I also draw on the fact that my parents did not talk about their parents very much, or more especially about each other's parents, though in view of their early departure from my childhood that is not surprising.

CHILDHOOD

Perhaps more to the point, did my two pairs of shadowy grandparents get on with each other as husband and wife? During those distant times the chances are they had to, like it or lump it. Looking at photographs, I get the impression that Mr. and Mrs. Forsyth and Mr. and Mrs. Morley back in the 1860s were the opposite of each other in physical presence and in personality. That may well have led to a happy union of opposites, which includes a contrast in husband and wife dominance in domestic circumstances.

The Forsyth branch of the family owed allegiance to a lowland Scottish clan and, like many self-exiled wanderers, romanticised the connection. **James** was one of six children sired by Alexander Forsyth, a Scottish ploughman who neglected to record his son's birth in Scotland. James's mother Mary came from (or was born in)[1] Warwickshire, England, which may explain how James Forsyth in mid-Victorian times happened to be staying in Worcester. It seems likely that James met his bride-to-be there, for the Corsons of Kirkcudbright had family connections with Worcester, where a brother of **Agnes** Corson was working as a draper. This would mean, so I am informed[2], that he was a so-called 'Scotch draper', i.e. he had a horse and trap and hawked his wares around the farms of Worcestershire. James no doubt would help a fellow Scot at his trade and thence worked at the same trade while he courted Agnes. Judging by photographs, I imagine my Grandfather James was slightly built and not very assertive, though clearly in his prime he won the hand of Agnes (my Grandmother), and in the tiny village Presbyterian Church of Garocher, they married on the last day of 1884. He was 30, she 24. It seems from the marriage certificate that his parents were deceased but hers were present at the ceremony. Her father was George Corson, a ploughman, and her mother was called Margaret (née Anderson), after whom my mother was named. The happy couple moved to Worcester, England, where Agnes's brother Thomas was presumably still working.

Apart from this, my knowledge of the Corson heritage seems to have been subsumed into the Forsyth family of mid-Victorian fecundity. **Agnes** and **James** produced and raised seven children, four girls and three boys, and the Forsyth

---

[1] Cousin Ian kindly supplied me with research genealogy on the Corson and Forsyth family links in Scotland. The 1861 Parish Census registers Grandfather James aged 7 as the fourth child of Alexander and Mary Forsyth, born in Kirkmaiden, but there is no record of his birth there in 1854. Probably the family skipped church in this remote southerly parish or possibly attended the 'Wee Free' church in Kirkmaiden (set up since the 1843 'disruption' caused by the formation of the Free Church of Scotland) though no records have survived, nor for James's two younger siblings also born in Kirkmaiden.

[2] Ibid.

family became established in Worcester. Agnes in appearance was plump, no doubt due to child bearing, and full-faced with a twinkle in her eye and a soft smile that suggested a humorous, comfortable personality. She was much more self-assured and physically strong than her husband James, who in family groups at his children's weddings does not appear a very imposing figure. He probably never recovered from the financial setback in middle age[3]. I get the impression that the Forsyths were in decline financially through the years; though I must say the first three of the Forsyth girls were able to land 'professional' spouses. I reckon Agnes, née Corson, made the most of her motherly skills in bringing up the family.

That doesn't imply that the distaff side of the Forsyth children was necessarily dominant. Of the three boys, **James** the eldest became an infantry officer killed in the trenches in 1916 and was mourned deeply thereafter. **Alec** endured but survived the Gallipoli campaign, though he rarely spoke about it, and he married Hannah (their son is Cousin Jim)[4]. And **Norman**, the youngest, pursued a career in banking. He married Freda (their son is Cousin Ian)[5]. All of which explains nothing about their character though I find it interesting that my mother is the

---

[3] Cousin Muir comments: James Forsyth wasn't even a tailor at all, in the usual sense. He was a so-called Scottish tailor, i.e. he had a horse and trap and hawked his wares around the farms of Worcestershire. It was his undoing that he came north to start a proper tailoring business in partnership with a man who promptly absconded with the money they had put together. That's why he was forced to revert to type, as it were. (In those days country folk didn't go to town to shop, they ordered and bought from travelling salesmen. The wheel seems to have turned fully now, what with postal shopping and the internet.)

[4] Cousin Muir comments: Alec was a disappointed man. He had hoped to teach but his mother (so my mother told me) wouldn't hear of it. So he became a clerk and never rose very high. His marriage was a disaster as both Hannah and her parents concealed from him that she had had mental problems and treatment. She was very unstable even before she began to threaten neighbours with a knife. Jim's boyhood must have been a nightmare at times.

[5] Cousin Muir comments: Norman became a bank clerk and, though he got a small managership (Yorkshire Penny in Castleford), he was dogged by illness, had several operations on his stomach and was more often off work than on. He married Freda Liversedge whose family made it clear that they considered she had married beneath her. She publicly humiliated Olive, who was one of her bridesmaids, at the wedding, thus causing a rift that was never healed. She later contracted T.B. and Ian lived with us in Adel during part of her hospital treatment. Later she disapproved so strongly of Ian's marriage that she and Norman refused to attend his wedding and, as Ian freely admits, continued to make trouble to the end.

CHILDHOOD

only Forsyth to give birth to a daughter and the only one to create a family with more than one child (and all of these were sons).

My mother was the eldest daughter of James and Agnes Forsyth and her younger siblings called her **'Cissy'** because they couldn't pronounce 'Margaret', which indicates that she often helped to look after her brothers and sisters. She was born on 2 May 1889; I possess her Certificate of Registry of Birth, a precious relic that confirms that she was 24 when she married my father, a Civil Servant (Inland Revenue) who was 5 years older than my mother. **Gladys** (her favourite sister) married Leslie Temple, who moved from Lincoln to set up a dental practice in Leeds in the early twenties. Meanwhile her younger sister **Nessie** went on to marry Frank Capes, a solicitor based in Doncaster, which is where she moved and so did the youngest Forsyth sister, **Olive** (who never married) in the twenties. Aunt Agnes and Uncle Frank had no children and were divorced after 20 years, allegedly on the grounds of failure to consummate the marriage.[6] Of course we knew nothing of this and actually saw little of them but once I did travel by bus on my own to stay for a week. I threw away the return half of my bus ticket to Doncaster on arrival, so at the end of my stay they drove me back to Leeds, which was a novelty for me. Uncle Frank took me to watch Doncaster Rovers; he was a Director so we had seats but, ignorant of football, I found the game boring and was puzzled by the frequent shouts, "Keep it on the island!" As Uncle Alec (who married Hannah) was already living in Leeds and Uncle Norman married Freda and moved to Huddersfield, there does seem to have been a clear plan to deploy the various branches of the Forsyth family in the West Riding.

5. Grandparents: The Morley Line

The **Morley branch of the family** was based in Nottinghamshire, centring on Edwinstowe and then Ashby de la Zouch, though there are other branches and twigs I know nothing about. The most significant document I possess is the Last Will and Testament of my great-grandmother, Fanny Morley, dated 11th August 1886. This is both succinct and interestingly written.

---

[6] Cousin Muir comments: The reason behind the Capes divorce may have been non-consummation but the legal grounds were adultery between Frank and a publican's wife whom he subsequently married. After his death in 1977 I had a lengthy correspondence with the solicitors on behalf of Nessie concerning the divorce settlement, his blatant failure to keep up payments and other matters which show him in a very poor light. I had the distinct impression that he was not highly regarded in the profession.

IRONS IN THE FIRE

This is the Last Will and Testament of me Fanny Morley of Edwinstowe in the County of Nottingham Widow. I devise the dwelling house and premises belonging to and occupied by me situate adjoining the Town Street of Edwinstowe aforesaid And also the Four Cottages thereto adjoining and abutting upon the Town Street of Edwinstowe aforesaid to my son Frederick Morley absolutely subject to any mortgages or charges to which the said property is subject. I bequeath my household furniture money ponies goods chattels and effects and all other my personal estate of whatever description to my Executor hereinafter named. Upon trust at his discretion to divide the same and every part thereof equally between my children or to sell and convert into money such parts thereof as shall not consist of money and to pay and divide the proceeds thereof and also the ready money of which I may die possessed unto and equally amongst my said children. I appoint my said son Frederick Morley Sole Executor of this my Will.

In Witness whereof I have hereunto set my hand this Eleventh day of August 1886 Fany (sic) Morley.

Signed by the said Fanny Morley as her Will in the presence of us who in her presence at her request and in the presence of each other have hereunto subscribed our names as witnesses.

                                       A J Curshaw Sol. Mansfield
                                       S Baguley   Sol. his Clerk

    Fanny Morley, my great grandmother, died on 15th September 1886. She left a gross Personal Estate of £71.13.6. though I am uncertain whether this included the value of the house and four cottages. The mention of 'ponies' in the Will suggests that there was some kind of carrier or hostelry connection. I have no knowledge of Fanny Morley's husband's demise but I'll bet he was called Frederick. The Edwinstowe branch of the Morley family currently operates a coach and taxi business from these very same premises.
    Frederick Morley, her eldest son and my grandfather, was clearly entrusted to execute his mother's will, which allowed the Morley family to continue in business in Edwinstowe. Frederick, however, had already left home and had become the (head) teacher at the Ashby de la Zouch Blue and Green-Coat Boys' School. He had also recently married a teacher called **Charlotte** Sones who taught at the Ashby de la Zouch National School until 1882, which was probably the year of the wedding, as she would have had to leave teaching upon marriage. Charlotte bore two children. My father was born on Christmas Day 1884 and was duly christened **Noel** Frederick. A daughter, my Aunt **Winifred**, followed a

CHILDHOOD

few years later. My grandmother Charlotte occupies a rather intriguing place in my mind, for she seems to have made the leap from being a governess to being a qualified teacher in the newly formed elementary schools of Forster's Education Act (1870). The Sones family, however, like the Corsons, are almost totally missing from the archives. I remember an Aunt Kitty Sones who visited us in Leeds once or twice, but that's as far as it goes.

Interestingly, photographs of my paternal and maternal grandparents seem to reveal them as the opposite of each other in character and personality. On the Forsyth side, I see Grandmother **Agnes** as the dominant partner, definitely confident (all those children) and accommodating, bright-eyed and relaxed, while Grandfather **James** Forsyth (being Celtic?) seems slightly built, wiry but not exuding the confidence of a successful merchant. On the Morley side, however, I get the impression that Grandmother **Charlotte** is more detached, slimmer in build and cooler in manner than Agnes. As for the Grandfathers, **Frederick** Morley (being Anglo-Saxon?) is of much heavier bulk, a larger frame, perhaps ponderous but self-assured, as befits a man in authority. He may well be more dominant than his wife, Charlotte. Somehow I can't see the grandmothers getting on together any more than the grandfathers, but who is to tell? In each case there seems to be a union of opposites and I hope they were at least happy with their partners.

I don't doubt that the Morley line benefited from qualification as Teachers. In status in the community, in their personal education and in the security of employment, they had moved nearer to being 'professional middle class', though of course I have no idea if they 'fulfilled' themselves. With fewer problems than the Forsyths, the Morleys would expect their only son to proceed to the Grammar School for Boys and I presume sister Winifred also stayed on at a girls' school. As for the Forsyth children, I know nothing of their schooling but, despite the lack of success in the tailoring trade, James and Agnes did create a happy family from which my mother emerged.

6. My Mother and Father

They were, I think, happily married. They were known as Cissy (= sister) and Doe, a soubriquet derived from Noel (I guess), which suggests a settled and socially accepted relationship. Although Dad had a short fuse on his temper he never gave the impression he was angry with her. In these pre-teen days, I once blundered into the dining room and found my mother in tears and my father standing opposite with a surly expression on his face. I don't know what had caused the quarrel but I was told to leave the room and I did. It is the only time I remember an emotional conflict between my parents. Usually there was harmony, my mother able to tease Dad when he was too high-handed and in many ways get the better of him in domestic matters. She was definitely in charge of the home, though it was clearly Dad who was head of the family. In a rare exchange of confidences years later, Dad told me with remarkable conceit that he had been responsible for Mum becoming such a firm, confident and attractive person. When he first courted and married her, she had known nothing, he said. I was silenced by such presumption, though I know he intended to express pride and admiration for the mature woman. Typically he would be thinking of intellectual, cognitive intelligence; he wouldn't really rate emotional intelligence which Mum innately possessed in far greater abundance than he did.

During the thirties Mum employed a live-in maid. I wouldn't want to boast about it; in fact, looking back I am more inclined to feel embarrassed. I remember only two maids; one who was pretty, very capable and soon to depart, and the other plain, clumsy and staying five years, leaving because she could earn more money in a munitions factory when war broke out. Living conditions in our house were really primitive for any maid. She was given a small room at the top of the house. A thin carpet, drab curtains and perhaps one chair and side-table. There was a single iron bedstead and a chest of drawers on which a basin and jug resided for her washing, with water brought up from the kitchen. The nearest toilet was down in the cellar – at least I assume this is so, for I do not recall the maid ever using our toilet or bathroom. Such is my ignorance, I don't know if she went to the public baths in the centre of town when she needed a good scrub. Nor do I know how Mum advertised for a maid, but she actually took pity on Eva, who was an illegitimate girl from a mining village with an unhappy home life. She was dumpy and thick-legged, placid and dispirited, but grateful for any place to call her own. Why otherwise would she have put up with the mean life, with the kitchen as her only rest room and so many stairs to climb? Little more than five feet tall, she was a comical sight in her maid's bonnet and apron but she became, if not one of the family, then at least a familiar part of home life. We teased but never mocked her; she laughed with us and enjoyed our company. I think we gave her something she had never had. It was a kind of love after all, though I took her for granted and only wondered about her after she had long gone. No one used that little garret room after her. I have no idea what became of Eva.

Washday on Monday morning was always shared between the maid and Mum, both down in the cellar with the boiler and the dolly, the Robin starch and the big mangle. The boys kept out of the way and after the washing was on the line, we always ate a cold dinner (lunch) in the kitchen with Eva. We moaned about this: "Why must we eat horrible gristly cold meat and pickle on Mondays?" "Because..." Eva would explain and then say no more, which made us fall about laughing. Was Mum out socialising or just resting? A little circle of women friends, a few perhaps Presbyterians, came for afternoon tea very conventionally.

CHILDHOOD

Mum and Dad dressed up occasionally for dances, or more likely balls, but they were not fond of whist drives, canasta or bridge gatherings (or daftest of all, Beetle drives). Both enjoyed tennis socially at the club just up the road. Above all Mum was the mother of four boys, a loving wife and a good housekeeper, which may look like three clichés in a row but that's how she seemed to me. She ran a fairly orderly household, considering there were five males to cope with. Only once did she clout me: I wanted a quiet place to read and so slunk into the spare bedroom with a book and a juicy apple. When eaten, I chucked the core in the grate and read on. I was disturbed by Mum entering to show Aunt Olive into the newly cleaned room, she being an expected guest. There I was, comfortably installed with my feet on the bed. No wonder she was annoyed and clearly Aunt Ol approved of my mother's reaction. It was easy to talk to Mum, for she was on our (boyish) side, even though she could criticise. With four boys, there was no point in being house-proud. The furniture had to endure hard knocks. Dad liked to tease Uncle Les who once protectively rebuked us in his home, "Now, boys, respect the mahogany!" Mum liked us being robust but encouraged sensitive concern for others: "do unto others as you would have them do unto you." I don't claim a special relationship with my mother, for we all enjoyed cuddles and shared intimacies, but I doubt if John or Neil can remember (as I do) lazily embracing her in an armchair and starting to manipulate her breasts rather lecherously (for a seven-years-old) until she told me to desist (either I was over-excited or maybe she was roused). She was a warm and impulsive person with a firm moral sense though she never favoured Presbyterian strictness. A curious memory floats into mind – a plain-clothes detective stands in the drawing room interviewing my mother who is insisting that someone must have entered the house and stolen a purse containing money. The detective asks questions and writes notes. I sit quietly fidgeting on the Chesterfield sofa and my hand strays down the side and touches something soft hidden in the folding part of the Chesterfield. It is the purse, which I flourish triumphantly. Exit a somewhat cross CID 'tec, leaving my embarrassed mother hardly able to believe that I hadn't known where it was.

For a young son exploring the parents' bedroom, Mum's dressing table was always alluring with an invisible aroma of face powder in the air; so many drawers and secret pouches, the powder puffs and make-up cases, scent bottles and perfumes, the beads and bracelets, but I don't think she owned much jewellery of any value. Searching their bedroom for signs of hidden Christmas presents was always fair game, but we never broke the rule that forbade looking in Dad's bedside table. When adolescence made me furtive, I borrowed a lurid paperback entitled "Lady, don't turn over" from someone at school. I read it secretly in bed and kept it well concealed, but Mum found the hiding-place. She asked me where I got the book; embarrassed, I told her, expecting to be scolded but she simply laughed at me and changed the subject. She didn't remove the book; that was left to me. There was a loving trust between us built up over the years. She was the only woman in our lives, and we didn't need another!

Whereas there was always a hesitancy in confiding in Dad. He would be more censorious, more concerned that we should not waste our time, more inclined to consider us 'fools', while still being fairly tolerant of (or resigned to) our youthful indiscretions. I enjoyed sitting on his knee and reading a family hand-me-down called "The Hey Diddle-Diddle Picture Book" (still in my possession). During the school years he took an interest in our homework and creative activities. His office work in Leeds prescribed a regular routine but throughout this period he was able to play evening cricket games with a Civil Service X1 (I got some early innings with them) and watch County cricket at Headingley (with me later on), join a local tennis club (with Mum), relax with chess and the piano, and sing baritone in choirs. I can still hear him chanting "the monster Polypheme, the monster Polypheme!" as he went up the stairs but I don't know from which opera or oratorio it originates. He played golf occasionally and was very fond of wearing baggy plus-fours on all occasions, which may have shown off his ankles but made his shoes seem larger (size 12). He was left-handed with golf clubs and at cricket he bowled with his left arm, but he batted right-handed and signed his name with a right-hand. Very odd. I'm not sure when he began cold baths first thing in the morning; he never wore pyjamas and he would leap straight out of bed into the cold water. None of the children followed his lead; he was over seventy when he ceased that heart-stopper. Dad was a walker, six foot three but not heavily built. He became a keen crown-green bowler (left-handed) once he moved to Otley.

He cycled to his office in the city centre each day. He rode a very tall bicycle which had a double bar across the frame as well as the obligatory sit-up-and-beg handlebars. He could have taken a tram of course, but he preferred the exercise and the thrift. He was a man who seemed to count the pennies. "A fool and his money are soon parted," he would warn me. He was not tempted by motorcars, nor the telephone; he bought Mum a washing machine just before the war in 1939. I can't think of any other extravagance though he seemed a loving and caring husband and father, though perhaps a little selfish. Dad was short-tempered and could fly off the handle with ranting rages as he stamped about the house shouting, "Damn and blast and hell set fire!" I was with my mother on one occasion when he was to be heard sounding off in another room and she confided in me, "Listen to him! Someone should have given him a good smacking when he was a boy!" I was able to look at Dad and see the sulky little boy behind the tall, dominating figure. He certainly didn't suffer fools gladly and would tell his sons they were fools very often. I'm not sure he wasn't right – I was a fool in many ways but it didn't help self-confidence. With regard to Brother John, my

CHILDHOOD

father was the fool because his attitude was so blinkered. John needed special attention which Mum could give; Dad was often too impatient and critical to contribute.

Such arrogance and impatience was probably engrained as a child in Ashby de la Zouch. He never forgot the pain and suffering when as a child he slipped on autumnal leaves in the street and broke his leg. After the fracture had been set and healed, the doctors discovered one leg was shorter than the other, so they tied a weight to it and stretched it over weeks while he lay in bed. I suppose this tough ordeal was worthwhile for there was no discernible limp in adulthood. The only son of the village schoolmaster, clever in class, clever at home, the apple of his parents' eyes, he was brought up conventionally. While still at Ashby de la Zouch Grammar School, a promising scholar in Mathematics, Latin and Music, Dad wrote a long poem celebrating the local Castle, and it was rated so highly that copies were printed and actually displayed in the railway station for sale to visitors and passengers. I have one surviving copy – though I must search for it. It is imitative of traditional odes, full of poetic diction and imparting much historical information about the Castle. It was remarkable if only for the intricate rhyming stanzas but I imagine an admiring father would be behind its publication. I wonder how many copies were sold. After leaving grammar school, he opted for the Civil Service, via London University, which provided a first-class certificate dated 1905. His career in the Inland Revenue, as an Inspector of Taxes, was successful indeed, though it does suggest a certain preference for isolated prominence.

If you have fathered four boys, domestic conditions must be pretty constricting. The house was not all that spacious and there was only one lavatory, a tiny room at the head of the stairs. One of Dad's stock phrases was "There's always a boy there!" He liked to sit in private doing the crossword. Actually there was another toilet at cellar level under the back door steps, but this must have been reserved for the maid; certainly we boys never used it, except in an emergency. Dad also liked playing the piano loudly, invariably the great composers' works, and sometimes this would drive me from the drawing room where I was quietly reading. Once, when I was listening with some interest and enjoyment to Jack Payne and his Orchestra (or perhaps Henry Hall), Dad entered the drawing room and immediately switched off the wireless. "You don't want to listen to rubbish like that," was his comment as he left the room. Perhaps he had my neglected classical education in mind, but it seemed more like puritanical repression and intellectual snobbery. On the whole, though, he tolerated and encouraged our personal interests and often joined in our games and sports. He called Neil and myself 'Spot' and 'Todger' respectively, pleasantly affectionate nicknames – but no name for John that I remember. I suppose we were rather afraid of him. He was after all a tall aloof presence whether he was encouraging or disapproving, which is not to say that he was cold and distant; there are pleasant memories of sitting on his knee being fed thin slices of apple cut with his little pocket knife or his laughing immoderately at our antics. I remember only one occasion when he smacked me for wrongdoing and he seemed to find the physical punishment as distasteful as I did because he stopped smacking almost as soon as he started. He was a gentle giant who could be an overbearing bully.

Two small problems persist. One is the hoary chestnut of what father did during the War. Any boy brought up during the twenties and thirties absorbed stories of trench warfare and conscription. My father did not join up; he was not a volunteer offering his services in uniform and when conscription was introduced in 1916 he was on the borderline of compulsory calling-up. Born in 1884, he was 30 when war broke out and was able to back away from the carnage, surely much to my mother's relief. I have no quarrel with this conduct now, but back in the thirties my friends in Ashwood Terrace asked me why my father 'had not been called up'. When I consulted my mother she grew angry, aware that behind the question lay the attitude of Dr. Willcock, my friends' father (and Presbyterian) who had been in the R.A.M.C. in France during the War. She irritatedly told me that Dad had been in a reserved occupation, which I vaguely reported back to my friends who no doubt reported it back to base. Sometimes I wonder if Dad carried any 'guilt' through his life; not that I think he should have, but did he feel there was a dreadful retribution in the deaths of his beloved wife and children later on?

The second problem is much less ambivalent and concerns his unaccountably callous attitude to the disposal of kittens. Perhaps we were an odd family for we never named our tabby cat. We were nevertheless very fond of her and approved her natural sex life which produced annual litters of kittens during the thirties, and although we found the newcomers delightful, very few could be given good homes. Perhaps my father's reluctance to pay the vet's sterilisation or termination fees played a part in his decision to drown the kittens himself, preferably before they opened their eyes, which at least suggests he had some qualms about killing helpless animals. It is the method of execution that is so heinous, however. He filled the dustbin to the brim with water from a bucket. He dropped the litter of unwanted kittens in the water where they would start paddling round and mewing as they struggled to keep afloat. He upturned the dustbin lid and placed it over the top of the bin, using a brick to keep it in position. In theory there was no pocket of air for the kittens to breathe. He then cycled to work and returned in the evening to bury the inert bedraggled corpses in the garden. Having emptied the bin, he put the lid on correctly. No doubt he would stroke the cat comfortingly as she plaintively searched for her children. I have no excuses ready. Dad was country-bred and no doubt drew a distinction between animals

CHILDHOOD

and human beings, but such indifference to the situation he was creating is difficult to comprehend. For the whole family was implicated, we were all guilty because we knew it was happening, we occasionally actually saw what was happening and we walked away and let it happen again. My mother must receive criticism not just for allowing her husband to do the deed over a number of years but also for being lax in not protecting her children from such brutal behaviour. But the crudity and incompetence of filling a dustbin with water and using the lid to seal the top takes some beating. Why not use a big saucepan and lid? Today such action would be considered chargeable and morally beyond the pale. Most people in the thirties surely felt similarly and indeed it was a protest from our next-door neighbour, whose daughters had been upset hearing mewing sounds coming from the dustbin (the lid had slipped), that caused my father to cease his activity. I certainly feel guilt that I, like my brothers, condoned such standards as part of normal civilised conduct.

7. Cousins in the Thirties

Contact with our cousins was spasmodic. Muir, only son of Gladys and Leslie Temple, was a good chum of my youngest brother, Neil. The only early event I recall was painting each other's bottoms with water colours and cavorting about naked in the spare bedroom, unaware that brother Fred could see us distantly as he walked with friends up the drive next door. I thought it was jolly nice of him to take me aside next day and simply advise me to draw the curtains next time. In the mid-thirties the Temples moved to a more spacious house in Adel on the outskirts of West Leeds beyond Headingley. There was an extensive playing field adjacent to their house which was an additional attraction but social contact between the families must have been restricted as we had no telephone installed and no car either. We had to take a long tram journey to Lawnswood and then walk half a mile.

The same applied to visiting Cousin Jim, Uncle Alec's only son. Tramcars or buses took circuitous routes; it was best to walk over and down the Ridge and through various estates to reach his home in Chapel Allerton. I didn't have a bike at this age and cyclists had to follow the roundabout route by road. Jim's interests were adventurous; he kept pets in cages in his garden, lots of rabbits and mice and guinea pigs and hamsters. He was also a Cub and then Boy Scout during the thirties, and clearly motivated to achieve activity badges. Neither pet animals nor scouting appealed to me, but he was a year and a half older than me and a good deal more 'street-wise'. He took me once to his local Saturday morning Children's Film Programme; Jim at ease and me uneasy, sitting in the middle of a swarm of kids of all sorts and sizes, shouting, cat-calling, throwing apple-cores, climbing over seats and screaming when the lights went low and an image flickered on the screen. Jim was quite used to the rough and tumble but I had not experienced crowds of kids like this before and did not like the appalling crudity and boisterous conduct of the audience, any more than the cinema attendant who was running around cursing and swatting the offenders. When Tom Mix galloped his horse across the screen the audience almost wet themselves with excitement (some did no doubt); everyone cheered the cavalry charge but when the hero held the girl in his arms and kissed her, a deafening bird-whistling sounded all round, almost hysterical in its vehemence. I succumbed to the enthralling longer feature entitled "The Tunnel: episode four" but both of us suffered nightmares about poisonous gas advancing along an enormous tunnel under the Atlantic Ocean. My curiosity about episode five lost out to my distrust of the audience and the terrors of the tunnel. I did not attend any more Saturday morning cinema shows but Jim did.

Cousin Ian was about five years my junior and not really much in evidence as Uncle Norman and Aunt Freda lived distantly in Huddersfield. I think we were polite to each other. I remember once reading to him and stopping because he seemed to be looking intently at me. "What are all those spots on your face?" he asked. I was put out at first until, after checking in a mirror, I realised he was referring to my freckles. That's about all I remember of little Ian in those days, except for the occasion when he was caught handling his crutch (as small boys will) when we were with the Aunts and his mother reproved him. He gave an extra pull and complained, "It wants stretching," which sent a titter rippling round the assembled ladies, who exchanged knowing glances. While I looked on, wondering.

Cousins Margaret and Kathleen lived in Nottingham, the daughters of my father's sister, Winifred, and her husband Ro. Kathleen was about my age with her sister three years older. I count on one hand the times we met in the thirties, but I was very fond of Kathleen who seemed to get a great deal of pleasure from brushing my hair. Neil and I made the journey to stay with them; being bossy I arranged a number of signals, such as a raised eyebrow or a kick under the table, to rebuke my younger brother if he should show ill manners, but he (or I) got confused about the detail and only made matters worse. When our girl cousins came to stay with us in Leeds, so they told me later, I objected to the shorts they wore and insisted on them wearing dresses all the time – examples of my ignorant arrogance indeed!

8. Neighbours in the Thirties

Despite the planned isolationism of the Villas and Terrace, in the thirties there were no neighbourly garden parties or social gatherings, not that I can remember anyway. There were some houses which had windows and doors that never

CHILDHOOD

seemed to open and front gardens devoid of human habitation except for small boys looking for lost balls. Unless there were children there, I was unlikely to take much interest in the households. Our family GP lived lower down the Villas, Dr. Muir by name, a dapper Scotsman who wore spats and morning suits (black jackets and striped trousers) with a grey homburg and gloves. We met as patient and doctor rather than as neighbours.

Next door (the other semi-detached part) lived Professor Cobb, a historian at Leeds University, one of the most self-effacing academics I have ever met (if I did meet him). He had a wife and two teenage daughters who, I suspect, were appalled by the noise and occasional sight of four uncouth boys living so near. They were a very blue stocking family, entirely worthy citizens but I see them almost as pale wraiths, except for the one extraordinary entertainment that the two girls presented to their parents in their back garden. There was a seesaw and a swing upon which they performed a series of 'exercises' which might be called gymnastic and which were solemnly applauded by the parents seated comfortably in deck chairs. And by John and me too for, hearing the rare voices of the girls, we climbed the fence between the gardens and started to watch and join in the applause. The girls were momentarily embarrassed but I think we showed considerable tact by asking if we could continue to watch the show. The parents gave approval; the girls made the best of it. I was impressed; I didn't realise girls could do something so unusual and interesting but there were no repeat performances. Did I ever notice the girls again?

A more worldly family lived in the next semi-detached house with two boys and a girl who never played on the Terrace, which must mean something. The father was in business, the mother was a somewhat flamboyant Hungarian ex-beauty who gushed and spoke broken English. My parents were not attracted to what seemed like pretentious extravagances. Eventually they were annoyed that brother Fred had to abandon his architect's training when War broke out in 1939, while the playboy son next door, who had twice failed his medical exams, was allowed to continue trying to qualify. But later the other son was killed in the war. The girl, Anita, was groomed for the marriage stakes and did well. At my age, however, Anita was not very interesting and she never put on performances in the back garden.

I'm not sure whether it was coincidence or planned that further up the Villas another Tax Inspector moved in with his family. The Dunsmore parents are totally lost to my memory but I remember twin (non-identical) sons called John and Robert and a younger daughter called Jennifer. The boys were my age but very different personalities. John was bespectacled and not a games player; Robert was fiercely competitive and quarrelsome. He nearly killed himself smashing a glass door with his fist. I met him in Oxford seven years later quite by chance in the street. How we recognised each other I can't imagine but after a

IRONS IN THE FIRE

few words of astonished curiosity we parted without renewing the past. Jennifer Dunsmore was at least two years younger than me; she made a pass at me on the sofa when we were all messing around but I didn't respond. The Dunsmores vanished at the end of the thirties and were replaced by another Taxman, Mr. Barton with his wife and one son, Brian. They were suburban Londoners and spoke disparagingly of Leeds City shops in comparison with Knightsbridge but they became resigned to northern standards and quite friendly with the Morleys. Brian Barton was to be an important influence on me during the early War years (see the next chapter).

The three Willcock boys lived in an Ashwood Terrace house and in many ways they were our best friends, being more or less our age. John, Malcolm and Croom were their names; their father was Dr. Willcock, originally from the Shetlands and very dour with it and Chief Medical Officer for the City of Leeds. Mrs. Willcock came from Bristol. Unfortunately the Morley parents and the Willcock parents did not 'get on'. Perhaps lack of congruency is illustrated by the fact that we played far more often in our house than theirs. We always kept a well-stocked fruit bowl in the dining room, which is where we mainly played. The Willcock boys annoyed my mother by asking frequently for fruit, which they were always allowed. At the Willcock's, a fruit bowl was conspicuously absent.

There was one early evening at Christmas when I was unusually in their house playing 'dinky toys' with Croom. A real Christmas tree stood in one corner with unlit candles and no other decorations. It was the first time I had seen an authentic tree and I thought it very gloomy. At home we had an artificial tree crammed with baubles and tinsel; not very large but it was placed on a cabinet in the window where it could be seen glittering from outside. Mrs. Willcock entered to ask if I would like to stay for supper, as we were playing so nicely together. I trotted down the Villas lane to tell my mother that Mrs. Willcock had invited me to supper so I would miss my normal tea. Mum was more than a little surprised that Mrs. Willcock has shown such friendliness and of course agreed to my absence at the table. Croom and I played very happily and then, bearing a tray with two mugs of sweet cocoa and two baked potatoes, Mrs. Willcock graciously entered again. It was not the kind of food I was used to. A little later, I left the Willcock's house, having thanked Croom's mother, and ran home with an increasing queasiness in my stomach. I just had time to rush up the stairs and fall in front of the bath before I vomited an ocean of brown gunge with bits of potato skin floating in it. I have not been partial to skins of any sort since then. Mum was not amused by the hospitality offered to me.

Next door to the Willcock's lived a tetchy old man called, I think, Mr. Laurie. He was no friend of the games-playing boys on the Terrace and complained regularly about noise. The Willcock boys one afternoon asked me to join them when a friend from West Park was visiting and their parents were out. Led by

CHILDHOOD

this visitor, the boys had just started a game of teasing Mr. Laurie who lived next door behind a high garden wall. They were throwing things over the back wall, knowing that Mr. Laurie was sitting peaceably on the other side. He was growing increasingly enraged by the rubbish that got flung over the wall. I certainly didn't begin the game but no doubt I joined in. Eventually their friend from West Park started throwing water, at first a sprinkle but finally buckets of water. Mr. Laurie got drenched and retired. I went home. Later that evening there was a knock at our back door. There stood Malcolm Willcock, still panting from running, to tell me Mr. Laurie had complained to his parents who rightly had been very angry and had cross-examined the boys about such atrocious behaviour. Who was responsible for starting it all? they asked. Malcolm said he knew it was really the friend from West Park who was to blame but as his parents were friends of the boy's parents (West Park being snobbishly superior territory) he had decided not to name him. Instead, said Malcolm, he had blamed *me*. Poor Malcolm, full of guilt, confessing to me on my doorstep, scared that I might make a fuss!

I regret now that I simply shrugged my shoulders and said it didn't matter, it was all right as far as I was concerned. I think the fact that he actually came and told me about his betrayal seemed jolly decent of him, but I was aware that he was no true friend of mine. Both older Willcock boys went to boarding school but not Croom for some reason. Later, Malcolm from Fettes won a Scholarship to Cambridge University (Classics); he was by this time rarely one of my confidantes. On the other hand, Brian Barton who was a closer friend also won a Scholarship to Cambridge University (Mathematics) from Leeds Grammar School.

9. Pastimes in the Thirties

Early childhood was full of card and dice games played in the drawing room with Dad (and Mum when she wasn't sewing or darning). Dad was a infectious card player, making 'Donkey' and 'Old Maid' and 'Beggar my Neighbour' exciting as we passed the cards round, though I think he began to duck out of dice games like 'Snakes and Ladders' which never seemed to end. We needed the dining room table for large-scale board games like "Monopoly", though the London-based property market meant little to us when compared with "Buccaneer", the Waddington game we loved passionately. The romance of sailing to Treasure Island to load our little ships with rubies, diamonds, pearls, gold ingots and barrels of rum was irresistible, particularly as you might meet pirates. You unrolled a chart from a cylinder and sailed the ocean blue with crew cards controlling movements (no dice!). When the Yellow Fever card struck, you felt like the Ancient Mariner…well, that came later, but assuredly 'Buccaneer' was on the same ocean-wave length. When Neil in middle age purchased a nearly pristine copy of this obsolete game at a Church fete, a full tide of nostalgia flooded our memories. We tried to set up a session with members of our families but while Neil and I crooned over each jewel taken on board, the younger generation soon deserted and returned to their Action Men or Barbie dolls. Since then, time has slipped our moorings though surely Marion, Neil's widow, keeps 'Buccaneer' alongside 'Fred's game' in the family vaults, the latter being a fine (and unique) transformation of a tame 'soccer' board game into a scintillating rugby contest.

A totally homemade game we called 'Invisible Cricket'. We used a large cricket scorebook abandoned by Dad's Office team and started by writing down the Yorkshire cricketers' names and then the Lancashire team. The match was played across the landing of the house. The batsman took guard in the bathroom; and the bowler did a little run-up and bowled from the bedroom, where the scorer (next man in) lay on the double bed and wrote down the score after each ball was bowled. The batsman improvised his scoring shots or decided to lose his wicket. Both teams batted - but there was just one little oddity. All the action was mimed. No ball literally existed, though the bowler pretended to grip and spin one. No bat was wielded but the batsman mimed his strokes. Somehow or other we three brothers combined imaginations and a cooperative willingness to suspend disbelief. And all was recorded in the scorebook. For two or three years, on many a wet or cold afternoon, a game of 'Invisible Cricket' would proceed elaborately and logically like a solemn ritual prolonging summertime.

Do I curl up in embarrassment at its ludicrous naïveté? No, I applaud home-grown imaginative activities, even early attempts at entertainments such as 'Ink Writing', performed (so we were told later) by the three brothers to Mum and Dad who sat in armchairs by the fire and gravely watched as we entered the room, each carrying a piece of paper and a nibbed pen. A bottle of ink was somewhere and we dipped the pens and sat at a card table applying ink to paper, presumably writing words. This went on for some time, until we were asked what happens next. Apparently nothing: putting ink to paper was the total dramatic experience. On another occasion the whole cast, faced by neighbours invited to attend some kind of show, broke into a fit of hysterical nervous screaming from which the performance never recovered.

Cousin Jim enlarged our dramatic potential at Ashwood Villas as a direct result of attending one of his Scout Concerts. We extemporised a dance band using combs and toilet paper (this was long before skiffle) and hung wallpaper drapes over the back of chairs behind which we tootled. Jim stood in front, jerking his arms about like Jack Hilton or Henry Hall. This was followed by a little melodrama in which a miserly character called Ebenezer duped a number of other characters. Cousin Jim played Ebenezer in masterly fashion and I was a

CHILDHOOD

little piqued that Dad laughed his way round the house afterwards, rubbing his hands and tittering, "Old Ebenezer wins again!" as if no other role was worth imitating (which they weren't).

Old-fashioned 'Charades' became a stock entertainment after a grown-up family party. 'Dumb crambo' is a mime version but we preferred the spoken word, mime not being an art we recognised (outside Invisible Cricket). In our hands Charades became quite sophisticated. We spent hours at the game, often with friends; two-a-side was possible but sometimes without an audience to guess the word – pretty pointless really. We were, however, not a theatre-going family. For many years there were special family outings with Aunt Glad and Cousin Muir to see the annual pantomimes at the Grand Theatre or the Theatre Royal. That always gave us stimulation though one Christmas the Theatre Royal staged a Big Top Circus which was a flop for us. I never liked Circus smells or animals in the ring; the clowns were too grotesque to be adults and too silly to be children. What we enjoyed most of all were the variety entertainments put on by Fred's Co-optimists Concert Party. At the Presbyterian Church I took part in a weird performance of "Alice in Wonderland" (it made no sense to me). In it I painted roses briefly, but all I remember is ducking to avoid cardboard plates thrown about the stage by a girl-Cook.

Probably my first film was "A Midsummer Night's Dream" with a star-studded cast; I made neither the ass's head nor tail of it. The mixture of 'real people' and fairies was bewildering; I was much too young for Shakespeare surely! And I cannot imagine why I was taken to see a film about a submarine sinking or by whom. Images of sailors drowning in a ship's hold haunt evermore. I was the right age, however, for Disney's 'Snow White and the Seven Dwarfs' in 1937. This provided romance, adventure and comedy in abundance though by this time I was well used to the delights of Laurel (especially) and Hardy. We had a family wind-up gramophone that gave access to some popular melodies of the day. Gracie Fields sang for us "Red Sails in the Sunset" and I never found out if she meant Thames barges at dusk or ruddy clouds blowing across the evening sky. On the reverse side she sang "One of the Little Orphans of the Storm", or was it "The Biggest Aspidistra in the World"? We played a mysterious ditty advising "You must say 'Yes' to Mr. Brown!" but I don't remember any classical music on record. The crunch came one morning when we opened the gramophone lid to discover that the playing parts had disappeared. Fred had taken the turntable for some Co-Optimist Concert act and we never got it back. That is the only grudge I hold against brother Fred. He deprived his younger brothers of a musical upbringing!

All is forgiven though, because Fred created 'The Ghost Train' in his attic. The train was actually a child's pushchair which he thrust along a pathway that wound its way round the room and in and out of corners till the journey came full circle. Suspended sheets and blankets helped to create scenic divisions. En route were various horror images, ghosts and ghouls, trailing wet strings, swinging axes and buckets of dripping blood, luminous spectres and ugly monsters who menaced the single passenger in the pushchair. Of course the Ghost Train operated in the dark, with one or two candles at strategic points, though the spooky illumination came from Fred's hidden assistant who lurked under the bed and scrambled around shining a torch on one terrible image after another, jerking at strings and activating skeletons. This was John, poor chap. It was not easy to remember the sequence of spotlighting and string-pulling, and Fred sometimes had to stop groaning, squealing, gibbering in the ears of the passenger in order to scold John for getting it wrong. Neil and I loved the Ghost Train, especially as it was just for us. I'm not sure that John did, press-ganged into helping. The ingenuity of the 'special effects' was admirable but it all had to be dismantled after a day or two and vanished like a chimera.

Reading was of course a constant companion; I could sit for hours with my thumb in my mouth. Dad had a glazed bookcase with his own contents, including some fairly stuffy but well-bound prize books from Ashby de la Zouch: for some reason the works of Thackeray in fifteen volumes, and also Chambers' Encyclopaedia all twelve of which provided information for schoolwork. But I don't recall many more books on shelves, and both parents borrowed from libraries, Mum using Boot's library (mainly novels) and Dad the Public Library (mainly not novels). In the bedroom which we three boys shared there was a cupboard for our own collections of favourite books. Early titles elude me but we liked Albums and Bumper Books for Boys. What were early influences? Well, we were not brought up on Christopher Robin or Beatrix Potter's delicate stories. One of my treasures was the story of Robin Hood but I think I came late to the King Arthur legends. 'Peter Pan' and 'The Wind in the Willows' became favourite tales to read. The *Just William* stories were collected and absorbed avariciously though not always totally understood, for Richard Crompton used a fairly adult vocabulary. Captain W.E. Johns created real juvenile heroes with Biggles (and Ginger – my look-alike). And Leslie Charteris made the Saint an attractive role model as I approached my teens.

Probably I was eight when Thompson's tu'penny 'bloods' provided magazines for each day of the week: Monday *(Adventure)*; Tuesday *(Champion)*; Wednesday *(Wizard)*; Thursday *(Rover)*; Friday *(Hotspur)*; Saturday *(Skipper)*. Not that I read all of them; my favourite was the Hotspur. I was never addicted to Greyfriars and St Jim's in *the Magnet* and *the Gem*, which puts me on the right side of George Orwell. What amazes me now is the sheer volume of words in those 'bloods', often in small typeface. The arrival of comics like *'Beano'* and *'Dandy'* meant that pictures superseded words. *Film Fun* had already favoured

CHILDHOOD

the strip cartoon style, but I was not interested in celluloid 'stars' and by now I was reading longer 'hard-back' books.

There was a wireless (the wires were inside the cabinet) which depended on a large, heavy D.C. battery to operate it. I went once or twice with my father to the local car repair garage where big batteries were re-charged. He used a little trolley but it still took some lugging. We listened to *Children's Hour* of course, mainly for *'Toy Town'* which gave us plenty of characters, but memorably for L. du Garde Peach's plays about the adventures of a hero called Armitage which had me glued to the set. I liked writing stories and remember filling a reporter's pad (for a tenth birthday?) with the exploits of my intrepid boy detective named Sandy Macpherson. Grown-up readers never showed the perseverance needed to master my juvenilia. Years later, Sandy Macpherson used to play a Wurlitzer (or Hammond?) organ on the wireless but he sounded nothing like my boy hero.

At least one attempt at improvising an adventure left its mark on me. A pile of sawn logs, kept by the steps leading to the washroom in the cellar, resembled ship's cannons if laid out in a certain way and before long we were setting sail and encountering privateers in the back garden. At one point I was captured by pirates and dragged into the washroom where I was threatened with torture. Stubbornly I refused to say where the gold was, so someone pushed my hand towards the mighty mangle and in the excitement turned the handle. My fingers were caught between the wooden rollers and I lost interest in the gold. Yelling with pain, with blood issuing from a split finger, I struggled upstairs to the kitchen and, thanks to a cool-headed maid who took control, held my hand under a cold tap. My right little finger is scarred forever but I can't remember which of my friends confused make-believe with a somewhat grisly reality.

Improvisation has its dangerous side. When Neil and I were playing cop and robber we were in need of a revolver, so we half-opened a clasp knife and held it in hand, gripping the blade as if it were a handle. In the excitement of the game, Neil pointed this 'gun' at me and threatened to shoot. Quick as a flash I feinted, seized the knife and wrenched it from his grip. I nearly fainted when he opened his hand to reveal a deep slicing cut across the inside of his fingers, with blood just beginning to well out. That wound required stitches. I deserved dire punishment but it was so obvious that I was crying in remorse that all was forgiven – at least I think Neil forgave me.

One unusual flight of imagination I remember vividly because there was an 'epiphany' attached to it. One Sunday morning our house in Ashwood Villas became a ship, not a warship but a liner, and I was the Captain responsible for every part of it. Down in the cellar was the engine-room where machines pounded and the propellers drove the ship through the ocean. Having checked all the gear, I ascended to the galley and checked the food being prepared for the passengers. Into the dining room and the drawing room I strode to ensure that all was shipshape and Bristol fashion, before mounting the stairs to view the cabins and bathroom. Then up the enclosed stairway that led to the attic where I stood on the bridge of the ship, with light pouring through the portholes and the water tank perhaps bubbling. I was alone and suddenly felt that this was for real, it was no longer a house, and I actually was the captain of a great vessel. For a brief moment, I was part of a kind of virtual reality and aware of myself dominating a pretended environment. Then of course I was interrupted (by Fred probably – "What d'you think you're doing in my room?"), the ship's bridge collapsed, normal life resumed and I could smile at my own vaingloriousness. Yet that intense moment of imagination remains in my mind.

10. Out and About Ashwood Villas

The walls and fences delineating the layout of the neighbourhood were accessible to any young explorer worthy of the name. Looking back, I am surprised that so few adults seemed aware that little boys were crawling along their walls, scaling fences and climbing up trees and along branches that took them round their gardens, some of which were quite large. I suppose we were harmless, not scrumping nor hurting plants but we were certainly trespassers. Who accompanies me on these adventures? Certainly not my brothers, but what starts as an exploration could become a tense challenge to travel as far as possible without setting foot on the ground, or to take part in a risky 'dare'. Sometimes I would explore on my own. On one such expedition I forgot time and place, arriving home quite unaware that I was an hour late for my dinner. Mum scolded me, fearing for my safety.

I am not sure if she curbed my exploration of neighbouring gardens but I was cured of such escapades after a real scare. My companion (who?) and I have journeyed through the jungle of a neighbouring estate and have reached the wall overlooking the main road. It is dusk and, concealed by bushes and trees, we look down on the pavement which is lit by a street-lamp. On this occasion we carry peashooters and plan to pepper passers-by as they walk along the pavement. As we are well concealed no one will know where the stings come from. We wait for victims and all goes well; we silently enjoy the surprised exclamations and mutterings. Next, two burly men walk by and we shoot peas at them, then snigger and lie still, waiting for the next customers. Suddenly there are movements in the bushes behind us; the two men have entered the garden and are tracking us down. Panic! We race for safety, across the lawns, through the trees, along branches and over the high fence into the back garden of 9 Ashwood Villas, the men hot on our heels. We elude them and tell no one but next day my father sternly calls me to account. These men have found out my address and

CHILDHOOD

made a complaint. I am contrite, but thankful we had not been caught. They were really big, rough men by the sound of it.

Another earlier visit to that same garden led to a lifelong distaste for dogs. Which summertime was it? I know I wore only a flimsy swimming costume, sandals and possibly a sun hat. My play-ball had gone over the high fence and I wanted to retrieve it but lacked the climbing skills of later years. Dad, aware of my dismay, decided the two of us would visit the adjoining estate to ask for our ball back. We walked down the Villas into the main street and entered the gates that led to the mansion, an early Victorian edifice. Dad held my hand as we advanced up the drive, a tall protective father figure and a fairly naked, white-skinned lad who had lost his ball, aware that people on the veranda were watching. We could hear the gruff barking of a dog as we advanced out of the trees and bushes and began to walk over a lawn. The barking of the dog became frenzied. I could see it by the house, fiercely barking and challenging us until it lost patience and started to sprint towards us, jowl open and eyes blazing. It was a big dog. It came straight for me, and Dad and I stood petrified. I don't know how my father would have coped if the dog had actually landed on me but just as it launched into the air for the attack, its head jerked back, its powerful body lost coordination and it collapsed in a heap, yelping instead of snarling. All this no more than a yard from me.

The dog's lead could travel along thirty or so yards attached to a pulley. At its limit, the collar round the dog's neck simply tightened and stopped the creature in its tracks. By luck, Dad and I were just beyond the reach of the dog. One step forward and I would have been dead meat. A distant voice cursed the dog which retreated sullenly, my father tried to protest, and someone came forward to apologise and make light of the matter. I went to retrieve my ball and we returned to normal life. The trauma lay in what might have been rather than what happened and I did not lack imagination. Forever after, though I put on a brave face when confronting (big) dogs, part of me is remembering that narrow escape. Dad was visibly shaken, aware just how helpless he had been at that moment.

Ball games, and other pursuits like Hide and Seek, were possible in the secure surroundings of Ashwood Villas, or more correctly Ashwood Terrace, which was the top part of the T-junction shape of the lay-out. This was completely level, cobbles at one end and compressed grit the other, like an airstrip. Though we lived in the Villas, we claimed the Terrace as our private playground. At first Fred and his friends were in charge and we kids played at home but the day came when they moved on to adolescence and we took over. A succession of games could fill a day – much to the annoyance of some local residents who resented our raucous voices and searches for lost balls in their gardens. I suppose they lost the battle years ago; we were just one more generation of rude, noisy youths claiming territorial rights. I don't remember any misbehaviour. And I can't recall any girl(s) taking part.

Four minutes walk from the Villas were shops at Hyde Park Corner (for sweets, ices, pop, bloods, what else?). Beyond the shops lay Woodhouse Moor, a vast expanse (to us) of incredibly flat, grey crushed coke deposit (remains of a century of heavy industry), not a pleasant playing 'field' nor hygienic if you fell and scraped your knees but it was the scene of the annual Fairground, ideal for roundabouts, swings and the long lines of booths and stalls offering a variety of attractions. By the time the thirties were ending, I was blasé about swings and roundabouts but there was a creepy interest in some of the sideshows like Boxing contests, Ghost Trains and Flea Circuses. This was a crazy, potentially violent world but I never envied the gaunt youths who collected the fares for the rides. I wasn't taken in by the glamour of the Fair.

On the outskirts of Leeds there was Golden Acre Park, a kind of 'leisure centre' which attracted the interest of youngsters as well as adults. It was simple and rural in comparison with Woodhouse Moor Fair which offered the temptations of urban life, and we occasionally had family outings there, but never on our own which was very annoying. At the end of one Summer holidays two friends and I broke the rules, so desperate were we to enjoy its attractions. It was a devious and cunning little plot that we hatched. I was the instigator of the tangled web of deception but the Willcock boys who lived in the Terrace were equal participants. The outing ended unhappily and I have strong emotional feelings about it, so much so that first-person autobiographical narrative seems unlikely to convey the personal significance of this event.

So I must hide behind fiction, and allow some embellishment of the facts. For example, the names of the boys are changed, dialogue is invented and most crucially the visit to Golden Acre Park has been transferred to a Fairground resembling that on Woodhouse Moor. I wrote this short story fifty years ago for a school magazine when I was teaching at Sevenoaks, since when it has lain in a nearly forgotten file. It seems to me still a sincere account of what happened back in the thirties.

THE CONSPIRATORS

> All three of them squatted in a circle and John moodily scraped lines on the pathway with his notched elm stick. They ignored two mongrels that scampered down the lane, deaf to the tram that rumbled along the rails on the distant main road.
>
> "It isn't as if we're broke," said Richard suddenly, his lower lip protruding beyond a snub nose.

CHILDHOOD

"Or just kids," added Peter, trying to make his rotund face severe and grown-up. "It takes more than a few goes on a roundabout to make me sick."

The two brothers looked at John as he stabbed at a pebble; then they watched as it rolled over, the dark shadow of John's head making it change colour. Richard and Peter exchanged glances and waited. John was obviously thinking hard.

"They won't let us go by ourselves, that's flat," he said at last. "They just won't listen to us, not even when we tell them it's the last day of the fair and we won't get another chance before school starts. And I'm jolly well going, whatever they say."

He looked sidelong at the brothers, as if sizing them up. "Let's pretend!" he said. "We'll say someone's going with us. You go home and say my mother is taking you, and I'll go home and say your mother is taking me. We can meet at the tram stop and – there we are! I'm going on the Moonrocket five times."

The two brothers made no move. "Can't be done," said Peter bluntly, "they'll see us leaving alone." There was a heavy silence.

"Anyway, it would be lying," said Richard, blinking rather quickly.

"But it wouldn't be a big lie," replied John persuasively. "I mean, why shouldn't we go to the funfair? In any case we won't get caught. We can't see your house from ours, so you can pretend to walk down to mine; and I can pretend to walk up to your house. When we get halfway we'll all sneak through old Thompson's garden into the next street. Nobody will know then."

Again there was silence; then the two brothers looked at each other, nodded and stood up.

"We'll have a shot," said Richard.

"It may not work, though," warned Peter. "Our mother's a bit more suspicious than yours."

"You'll be all right," said John encouragingly. "Just look pleased about my mother's kindness and you'll get away with it. S'long then, see you at quarter past two at the bus stop."

The conspirators parted, as the distant church clock struck one.

Richard and Peter were the first to reach the tram stop, flushed and breathing heavily from the excitement of their success. They waited impatiently, both recalling rather uneasily their instructions to thank John's mother after the trip. Then John arrived, walking quickly, his eyes gleaming happily.

IRONS IN THE FIRE

"Smashing!" he whooped, "It was easy as winking. Nearly got seen by old Thompson but Mum fell for it completely, she even gave me two bob to spend. I'm going on the Moonrocket seven times!"

But three times were enough, for although stolen fruits are sweetest, there is a limit to the sweetness of the Moonrocket. Round and round, swinging and swaying, dazed by the din of blaring loud-speakers, steam engines, drums, bells and hoarse-voiced showmen, starry-eyed from flashing lights and bright colours, thrilled with the flight through space, gazing up at the sky and the twisted chain that held the fragile chair, punch-drunk with the thumping of bumper cars, sweetly sick of the gob-stoppers, the candy-floss and watery lemonade... until, tired at last of the dazzling cavalcade, the three friends slowly trudged towards the bus stop, hands in pockets, whistling cheerfully in chorus. It was almost dusk; red and orange streaks lined the lower reaches of the sky. The subterfuge behind the giddy afternoon was barely remembered. It was a grain of sand irritating the green and tender conscience, and already time was secreting a hard cuticle round it, transforming it into a lustrous memory. Leaning back on the tram seats, bouncing their way home, they excitedly re-lived the afternoon's thrills "Abyssinia!" shouted Peter and Richard, as they jumped off the tram.

"Thanks! See you tomorrow."

"Ethiopia!" yelled John. "It was worth it, wasn't it?"

He walked up the lane in the gathering gloom, opened and shut the gate with a flourish, and raced up the path to the door.

"Here I am! We've had a super time!" he cried, and stood in the hall regaining his breath

"Hello, John," a quiet voice answered from the front room. "So you had a good time."

He found his mother sitting by the window, trying to catch the last of the daylight for her needlework. She was looking down at the work, the needle passing through the linen with a quick glint as her fingers moved incessantly.

"Yes," he replied, looking at his mother confidently, his mind still spinning with the roundabouts.

"And did Richard's mother go with you?" said his mother quietly, her eyes still fixed on the needlework.

"Oh yes," he said carelessly, "She went with us."

CHILDHOOD

He was turning away when his mother put down her work and spoke again. "Was Richard's mother there?" she repeated, and her eyes rested upon his face suddenly, surprising the guilty shadow that passed behind his eyes. There was a silence as he looked at her. He could feel roundabouts spinning inside his head, whirling out of control, disintegrating inside him. He suddenly realised what he had done. He had betrayed the trust between himself and his mother.

He bowed his head, wretched with guilt, suddenly full of remorse, thoughts tumbling down his mind until one hard fact was beaten out of the turmoil. He condemned himself for the deed itself and not the exposure of the deed, the sin and not the confession.

"No," he whispered.

His mother looked at him steadily.

"Go to your room and stay there. I met Richard's mother out shopping this afternoon."

John turned and left the room. As he mounted the stairs he knew that whatever punishment lay in store for him, nothing would remain in his memory like the sadness in his mother's eyes.

Next to the wasteland of Woodhouse Moor, and in contrast, stretched Hyde Park. This was tree-leafy with grassy acres where we could improvise pitches for cricket and football but otherwise it was not particularly interesting. I recall no children's playground and the bandstand at its centre seemed to have no function, but the pathway I followed through the park to reach the Grammar School on most schooldays still seems familiar to me. It took 15 minutes to walk there.

In contrast, on the northern side of Ashwood Villas, there was a mile-long escarpment called The Ridge. There was a steep drop to a valley and, though I was never fond of uphill walking, I used to love dropping down the Ridge pathways to reach the stream at its foot. Sticklebacks and tiddlers, water boatmen and skaters, dragonfly larvae and caddis worms were in abundance. With a fishing-net and a jam-jar, you could dredge for pond-life for hours. In season, the frogspawn just had to be transported home and kept in a tub. It's a pity such simple resources are hard to find these days.

Dad took all four boys sledging on the Ridge one snow-time. We were going to try a new sledge he had just bought. We trudged towards the point where a steep incline started and heard cries from the bottom of the run where many sledgers were gathered. Someone told us a boy had broken his leg and was awaiting an ambulance to take him to hospital. When we launched the new sledge, with a Morley load on board, it couldn't take the strain and collapsed. End of outing. The boy's cries followed us as we wended homeward.

IRONS IN THE FIRE

To reach this Ridge you snaked through a ginnel beside a big house with a spacious terrace on top of a sheer wall like a battlement from which the view was spectacular, though when I was there I wasn't looking. It so happened that, aged about 9, I lost a ball that bounced from the road into the extensive gardens adjoining this mansion. Deciding to retrieve it, I went through a green wicket gate and found myself in a market garden not unlike Mr. Macgregor's when Peter Rabbit sought juicy lettuces. I could see my ball lying next to a bushy-leaved patch of plants, and so trod boldly forward to take it and nearly jumped out of my skin when a rough voice shouted, "Hoy! What d'you think you're doing?" In the distance a burly man was shouting at me and when he started to rumble forward like a tank, issuing expletives, I grabbed the ball, turned and ran for my life, leaping over lettuces and cabbages, sprinting down paths and past wheelbarrows, not caring where I was going as long as it was away from my pursuer. I came to an open door, ran through a passage and found myself on a terrace with stately urns and flowers and a lady who held a watering can with a look of astonishment. Ignoring her, I dashed to the front of the terrace and halted, for I was now looking down at the Ridge from a great height. As the gardener came clattering on to the terrace, still growling, I jumped over the wall and landed on the ground below. Without stopping to look back, I scuttled up the ginnel to safety, clutching my ball triumphantly. I was unhurt; I told no one about it.

I have visited that scene. I know the wall was about 20 feet high. My father, informed by the gardener about the incident when they met at the adjacent tennis club, was appalled by my panic reaction to the emergency. The gardener was apparently a jovial sort of chap. To me, it is like a sequence from an old black and white film set in Victorian times. I can see the hue and cry as the boy races for his freedom but was that boy really me?

11. Schools in the Thirties

John, Neil and I attended St Michael's C of E School in Headingley during the early thirties. To get to it, we crossed the road at the bottom of the Villas and walked a quarter of a mile up and down hill along the main road until we reached the Church and then the School nearby. A State Elementary School was situated a further quarter mile on but my parents were eminently sensible to send us to the nearer Church school even though my father was a lapsed Anglican and my mother a firm Presbyterian. St Michael's was not a bad school at all, though I remember smelly outside lavatories and a little bullying. I guess there would be 200 pupils at any one time. I have one abiding memory of a visit to the Church itself; we were in the Choir stalls and sang all six verses of "There is a green hill far away without a city wall". I had trouble with the meaning, wondering how important it was to have a city wall, but I was overwhelmed by the plaintive,

CHILDHOOD

plangent tune. We were a choir of angels (or cherubim) at Eastertide, rejoicing in the blood imagery of Mrs. Alexander's lines. Seventy years on, I still feel the emotional pull though I resist the message.

I remember two teachers. One was the headmistress, a small busy motherly type who delighted classes by reading Kipling's Just-So stories. The other was Miss Green, a somewhat severe angular figure with a beaky nose. She was consulted when Brother John lost his school cap and Dad came to the school to help sort out the problem. I wasn't present but Dad laughed his head off afterwards imitating Miss Green bending over John, her beak almost touching his anxious face, repeatedly asking him where he had lost the cap. John, no doubt in fear of being pecked, couldn't answer. "If he knew where, he would have found it!" said Dad, a little unreasonably.

I did not respond to Miss Green's personality and once I took a piece of chalk and on my way home chalked rude words on wooden boards in the street, like "Miss Green is a pig" sort of thing. The friend I was with tormented me by threatening to tell Miss Green next day. He didn't, but I was so terrified that when I saw Miss Green at school that morning I burst into tears and made a full confession when she asked what was the matter. I don't remember how I was punished. I was told to rub out the offending words on my way home and no doubt I did.

A somewhat different light on these early school days (I have no memory of attending any kind of nursery school) is shed by my kidnapping of a little girl. Bear in mind that I was not used to girls and this one was remarkably attractive, if you like dolls that look like Shirley Temple. I was fascinated by her circular blue eyes and golden curls and she didn't mind when I took her hand and started walking round the playground with her. She was younger than me and I guess I felt proudly protective. At the end of afternoon school I asked if she would like to come home with me and without a demur she came, two toddlers holding hands, trudging together quite a long way, up and down hill, and finally arriving at Ashwood Villas where I introduced my friend to a totally astonished and alarmed mother.

The trouble was that the little girl didn't know where she lived, nor was there a telephone at home to send an urgent message to the school. And what about her parents, probably distraught with worry? I sat sipping lemonade and chewing biscuits with my delightful doll-friend while Mum found a solution to the problem, probably involving neighbours and I seem to remember waving to a taxi or car. The child vanished from my memory but I haven't forgotten my Mum, a twinkle in her eye, telling me never to do that again.

I was well behaved in class usually but I kicked up a quite unnecessary fuss over swallowing the metal cap to a retracting pencil one afternoon. Maybe I didn't swallow it but no one was able to find it. I went home convinced that I was in mortal danger and alarmed my mother so much she insisted on Dad taking me to the Leeds Infirmary to be examined. The size of the metal grew each time I described it but the doctor couldn't locate it even though he panned my abdomen with a huge X-ray machine. Dad was there, marvelling at the sight of my innards and lingering over my guts for so long the metal cap was forgotten. The doctor enjoyed showing off his machine but what the hell, in those days down the road at Lewis's Store you happily put your foot under an X-ray to test shoe sizes. It was some time after that I discovered the metal cap in my pocket. I think I kept quiet about it.

The time came for me to move to the Grammar School. I remember the St Michael's head teacher withdrawing me from class to ask if it was true I was going there. She seemed very impressed by this, as if hardly anyone ever did from her school. She wished me well and I went back to my class wondering why she had been so nice to me, not really appreciating I had made her day. In those days children left school at fourteen.

I must have sat an entrance exam in 1935, though with Fred and John already there I doubt if I would have 'failed entry'. The school fees were £7.00 (or guineas) per term, with a reduction for younger brothers (£5). I hardly thought about entrance problems until I met a boy at Sunday School who had tried for a scholarship unsuccessfully and his parents had been unable to afford the fees. All I could offer was sympathy. Overheads like books and uniform could put off many a working class family, even if their son had gained a scholarship, but compared with private and boarding schools the fees were amazingly low. I don't know how they did it back in the thirties; maybe there were legacies and direct grants subsidising the middle class beneficiaries. When the 1944 Education Act revolutionised secondary education in U.K., post-war changes were inevitable and Leeds Grammar School, like many other old foundations, decided to withdraw from 'maintained' status and became 'independent direct grant'. In the 1990s the Grammar School sold its site to the University and built a brand-new campus on the outskirts of northwest Leeds, which I have not visited but there's no doubting the improvement on Victorian Gothic blackened by the soot of ages.

Leeds Grammar School was founded in 1552 in the reign of Henry VIII. In the 1930s the Headmaster of Leeds Grammar School was a member of the Headmasters' Conference. This was an august independent body that issued invitations to Heads of 'the best public ' schools, something of a misnomer as most were 'private' and not always 'the best', though quite frankly we pupils knew little about such matters. In any case the Grammar School belonged to a prouder, more worthy tradition – originating in the education of poor scholars, with a fine academic standard and strong local ties. Which is not to deny that sometimes it could be oppressive and hidebound. The buildings were hardly aesthetically pleasing though the Victorians probably thought they were.

CHILDHOOD

For the Morleys of Ashwood Villas, the Grammar School was very conveniently situated. I think the walk through the Park took 15 minutes, but maybe we should have allowed 20 to be punctual for roll call. There were about 700 boys on the roll in the thirties; if I was aware of older pupils it was largely through the remote activities of Fred at the 'top' end, playing cricket and rugby. On special occasions the whole school watched matches from the touchline or the cricket field boundary. In 1937 Herbert Sutcliffe brought a County team to play the 1st XI one summer day. He was out when he skied a shot miles high and the bowler held a fantastic one-handed catch over his head. We screamed our delight.

Recollections of events and happenings between 1936 and 1939 at school are not easy to qualify in terms of influence on my upbringing; or to quantify, as so many personal experiences turn into amorphous strings when looked at closely. I was absorbed in the normal processes of learning and playing, achieving a steady 'middle' status in classroom rating. Each year a substantial booklet recorded the marks and positions of all pupils and our parents received it. This implies a rather competitive regime controlling our learning; and certainly it was fallible as a measure of 'success' but it did include everyone – comprehensive to that extent! I recall the teachers with affection and respect. For every unpleasant memory there are half-a-dozen good ones. If I now itemise events which seem trivial, it is because they left a mark on me and/or because they provide insight into my character and personality.

So I start with the Lord Mayor's Quarter Mile Race, a 'one-off' event for I can't recall it in succeeding years; it was an extraordinary and somewhat deflating experience for me, as I had not yet joined the Grammar School. Young runners were invited to take part in this handicap race, the culmination of Sports Day with many parents and visitors present. According to your age you were given a few yards start in a race round the circular track. So a scattering of young competitors were placed at various positions on the track and the nearer to the starting point you were, the older (possibly the more athletic) you were. As befitting a younger runner, I was near the front, with perhaps 15 or so in front of me and up to a 100 behind me, a veritable army of older boys with a massing of maturer runners at the line-up waiting for the Lord Mayor to fire the starting pistol. There were crowds watching the mixed bag of runners.

Sprinting round a track was something new to me but I realised the idea was to overtake anyone in front, so at the crack of the start I raced ahead and began to overtake the string of front runners. Then, bursting into the lead, I rounded the bend and, with the crowd cheering, I headed for the winning post but – a fatal mistake; I looked round and got the fright of my life. A wild horde of grimacing runners was bearing down on me, like a pack of baying hounds. I almost stopped in my tracks, then picked up pace and surged ahead, but alas, now I could hear

IRONS IN THE FIRE

and feel their hot breath on my neck and all at once I was swamped in a tidal wave of hustling and pounding feet. The winner was a boy not much older than me but he was a real sprinter. I finished well down in the order, still feeling foxed.

My father arranged for me to start one term early in 1935. He thought it a good idea for me to get the summer term's cricketing experience, which says as much about my father as about me. Apparently I was a 'promising' bat and I became a 'demon' bowler that term because I specialised in bowling 'donkey-drops' which arched without bouncing straight for the wicket. I was banned from bowling during games periods because no one knew how to deal with them. At the end of term I was chosen to play for the Sheafield House Junior team against the rival Nicholson House team. (All the Houses, 2 Junior, and then 7 Senior, were named after famous old boys). It was a memorable match.

Nicholson House team batted first and scored 54 runs. That total is authentic and was displayed on the scoreboard. When Sheafield House batted, the score crawled along until we had reached 46 for 9 wickets. As befitted one of the smallest and youngest, I was last man in. The pads were more impediment than protection but I knew my job was to stonewall while the other batsman (who was quite good) tried to score the nine runs for victory. I played a straight bat. The scoreboard showed our runs slowly advancing to 54 and the scores became tied! The bowler trotted to the wicket and my co-batsman struck the ball through the covers. We sprinted the length of the pitch and that was it, we had won! I started dancing down the pitch waving my bat and cheering (so were the spectators) until I saw my co-batsman charging back for a second run, shouting at me to get to the other end. I was miles out of my crease but I ran for the line, only to be overtaken by the ball which a fielder was throwing at the stumps. Bails scattered and I was out but I didn't care, we had won the game by one run.

Or had we? As we left the field, the scorers were arguing, the scoreboard was changing. It seemed they had made a mistake, Sheafield House were on 53 runs not 54 and as only one run had been added before the last wicket fell, the game must be declared a tie. Hardly the conquering hero's deserts!

Mr. Kent was the Sheafield Housemaster. He was old, testy and a little threatening for he wielded a sawn-off cricket bat as an aid to class discipline. I don't think I was ever 'batted' but he once had the class on tenterhooks when dealing with one offending boy who was brought forward to receive punishment. Building up the tension by making the boy bend over, then straighten, then change position Mr. Kent finally struck the blow – and hit the side of a desk with the bat. He had placed the boy next to the desk and meant to miss. The boy stood up in surprise and was told to sit down. The rest of the class had hysterics in relief. Mr. Kent had a sense of humour! It was a sadistic little joke, though, and it preyed on fear.

CHILDHOOD

Mr. Kent it was who allowed a University Maths student teacher to take charge of us for a few lessons. He looked Nordic (or Aryan) with blonde wavy hair, fine bone structure, handsome and haughty; he was learning classroom skills, though it was clear he didn't like teaching fractions and decimals to us. Having used the double blackboard to explain what to us was an arcane arithmetical point, he set us tasks from the textbook.

I raised my hand to ask a question and he started to go through details again. As I listened, my eyes strayed to the other blackboard to check figures. The teacher glared. "Stand up, Morley! You are not paying attention!" he shouted. "Come out here!" I approached and protested that I had been listening to him. "You were looking at the other board," he said. Before I could reply, he raised his two hands, open-palmed, and slapped them simultaneously on either side of my cheeks hard. There was a stunned silence, I reeled under the unexpected blow and was told to sit down. End of assault, and the response to my question. The class was as astonished as me. I don't think I told my parents; learning went on. I wonder occasionally whether that arrogant bully ever became a qualified teacher. Or whether Mr. Kent ever heard about his methods in the classroom.

Miss Christie was one of two junior school lady teachers. I stress 'lady' because she was very keen on her pupils showing the right amount of respect for her. Short and fierce at times, she demanded attention and usually got it. Once or twice we met in the park, both of us school-bound, and I had to carry her briefcase and talk to her, which wasn't that simple but she seemed to like me. I was a little hurt when she compiled a weird article for the school magazine which contrived to include the names of lots of her pupils, but which failed to contain my name. There was a prize for counting how many pupils' names you could identify but what annoyed me was the inclusion of Cousin Muir's name (Temple). No matter that 'item pleased' is easy whereas 'Morley' just doesn't divide, Muir had been at the school a mere year and in my estimation didn't warrant a mention, not at least if I didn't. I was a vain little boy.

I mention Johnny Lee because he was a good teacher. In my first year in the middle school (1938) he taught us Biology – or it may even have been called Nature Study, which definitely included learning about the life of earthworms, crane flies and frogs. In the summer term, however, Mr. Lee concentrated on wild flowers and off we went to meadows, hedgerows and marshes to collect our specimens, press them in big books and display them in special exercise books. It was wonderfully educational and though something of a competitive game to collect the most wild flowers, there can't have been a boy in that class who didn't grow to love his obsession with nature or share Mr. Lee's enthusiasm. It's sad to reflect that I can't remember one tenth of the flowers I so lovingly pressed and named when I was eleven years old

IRONS IN THE FIRE

I was in Middle Three Class in 1939. Mr. Montagnon (the Maths teacher) was a good form master and he enjoyed our company. My favourite lesson was English with Pip Kelsey, a young teacher who had been a Grammar School boy in Fred's time, though I balked at clause analysis. These were good days and the class mixed well. I made my first real friend in Peter Lupton. He was the son of a dairy farmer in a village north of Leeds and travelled to school by bus. We exchanged visits to each other's home. Our parents approved. During the midday break, while I walked home to dinner, Peter stayed at school and thus stole a march on me by getting picked as wicketkeeper for the School Colts XI. He had been at the Cricket nets and Pip Kelsey, the coach, had 'spotted' his talent. I admired and wasn't jealous but became aware that his was suddenly a bigger world than I occupied. It had never dawned on me to take part in a responsible, serious task, or to volunteer for extra-curricular activities. It was perhaps a salutary hint that I had to start growing up.

The summer Term ended. After our holidays we would be back together in the Fourth year. Unfortunately war intervened.

12. The Presbyterian Church

Dad had distanced himself from church religion long before my time. He had been a choirboy in Ashby de la Zouch Parish Church but his love of music benefited more than his devoutness. Early days in Newry (Ireland before the Great War) as an Inland Revenue Inspector had made him very aware of the absurd extremes to which Sectarian rivalries drove Catholics and Protestants. He wasn't in favour of taking sides but he did become a Mason of the Newry Lodge, which was certainly aligning himself with the Protestant cause. After returning to the mainland, he became a lapsed Mason as well as lapsed Anglican. I have his little apron in a little leather bag to prove it. I guess it was a fast learning curve as the bachelor apprentice tax-inspector came to terms with Irish realities.

Mum was a loyal rather than devout Presbyterian attending 'the Church of Scotland in England'. If the origins were Calvinist, no one said a word. The congregation came from all parts of Leeds once a week, an act of bonding as much as worship. Friendly contacts were made and kept, but it was very much a middle-class gathering with a preponderance of professional men and their wives, and prosperous business men who drove cars to the Sunday services from the outskirts of Leeds. The Church in Cavendish Road adjoined poor quality housing with working class residents, but few of the locals attended services or appreciated help from Church members as far as I know. Charity is not next to love.

The only service the Presbyterian Church successfully offered local families was Sunday School. The Morley boys attended regularly and it was certainly a

CHILDHOOD

thriving institution that mixed the classes and made us aware of children from very deprived households. I reckon we learned quite a lot through Bible stories from earnest, young Presbyterians, dividing into small groups for 'religious instruction' in the big hall; we learned about social divides too.

I recall one Sunday School event because it shows me in a good light, but there is an instructive side to it. A local boy who was clearly the bullying type occasionally attended Sunday School. He was always surrounded by his gang and between them they disturbed some of the teachers and some of the pupils without causing serious trouble. I was not really concerned as I belonged to another group of boys, most of them from 'Presbyterian' families, but trouble started at the Sunday School Christmas Party when this boy began throwing his weight about. He challenged our group and picked on me. I answered back and we squared up for a fight, while a crowd of cheering kids gathered. Somehow I managed to wrestle him to the floor and straddle him but by this time a couple of teachers were coming across to separate us. We received a severe ticking-off but the result was we shook hands, talked and parted amicably. The bullyboy was as docile as a lamb and peace reigned but he never came to Sunday School again so I don't know how he felt. As for me, later at the party I overheard the girlfriend of one of the teachers excitedly telling him, "But he was winning!" and I think she was talking about me.

Every Sunday Dad looked after the cooking of the roast dinner though Mum did most of the preparation before taking her brood to Church, either walking or by tram. We always sat in the same pew: Fred, John, me, Neil and Mum. The deliberately long (winded) sermon could be avoided by retiring to colour pictures or something in an upper room, but it was difficult to avoid being present when the Choir sang their anthem for the week, unfortunately. The Presbyterian connection lasted well into adulthood, and kept me ignorant of Anglican procedure and custom. Attending the Sunday service at the Parish Church when at Sevenoaks School, I was out of my depth. Kneeling to pray never seemed right and I couldn't cope with responses and collects. Chanting the Creed was embarrassing, if only because I didn't know the words. Having been brought up a non-conformist, I tend to take the outsider's viewpoint, and I have never been a committed 'joiner'.

13. Holidays in the Thirties

The ones that mattered were summer holidays when the family assembled at the Leeds City Station to take an L.N.E.R. train to the Yorkshire coast. There were of course local and short holidays but they don't register much. I recall a vague Empire Day in Roundhay Park, probably in 1934 when Hitler was rallying his troops at Nuremberg. Did I understand the message? 'Look at this map of the world, children! The red bits are British!' All elementary schools were represented at this gathering; there was some kind of flag-carrying procession round the running track and we watched a few races and sat on the grass for a family picnic but I don't think I was involved in running. I went one Easter to the Grammar School Holiday Camp but I wasn't convinced roughing it was quite my style, particularly having to sit on a crude bench to crap into a festering pit. Imagine toppling over! The next year I had veruccas and chickened out.

Dad took us all for family walks. There were regular Sunday afternoon strolls to Sugarwell Hill, for instance, about 3 miles there and back, though I forget where it actually is. A more ambitious walk in the Skipton area was sabotaged unintentionally by me. There were crowds in the market square, mostly hikers and day-trippers for it was a public holiday, and we had to wait for the right bus to take us further up the dales. Dad was getting impatient to be off and we boys wanted ice creams from the cafe opposite the bus stop. Mum took our side and gave me the money to get cornets. In the cafe, there was a long queue for ices so I decided we should go upstairs and get them from someone up there. Plenty of people sat at tables eating ice creams and drinking tea so we sat at an empty table by the window. I could see Mum and Dad in the square so I waved to them happily. To my surprise Dad jumped up and down furiously, shouting and waving his arms. "Come down, you fools!" he yelled, "The bus has gone!" We ran out into the road without ices or understanding. Apparently we had been waiting ten minutes in the shop; the bus had arrived, picked up passengers and departed. Dad was still dancing with rage and frustration but Mum couldn't stop laughing. "You should have seen your face, Harry," she said, "grinning like a Cheshire Cat!" Not for the first time I thought my mother had a superior sense of humour, but I admit my father had a point when he called me a fool.

No comparison with two weeks in a boarding house on the seafront at Saltburn, near Whitby! The Misses Burton had everything well organised, a room for Mum and Dad with a spectacular view seaward and I don't remember how the boys slept but we got packed off to bed just before the evening meal. Our dinner was midday. If you went down to the beach in the morning it was quite a climb up the cliff-path for dinner, then down again for the afternoon. There was an electric cable car but only occasionally were we allowed to use it. We took the steep climb in our stride and raced downhill with buckets and spades, cricket bats and balls. Having a fair skin I regularly got sunburnt across the shoulders, with raw patches of flesh and plenty of calamine lotion. The weather must have been exceptionally warm in those days.

In four successive years (from 1933 to 1936) the Morleys holidayed in Saltburn at the same boarding house. The same returning visitors greeted us; the same regulations would be framed in our rooms, the same games on the beach, the same entertainments. Chief among those were The Pierrots who performed

CHILDHOOD

their shows every year on a ramshackle stage on the beach. The final time we went to Saltburn, they had moved indoors to a proper theatre but the real magic was performing in the open air, the gulls competing, the salty breeze blowing, waves breaking in the distance, the dusty sand we sat on. The Pierrots really seemed to enjoy entertaining kids. Two of them clowned like Laurel and Hardy, two others provided romance and song, there was one pianist and no one else mattered. They were innocent funsters and we loved them. You won't see their like these days – nor ever will for the world has grown up since then.

Usually I was so preoccupied with family happenings that I took little heed of other children but I had to take note of the Todd boy who stayed at Misses Burtons' boarding house with his parents. He was my age, and a chorister in Durham Cathedral; he possessed a fine treble voice and with his curly golden hair and angelic expression he was adored by the elderly folk on holiday. They wanted nothing so much as a song or hymn solo from him at teatime and as he stood by the piano and held forth like a linnet all eyes and ears were fixed on him. The applause would turn anyone's head, even mine. Consumed with a desire to emulate the Todd boy (name forgotten, significantly) when he sat down I asked my mother if I could sing to the assembled grown-ups. Surprised, she probably demurred but someone next to her had overheard and urged me forward. The hymn is forgotten ('A green hill far away'?) but I stood by the piano and held forth, buoyed by my vanity and ignorance, before the audience. Even I knew my singing was flat, the voice like a broken reed. Desultory applause followed and I lapped it up. Returning to my mother's side, she hugged me. "Well done, you tried really hard!" she said. I was grateful for small mercies. I lived and let live with the Todd boy.

Needing a change, we tried Colwyn Bay in North Wales in 1937. I reckon this is the right year because Len Hutton scored a record 365 runs in the Test match at Lords. England amassed more than 900 runs and effectively demoralised the Australian cricketers. I think this was one of those matches without time limit and they were experimenting with eight ball overs. There is something unreal about the nation being gripped by such trivialities while dictators stalked the mainland but I listened avidly to the little wireless owned by the miniature golf course attendant at Colwyn Bay. I remember very little about that holiday but for some reason or other we were disappointed with the guesthouse we stayed at – it was clearly different from the cosy, uncritical atmosphere of our boarding-house in Saltburn. Perhaps the proprietor didn't like boisterous boys but one of the men visitors taught me the backhand flick at table tennis, so it wasn't entirely wasted holiday time.

The following year (1938) it was back to the Yorkshire Coast, this time trying out Bridlington and staying at a familiar kind of residence, though it wasn't on the sea front. Unusually, Brother Fred had a friend joining us for a few days of the holiday but I knew nothing of this before meeting him on the stairs of the boarding house. Really the story starts on the beach where I am becoming aware that I need a pee but I can't find a toilet and I am wearing only my swimming briefs and sandals. Does it occur to me that I should simply pee in a corner? No, I have decided to trot up the cliff-path to our boarding house and by the time I arrive there I am bursting for relief. I dash up the stairs, and meet Dennis Richard who greets me, smiling and asking how I am. Now Dennis Richard is a hero because he is one of the Co-Optimists Concert Party in Leeds, so I must stop and answer his question politely. He persists with his questions, I twist and turn, itching to get past him and dive into the lav. With horror I feel a warm liquid trickling down my leg and my self-control breaks down. There is a telltale pool between us and I have to hop past him, covered in embarrassment and humiliation.

Fred and Dennis are old enough for dancehalls, pubs and flirtations but one evening they spend a little time with us. Sitting in a dim little parlour with an aspidistra in the window, Dennis tinkles on the piano. He wants us to play a quiz game: we have to name the song or melody which he plays. Brothers John, Neil and I have not a clue. He gives us the latest 'hit', the sweetest romantic lullaby; the new swing number and draws a blank each time. I resent his incredulity; he is showing off and probably thinks we have had a very deprived childhood. Maybe I should have blamed Fred for pinching our gramophone, or Dad for playing only classical music at the piano or for stopping me listen to Henry Hall's band on the wireless. It seems that Bridlington and this boarding house were not up to Saltburn standards either. Maybe it rained too often. Whatever the reason, for the next year (August 1939) my parents decide to branch out – they booked two or three weeks on a working farm at Grimthorpe, a village near Filey. It was to be our last family holiday.

War clouds gathered but the sun shone on the Yorkshire coast. The farm was isolated with magnificent views towards the sea; farm life was interesting and though grown-up anxieties and fears filtered down to our level, there was so much to do we gave little thought to what might be in store. Mum and the farmer's wife got on like buddies; Dad no doubt rambled. And I made friends with the farmer's daughter who was perhaps a little older than me and certainly more aware of what goes on in the farmyard or elsewhere. I was now 13, but totally ignorant of the facts of life, and yet to actually kiss a girl. I still thought babies were delivered by some agency, possibly by doctors and left under bushes or at back doors. Observing farmyard activity I told my new friend I thought the cock was a great bully standing on top of hens so brutally and she was amazed by my naïveté – if she tried to enlighten me, she failed. I had yet to be disturbed by pubertal changes; and girls were not important in my self-sufficient, self-promoting world. The friendship persisted but I remained ignorant.

CHILDHOOD

There was an elegiac quality to our final day on the farm. We put on a little performance for the grown-ups in the garden. Fred directed the show: sketches from the Co-Optimists, some comic songs, some clowning and tricks. I seem to see the sun setting as chairs are taken back to the garden shelter; we are packing cases and bags for the journey home, there is talk of Fred being 'called-up' and my parents dread the future. August ends and the puffing train takes us back to Leeds.

On September 3rd we listen to the Prime Minister telling us we are at war with Nazi Germany, speaking so sadly you feel his heart isn't in it. 'Peace in our time' is no longer possible. Holidays are over. I wander in and out of the drawing room as Chamberlain's quavering voice emanates from the wireless. The full meaning has not yet dawned. At least I had to take note when it was announced that all Grammar School pupils were to be evacuated immediately for fear of bombing raids on Leeds. Everyone was issued with gas masks to be carried in flimsy cardboard boxes slung from our necks. The School had announced evacuation plans to send Junior School pupils to Wales and the older boys to two separate country houses in Upper Wharfedale. And Dad announced that he was opting out of this plan; both Neil and I would stay at home in Ashwood Villas and if the School was closed, any teaching would be handled by Dad.

I am aware that I passed through the thirties in a kind of dream, registering very few of my experiences with anything like consideration of their significance. A life of sensations was sufficient to satisfy my childhood aspirations, but I had only partial sensitivity or indeed participation. A memory of my love of birds flashes across my mind – the exquisite forms and colours, the sense of wonderment at such beauty – kingfisher, bullfinch, eagle, albatross – and yet I was looking at cigarette cards stuck in an album. I didn't transfer that romance and devotion to the birds on the other side of the window. I preferred the idealised and the simplified version to reality. Without too much pretension I draw a parallel with my childhood in Ashwood Villas: they were happy days and I was content to stay within the confines of love and protection. But this was the end of the decade. Times were changing.

CHAPTER TWO

ADOLESCENCE

1. Outbreak of War

I was 13 at the time. Neil was 10. John was 16 and had left school to start work in Wilkinson's, a wholesale clothes manufacturer and supplier in the city centre. They marketed Caressa underwear, which struck me as very punny. John worked in the packaging department without showing much enthusiasm either for goods or fellow workmen but he stuck at it. I don't know how he got that job, which meant that only the two youngest boys were now at school, in theory at least.

In practice, Neil and I were stranded in a no-man's land of home education as Dad had decided that the plan to evacuate the whole school from Leeds to rural backwaters was an absurd panic reaction, which would badly damage his sons' education. In effect, however, he disrupted it, particularly in the delicate area of identity with a peer group. I suspect that he didn't want to pay boarding fees; or he disliked the boarding school ethic; or possibly he thought he could be an excellent private tutor for his own children. He was right about one thing; the evacuation of the whole school was unnecessary. After two terms there were classes being arranged for those who stayed behind. The school buildings re-opened in September1940, by which time France had fallen and the Blitz was starting, which was probably why the boarding arrangements kept going for those who wanted to stay out of Leeds. We were not the only children with schooling problems.

Fred meanwhile had packed his bags and headed for the poor bloody infantry. He had to abandon his studies in architecture and 'join up'. What a waste but he was in the first batch of conscripts (22 years old) and that was that. I don't think he volunteered for officer training. He was Private F.J. Morley and that was how he stayed. He had no taste for war. One of his best friends, Dennis Richard, was very much 'officer-like' material and got rapid promotion to Staff Captain. I don't know whether this killed their friendship but there must have been a big contrast when they met on leave together, which wasn't often.

My first reaction after war had been declared was to dig a hole. Perhaps the images of trenches and air raid shelters being created elsewhere spurred me on; all I can remember is not stopping till I had dug something like four feet down in a part of the garden that was raised to form a terrace with a stone wall. My hole was about five feet long and three feet wide, dug into heavy clay. I think it was impressive as a feat but what the point of this burial site was I did not, and do not know. It ended after a week of activity with the displaced soil being returned to its previous position. Curiously my parents expressed no criticism or astonishment. They were probably too absorbed in their anxieties as the year drew to a close.

There followed a period in which Neil and I adjusted to spending the days on our own. It didn't feel like holiday time and there was hardly any contact with other boys. Dad would set us schoolwork – he must have got hold of some textbooks surely – and then rode off on his bike to the Office. I am not sure what Mum thought of the procedure. She certainly encouraged us to take daily exercise by going for afternoon walks, though I don't recall her accompanying us and I don't think she actually taught us. I suspect she wasn't in favour of home tuition and she was now without the maid of all work, Eva.

Our walks were not very interesting; after all we were trudging over familiar ground most of the time but I developed an unusual motivation for exploring the highways and byways of Headingley and beyond. I started collecting cigarette packets - not cards, which had become a redundant means of selling cigarettes as smoking became the universal palliative, but the packets. I didn't smoke of course but simply picked up empty packets thrown in the gutter and elsewhere. There was a proliferation of names and designs on the market. Some, like Woodbines, Goldflake and Player's Navy Cut, were obvious and numerous; others, like de Reszke and Passing Cloud, very recherché and rare. Neil was a willing accomplice in the game; it kept us on the move, two ex-schoolboys nosing along streets and parks, heads down and occasionally pouncing on prey. Of course the packets had to be as pristine as possible, so I was constantly replacing one specimen with another in better condition. I kept my collection in a suitcase under the bed. It got pretty full; maybe there were thirty different brands to gloat over but no one was impressed. Eventually I decided there were better ways of spending time; no doubt the supply of rare packets ran out. I threw them in the dustbin. Neil remained unmoved.

The 'lessons' that Dad set for our morning sessions were not based on a balanced curriculum of subjects. Dad had a firm notion, gathered from his own experience of schooling fifty years ago, that Maths and Latin were the two vital subjects for any aspiring youth. Consequently most days we had to answer arithmetical questions and translate passages from Latin, which hardly enthused us with a craving for knowledge, especially when we were working on our own. The amount of tuition that Dad gave us was limited to the marking period in the evening when he returned from work; the crosses probably exceeded the ticks but I learned little from the exercises or explanations. In any case, as far as I was concerned this was education under duress. We needed and craved for companionship, the rough and tumble of schoolmates.

Dad intended well; he realised that neither Maths nor Latin were my favourite subjects and wanted to improve my ability but he had no idea how to teach or educate. Neil and I wrote a few stories (English) and looked up places in an atlas

ADOLESCENCE

(Geography) and learned irregular verbs (French) but there were huge gaps and little continuity. Up in Wharfedale (Burnsall) the evacuated fourth-formers were being introduced to Chemical equations. I missed out there and never caught up in Science for School Certificate.

This period was known as the 'phoney war-time' as there seemed little British military activity for six months, and each week I bought a magazine called "War Illustrated". With a dearth of exciting news and photographs about the 'western front', this black and white journal covered the Russo-Finnish war in horrifying detail. Pictures of frozen bodies, some with limbs breaking off in the intense cold, showed The Russians as incompetent assailants oppressing the heroic Finns. Everything was grim, ugly and atrocious, yet fascinating to behold; and the baddies were victorious. It was far removed from our own war, which had hardly touched us as we lived our somewhat confined lives, making minor discomforting adjustments.

We had to buy blackout material to cover the windows at night. Mum was busy making black curtains. Sealing tape formed a network on panes to stop glass splintering though this was never put to the test in the Villas. Dingy yellow close-knit fabric (or plastic) was stuck to the glass panels of all public transport. You couldn't see in or out, but there was a small rectangle in the fabric through which to peer when you got near your destination. One of the neighbours was appointed Air Raid Warden; she sometimes wore a tin hat. One evening she knocked on our front door to tell us the upstairs lights were blazing a clear signal to bombers. We hastily blacked out the offence. Each home had been supplied with a metal bucket (marked Water) and a stirrup pump fire extinguisher to put out incendiary bombs. We argued about where to store it as we kept kicking the bucket. One neighbour was seen using the pump to clean his car, an unpatriotic abuse no doubt but we didn't have a car to clean anyway.

On one occasion my father, fiddling with the dials of the wireless, tuned in to news being announced by some man with a peculiar singsong accent, a kind of cut-glass finicky speech. He was telling us about the rationing of food in England and how sorry he was for us. Dad said this was Lord Haw-haw who was a collaborator with the Germans and wasn't he a silly idiot if he thought we were going to take him seriously. Some outrageous lies were blandly told but at the end of the programme the sound of Elgar's Pomp and Circumstance no 1 boomed out of the wireless. Dad nearly went crazy. 'How dare they play our national music!' he shouted at the wireless. I hadn't noticed but apparently the German broadcast was defiling one of the greatest Britons who had ever lived! That treacherous Irish swine ought to be shot! The Germans should stick to Beethoven and Wagner. Damn and blast and hell set fire! Switching off the strains of Elgar's music, he went rampaging up the stairs very seriously.

IRONS IN THE FIRE

2. Escape to the Farm

Perhaps Dad didn't try very hard to be a home-tutor, he was simply playing a waiting game until the chickens came home to roost. But it was no damn good educationally and the crucial factor was always the break with our contemporaries at school. Peter Lupton, my third year friend, had gone straight to nearby Knaresborough Grammar School on the outbreak of war, swapping one peer group for another. Peter, wiry and quick on his feet, his bony face usually wearing a happy grin, fitted in at once. He was a farm lad, I a town boy – but he was getting involved in practical living on the farm while I was still marking time. I took the bus once or twice to see him.

On one visit to the farm at East Keswick, Peter took me out to the cowshed to watch what was going on. It was evening time and the electric light was dramatically primitive, a single bulb hanging from a rafter and hand-held torches flashing thin beams on the scene. A cow was having trouble giving birth to its calf. It was standing still while two workers and Mr. Lupton heaved and pulled on ropes. I was suddenly aware that a compressed mass of flesh and blood was sticking out of the cow's rear end. The ropes were tied to the folded front legs and to the shoulders of the calf and the men were gradually freeing it from the position where it had got stuck. They had been working for some time, sweating with their efforts and talking quietly. I gathered that Mr. Lupton wanted to save the calf and that's what they concentrated on. One more tightening of the ropes, a heave in unison and suddenly, with a slither of caul and fluids, the rest of the calf burst through the cow's rear and flopped to the ground. It seemed to unfold neck and head, and four legs became visible. The men were quickly untying the ropes, wrapping a blanket round the frail body and the cow, turning its head to look at the fuss, mooed and seemed quite indifferent to the sudden relief from its suffering. I was told next morning that the cow had died. It had simply keeled over after we left, but the calf had survived. It was all very surreal and unexpected. I was a very astonished observer of natural forces at work – or unnatural perhaps.

The sudden blitzkrieg that scuppered the western front mid-1940 was hardly credible to us. We were still adjusting to ration books, shelving our gas-masks, and going to the pictures where Gaumont British News brought us clips of British troops near the Maginot Line being entertained by celebrities in the open air. Gracie Fields was there, filmed cooing and waving and warbling "goodbye! goodbye!" (her Italian marriage not yet a disgrace to the good name of Rochdale, Lancashire) and I laughed with thousands of British soldiers listening to George Formby twanging his ukulele on a makeshift stage, singing about some Mademoiselle: "I know what she means when she says 'oui oui!'" Very funny

ADOLESCENCE

when you are in Cottage Road Picture House, Headingley. George Formby was one of our heroes.

When the Panzers rolled across the Netherlands and Belgium the smile got wiped off our faces. Lord Gort, looking very like one of the Great War generals, appeared moonstruck as he left the War Office (Gad, sir, they've stolen a march on us...). Politicians in dark overcoats and trilbies (Lord Halifax in a top hat) were filmed entering and leaving Parliament purposefully. Chamberlain was remaindered, Churchill still moving in. Suddenly I was reading below the headlines on the front page of 'the Yorkshire Post". Over there, French defences crumbled; in June France surrendered and Italy tried to annexe the Riviera. It was the Axis versus the dislocated Allies.

Dunkirk happened. It was impossible to ignore the sombre, worried mood on the Home Front as news of the 'little ships' crossing the Channel filtered through. I doubt if my grown-up neighbours could imagine the reality any more than I age thirteen but we all knew the significance of the defeat. And then suddenly it became a victory, almost overnight. God was on our side, the escape was a miracle, and our gallant troops had been rescued from the edge of disaster. It meant we would survive in our island kingdom. Churchill manipulated the sound waves more brilliantly than Goebbels; the bulldog outwitted the sausage dog. The Local Defence Volunteers rallied to the call, including some schoolboys older than me. After a while they were re-named The Home Guard. How this became Dad's Army is the stuff of mythology.

Survivors of Dunkirk's retreat were deployed around the country, mostly in small groups. Lorries brought them round the estates looking for emergency lodgings. My mother volunteered to take some soldiers but she suddenly fell ill – I think no more than 'flu – and she was in bed when the officials came round to take up her offer. Dad had to tell them we couldn't oblige. I remember Mum weeping in bed about it but two weeks later two soldiers were billeted on us and they stayed for about a month. One was a pretty wrinkled Cockney character who had served in the first War, the other a young Brummager placid and gentle. Neither of them were professional soldiers. They wouldn't tell us about their Dunkirk experience because they had orders to say nothing that might lower morale; but they shook their heads meaningfully. I remember the Brummager mending the dining room lights. He had to stand on the table and fiddle with a screwdriver. I felt it was only polite to stand and watch him doing this DIY job. He seemed to take hours, with me looking up at him, as if admiringly: I was actually willing him to finish so I could get on with reading my book.

Somehow the two mothers had got together to arrange my stay at the farm at East Keswick during the summer holidays. This must have been harvest time, late August in 1940. Mrs. Lupton was warm-hearted, smiling and welcoming and Mr. Lupton, much occupied with his TT protected dairy herd, showed a lot of patience and humour as I reacted to the challenges of arable farming. There were about seven locals recruited for the harvest and I was expected to fit in with the field-work. I remember Fred describing the backbreaking, bleak routine of potato picking, which he had done the previous winter before enlisting. My experience of farm-work was nothing like that. The weather was warm, dry and balmy; the fields glowed gold and I watched with awe and admiration the clanking combine harvester cutting edges off the wheat crop. What fascinated me was how the sheaves dropped out of the back already tied with twine, loosely bundled straw stems with heads of nodding golden ears. Our job was to follow the harvester to pick up the sheaves and form stooks by stacking them together. Each stook had eight leaning sheaves, a perfect back-rest for a break after hours of stacking but actually for the practical purpose of keeping them dry and aiding the transfer of sheaves to the wagon. With pitchforks we loaded them, a task that got tougher the higher the pile rose, for the sheaves were quite heavy to hoist aloft. The best part was being allowed to lie on top of the wagonload, slowly being pulled along the cart tracks to the farmyard, brushed by trees and slightly swaying from side to side.

The sun was sinking as the combine harvester whittled away at the central block of wheat. I noticed the workers took up new positions and weapons, standing at corners and along the edges of the field, carrying sticks or guns with barrels pointed down. All watched the shrinking rectangle of wheat. A few rabbits had scuttled from the centre to the surrounding undergrowth and were picked off by dogs or men but I wasn't expecting the sudden mass appearance of scores of furry bundles leaping and dashing for safety. All was confusion - am I wrong to remember guns, the danger being obvious? I do know that the random action of the rabbits helped many to escape but one of them suddenly stopped and huddled close to the cropped ground, clearly paralysed with fear, no more than ten yards from me. I stalked the pathetic little creature as it quivered, hunched up and beady-eyed. One sprint with a side step could save it but it stayed frozen. I stepped slowly towards it, stood still and then fell forward with my hands outstretched to seize the warm bundle. It squealed as I held it aloft, astonished and delighted. "Rabbit punch it!" shouted Peter, and I grabbed both hind legs and up-ended it as I had seen others do. It jerked feebly with stretched legs, but my karate chop did for it.

I don't remember if we had rabbit pie for supper but it is quite likely. It had become quite a delicacy, though I hated seeing rabbits (and hares) hanging upside down in butchers' shops with little bloody bags tied round their heads. My own unexpected skill in dispatching a rabbit single-handed (well, both hands) was just one of the pleasures of the day and I would have no qualms about eating it. But there were other pleasurable events. That Saturday evening the Luptons had a family party, perhaps celebrating the end of the harvest, and I was there to

ADOLESCENCE

join in the fun. After a meal, the young folk were left to their own devices in the sitting room while the grown-ups got down to some serious drinking in the farmhouse kitchen. This was to be my first encounter with what we now call 'sex'; I had no idea what to call it back in those days.

There were perhaps seven or eight of us, including girl cousins of Peter Lupton, one of whom was a fifteen-year-old beauty both buxom and high-spirited. I shall call her Rosie though I don't think we drank any cider. Neither did we play charades or cards, though 'Postman's Knock" is surely equally venerable and Victorian. Not that I had ever heard of or played the game but it was clearly designed to facilitate an exchange of kisses when the 'postman' knocked, and that was an amusing novelty though I can't remember the procedure. I found kissing very enjoyable. "Hyde Park Corner" was something more sophisticated, for this involved the lights being turned off and the 'odd one out' going round with a torch trying to catch couples kissing as they cuddled together in an armchair. Once caught, you swapped places. The interesting thing was, Peter's lovely cousin (who had obviously played this game many times) was set on cuddling exclusively with me and keeping it that way. The poor guy with the torch got ignored, we cuddled and kissed and I had one of the most exciting hours of my limited life. I have to add that our behaviour was zestfully innocent. The age of underhand groping had not been reached.

When I returned from my farm holiday, one of the first things I wanted to tell my mother was how to play 'Hyde Park Corner' (though this was not our local Hyde Park). She didn't say much, though she smiled encouragingly when I described Peter Lupton's cousin. Sadly, I was not to see Peter very often after this (and Rosie not at all) but I salute his memory. Perhaps puberty was beginning to send us into our shells; possibly Peter was drawn to farming more intensely. I think his father died unexpectedly. Travel was always a problem ("Is your journey really necessary?') and changes were taking place in Ashwood Villas.

3. Brian Barton

I can't remember exactly when Brian Barton arrived with his Tax Inspector father and mother. It was probably mid-1940. He was an only child and delicate in health, mainly due to dyspepsia. There were times when his sickly breath sent me reeling back, but as friendship grew a compromise was reached: he took table-spoonfuls of medicine and I kept my distance. He was pasty-faced and rather clumsy. He wore metal-rimmed spectacles and looked brainy. He was about a year older than me but streets ahead in accomplishments and possessions. He played the piano and the harmonium, which his parents had bought him for his thirteenth birthday. The nearest I got to music making was pedalling the footrests and pressing a finger on the keyboard.

He played the three Bs at times (Bach, Beethoven and Brahms) but he also had a big book of English Music Hall songs which he enjoyed pounding out and singing. I joined in these quite happily but he also revelled in Gilbert and Sullivan, of whom I had never heard. I was not impressed by the tunes or the words. "The Mikado" was a bit too exotic for me. But the Bartons had come up from Basingstoke where there had been contact with a more advanced culture, or so Brian implied. Even the Leeds shopping centre was disappointingly small for his needs at first. He was undoubtedly precocious but I found him interesting.

Brian owned a portable epidiascope and a collection of picture post-cards, which could be projected and enlarged on the wall. This was fascinating. Visually, I was sharp and perceptive; going through his stacks of pictures (some views, some portraits, some paintings, some oddities) became one of the interests that drew us together. It was an ingenious little machine, all worked by mirrors, but I can't remember any particular images. We swapped books; he was probably the first person I talked to sensibly. About this time I was reading steadily through the works of Jeffrey Farnol and even collecting them. No one reads his romantic stories, do they? Most of them were loosely historical in setting and detail but the emphasis was always on boy meets girl – which of course is what I wanted. His heroines were invariably spirited, eye-flashing damsels and the villains cruel and devious seducers, and as for the heroes, well, I could identify with all of them. These easily-read pastiches were meretricious and presented society in melodramatic terms. As far as understanding the opposite sex is concerned, Farnol's novels led me up the garden path, though I enjoyed the flowers on the way. It took the last fifty pages of James Joyce's 'Ulysses', encountered more than ten years later, to redress the balance. However, I was already turning from Farnol to Conan Doyle's historical novels when Brian Barton moved to the villas, and also (thanks to Malcolm Willcock's enthusiasm) to Rafael Sabatini; but it took more than immersion in historical authenticity to erase my Farnol-inspired idealization of the fair sex. One of the interests we shared was sea stories by writers like Percy F.Westerman, Captain Marryat and Jules Verne. Out of this came a very Brian Barton kind of proposal

He had the run of his attic which became a kind of headquarters for the Villas boys, meaning Brian, Neil and myself, the Willcock boys and occasional visitors like cousin Muir. One day when we were alone, he broached the subject of the Boys Boating Club or the B.B.C. God knows where he picked up this idea: Arthur Ransome perhaps, and my first reaction was to scoff, particularly when he referred to himself as Commodore of the B.B.C. Cleverly, however, he suggested that my rank would be Commander. Neil, if I remember rightly, was a Petty Officer, a casual visitor like Muir an Able-bodied Seaman. He explained

ADOLESCENCE

that we could study seamanship in various ways, tying knots for example, learning semaphore, using nautical terminology, collecting model warships, knowing flags and funnel colours, etc. Remarkably, we launched the Boys Boating Club with no more than six or seven members. It became a regular feature in our lives, with meetings to absorb information and ceremonies to colour our proceedings. Brian's father erected a mast and yardarm in their front garden. We hoisted the Red Ensign, which was saluted when we passed by. There was little drilling in the attic but some quite absorbing studying of nautical manuals. I suppose we took an informed interest in the war at sea. The Battle of the River Plate was an early example – very epic with ships' names like Ajax and Achilles – but most of the naval news was depressing, with merchant ships being sunk by U-boats.

Regular trips, travelling together by bus, were taken to the river Wharfe at Otley bridge where rowing boats could still be hired in season. Usually we hired two skiffs, rowed up river and practised landing-craft exercises out of sight of the park attendant. We learned how to feather blades and avoid catching crabs, how to reverse in your own length and how to hoist blades when you came alongside. Awards were made for skilful boat handling, and a few promotions were confirmed by the Commodore. I compiled a B.B.C. magazine, crammed with information and yarns about the sea; all hand-written, the single copy being passed around and probably ending in some landlubber's waste-bin. The B.B.C. was kept going for two years at least and provided a self-made educational motive. My interest in a life on the ocean wave got a cautious and limited boost.

Brian Barton was also influential in directing our thespian tendencies. There was a bay window to his drawing room (or did the Bartons call it a lounge?) which was closed off when the curtains were drawn across. This bay space became an acting area. Brian decided we should make up an afternoon entertainment for our parents and friends. Goodness where from, he had copies of a French's acting edition farce called "India is *so* hot". Indian Army officers and native servants cavorted about but the play's climax is beyond recall. My character was named Carruthers and I kept ordering chota or burra pegs from the Indian boy (played convincingly by cousin Muir despite a loose head towel). I think this was our first scripted performance but more interesting was the second part of the show, viz. two scenes presenting Shakespeare's 'Julius Caesar' in Ancient and Modern form. First we acted the original version, dressed up in various old bed sheets. Then we boldly changed costumes to become Chicago gangsters with homburgs and American accents. I concede the brilliant idea to Brian but I concocted the dialogue for the modern version and, taking the 'lead' in both scenes, I was much involved. Hence my sensitivity when the actual performance did not go quite as planned.

IRONS IN THE FIRE

The scene in both versions was the assassination of Julius Caesar at the Capitol. A plot had been hatched to stab Caesar to death when he stands before various senators to answer their petitions. "Et tu Brute? Then die Caesar!" says Caesar as Brutus knifes him. He collapses and dies; the conspirators celebrate the death of a tyrant. Unfortunately our company could provide only five of the six conspirators (Cassius, Brutus, Casca, Cinna, Metellus Cimber) so brother John was asked to stand in as Decius who had only one line in the scene: "Great Caesar!" before stabbing him. This assassination of course was to be repeated with Al Capone as the central character and the gangster mob shoot him dead with guns. I learned my lines as Caesar, no doubt struggling to master two fairly long speeches which isolate him from the underling conspirators. I still recall (with a few nudges) these lofty sentiments:

> I could be well moved if I were as you;
> If I could pray to move, prayers would move me.
> But I am as constant as the northern star
> Of whose true-fix'd and resting quality
> There is no fellow in the firmament.

And so on ... for another eleven lines.

Immediately after this pretentious speech, Casca gives the signal: *"Speak, hands, for me!"* and the conspirators draw their daggers for the kill. I am sure the audience was very glad to see me getting my come-uppance. I reacted to the stabbings dramatically and, holding the bed-sheet tight to my bosom, awaited the final blow from Brutus. Unfortunately no one had noticed that John hadn't stepped forward to stab me; remembering the instructions in a rather confused way, he chose this moment to pull out his gangster gun, point it at me and shoot me with a kind of explosive noise from his mouth.

Everyone froze. What was he doing? That was the next scene! The audience burst into laughter. I'm afraid Caesar lost his cool and stepped out of character to tell John he had ruined the play. Then Brutus took over, probably played by Brian Barton, and stabbed me and I had to make the best of a bad job by lying doggo. The scene ended with the conspirators leaping about shouting *"Liberty! Freedom!"* and after a brief interval to change costumes the gangster play proceeded smoothly enough but some of the drama had evaporated. At least John, aware now what was going on, did not pull out his dagger in this scene.

John was called up in mid 1942 and joined the R.A.F. He was six foot seven, long and thin. All the Morley boys were over six feet but John was over-grown and later would suffer for it. He took size 14 in shoes but the R.A.F. coped. He was Aircraftsman John Morley though I don't think he had much to do with aircraft. In the mean time, Private Fred Morley had been stationed in Scotland

ADOLESCENCE

and was enjoying the warm hospitality of Glaswegian friends. He wrote to tell us he was unofficially engaged to a Scots lassie called Charlotte and he would be travelling down with her on his next leave. My parents were excited at the prospect of meeting Fred's fiancée. She started well by having a known familial name, but her visit was not a success. Charlotte was tall, dark and slender but very shy and nervous. Her strong Glaswegian accent was difficult to understand. I thought she was nice though she wore too much lipstick, perfume and had red finger-nails. Mum and Dad were privately convinced she was not right for Fred and they were a little relieved to learn Fred's regiment was shortly to move down to Salisbury Plain to start training operations.

Out of this Scottish romance a warm friendship between my mother and Charlotte's Aunt flourished. This formidable lady came to stay with us, perhaps reconnoitring for her niece but we were all highly entertained by her lively personality. When the time came for her return to Scotland, she asked us to sign her autograph book. I made a drawing of a black Scottish terrier following a lady walking along the road and captioned it: "May happiness dog your footsteps… Love to Mrs. …" I forget her name but she was charmed by my effort. She said I had got her legs exactly right – black stockings, flat heels and thick ankles.

A couple of months later, a large and mysterious package arrived, addressed to Mrs. Cissy Morley, but no other indication of sender or contents. It was wrapped in many layers of brown paper and tied very securely with string. Heavy and bulky, you needed both arms to lift it. The cost by parcel post must have been phenomenal. Trying to guess what was inside, Mum started to cut the strings and unwrap the layers of wrapping. There was a peculiar smell and then the contents were exposed – a sagging, sprawling mass of raw flesh, red meat with fatty edges and bony parts, positively unpleasant to behold. It so happened that about this time there were lurid accounts on the News and in the daily papers about a dismembered human torso wrapped in a parcel and posted somewhere, evidence of a ghastly murder. On exposing this gory parcel, Mum began to imagine all kinds of horror – none of us had ever seen such a mass of meat before, but a little later that day all was explained. A letter arrived from Glasgow. Charlotte's Aunt was sending us a special thank-you present of a huge sirloin of Scottish beef. She hadn't wanted to enclose any information or the source because, well, I suppose it was black market meat. And it was illegal to send perishable food by post, but how else could she get it to us? It certainly dwarfed our paltry weekly meat ration. We had some lovely dinners of roast beef and Yorkshire pudding for weeks afterwards and thank you very much, Charlotte's Aunt. Incidentally, in those days without fridges, a cold cellar could be relied upon to preserve meat very successfully.

IRONS IN THE FIRE

4. Leeds Grammar School Re-opens

The return to school actually started in mid-summer 1940, when we were told to register at the sports pavilion playing fields at Lawnswood (which was way out of town). I was placed quite properly in the middle stream of the fourth year but did not relate easily to the unsettling mixture of known and unknown pupils swarming into the classrooms. Quite a number of boys were entering the Grammar School for the first time as well as some ex-form mates returning from evacuation. I felt separated from either category, but at least it was a relief to get back to the school routine, though I seemed to be behind in some subjects.

Really I lost touch with Neil who was in the first year class. I don't recall anything about his activities or Cousin Muir's, who had returned from being evacuated to Wales, had become a boarder at a prep school and then transferred to Sedbergh School high up in the Pennines. Meanwhile I was seeing very little of Cousin Jim who was a pupil of Roundhay School, Leeds, which had endured no mass evacuation policy. At the Grammar School there was only one boy in my class I remember with affection. His name was Tebb (we did not use first names in those days) and he was the class clown, mimic and buffoon. He could provoke the teachers with his antics and I laughed a lot but he must have left after that one term and I think I felt rather isolated.

After my farm summer holiday at the Luptons', I was approaching the fifth year, which would culminate in School Certificate in June 1941. Things started badly when I was selected for the Latin set despite the fact that I had opted for the alternative subject, Geography, which was one of my favourite studies. Latin! I had struggled the previous year with it; I couldn't see the point of it and one of the Latin teachers gave me the creeps (he was famed for whacking boys with a backhand stroke). And worst of all, I was being denied Geography. And why? Because too many fifth formers had opted for Geography and the Latin set had to be completed! So I must take Latin for my School Certificate. I rebelled by cutting off my nose to spite my face. I attended the lessons and did no work; I simply divorced myself from the class, many of whom conformed to the system and were destined for university places. I had no such ambitions at this stage, but I offer apologies to Mr. Scott, the kind Latin teacher, who sympathized and let sulking dogs lie; I actually liked him and did not attempt to disrupt the class.

On the positive side, however, there was Stanley Fisher taking us for English Language and Literature. Take him all for all, I shall not look upon his like again. He was the most charismatic and humane teacher I have ever known. I first identified him as one of the Staff team playing against the 1st XV in 1939, which was in itself a remarkable event. At that time a former England three-quarter named A.L.Warr coached the 1st XV and it was he who persuaded fifteen members of the Staff to play one game against them. The Staff team actually

ADOLESCENCE

won, largely because Mr. Warr scored a late dazzling try, though my admiration goes to the Staff forwards who buckled down to the scrums and lineouts. And there, hanging on to the back of the scrum (wing forward) was a lean, swarthy young teacher who was new to the school and perhaps fairly new to the game of rugby. Stanley Fisher disappeared from my sight on the outbreak of war, most likely deployed to teach evacuated pupils in Wales, but this is only a hunch based on his confiding (to Sixth formers later) that the Headmaster (Dr. Terry Thomas) has asked him to arbitrate in a case of one Junior boy caught hopping into another boy's bed. The point was that Stanley Fisher was ordained, though he hardly ever wore a dog collar, and was advanced in his knowledge of sexual behaviour.

He was an entirely new kind of person to me. I was used to a fairly rigid conformity to a middle class norm; on top of this, everyone accepted the necessary strictures on everyday life in wartime Britain. The result was a uniform greyness over everything. In some cities and towns spectacular outbreaks of abnormality erupted as the bombs dropped but in Leeds people seemed to keep to the even tenor of their ways, with a traditional stoicism that was both boring and self-sufficient. There is one memory that dispels the greyness. I am sitting at the Headingley Cricket Ground watching an unusual game between professional and amateur cricketers. I can't recall which players are my heroes but on this hot afternoon the cricket has been entertaining. One team has batted and there is an interval before the other team starts its innings. An announcement over the speakers tells us there will be a collection for the War Effort and some of the cricketers will come round for our contributions. I can see various white-clad figures moving up and down the tiers of seats rattling collection cans and I am suddenly aware there is a cricketer bearing down on me. I don't know who he is, but he is like a film star, handsome with dark wavy hair and wearing a smart light blue blazer and flannels. He sports a cravat and really I think he is too theatrical to be a cricketer in Yorkshire. He holds out his tin and I put in my measly two pence but he is looking over my shoulder and speaks to someone.

"You go down the next line, will you, darling?" he drawls, and it is obvious he is from the South. I turn to find the most beautiful woman I have ever seen standing behind me, nodding and going towards more of the spectators with a collection box. She is dressed for a summer's day, she is bright, colourful and graceful, she wears high heels and walks like a princess, she bends and condescends kindly to the task she had been given. And I am thinking she can't be real, she has just stepped out from a silver screen and doesn't belong here in my life. The two visitors from outer space fade into the distance; the umpires are out, the field is set and the opening batsmen walk to the crease. While I muse about the difference between shades of grey and multi-coloured glamour; and how the foppish gay Lothario manages to attract the beautiful girl; and how there is a whole world out there I haven't noticed before.

It was like that with Stanley Fisher. He carried with him an aura of Bohemian life, mainly because he wore corduroys, coloured shirts and contrasting ties. In summer he even wore sandals. He was lean and brown-skinned with black hair that fell lankly over his brow. When he smiled, and he had a ready wide grin, it was as if he shared the fun with you. He was a published poet and I thought his poems great when introduced to them in the Sixth Form. He had been at Oxford in W.H. Auden's time and called him Wystan. I think he was in his early forties. He was a practising nudist and had sunbathed in secluded Parson's Pleasure on the river Cherwell, and elsewhere. When I met him with his wife, I was again jolted into an awareness of other worlds – a kind of cultural dichotomy. Mrs. Fisher was from an environment both artistic and sophisticated, she was self-possessed and assertive, very much a Lawrentian type of heroine. She swept her hair back à l'espagne and strolled like a panther. They were well matched, alike in many ways but she kept herself aloof from the school; she did not share his proselytising fervour. He took his responsibilities as an Anglican parson very seriously, though he alarmed some cautious clerics with his unconventional conduct.

He had already established his reputation for encouraging nude swimming in the River Wharfe near the buildings where the evacuated school was housed. My own experience of this was limited to one short holiday spent there. I retain a clear-cut image of a group of boys, between the ages of fifteen and seventeen, lying in a circle on the banks of the river. We have bathed and found the water cold but we sprawl at leisure round the focal figure of Stanley Fisher for it is warm in the sun. He relaxes, with his feet crossed and expounds on the problems of life to the boys. Everyone is naked. We are all shapes and sizes but we pay little attention to each other; our eyes are directed towards Mr. Fisher. He lies like a pagan god, like Dionysus surrounded by myrmidons, a slender, graceful, masculine figure, well tanned and confident, and his penis is magnificent. It lies long and strong under a black bush, uncircumcised and tubular; when he changes position it rolls lazily to one side. It exists at the very centre of the line between head and feet. No one can match this splendour. I am aware I can never be like this superior being and I pay homage to the priapic principle. But deep down, repressing the penis envy, I question Stanley Fisher's motives for encouraging nudity amongst young boys. It was not paedophilia, of course but possibly a supreme egocentricity based on his pride that his Maker has endowed him so well. I am not sure how to assess the impact of nakedness on youngsters. No doubt we all enjoyed the freedom and the licence but did any of us convert to nudism?

ADOLESCENCE

Stanley Fisher had a Pied Piper attraction for adolescent boys. There was a knowing understanding between him, as the source of so much information about sex, and the empty, parched young vessels waiting to be filled. He wanted us to know more facts about 'SEX' but more importantly the personal and social responsibilities. My own ignorance about human relationships had not been shifted by studying the rabbit's reproductive system in Biology in the fourth year. Perhaps experiences down on the Lupton's farm had been salutary but I imagine puberty simply arrived unannounced. I can recall sitting in the upper deck of a tram and being gently rocked into an erect condition that was impossible to conceal when standing up to get off the tram but I don't remember any sudden masturbatory frenzy at this age. Sex was still more or less theoretical.

Stanley Fisher played his pipe and we danced before him. Many an English lesson became devoted to the enlightenment of our minds on matters sexual. He would quickly still the vulgar guffaws and prurient giggles. He was being serious, not arch. He would draw diagrams of male and female anatomy on the blackboard, carefully explaining the way sexual intercourse happened. He would issue slips of paper to each boy and ask for questions to be written down for him to answer. Nearly always the question concerned 'sex' and he would choose the most interesting, on prostitution, pre-marital sex, foreplay, masturbation, incest and so on. He thought sex education was virtually ignored in the pursuit of swotting for the examinations, and he did his best to rectify the situation. With some classes I think the tail wagged the dog, that is, the boys clamoured for more information so Stanley Fisher obliged, but he had a totally liberating effect on grammar school classroom life. And in the playground too. He would be cheered or jeered at by some of the bullyboys who swaggered about in small gangs during these war years.

Because many pupils were still continuing their education at the boarding establishments up Wharfedale, some pretty rough types were being allowed in to complete the roll call at the School. Standards of behaviour certainly had dropped. One of the most degrading activities was what we called 'pilling'. Two boys would square up like fighting cocks in the playground and the rival gangs or classes would surround them, shouting and egging them on. Cock fighting was illegal but these two boys were engaged in an ugly parody, both of them bending forward as they faced each other and extending an arm in front with hand in a kind of hooked position. They would move round the ring, every now and then making a grab at the crutch of the other boy. The idea was to snatch the balls of the adversary, but never to hold on to them. It was a grotesque spectacle and dangerous. The Headmaster, Dr. Terry Thomas, had to announce a ban on such stupid behaviour and it gradually died out.

IRONS IN THE FIRE

Another of Dr. Terry Thomas's pronouncements led to Stanley Fisher receiving the doubtful honour of a nickname. Our Headmaster in Assembly issued an edict about the salute that a pupil should respectfully give to any teacher whom the boy might meet in a public place. He was not referring to the raising of the pupil's cap, which was too elaborate a gesture and sometimes the boy would not be wearing his cap. No, said Dr. Terry Thomas, if you meet a teacher you should politely bend your arm and raise your clenched fist to shoulder level. The teacher would respond to this salute with an approving nod. You didn't need to be a scholar to find this a hilarious suggestion and the gangs of middle school boys roaming the playground started to look for teachers so they could demonstrate their version of the salute. You would see them all stand and greet the passing teacher with bent arms and clenched fists which were slowly lowered, as if they were miming the pulling of a lavatory chain. As they flushed the toilet, the members of the gang would make a derisive flushing noise.

There came the time Stanley Fisher was greeted by a noisy bunch of middle school yobbos. They hooted at him and went through the mocking ritual of the bent arm and chain pulling, ending with the flushing sounds and laughter. Mr. Fisher watched them with a smile on his face and raised his eyebrows. "Boys," he said, "I don't know why you are greeting me like this when I know your regard for me is no more than a flush in the pan." Everyone, even the yobbos, thought that a brilliant riposte. The boys cheered, Stanley Fisher retreated with another smile and forever after was known as "Flush".

As might be expected, the gang mentality led to some fairly unpleasant bullying and I became involved because I was friendly with Brian Barton. Brian, one year ahead of me, always wanted to meet at the eleven o'clock break each day. He seemed to have few friends in his class, and the same went for me really. We would walk right round the school grounds and eventually stand talking in the playground. Something about Brian Barton unsettled the bullyboys of the school; he was obviously a brain-box and a swot, but he was also a soft target for a sustained session of teasing and jeering. As his companion, I was a protection against personal attack, which worked most of the time, but when the mob's blood was up we would be approached by an extraordinary set of boys gathering round us, baying and hissing – never right round us, for we chose to stand against the wall. I imagine it was something like this in Germany when the Hitler Youth turned on Jewish children in early Nazi times. There was never any attempt to attack Brian physically, and I am pretty certain the resentful jeering and snarling was not directed at me. The mob hated what Brian represented, intellectual elitism. It was simply a display of spiteful sarcasm. There were times when I was tempted to hit out at one of those sneering, yelling faces but Brian urged passive resistance. The mob jeered, an indifferent crowd gathered and then dispersed, and suddenly we would be on our own, and could part, Brian

ADOLESCENCE

to the Lower Sixth, and I to the Fifth year. I suppose this happened three or four times, and Brian's Ghandi-like response paid off.

It must have seemed a peculiar friendship for I was certainly no intellectual power-house. Brian went on to gain a Major Scholarship in Mathematics and eventually became a Cambridge Wrangler; but I was more of an all-rounder, with weak spots in some of the eight subjects I was studying for School Certificate. Team games were just beginning to dawn on me. I had little interest in athletics, and cross-country running I loathed. Back in the lower school, my Housemaster had reprimanded me after I skipped one of the runs. In front of a House assembly he said with a scowl, "Morley! You are an absolute slacker …" He paused and I looked resentfully at him, and he continued "… where cross-country running is concerned." That's all right then, I thought, he knows I don't slack at games, so I took the punishment uncomplainingly.

Actually, on another occasion I hatched a plot with two pals to cheat on a House run. The three of us started the run very purposefully and got as far as the wood, which took us out of sight of the main Pavilion where the referees and counters were situated. When all the runners had gone ahead of us, we ducked into a ditch in the wood, and cunningly crept through to the other end of the wood, which is where the final stages of the run were encountered. All we had to do was lie hidden and choose the right moment to re-join the race, putting on a display of exhaustion and determination to reach the finishing post. Unfortunately we misjudged that moment and our acting was pretty flabby. We watched as the race leaders ran past and decided to emerge from the bushes when no one else was in sight, forgetting that the race involved thirty or forty boys who would be behind us. We crossed the finishing post in a remarkably quick time, judging by previous experience. Our Housemaster, Drip Wood (his nickname from his initials: C.W.W.- City Water Works) made sarcastic comments and accused us of cheating but there had been no one to check progress through the wood, and we found nobody really cared which House won the race.

Rugby however was a team game worth playing. At first I was lost in the scrum, not knowing what I was supposed to be doing. I was detailed to play loose forward in a Colts match against another school and I helped our team to lose by breaking illegally from the scrum to tackle an opponent. The referee's whistle blew (he was a soccer man, I found out later) and I was adjudged offside. Penalty kick: 3 points to them. I still don't see how I was offside when the ball was clear of the scrum. Eventually I moved to the open spaces of back-play and that was much better. In the summer of 1941 cricket took a minor role as the examinations were to be faced and I admit to some rather uncertain and desultory preparation for the ordeal; and not feeling at all well for at least one of the Mathematics papers. When the results came out I had scored two credits (in Physics & Chemistry and Divinity) and four passes (English, Literature, French,

IRONS IN THE FIRE

History). I failed in Latin and Mathematics. My father said little, my mother praised me and Private Brother Fred sent me a note of congratulation, adding "Comparisons are odious" by which I think he meant his results had been worse! But I knew these were bad scores and by pre-war days well below Matriculation standards. I owed my Divinity credit to Stanley Fisher (and St. Matthew) but what happened to the English results? I remember writing a feeble essay on "Voluntary Service during the War". We had studied three books with 'Flush': "Julius Caesar, Methuen Book of Modern Verse' and 'Eothen' (a totally inexplicable choice of text). I had every intention to stay down a year and re-sit School Certificate but Johnny Lee brushed this idea aside. "Move into the Sixth Form and start your Higher Certificate Courses," he advised. "Nobody is bothered about these exams. And you can get back to Geography!" Johnny Lee taught Geography of course. So I took his advice.

My principal H.S.C. subjects were English, Geography and Economics. I chose History and Art as Subsidiary subjects (one year courses). In the second year I changed my Subsidiary subjects to Biology, Economics and Art. I approve the system that allowed subsidiary courses to be swapped over two years, as it encourages a wider range of subjects, but there were practical problems as there were not enough teachers to cope with the variations. The solution was to accommodate the Upper and Lower Sixth formers studying a particular subject in one classroom. The teacher had to divide his time between these levels and one group often marked time while he was teaching the other group. It was hardly efficient but at least it enabled the system to work. However, there were two exceptions where I was concerned. As the only student taking Art in the Sixth Form (incredible now!) I was allowed the run of the Art Room by Mr. Andrews, the Art teacher. I thoroughly appreciated this for though I drew or painted very little (the Course he chose for me included Design, Furniture and Costume) I was able to ramble round the Art books freely. Mr. Andrews was a temporary appointment, a middle-aged, arthritic artist not much interested in teaching nor me really. He kept an easel and oil paints beside his desk and whenever he had a spare lesson (or I was present) he propped up one of his canvases and continued painting landscapes of dramatic mountain scenery reminiscent of the Swiss Alps, always from memory and invariably rather too chocolate boxy to be approved – even by me. He shrugged off criticism; there was a market for mountain scenery and he needed the money. I liked him, but he wasn't really a teacher and he moved on a few years later.

The other exception was English Literature with Stanley Fisher in the School Library, sitting at one end of a long table and no sharing with another class; it was like attending a tutorial. How was it we had this double privilege? Had our revered teacher some extra persuasive power? It could be because there were only four of us. I remember the names of only two fellow-students. One was

ADOLESCENCE

Geoffrey Backhouse, son of an architect (why does that fact stick?) and the other was called Gunter (but his first name is missing). Who the fourth student was I have totally forgotten. Given Flush's charismatic appeal, I would have thought more students opted for English at Leeds Grammar School but in the middle of a tense war (1941 and early 1942 were particularly disheartening) not many youngsters were interested in studying Shakespeare and poetry. I don't think it was due to the decline in Classical studies and the compensatory expansion of English as the most popular 'arts' subject in Sixth forms, for this happened only gradually, and much later, for when I started teaching, the average Advanced level class still remained in single figures. The English revolution came about through co-education.

Stanley Fisher was a keen thespian and excelled as King Lear in the Library where he could let loose his finest declamations. He was obviously capable as Sir John Falstaff too. What a splendid duo of Shakespeare texts – "King Lear" and "Henry IV part one"! There were quieter moments too when the English set would discuss life and all its adolescent delights, few of which we had sampled. Thanks to Flush's enthusiasm we staged a production of "A Midsummer Night's Dream" in the School Hall, quite an undertaking in wartime as the stage had to be re-equipped. Geoff Backhouse was a lively, galumphing youth with a strong personality so he was inevitably chosen to play Bottom. I played Egeus, an elderly character, and the following year 'Flush' wanted me to continue in that age-group as Belarius in 'Cymbeline', which was the next play he produced. I rebelled, however, and would accept only a straight part so he offered me the boring role of the King. Having been a minor character early on, the King came into his own at the *denouement* when all was laboriously revealed. I don't think the producer ever forgave me for messing up the final (and tedious) scene in the play by not knowing my lines. The Prompter worked over-time while 'Flush' fumed in the wings. I thought 'Cymbeline' a rotten play for a school but I can't excuse my irresponsibility. The boys playing Posthumus and Imogen were very good, actually.

As far as I recall, the Cadet Corps (pre-war Officer Training Corps) claimed all members of the school; if there were pacifists, I don't remember them. Once a week we attended school dressed as Great War soldiers, which involved knee breeches with puttees unravelled from ankles and wrapped round calves. Army boots, jackets buttoned to the neck with brass buttons to be polished and peaked caps completed the costume. I hated this uniform because it tickled my skin, particularly round the thighs. I had the same problem with flannel trousers, which itched. I always wore worsted normally. This was no fad, I had a very fair skin! The only practical solution was to continue wearing pyjamas when donning the uniform so on Corps day I arrived at school under two layers. If a puttee worked loose, the striped pyjama leg would be revealed. What a business,

IRONS IN THE FIRE

constricting your neck with the rough collar, regularly polishing your boots, badge and buttons. Drill was bearable at first. Cleaning old Enfield rifles was smelly, dirty and confined to a cramped Armoury.

And then there was the Field Day spent out in the wilds of Lawnswood (memories of cross-country running) on a fine summer's day. There was a grand parade and for the Field Day we were transported by Army lorry to our destination. Two or three cadets keeled over when disembarking; too many, too close on a hot morning. Recovering, we listened to our instructions. The rest of the day would be devoted to a mock-battle between Defenders and Attackers. The Defenders would be protecting a barn in a secluded neck of the woods. The Attackers (and I was one of these) would be attempting to capture the barn. The Commanding Officer had a lot to say about the rules of the contest, not quite Geneva Convention stuff but fairly complicated. The other teachers stood around in smart officer's uniforms, looking knowledgeable though not necessarily about military matters. Most of them wore tabs denoting 'Umpire'.

Zero hour was eleven. At half-past ten the Defenders marched away and disappeared behind the trees and bushes; they had 30 minutes before we attacked. I was part of a platoon of eight raw recruits led by a lance corporal from the Upper Sixth. We marched to the edge of the wood, synchronized watches and waited. Our lance corporal said we were part of the advance guard. At zero hour he jumped up and ordered us to form ranks, two abreast. Quick march! There was a track leading into the wood and we advanced a hundred yards with thrushes and chaffinches whistling at us. There was nobody about, we could commune with Nature. Suddenly an officer with 'Umpire' on his cap stepped out of the undergrowth and told us to stop. "I'm awfully sorry," he said, "but you're all killed. There's a machine gun nest covering this trail and he's shot all of you." The lance corporal looked bewildered. He had heard nothing. "I'm afraid you'll all have to report back to base," smirked the Umpire. "You are all dead, the battle is over for you."

The time was eleven five. We had been wiped out, without even going over the top. Theirs not to reason why, theirs but to do and die. So we sauntered back to H.Q. and reported the demise of the platoon to our C.O. Then we lounged around for the rest of the day doing precisely nothing. Apparently it was against the rules to resurrect the dead. My pyjamas felt very hot and sweaty. I have no idea which side eventually won; nobody, not even our Lance Corporal bothered to tell us. Perhaps he was sore about being demoted.

I transferred to the Air Training Corps soon after this. I was actually head hunted by Squadron-Leader Drip Wood, who wanted to build up his power structure and was looking for potential Flight Sergeants. He claimed to have more interesting activities for the likes of me. No Field Days and some super visits to airfields instead. I didn't actually ask him if the uniform tickled but I

ADOLESCENCE

was reassured by the puttee-less trousers and the forage cap so I made the transfer. I'm afraid I was a sad disappointment to him. There was very little about aircraft that really interested me. I could recognize a Spitfire though it might be a Hurricane actually, and I appreciated the bravery of the 'few' during the Battle of Britain but identifying German planes left me cold. What excited me was Paul Nash's marvellous painting of an air battle over the Kent coastline, all vapour trails, smoky clouds and dropping aircraft. Mr. Andrews exhibited that example of War Artists at work.

To get on in the Air Training Corps, it was necessary to learn the Morse Code and be adept at sending and receiving messages on the transmitter. I found this very difficult. Perhaps there is some deficiency in my brain that prevents me from abstracting myself from surroundings and concentrating on a series of sound patterns like the Morse Code. I admired the remarkable skills of some boys without wishing to emulate them. Maybe it has to do with the right and left hemispheres of the brain. Good Morse operators are able to switch off the right and focus entirely on impulses in the left hemisphere.

All members of the A.T.C. were expected to attend the weeks' annual Camp at Driffield Airfield, situated in East Yorkshire. This was to be our first taste of life in the Air Force and a number of events would be laid on for our benefit, including a flight in an operating aircraft. Without much enthusiasm I signed up for this visit, which would start early in August and continue for a week or more. It would be something of a holiday. Perhaps my parents were glad to see me getting away from home because they wanted to concentrate on Private Brother Fred who was very much a cause for concern. During training operations on Salisbury Plain, which understandably involved rough and ready sorties, Fred had collapsed and been diagnosed as suffering from pleurisy, a possible killer. After surgical treatment in a military hospital, he was sent to a Convalescent Camp at Richmond where he enjoyed perhaps the only real break from his military service since joining up. Whilst there, in the space of perhaps ten days, he was able to benefit from occupational therapy each day. He became an itinerant artist, travelling round the district of Richmond and Kingston, making brilliant pen and ink sketches of local buildings and sites. Just before he rejoined his regiment he collected these drawings and bound them into a beautiful hand-illuminated book, which I now keep as the most precious memento of my brother and his artistry. Fred left this with Mum and Dad obviously for safekeeping and after a short leave he continued training operations, this time on Exmoor. Imagine their alarm when a telegram came from his Commanding Officer advising them that Fred had been transferred to Truro Hospital for an emergency hernia operation. He was seriously ill again. Shortly after my departure to the Cadet Camp at Driffield, my parents decided to take a train to Truro to see what was going on. I have no recollection of being worried about anything but my anticipated discomforts at the Camp. Neil was staying with Cousin Muir; John was away on holiday. My parents could be well satisfied that the children were being looked after while they went down to Truro to see Fred.

5. Events at the Airfield

Great Driffield is actually a small town in the East Riding where R.A.F. Driffield evolved; it's the airfield that's great, though not metaphorically. In my memory it is a vast open space with tarmacked runways expanding in all directions and bleak cavernous hangars dropped more or less arbitrarily by their side. In 1942 it was a busy place for bomber aircraft but I have no recollection of squadrons taking off on missions. There were Halifaxes and Wellington bombers ticking over very noisily by the hangars and technicians climbing all over them, but no sign of pilots and crews. Maybe our pseudo-officer-teachers could find a little more of the action, for they were guests of the Officers Mess for the duration of the visit. Drip Wood was our Commanding Officer. I don't remember the others.

The Leeds Grammar School Air Training Corps occupied canvas tents erected some distance from the active airfield. There were two other groups also under canvas, both from town A.T.C.s, but we hardly ever met their personnel apart from the morning parade, which was held on a large flat concrete raft big enough for a county cricket ground. A telephone kiosk was bizarrely placed on the edge of this wasteland. The daily parade was really a device to unite the assembled cadets as one disciplined body. There were lots of orders shouted, officers saluted, ranks standing to attention, marching up and down; I don't think we raised a flag as there wasn't a flag-pole, there was certainly no band and nothing much was achieved except an absorption of time. I have no memory of what we did all day but no doubt the authorities laid on demonstrations and instructional sessions for our benefit. One of the highlights was supposed to be a flight in an aircraft, for none of surely had ever 'flown' before. There was some difficulty about the supply of these flights. Who was responsible for arranging them? Which aircraft and who flew them?

I imagine the trouble was that there was a war going on. Who the hell wanted to give kids joy rides when they were due for serious sorties? In the end, Drip Wood moaned until special arrangements were made to take the Grammar School cadets on their promised flights. When my turn came it was late afternoon, grey and gloomy. There was this huge carrier-type aircraft thundering away in neutral, waiting for the next batch to enter its belly. About seven of us were strapped inside this shaking roaring beast, no seats, we had to squat, the door was closed and off we went, trundling noisily into the unknown. It was dark, we could see faintly the cockpit lights but we had to stay where we were, in

ADOLESCENCE

the gloom, no windows or portholes to look out of, trying to conjure up some excitement about the experience. That was it, a bumping and bouncing as we landed and thus we were delivered back to our starting point little the wiser for our treat.

There were repercussions, however. Towards the end of the visit hostilities broke out between the A.T.C. groups. One of the town Corps complained that preferential treatment was being given to the Grammar School cadets. While they had not been offered any flights, or enough flights, the snobs had been given all the perks. This may or may not have been true but the outcome was a mutiny organized by members of the town corps staged on the last day of the camp. They refused to obey orders when on parade. This was serious stuff! Unfortunately the School A.T.C. were wheeled away and pre-occupied. I don't know what happened to the mutineers but I sympathized. The next morning we were on our way home.

Halfway through this weird sojourn at Driffield my life was changed forever. Morning parade on the concrete wasteland was taking place and we stood in line, probably accepting the routine with good-humoured boredom. There were officers positioned at the front; senior ratings marched about, stamping feet and saluting. I saw our Commanding Officer suddenly leave the parade and enter the telephone box. Presumably someone had heard the phone ringing and told Squadron Leader Wood the call was for him. We watched him talking into the receiver and nodding two or three times. Then he left the box, spoke to other officers and someone told me to fall out and report to Squadron Leader Wood. He was looking shifty and disgruntled as he often could do. He was not called Drip Wood for nothing.

He took me for a little walk, leaving the cadets marching about. He suddenly put his arm round my shoulders, lowered his voice and told me I had to brace myself for bad news. I of course had no idea what he was talking about. He called me "Harry'. He knew my family, he had been Housemaster for all the Morley boys, he spoke highly of Fred and here he was having to find a way to tell me something unpleasant. He said my mother and my brother had both been killed by a bomb dropped by a German plane on Truro Hospital. He didn't know the full details but my father was in Truro. He said it had been decided that I should stay at Driffield until the end of the A.T.C. Camp as no one was at home. He said I should try to take part in activities but if I wanted to be alone it could be arranged. He would ask two cadets to accompany me. He said he was appalled having to give me such terrible news. He was sorry, it was all terrible.

What more could he do? He was simply passing on messages already formulated. He was gentle, considerate and genuinely upset. It was as if his part was done; he faded from sight, attending to A.T.C. matters, and I don't know whether he got in touch or enquired after the family afterwards. He selected two trusty senior cadets to look after me but neither could do much for me, I wouldn't let them. I didn't want to talk to them; I resented their clumsy goodwill and concern. "Why don't you cry?" they asked. As if I would gratify their desire to see me in tears! Actually I had no tears to shed. I had no understanding of what had happened. It was impossible to accept this news as real; someone speaks the words but they don't add up to any kind of truth. There was no one to relate to, I was isolated, I was in limbo. My mind felt numb and nothing seemed to have meaning. And this is how it remained until the end of the week. Like a zombie I walked through the life of each day. Two friends, Chamberlain and Sewell, did help by talking about trivial matters, but I don't remember any details of those days.

The last night under canvas was memorable. In our tent, we were on tenterhooks after the mutiny for fear of guy-ropes being released or raids being made by rival A.T.C. cadets. There was a frenetic half-hour, fuelled by bottled beer, of racing from one tent to another (though not by me) and then a period when (I think) mutual masturbation in the darkness reached orgiastic proportions, while I, grieving, clung to Sewell, my cheek pressed to his in some kind of sexual desire; at one point my hand strayed down to his crutch and recoiled in surprise on touching an erect penis, and then someone's fingers grasped the organ. Eventually sleep came to exhausted minds and bodies.

I think we travelled back to Leeds by train and I took the tram to the stop opposite Ashwood Villas and walked up the cobbled lane, wondering what was waiting for me at home. Dumping my bag in the hall, I called "Anyone in?" I heard a voice upstairs and went up to Dad's bedroom, where he sat at Mum's dressing table, sorting her belongings. He looked pretty shattered. He asked me how I was and I started to babble about the mutiny of cadets at Driffield. He said nothing and I went through to my bedroom. I had to move about, take myself away from the raw edge, avoid a head-on collision, and perhaps touch something that belonged to me. "I don't know what you boys are going to do now," he said when I came back. I had never seen him so listless before. The house felt very empty. I asked where Neil was; he was staying at Cousin Muir's home with Aunt Glad and Uncle Les and had been there since my parents had gone down to Truro to see Fred in hospital. And where was Brother John? He apparently had not yet returned from his holiday in Llandudno with a friend.

There was just the two of us in the house but we couldn't communicate: two loved ones had been blown out of existence and we couldn't bridge the gap, even reach out for mutual physical support. I don't think we actually embraced. He was frozen in his own grief and I was still trying to grasp the reality of our new relationship. He couldn't talk about the events in Truro and I didn't ask. We just stood for a while sharing the emptiness and then tried to carry on. John arrived home that evening. All week he had been kept in ignorance of the deaths of his

ADOLESCENCE

mother and brother. Only on the last morning, before catching the train from Llandudno, did the landlady tell him the brief facts. She had known them for some time but was requested to withhold the information until the last moment. "He may as well enjoy his holiday," she had been advised. And it was preferable to keep him away from home when there was no one there. John and I met but we had little to tell each other; each of us withdrew into a personal grief, and a personal resentment too.

Who was making these decisions for us? Why should I be 'told' and then made to endure a miserable interim before facing the reality? Why should John 'not be told' and then feel cheated and guilty about his week's holiday? I would not have wanted to be kept ignorant like John but then I loathed having to play the stoic until released from that Camp. In considering our various predicaments, it had been taken for granted that children had no voice; in such matters the adults managed things as they saw fit. I think we did have 'rights' that were overlooked in pursuit of convenience. John was 19, I was 16 and Neil aged 13: we were brothers deliberately kept apart and not permitted to bond emotionally until it was convenient. There was never a family gathering to share our grief; I remember only one emotional embrace when Aunt Glad and I stood together, our arms round each other. "I don't know what we can do," she said. It was an awkward moment because I had never held her close before and I felt somehow it was me having to give comfort to her. Apart from this, the Forsyths were unexpectedly mute. Maybe my father, after years of contact with my mother's side, rejected the idea of a family bonding ceremony.

Beyond the sheer frustration of being kept in isolation, there is our obvious inability to comprehend the facts. No one actually sat down and explained what happened in Truro. I have had to piece together my version but, because we never spoke about these matters to each other, John and Neil may have had different opinions. Perhaps the best way to describe events is to follow my father's moves:

i. My parents, on hearing that Fred is seriously ill after a hernia operation at Truro General Hospital, take a train to Truro. They arrange to travel on Wednesday 4th August 1942. They can take this trip because the boys will be conveniently away from home. John, about to be called up in the R.A.F., is in Llandudno. Harry is attending an A.T.C. Camp at Driffield. Neil is invited to stay with the Temples in Adel.

ii. My parents, after a long, tedious journey on 4th August, stay in a Truro boarding house and visit the Hospital on Thursday 5th August. Fred is responding to treatment - and their visit.

iii. They spend another day (Friday 6th August) visiting Fred at the Hospital. Dad decides to travel north that evening on the night train to Leeds.

iv. My mother, staying on, is by Fred's bedside that evening. (Friday 6th August). A lone German bomber aircraft (en route for or away from the Midlands?) drops a single bomb on the Hospital. Nine people are killed, including Fred and Mum.

v. Early on Saturday 7th August at Leeds City Station Dad arrives from Truro and receives an urgent call to return. He takes the next train back to Truro and learns what has happened.

vi. On Sunday 8th August, Dad telephones the Temples and Uncle Les makes the necessary contacts concerning John and Harry. Dad attends the official proceedings in Truro.

vii. On Monday 9th August the funeral and burial of the victims.

viii. On Tuesday 10th August Dad takes the train from Truro back to Leeds.

ix. On Wednesday 11th August Harry returns from Driffield, John from Llandudno. Neil remains with the Temples. Dad is at home.

Wartime travel was always slow and tedious, cold and dirty. Physical exhaustion from the journeys must have affected Dad, but the sheer enormity of the chance event would undermine anyone's morale. I imagine him concluding his association with Truro in a state of shock, feeling very much on his own and wondering how he can cope with the future. A letter Dad wrote to my mother's sister, Aunt Gladys, thankfully preserved by Cousin Muir, becomes a moving testimony to his sensitivity.

Dad's letter, which came to light very recently, helps me to understand my father more sympathetically. He obviously was unable to unite the family, so far from home. At the time it must have been sensible to 'let the poor boys get on with their holidays', though retrospectively I think it damaged family relations. I find the sentence: "They are too young really to know what has befallen them" somewhat self-conscious and evasive. 'Too young *really* to know…' (How old does one have to be?) …'by what has *befallen* them …' (isn't this a pretentious phrase?). But there is a lot in the letter that is genuinely moving.

ADOLESCENCE

Red Lion Hotel, Truro
8th Aug '42

My dear Gladys

    This blow is almost too much to write about. I feel nobody should come here, it is too remote and I do not want people to send flowers.

    It happened so soon after I left. Cissy went straight back from seeing me off, to Fred and sat in his room. There was no warning. The bomb just came – a direct hit on the ward where they were and the acting matron said it would be better not to see anything of their shattered bodies but to remember them as they were in life. I agreed. They are believed to have had no pain but just to have gone instantaneously into unconsciousness.

    I have agreed to the local undertaker's suggestion about the joint funeral. There is no Presbyterian Church here and they will be buried together in Kenwyn Parish churchyard. It is a very beautiful situation but such thoughts don't really matter, I think, since the bodies of all of us are nothing without life in them

    I feel I ought to apologise for staying at this Hotel but I could not stand the jibber-jabber talking of our landlady in the circumstances and the place is so full I could not get anywhere else. The matron and doctor's wife offered hospitality but I do not think I ought to accept it so I am here for three days.

    I dare not think of the future and the poor boys without their mother. For the present I think they should go on (with) their holidays as already arranged. They are too young really to know what has befallen them. You cannot get this until Tuesday so I need not try to explain myself in writing.

    I return Tuesday night from here. There were 9 fatal at the Infirmary. This was Truro's first raid and I ask myself why I was left but I cannot really think what we call God can concern himself with one human being. All the lives lost in this war too!

    I am writing to Win. You will tell Alec and he will excuse me. I have a hard task to write Charlotte.

    Nobody is to come. I will phone you this evening. I don't know your phone no. though.

Doe

IRONS IN THE FIRE

Dad never did write to Charlotte, Fred's beloved. He asked me to do it instead, which I did however ineptly. I never heard from her but I don't think I expected a reply. If Dad couldn't communicate with his children (and I saw no evidence to suggest that he was talking to John or Neil) he was certainly ducking out of this one. His reaction was to withdraw into himself; he had no special friend to confide in and he continued like this until old age began to mellow him. He did keep the family home going, however.

6. Aftermath

So what should have happened and indeed what would happen today? The family would be encouraged to share grief and comfort each other. Efforts would be made to bring the children together immediately. The family branches would unite to mourn and express shared sorrow. Counselling, now an important branch of social welfare, would be available. And I think people would be generally more caring about the suffering of others. But this was August 1942. Deaths were occurring every night from air raids; bereavements were two a penny all over the country; personal responses had to remain private and individual. We were expected to keep warm under a thin blanket of silent sympathy and, as these were wartime conditions, we tried to avoid the chilly feeling that this could be mistaken for indifference.

It was literally years after August 1942 that someone kindly gave me a copy of the Monthly magazine of our Presbyterian Church in Leeds, published a few weeks after the Truro bombing. It contains the sermon preached by the Minister, the Rev. Robert Robertson, as a response to the tragedy. I had no knowledge of this evidence of public grieving. My forgotten benefactor thought it would comfort me. Well, I have no axe to grind but it offered cold comfort. Because it expresses the orthodox theological doctrine about such deaths and because the Reverend Robertson does pay fitting tribute to two of his flock, I include the second half of the sermon herewith: August 23rd 1942

"The Lord shall preserve thy going out and thy coming in from this time forth and even for evermore". Psalm 121, 28

> ... above all, the thoughts of many of us this morning go out to two of our number who went out, but will not here come in again, for mother and son, in that hospital far in the South-West, were suddenly killed by enemy action. Fred Morley was one of our most promising young members. Of splendid physique, of sterling character and of gentle disposition, he had borne a series of illnesses whilst in the Army with great gallantry and fortitude. His mother was beloved by all who knew her. Devoted to her

ADOLESCENCE

home, and to four sons of whom she was so proud, efficient, resourceful, tireless in her activities, and staunch in her friendships, she was a very gracious lady. To the Church she was unfalteringly loyal, and in the gallery of memory we shall always see a certain pew in Cavendish Road where she worshipped with her boys at her side. With her, loyalty to God was linked with loyalty to her motherhood, and there is pathetic significance in the fact that when the fatal bomb fell she was found at the bedside of the son who had put up such a grand fight against ill-health for over a year. Fred Morley and his mother were the kind of members we could ill afford to lose, and they could both have said with the Psalmist: "My help cometh from the Lord which made heaven and earth."

And are we then compelled to believe that God does not preserve them although they trusted in His guardian care? Not if we strike deep enough. I am sure it is a false comfort to say that God took them, as though God had willed their untimely end. Such things come not by the will of God, but by the evil will of man which fills the earth with hatred and bloodshed and strife and death. So long as man remains free, God cannot prevent such things happening, and the tragic thing is that the blow so often falls on those who least deserve it, so that Herod sits on the throne while Jesus dies on the Cross. But though God cannot prevent these things, he is not defeated by them. His guardian care is from the time forth and for EVERMORE. He who brought again from the dead our Lord Jesus could still preserve the souls of our dear friends even when man's sin had destroyed their bodies. In that last going out from this earthly scene was also a coming in, a coming in to the eternal world and the abiding city of His love. They have gone from us, but they have come in to Him: out of the Church militant but into the Church Triumphant. To the loved ones who remain, our hearts go out in sympathy for their tragic and sudden sorrow, but for them we need not mourn. God kept them in that last going out and coming in, and now they see Him face to face. May that knowledge be for the strengthening of our faith, so that amid all the chances and changes of this so uncertain and often tragic world, we may hear the voice which says: "The Lord shall preserve thy going out and thy coming in from this time forth and even for evermore.

IRONS IN THE FIRE

Every Churchman thinks his role and duty is to offer condolences to the bereaved and to give some kind of comforting explanation of violent and unexpected death. The Minister falls back on the time-honoured assurances. God is looking after the soul of man, which cannot perish even though the body does. The soul is called to another better world and therefore benefits from dying. Omnipotent God loves mankind but He is not to blame if evil occurs because He has given man free will. And after all, God can never be defeated by evil, however much the victims of evil have to suffer. So much unsubstantiated wishful thinking and irrationality!

The sermon wags a weak tail. 'out of the Church militant' ... meaning? 'our hearts go out to the loved ones who remain but for them we need not mourn' ... well, they haven't gone out and come in, have they? But should we mourn for their loss? 'God kept them in that last going out and coming in' ... 'kept' exactly how? And who is 'them'? We must strengthen faith by repeating the mantra: 'going out and coming in'. A bit thin.

Not being in favour of mothers and brothers being whisked off to paradise prematurely, I took a somewhat self-interested view of my personal situation. I had lost my mother (and brother, though this was a lesser grief) and I was bewildered. She had been blown away, more violently than 'gone away'. There must be some reason for the catastrophe. I believed in a God who cared, a God who cared for my mother (and now perhaps rejoiced with her in heaven) but who was also caring for me. Why choose this moment to call my mother 'home'? I felt it must be for my own good; I was to learn from the deprivation. My 'character' (let alone faith) was to be strengthened. Before I knew where I was, my mother and brother were being taken out because my ego needed a boost. If anything, this self-centred posturing focused attention on the need to get somewhere with my schoolwork but it made no sense of their deaths. I soon realized the absurdity of my reasoning but it was a long time before I dumped the pursuit of a logical explanation which exonerated God.

My brothers and I never came to terms with this catastrophe. John disappeared into the R.A.F. At some point he was posted to North Africa and was stationed in a barren airfield while Rommel mustered his troops for the big push towards Egypt. It was hardly possible to talk to him about our loss, let alone how he felt about life. Neil of course was still with me through these trying times but perhaps because he was only thirteen (and I was sixteen) we never exchanged intimate confidences or information. We knew we shared a common deprivation but our brotherly relationship could not bear an open reference to it. Even in adult years we never spoke of Mum or Fred. There was a vacuum where emotional bonding should have been, perhaps directly attributable to our separation during those first crucial days after August 6th. We had nothing solid to grasp; and scarcely a memory of what had happened for we had not been

ADOLESCENCE

present, we had hardly participated. In any case, I was retreating into my own self-centred world and eventually moved into Fred's attic, which had been vacant many months. In comforting isolation I sought (and fought) solace in masturbation.

The immediate aftermath of events in Truro was the need for a substitute mother, or at least a resident housekeeper. No doubt Dad sent out SOS signals and in fact it was the Edwinstowe branch of the Morley kin that provided a solution. Mrs. Ada Locke was available to move in. Previously unknown to us (she was a relative by marriage, but then we knew none of the Edwinstowe family), Aunt Ada had been widowed recently and was being given temporary accommodation. She needed a home and, without children of her own, the transfer to the north could be mutually beneficial. But what an undertaking! I don't suppose she was paid liberally for her services and Dad checked the housekeeping account each week. Both Neil and I resented her presence, though we knew it was necessary. She had no experience of adolescent boys or how to cook for a family. I remember at the beginning she served Woolton sausages three dinners in a row with potatoes and pickle which we ate in silence till Dad mildly piped up that a more ambitious choice of food might be possible. It took her some time to find the Maypole (grocer's) and Dewhirst (butcher's) around Hyde Park. She herself was a suburban Londoner and the rough banter of Yorkshire folk was not easy to accept. Looking back, we were lucky Aunt Ada was brave enough to respond to the emergency. She stayed on after we left home, though my father did not want her. He never really liked her nor, I suppose, vice versa; it must have been difficult having to share his home permanently with her, particularly after the need for her had more or less passed.

Aunt Ada was no more than five feet tall and round in build. It was comic to see her pattering along beside Dad and his three sons, all of whom were well over six feet. She vary rarely went for walks with us. Keeping up was one problem, our reluctance to treat her as 'one of us' was another. In the early settling-in days, we showed an embarrassed politeness, then an irritated impatience and only gradually a resigned tolerance. She had a cheerful disposition and would sometimes be caught singing sentimental songs. We got used to helping with the house-work and Neil and I enjoyed teasing her by washing up and throwing the plates to each other. She always rose to the bait when I told her that her drawers were filthy. Gradually she became part of number nine in the Villas; I don't think the neighbours took to her but then they took little interest in any of us. In 1946, when Dad eventually moved house from Leeds to Otley, she came too. I think she was happier in the new environment as she approached old age.

Dad took advice about a Christmas holiday for the two boys, a good idea to take us away somewhere – give Aunt Ada a break and keep away sad memories. John was stationed in some god-forsaken airfield in the North African desert but

IRONS IN THE FIRE

Neil and I went with Dad to a C.H.A. hostel near Grasmere for a week. The company was rather weird and eccentric, but perhaps we were unused to cheerful chumminess. The 'leader' was a toothy, animated, smiling lady who kept calling the fellowship to impromptu prayers. I don't know why Dad chose a hostel of this ilk but he enjoyed gently ribbing the establishment. No doubt it was quite cheap. Neil and I slept in a small dormitory with a man who snored worse than Dad. We got so frustrated we chucked our socks at him. I scored a direct hit when he choked on one of mine, coughed, grunted, turned over and went to sleep like a babe. I retrieved the socks in the morning.

We enjoyed pleasant walks and some hill climbing. I returned with school friends a year or so later and used a string of Youth Hostels as we overcame the higher peaks. Those were wonderful times for the Lake District – not too pestered with tourists. The memorable part of the C.H.A. visit was a final evening concert to which people contributed. Our 'leader' warbled becomingly and Dad played the piano, but the *pièce de resistance* was staged by four young hostellers. Neil and I were in it and there was another boy and possibly his sister, but the idea came from an older girl who suggested we dressed up as ballet dancers. She mocked up the tutus and a gramophone played for us. I was pleased because our 'producer' praised me for keeping a straight face whilst dancing – much funnier than grinning. I was able to use the idea of a cod dance routine later on when I started staging shows at school. That too brought the house down.

It was a pity John was far away in Africa and missed this 'break'. The next time we saw him he was very ill. He had been airlifted from the North African desert to a hospital in Southampton. T.B. was diagnosed. From the south of England, somewhat inaccessible for us, he was eventually transferred to a bleak, utilitarian sanatorium on the outskirts of Ilkley. Each day he lay in a bed looking at the green slopes of Wharfedale with the glass wall opened wide, breathing the sharp-edged breezes that penetrated the room and absorbing sunlight while nothing moved. He was slowly recovering as the dark patches on his lungs diminished. It took more than a year before they could release him into Civvy Street. Dad, Neil and I (Aunt Ada once) took the bus to Otley and another to Ilkley on Sunday afternoons to visit him but we were all pretty miserable company. I didn't go often. It was perishing cold in that open-air cell and John hardly sparkled. He lived in lonely isolation. When he was finally demobbed (with a small pension) finding a suitable job was a problem. For a time he worked in Parks and Gardens for the Borough, but then with all the bending he slipped a disc and had to retire. Back trouble and varicose veins plagued him constantly. At home we worried about his future – and yet all's well that ends well, as will become clear later on.

ADOLESCENCE

7. School in the Upper Sixth

My mother had remarked, as she stirred the lentil soup on the hob while I stood irritably waiting for food, "I don't know why it is but ever since you've been in that Sixth Form you have become surly and unpleasant!" That was me in the Lower Sixth and maybe I had been adjusting to newfound liberties or pubertal pressures. Now, deprived of her loving criticism, I was starting the second year, leaving a nightmarish summer holidays behind and entering the Upper Sixth. One thing was certain, I was not telling anyone about my personal tragedy. Perhaps there was no one I could confide in. Brian Barton had proved an unlikely confidante and was wrapped round with scholarship papers. In any case I didn't want to complicate matters with schoolmates.

The *esprit de corps* of the Grammar School was beginning to revive and there was a strong camaraderie between the boys now staying on in the Sixth Form. The bullyboys of the middle school had dropped out; my contemporaries were taking charge and, pardon the vanity, I was one of the 'forces for good'. By the end of the summer term in 1942 I was playing both cricket and rugby for the first teams. Frank Hoggett, a talented biology teacher, gave up his spare time to coach the 1st XV. He decided to play me at fullback and I proved my mettle when, in a match against Leeds University Medical School, I stood my ground against an adult fly half who broke through our defences and advanced towards me. I tackled him and all was saved! Now in the new season I was to play centre three-quarter and the team prospered. War or no war, we were able to travel round the West Riding mainly on Saturdays, by coach or train, enjoying a welcome break from routine.

To a large extent we ignored the war while noting the headlines. We knew that all the future could offer us was national service when schooldays ended and that spurred us on to make the most of our Sixth Form years, though the range was limited. We were able to take holidays in the evacuated school premises in Buckden, lower Wharfedale. Cycling there was definitely part of the fun. In Leeds, fire watching was one of the few encroachments on our leisure and even then we were paid for guarding the school. Two and sixpence per night. Each evening three boys and one teacher reported for the night watch. Special arrangements were made for them. In a part of the school normally closed to pupils (staff only) a dormitory was formed, with space for armchairs and an electric fire. Some distance from the H.Q., the Green Room next to the School Hall had been converted into a billiard room with full-size table. The early part of the night would be spent here. The game was usually snooker and, however poor our cueing, we enjoyed the contest. Sitting round the fire in the dormitory was perhaps another matter; all depended on the teacher's amiability. Stanley

IRONS IN THE FIRE

Fisher was always superb; he never played snooker but he talked like a sage. Thinking it over, most of the teachers proved to be interesting after all.

There was a raid on Leeds only on one occasion that I fire-watched. We donned helmets, checked the fire buckets and kept vigil on the school's flat rooftops. We could see flashes of light down in Kirkstall and flares in Hunslet in the Aire valley. There was a moon giving phosphorescence to the rooftops but we couldn't see the bombers even in the searchlights. Every now and then a dull c-crump and a shriek of incendiaries sent a cold shiver down me but I can't add more description because we observed from a distance and it was a small raid. As far as I know, the Grammar School buildings remained unscathed. We took the money and waited for the next snooker game.

During the summer of 1944 Leeds City Council erected Big Tops in Parks around Leeds and encouraged citizens to take 'a holiday at home'. They were splendid marquees and inside a parquet-type floor was laid for dancing. A live band played – none of this disc-jockey business. It must have cost thousands to hire these tents and few people were attracted to the Hyde Park Big Top, which was the one we used to patronise before crossing the Park to fire-watch at school. I suppose the entertainment was aimed at the young and as far as I remember the admission charge was very small. I danced with local girls there but never 'met' anyone I wanted to date. Whereas I did meet at least two girls (at separate times) at the Capitol Ballroom in Meanwood. This was a Palais de Danse of some style, with packed couples shuffling round to the Glenn Miller-type music of the local band. 'Moonlight Serenade' was their signature tune.

> Saturday night is the loneliest night of the week
> For that's the night my baby and I used to dance cheek to cheek ...

Saturday night at the Capitol was truly exciting. Everyone dressed up and behaved. No need for bouncers, as far as I recall, but no doubt a lot went on I never realised. The first girl I kept dancing with and finally dated was called Monica but she was a bit dumb. I made the mistake of inviting her round to the Villas after taking her to see "The Bartered Bride" at the Grand Theatre. I thought it would be nice to show her off to Dad but it wasn't. My intentions were honourable, though rigidly middle-class. My second girl was auburn and I forget her name but she was very responsive. We could embrace for hours, simply standing and cuddling, kissing and hugging without saying anything. Perhaps she needed loving as much as I did but I didn't delve. It was her father who broke up our beautiful friendship though I was going away to university anyway. We clung to each other at the end of her road, melding in long ecstatic kisses, when this man came storming along to drag his daughter away. He had been waiting up for her, had watched us embracing for hours and had lost

ADOLESCENCE

patience. I felt very sorry for her, wrote to her (and him) but somehow the spell was broken.

I had taken dancing lessons six months previously, thanks to Malcolm Willcock who was down from Fettes College for the Christmas holiday. He had booked in at a Dance Academy in town but was too nervous to go through with it alone. I spent some of my hard-earned cash (2s/6d a night) on lessons and became pretty good at the quickstep and foxtrot, as well as the ubiquitous waltz. I enjoyed dancing with the teacher; she was young, slim and temptingly perfumed. I think she enjoyed dancing with me too but Malcolm Willcock had two left feet. He went back to Scotland while I went to the Palais de Danse. Most Saturday nights I would wend my way homewards, every now and then leaping high and sprinting for sheer physical delight with the experience of another close embrace. But there was never any likelihood of 'sex' occurring. I sought a substitute for a mother's love.

I was in fact repressing my feelings fairly well, or perhaps channelling them into fairly harmless behaviour. At school I maintained a tight grip on the private grief that I kept 'bottled'. I don't think many boys knew that I was 'scarred'. The only time the grip loosened occurred in an English lesson in the Library with Stanley Fisher. The little class of four had been discussing what had happened to Gunter, one of the four. He had been to a C.C.F. course and was handling a dummy grenade when it exploded in his hand. He was lucky not to lose fingers and the main damage was via shock. He told us something happened that was awful, it was so embarrassing he didn't want to tell us in case we laughed. 'Flush' demanded to know and Gunter explained half-apologetically that he had 'shat his pants'. We responded by laughing because he expected it but 'Flush' became quite indignant and angry. "Of course you shat your pants! Anyone would do the same. It's an outrage putting you in such a position!"

We sobered up and talked about bombs and then someone mentioned he had heard that my brother had been killed by one and Stanley Fisher asked me if that was true. When I said yes he wanted to know more. "Come on, tell us what happened," he said. I didn't want to, I shook my head and said nothing. 'Flush' persisted and I broke into tears. I lost control and sobbed. "My mother was killed too," I was able to say and I just sat there crying while they looked at me, shocked and embarrassed. I think the boys felt 'Flush' had been clumsy and tactless; certainly he gently changed the subject. Later that day, he sought me out to apologise. I got the impression that he had found out more about the events of August 6th 1942, about which he had known nothing.

Behind the 'breakdown' lay self-pity and pathos. Here was my 'hero' and he knew nothing about me. All these classes and lessons, and there had never been a true understanding between us. No one, at school or elsewhere, had thought to tell him. It was the first time I had cried since the dropping of the bomb and it was for the wrong reason. I had to resume control as quickly as possible.

Of course I continued to attend A.T.C. parades but without enthusiasm. My brush with a maverick Luftwaffe pilot had not filled me with thoughts of revenge. Uppermost was a sense of futility. There was one occasion when we marched up and down the school playground in our uniforms being drilled by Sergeant Young, an ex-professional who had carved a niche for himself as School Secretary and instructor in the school C.C.F. He was Scottish and a dour Presbyterian to boot. His baleful eye fell on me as I slouched along obviously bored with the whole business of drill. He ordered us to halt and approached me with menace and a snarl. "Pull your shoulders back, Morley! Smarten up what's the matter with you? Put some guts into your marching!" I was taller than him but he could make me feel small. I just stayed still. "Discipline, that's what it's all about. What's the matter with you?"

He was expecting some response so I muttered, "It's all so unnatural!" and waited to be charged with insubordination. He glowered at me, turned purple and suddenly walked away. He obviously knew my personal predicament and decided to avoid a showdown. I was glad he was lenient. I wasn't a rebel, nor a pacifist; I was just sick of the whole business of being involved in the war effort. Maybe someone else would have relished the idea of getting his own back, hunting down the killers, committing himself to defeating the enemy, but I just didn't want to be concerned. I needed time out and could only retreat from preparations for adult commitments.

Games were the answer. Rugby in the winter months of 1942-3, there is no better team game! I developed skills as inside centre and for that second season was elected 1st XV Captain. This was democratically achieved at an annual meeting of players in the Headmaster's study. I flourished somewhat as a result of such support and even read books on rugby skills and tactics. Someone said a Leeds Rugby League 'scout' had been watching a couple of matches, but of course I scorned the idea of being paid to play. I think I was a successful 'captain' of an enthusiastic team though we did lose some games. Then there was Cricket for the summer of 1943-4. Since childhood I had always played a straight bat and now batted at no 4 or 5; unusually (particularly as I was tall) I took to keeping wicket, specializing in standing close up in order to stump batsmen who 'felt' for the ball on the offside. Was I consciously imitating Peter Lupton, my friend who kept wicket for the Colts in 1939? As I was elected Captain of the 1st XI, I found this central position greatly helped when organizing bowling and fielding tactics.

It seems odd that, in the middle of an increasingly intense war of global proportions, with the tide just beginning to turn against the Nazis, such traditions as photographs of blazered and smiling school teams continued to be honoured.

ADOLESCENCE

We tried to carry on as normal, I suppose. I now look at my collection of mounted photographs and remember enjoyable times at school. It is unlikely that any of these young men, posing for team photos so confidently, were killed in 'the war' though most of them, like me, were called up for National Service.

I remember a school cricket outing to Ripon in June 1944. As usual we had taken the train from Leeds and were walking up the road that led to the cricket ground, carrying in turns the heavy leather bag containing our gear. A warm summer jaunt for a cheerful bunch of youngsters, some like me sporting our 'colours' on blazers and all of us relishing the trip (do I recall a teacher with us? No.) We were passing an ancient monument, a cross or fountain, when a local gaffer stood in our way. He was looking at me and pointing. He shouted, "When you goin' then?" angrily. I stopped in my tracks, so did we all, and he repeated the question, "When you goin'?" He was addressing me but I didn't get the point until Geoff Aber, one of my teammates, started laughing. "He means 'joining up'!" he said, and the team moved on, ignoring the fellow cheerfully, but I felt as if he had presented me with a white feather. I was just 18, tall and perhaps peacocked in a striped blazer, and yes, I would be moving on in a few months' time, though I wasn't telling him that.

Mention of Geoff Aber reminds me of the Jewish 'problem' at school. Geoff and his twin Clive were two brilliant athletes and key players of our team. They were Jewish but who cared? They were fully paid up members of our society, good-looking and sociable. Other Jews (who, like R.C.s abstained from school religious services) were approved if they conformed to the normal behaviour of our peers or were clearly talented, but those who looked 'Levantine' or had suspect names were scorned, though not persecuted or assaulted. In a way we just ignored them, a thoughtless prejudice though not active anti-Semitism; it took the news from Dachau to alert me to my failings. Another of my personal prejudices came to light when visiting an open-air swimming pool in a London suburb on a scorching summer afternoon. I was about to launch myself into the crowded waters when I realized a huge black lady in a bikini was standing beside me, her grey-black nakedness over-exposed in the strong sunlight. Momentarily I was shocked; the thought of skin contamination made me shift to another part of the pool. On the other hand, maybe I would have reacted to an obese white lady in exactly the same way. I am not fond of fat people. Is that reprehensible?

I was made a sub-prefect towards the end of the first year of the Sixth Form but took little interest in prefectorial duties. Monitoring behaviour or checking attendances did not compare with activities on the sports field. As I did not like many of the select group of prefects who occupied the small room in the lower corridor and disapproved of the inquisitions and whacking of young offenders that were part of the prefectorial system, it was no surprise not to be promoted to full prefect. I had my own empire anyway; busily pinning school team lists to

IRONS IN THE FIRE

notice boards, treading the boards and editing the school magazine. I wrote articles, reports and even verses for the latter. A career in journalism was forecast on the strength of these writings but by this time I was set for Oxford and the Navy.

Dr. Terry Thomas, my somewhat aloof headmaster, had written a sensible comment on me in one of my final year reports. Written and signed in red ink was the Headmaster's considered opinion of me: *"Too many irons in the fire to do well"*. This can be re-construed in many ways whilst accepting the general probity of the comment. Yes, perhaps I was a jack-of-all-trades and master of none; yes, perhaps I was working for shallow breadth rather than profound depth; yes, perhaps there were too many cooks spoiling the broth of my activities; but each of my 'irons' was worth heating. Either as a result of TT's report or because I know no other way, I have made something of a virtue of this attitude. Those who specialize necessarily narrow their range of interests, the expert is bound to a narrow response, the treadmill operates, the ability to change is limited, variety is the spice of life etc. Is there not more opportunity for a varied, interesting career if I keep more irons in the fire? Well, it all depends what you are capable of, or interested in.

At any rate, when some kind benefactor offered students at the Grammar School twenty-five pounds for the best 'essay' on: "Victory for England", I entered the competition. I did a certain amount of research and penned a fairly wide-ranging essay on the patriotic theme. It was adjudged winner and I bought a number of books with the money (all marked with VE inside). And I shared the traditional Bacon's Essay prize with the only other candidate, which was very tactful of the judges. I bought the Complete Works of Geoffrey Chaucer, a sign there of my inclination to study literature.

Such 'achievements' were pleasing but I criticise one serious defect, which could be considered psychosomatic. I was often late! I became a late riser and a late arriver at school. Even when I had time, I would dilly-dally so that I was never early for any appointment. I see this as a failure of self-confidence; I was reluctant to buckle down to the tasks in hand. Compulsively I did not want to 'hang around' waiting for events to start. I found light conversation strained my nerves. I would arrive for a game with minutes to spare, change rapidly and dash out on to the field ready to play still tying my laces. This unpunctuality was obviously a weakness of positive thinking (it has continued!). To it I relate my habit of carrying a book everywhere I went. If there was a delay or spare moment, I needed to take comfort from the world within my control.

Two incidents from the final year at school illustrate the defect. I had been home to get my games kit during the lunch-break and delayed catching the tram to the playing fields. In fact the tram-ride was very slow and I arrived later than expected. The House game had started; the two teams were scurrying about the

ADOLESCENCE

pitch as I ran into the pavilion and raced up the stairs to change into my kit. There was a small man in a raincoat standing beside the line of clothing hanging from hooks. He seemed startled as I rushed past him to enter the inner changing room. So intent was I on changing for the game I gave no thought to the man. He was gone when, three minutes later, I rushed out to join the match. Next day there was an enquiry; various boys had reported money and watches taken from pockets in the pavilion. I had to confess my abject failure to realize what was going on; by making a citizen's arrest I could have been a hero but I ended up an ostrich or blinkered donkey.

Again, when our 1st XI was playing an away game against Giggleswick, the team met at the Central railway station early in the morning. Unfortunately the Captain was late and missed the train, which took the team to its destination without further incident. When I eventually arrived at Giggleswick, having caught the next train, the game was in progress and my Vice-Captain Geoff Embleton, was doing a cracking job with ten men on the field; he had varied the bowling skilfully and engineered a collapse of the home team's batting. It was not very clever of me to take over the captaincy upon my arrival; Geoff knew what he was doing and I didn't. In the event, it didn't matter that the Giggleswick team scored more runs than they should have done, for our batting proved too strong. Geoff Aber (or was it Clive?) struck a magnificent six that soared over the green copper dome of the School Chapel. But it was a Pyrrhic victory for me!

According to the Higher School Certificate for July 1943 my results in three Principal subjects and two Subsidiary subjects were:

Principal English Literature	Subsidiary
Principal Geography	Pass
Principal Economics	Pass
Subsidiary Art	Pass
Subsidiary Biology	Pass

I stare at this Certificate in disbelief. Did I really 'fail' my English exam after all that enthusiastic work with 'Flush'? Uppermost is the memory of opening an exam paper and realizing one of the two Shakespeare plays I had studied was not set for this exam; I could answer only half the questions. But I associate this gaffe with my second attempt at H.S.C. when, having stayed on for a third year in the Sixth, I was re-sitting exams for a State Scholarship to get me to university. Stanley Fisher had accepted responsibility for that blunder; he said he would report the error to the Examining Board but I don't know if he did. Whatever the reason for the poor showing in English, I thought to do better next time.

IRONS IN THE FIRE

I continued Economics but only at Subsidiary level. Later in my 'naval career' this qualification was to rescue me from the travails of minesweeping off Northern Ireland so I shall not disparage it; but Economics was never my interest. The teacher was an extraordinary fop who was blatantly homosexual; the streetwise Sixth-formers teased him mercilessly about this unusual sexual orientation. He was a brand new phenomenon for me. Stanley Fisher was very friendly with him (after all, he was very cultured) but I couldn't really approve. I doubt if he had much experience as an Economics teacher anyway. Dad, on the other hand, could sit me down and explain a specimen Balance Sheet fairly lucidly. He thought Economics new-fangled as an academic subject but far more useful than English Literature. Once, when I said I would like to be a teacher of English when 'I grew up', he advised there was no place for an English specialist in schools. Teachers qualified in Latin and Greek could handle all that mattered in English. And true enough; in my father's schooldays (and much later) there had been no English Department any more than there was one in Science. Well, no matter what the future held, I was determined to head for English studies; I had no other interest to touch them.

Johnny Lee had taught me a lot through the years in Geography lessons. It was he who pinpointed one of my failings in a report: *"He remembers facts badly ..."* I agree and I can't say I have improved much, though I did begin to make serious use of mnemonics after that reproof. I appreciated very much the extra work shouldered by Johnny Lee in preparing me for the Geography exams. I was surprised to be classified as 'Very Good' in the special Geography papers, but there was never any question of choosing this subject at university. The H.S.C. results for July 1944 were a little better. The Certificate records the following results:

Principal English Literature	Good
Principal Geography	Pass
Scholarship Geography	Very Good
Subsidiary History	Pass
Subsidiary Art	Pass
Subsidiary Economics	Pass

I was not awarded a State Scholarship, of course, but that fact becomes merely academic in the light of what was happening to Sixth formers who were about to start their national service in the Forces.

There was a big recruiting campaign to attract youngsters who appeared to possess officer-like qualities to choose the Army, the Navy, the Air Force or the Fleet Air Arm for their national service. I don't know whether rivalry or shortages were the cause; or perhaps the plight of the country's universities was

ADOLESCENCE

responsible. At any rate, teams of regular Officers descended on schools to interview those students about to be called up. They were preceded by doctors who assessed the physical potential of recruits, which is how I came to choose the Navy for my enlistment. I had sheepishly put down R.A.F. at first but the doctor who was testing youthful bodies rejected me. Maybe they had recruited enough would-be pilots for that day but I was somewhat alarmed to be pronounced unfit for the Air Force. Was it my heart? Or just my height? I had no alternative but to choose the Navy; the one future I was determined to avoid was life in the Army. So I attended an interview, in the Headmaster's palatial study no less, conducted by various gold-braided Naval officers, where I was asked how far it was from Portsmouth to Gibraltar. Somewhat startled and befogged, I suggested five thousand miles, upon which the officers broke into a series of exclamations and expostulations about how this answer confirmed the ignorance of the younger generation. Had they been betting on the answers provided? Had I just sunk my chances? No, they smiled condescendingly and bore me no grudge; I seemed to be favoured sufficiently to be selected for the Royal Naval Volunteer Reserve but – this was the amazing part of the offer – preceding this I would be spending two terms at university during which I would be expected to spend one day a week as a naval rating under training. After that interim I would become a full-time sailor.

There were a few universities involved in this scheme, which was of great advantage to them. During the war the number of undergraduates had dropped for obvious reasons. Many Faculties and Departments were threatened with closure. Universities were in desperate need of funds and the expediency of Short Courses had been operating for a couple of years. The Armed Forces presumably financed the scheme and benefited by recruiting potential officers. Politicians were planning for peacetime and our educational system was due for a major re-appraisal. The Welfare State was beginning to embrace higher education at universities.

My University was Oxford and my College was St Peter's Hall. When receiving notice of this wonderful news, I don't remember leaping for joy. I really had no conception of what it would be like. I would be studying English and assumed a continuation of schooling, but would this be like 'boarding school'? And how would the naval training fit into the college routines? I had never been as far south as Oxford. London was unvisited. My experience of the University of Leeds was limited to rough and tumble on the rugby field and stitches to my lower lip sewn by a medical student after a game. I had no conception of Oxford University life beyond that offered by Laurel and Hardy in "Two Chumps at Oxford', a film I had laughed my self silly over at the local Picture House. And, ah yes, Oxford was dark blue, Cambridge light blue.

IRONS IN THE FIRE

Dad himself was a little bemused by this turn of events. He had watched my conduct through the Sixth Form and sometimes attended matches when I was captaining the side. Coincidentally he had kept wicket for his school team (Ashby de la Zouch G.S.) in the eighteen nineties but the only helpful criticism he made was that I should not slouch between wickets at the end of overs. His reaction to my proposed university short course was very interesting. "What you will need if you are going away to college is a dressing-gown!" Did he have images of Noel Coward in mind? Anyway he took me down to Austin Reid's, a swell shop, and bought me a warm woollen full-length gown for which clothes ration tokens were not necessary. It cost quite a bit, though, and I still use it, sixty years old behind my bedroom door.

I was sorry to leave school not because I was shirking the new world, but because it seemed to be improving with every term's activities. The dark patch of the early forties had faded and the school was now functioning efficiently and more humanely. Brother Neil was himself now due to become a Sixth-former and part of a strong set of leading personalities. I think I had helped to establish a revitalised institution and probably in recognition of this I was awarded at the end of the school year a special certificate, not often given.

LEEDS GRAMMAR SCHOOL

CERTIFICATE OF MERIT

By the scheme of the Charity Commissioners of 1898, the Headmaster, in his Annual Report to the Governors, may mention the names of any boys who, in his judgement, are worthy of reward or distinction, having regard both to proficiency and conduct.

In accordance with the Scheme, this Certificate is awarded to

H.M. MORLEY

Date: Midsummer 1944

A.S. Reeve   Terry Thomas
Chairman of the Governors   *Headmaster*

CHAPTER THREE

PRE-ADULTHOOD

1. First Bite of the Cherry

My first impressions of Oxford University were confused because I apparently belonged to two Colleges. I was an undergraduate of St Peter's Hall but lived in Corpus Christi College. It seems that St Peter's had been loaned to London University for the duration of the war and the buildings were occupied by Westfield College, a strictly undergraduette institution which had been evacuated from London. Members of St Peter's were unwelcome at headquarters and on the one occasion I tried to explore the premises the residents eyed me with the utmost suspicion. It was best to consider Corpus Christi College as home for the time being as all St Peter's undergraduates were housed there. Tutorials were held in an annexe near to St Peter's and 'Huffy", the Rev R.E.C. Houghton, my tutor, was virtually our only contact with St Peter's authorities. After two terms at Corpus we would move into the R.N.V.R. for full time National Service. On returning to continue 'reading' English Language and Literature, I was domiciled in St Peter's Hall and very rarely visited Corpus Christi; so in many ways I had two bites of the cherry – though there were really two very different cherries.

In October 1944 Corpus seemed to be struggling to maintain an identity. There was an uneasy amalgam of undergraduates. A few of these were ex-servicemen who had been invalided out of the forces. Some students were straight from school and looked it. Others were deemed medically unfit for war service. Undergraduates studying special reserved subjects like medicine and sciences were in evidence. There were foreign students including Commonwealth representatives; and each year a group of short course students were present. To this motley band add the smaller but similar mixed bag of St Peter's undergraduates that shared the Corpus Christi amenities and it is perhaps not surprising that there was little collegiate spirit amongst this heterogeneous collection of academics from whom the senior common room habitués seemed to keep their distance as they walked round-shouldered and be-gowned through the college quadrangles.

The St Peter's contingent had rooms in the Thomas block, a recent addition to the ancient residential quarters. Undistinguished in architectural style, this building boasted the best plumbing in the College and undergraduates from far-off quadrangles regularly visited us for the sake of hot water and baths. The small group of short course students had single rooms here. I think there were eight of us and I record their first names as Jimmy, George, Harry, Geoff, Ron, Peter and Butch. And myself, a second Harry. By the end of the two terms I was ready to relinquish my first name and rename myself Michael or Mike, partly to avoid duplications but also because 'arry seemed perhaps a trifle lowbrow. When National Service was over, only three of us returned to complete our degree courses and interestingly none had been commissioned. George Gradwell became a distinguished entomologist at Oxford, Harry Spence a Foreign Office guru in Russian affairs and I became a schoolteacher. When I resumed studies I kept to Mike, which baffles those who knew me in Corpus days (and members of the family). I wasn't to know a princeling would bring Harry back into fashion.

Corpus Christi College is an ancient establishment in contrast to St Peter's. Rather like the Dormouse, it is squeezed between two much larger colleges: the Mad Hatter of Christ Church (Dodgson's base) and the March Hare of Merton, the melodious bells of whose tower woke me each morning. Merton was founded in 1264 and lays claim to being the oldest College in Oxford whereas both Corpus Christi and Christ Church were founded in Henry VIII's time, respectively 1517 and 1525; but the differences in scale and style of these two Colleges are striking. Christ Church was designed to be grand if not grandiose by Cardinal Wolsey at the height of his power (it was to be called Cardinal College but it got a holier name after he fell from favour). More humbly Corpus Christi College was named after a popular festival of the mediaeval Church when annual celebrations of the Feast of the Body of Christ took the form of Mystery Plays staged on pageant wagons in the streets of many towns north of Oxford. I wasn't expecting anything of that nature, of course, but there was certainly no sign of traditional festivities in 1944, though possibly on the first Sunday after Trinity there would be a commemorative service in the Chapel, by which time I was far away and not caring less. Corpus was always going to be an 'intimate' College simply because of its modest size and the small coteries of resident undergraduates seemed content to keep it that way.

Two architectural features perhaps contribute to the reserved ambience of the place. One is the Dining Hall, which is the main meeting-place for residents of the College. Corpus has a typical Oxford refectory, with serried tables flanked by long benches and a dais for the high table; dark oak panelling surrounds the diners and past dignitaries look down from heavy picture frames. Above them is the original hammer beam roof, which is a fine structure but in my opinion, rather oppressive because it hangs over a relatively small hall; those hammer beams carry the weight of the past as if discouraging unseemly or trivial behaviour. Maybe that was a good thing; there was a Corpus tradition (shared by other colleges) of a 'sconce' inflicted on any undergraduate who blasphemed, swore or mentioned a woman's name while at a dining table. The silver sconce bowl was filled with ale, which had to be drunk (and paid for) by the offender, but as this custom was in abeyance 'for the duration' I can't be certain I haven't made that up. Certainly dining behaviour was exemplary while I was there.

PRE-ADULTHOOD

The other somewhat cool feature is the Front Quad, which is deliberately kept plain and unadorned. In 1944 the surface was gravel, I think, and the more recent paving with flagstones is no improvement. There is no greenery and at the centre stands a tall sundial topped by the college emblem, a Pelican. Apparently a perpetual calendar encircles the column but I never found anyone to explain it, nor do I recall any legend about pelicans in Corpus. In 1944 this unusual (and useless?) device looked rather drab but after the war a coat of bright and varied colours gave it a much more cheerful appearance. The Pelican column was a proud symbol but not particularly vital to our concerns and the Front Quad remained rather uninteresting even though it was surrounded by casement windows, doorways and staircases leading to rooms for undergraduates. I was to grow very familiar with one of these entrances after a few weeks of term.

Oxford was the furthest I had travelled from home; it was a contrast to Leeds of course but I lacked criteria to judge its full greatness. Finding my way around obviously took time but the marvellous assembly of ancient colleges and institutions at the centre of the city was immediately impressive. Exploring the High Street and the Broad Street more or less defined the living space of my daily round but there was one special area to get familiar with: the river-side of the Thames (or Isis in Oxford parlance). Many Colleges owned extraordinary houseboats, which were moored permanently along the banks of the river. They looked more like the hulks of men o' war than the longboats seen on canals, without the masts and sails of course. Spruced by paint and varnish they were gaily-decadent indulgences but in 1944, after four years of neglect, rather dull and dingy. In peacetime they were the headquarters for the rowing fraternity of a particular college but I saw little evidence of eights in 1944 and indeed two consecutive houseboats alongside had been commandeered by the Naval Division of the University to be the training ground for naval cadets. Corpus Christi College was as near as any college to this watery retreat but I can't say that gave me any pleasure. Clad in bell-bottoms and round caps we reported for maritime instruction once a week, which usually meant sitting in rooms in the barges being told what seamanship was. Only once did we venture on the Isis, to experience life on a dinghy, but tacking between those narrow banks was, well, tacky. Being so far from the sea, such training was all a little absurd though there were times when I recalled the Boys Boating Club outings nostalgically. Still, it was quite enjoyable and we were all in the same boat. Frankly it was an easy introduction to National Service and I did not make a serious effort to absorb the finer details of the Manual of Seamanship, which was our textbook. For the rest of the week, I could be an undergraduate with a programme of academic study and a life-style appropriate to college wartime conditions.

As far as tutorials were concerned, I shared a regular session with Butch Conrad, the only other Corpus-based English student, at least once a week. As befits his name, Butch was a bit on the raw side. I can't remember where he hailed from, but he hadn't much time for the finer points of literary studies. Our tutor, Rev. R.E.C. Houghton (who had edited the edition of 'King Lear' we used at school) soon lived up to his nickname "Huffy" as far as Butch was concerned. I can't say I blame him; Butch was here for the ride. On the other hand, I was writing essays of some length and delving into Middle English very happily. I prospered and thoroughly enjoyed tutorials; there must have been a few other lectures and seminars but I remember only one stimulating session with Professor M.R. Ridley, who enthused about a popular hero, John Keats. At the end of the two terms, during which there were no exams, a modest and unexpected little ceremony for the short course students took place in the Dining Hall at St Peter's. I met and shook hands for the first time with the Master of St Peter's Hall, Canon R.W. Howard, after Huffy had spoken favourably about my studies. I was assured of a welcome upon my return from National Service; not that I had ever doubted this but there were rejects and it was nice to know I was approved.

Meanwhile I was thoroughly enjoying college life in Corpus. Enter Lewis Thomas, a State Scholar in Classical Studies, now in his third year at Corpus Christi. He hailed from Haverfordwest and spoke with a musical lilt. He had poor eyesight but there was nothing wrong with his perception of College life in 1944; it needed pepping up. Social activities were lacking, relaxations from studies were meagre; he was in a backwater and wanted to be in the mainstream. I think he rather envied the short course students who were able to move on to war service while he stayed put. Maybe he was just being polite, though no other undergraduate bothered that much, when he invited the short course students to tea in his room. Occupying the rooms adjacent to his in the Front Quad was Pat Bamford, a medical student with similar frustrations in social well-being, though caused by his intense workload more than boredom. The two of them played host and I don't know how long the guests were entertained but two of us stayed on to listen to more swing and jazz records: Jimmy Birnie from Glasgow and me from Leeds responding with increased heart-beats to the music the Yanks had brought with them across the Atlantic – Glenn Miller, Tommy Dorsey, Woody Herman et al. Lewis Thomas was up-to-date with his choice of discs; Jimmy and I were entranced.

Out of this mutual enthusiasm for new world sophistication a friendship developed that cast a golden glow over those two Corpus terms. It was an alliance of opposites, and a coincidence of separate needs being met at the same time. I don't think there were any homosexual undertones; in fact the presence of women was craved though not one of us had much sexual experience and our relations with female friends in practice lacked libido. Well, so it seems to me but I have to judge conduct on my own understanding of the past. For example, I burst into Lew's room to find Nina Bawden sobbing on Lew's shoulder as they

PRE-ADULTHOOD

clung together on his sofa, but this certainly didn't mean they were lovers. This was Lew as friend, with a touch of therapy thrown in. He could even comfort me, though we never talked about the bonding fact that both of us had been deprived of our mothers; we shied away from too much intimacy. Perhaps there was an emotional bond between Jimmy and Lew, for they shared enthusiasms and humour that excluded me but I was much more inhibited than Jimmy. They were both Celts and I was Anglo-Saxon. As for Pat, I hesitate to comment on his lineage; he was the only one of us educated at a Public boarding School (Ampleforth) but there was a strange green intensity in his eyes that hinted at an anarchic side to his nature. It seems to me the friendship allowed us the freedom to pursue pleasures together whilst resisting the temptation to pry into private selves.

Perhaps the point was that we got caught up in Lewis Thomas's struggle to survive the academic strait jacket that cramped his style. He was irritated with his brief as a Scholar ('Greats' was a four year course) while so much was going on outside the college walls. And yet he was still a provincial with simple tastes, grateful for being lifted out of obscurity in distant Pembrokeshire and with no ambitions to lead a Bohemian life or to emulate the Brideshead fraternity. Financially he was constrained in his range of outlets but that didn't stop his enjoyment of unsophisticated pursuits, chief of which was, I suppose, the gentle art of unpretentious conversation. So when Jimmy Birnie and I stayed on to listen to more Glenn Miller records and to hear for the first time the signature tune of the American Forces Radio Network, Ravel's *Pavane pour une enfante defunte,* we were not being tempted to indulge in dubious practices. This was an invitation to respond to our own impulses, and they were naïve enough. Lew's radiogram liberated us, so we could jig around and talk animatedly about American notions. We began spending time together, meeting in Lew's room mainly but often walking the streets light-heartedly. As far as I was concerned, belonging to a 'gang' like this was something totally new.

The leader was always Lewis Thomas, educated at Haverfordwest Grammar School, who had recently displeased his tutor by suggesting that he should change subjects to something more modern, but as he went straight back to his old school to teach Latin after Finals he must have become reconciled to his fate. I wrote to him during my time in the Navy but after he returned to little England beyond Wales we met very rarely. Yet both of us treasure the Corpus experience, and have kept in touch. Not so Pat Bamford who was visibly torn apart by the intense pressure of medical learning and the desire to relax and enjoy life. In the end he gave up medicine and left Corpus. After National Service in the Army he went into the City, very successfully. Only very recently, forty-seven years later, have we met again – very amicably but both aware that our HCC idyll was a long time ago.

IRONS IN THE FIRE

Jimmy Birnie, however, has disappeared seemingly forever. He was an RAF short course student but for the life of me I can't remember which subject he was studying. He and I related through Lewis really, and when we went our ways there was little to keep us in contact. Jimmy was enthusiastic for fun and games; he certainly sparked off Lew's pursuit of entertainment and it surprises me that he has never written since leaving Oxford. He did not say much about his Scottish family background to me, but nor me my Yorkshire background to him. He remains a bit of a mystery.

One morning Lew announced that we were founding the Habeas Corpus Club with the motto: 'ye can hae me body but ye canna hae me soul', which was witty enough for me though the sentiments certainly belied our intentions. H.C.C. was duly launched (no doubt with mugs of cocoa) and became part of our lives. The first tea party was held in Lew's room. Both Lewis and Pat had been around long enough to know a few interesting girls and invitations were issued. After tea and crumpets, we danced in the somewhat confined space but though I couldn't jive properly I knew how to slouch around the room holding my partner close. These were college or art school girls, very attractive though a little older than me, but I was not ready to 'date' one of them. It was very nice holding them in my arms. The entertainment was as innocent as a Sunday school treat.

There was a more sophisticated world out there. As a consequence of our socializing, we got invited to an event run by Slade School of Art students (another London educational establishment sheltering in Oxford during the war); there were alcoholic drinks in a big room but it was quite boring compared with H.C.C. After a while we followed people back to some lodgings in Walton Street, climbed the stairs and sat on the floor haphazardly with a crowd while Eduardo Paolozzi and a few arty types strummed on guitars and sang. We hummed along for a bit but it all seemed a bit pretentious and (never having sat on my haunches in the company of artists) I wasn't convinced the entertainment was worth the discomfort. Paolozzi, though, made a huge impression; he exuded a heavyweight mid-European culture and was clearly already an outstanding personality. I was aware of being small fry and not just because I had never heard solo guitars before.

The H.C.C. quartet sometimes wandered into the Kardoma café in Cornmarket Street, fashionable for elevenses, but we preferred our own resources, being short of cash nearly all the time. (I can't remember what financial arrangements were made for me. Dad must have given me 'pocket' money; I seem to remember £60, for surely the Navy wasn't paying me yet.) One place for free entertainment was the Record Shop in the High Street. The proprietors obviously found it profitable to provide cubicles in which one or two customers could listen to the latest records before deciding what to buy. These cubicles were soundproofed so you could often see a couple of frenzied

PRE-ADULTHOOD

undergraduates shaking and leaping about as if electrocuted behind the glass doors. It was possible to play half a dozen new discs without charge, simply returning them and walking out, having enjoyed an hour's free entertainment. If Lew was with us (me) he was likely to buy a record; not so me, but then I didn't possess a radiogram. Excursions were made regularly to the Cake factory to fortify our constant hunger, which College catering could not assuage. Queues formed outside this extraordinarily successful shop every day. As it was situated down a side street in North Oxford we had to ride bikes (Pat's or Lew's) or take the bus but it was always worth the effort. How else could we entertain our guests?

The Christmas break was spent in Ashwood Villas. No doubt Aunt Ada prepared the festive fare and I was grateful for whatever was placed on the table. Both Dad and brother Neil would be there and Brother John had probably not been released from the sanatorium by this time. If so, he would be convalescent and a cause for concern about his future, receiving a disability pension from the RAF, which was very small. No doubt I went dancing at the Palais in Meanwood. Did I go on my own or with friends? There was little social activity to breathe life into the domestic scene.

Back to Oxford for the second term and a continuation of the pleasures of HCC. The existence of a relic of the past proves that I briefly tried to keep a Diary of our activities though I had no recall of this even after the evidence was revealed. Lewis had kept the exercise book, which served as Diary and recently sent me pages torn from it. My handwriting records events during one week in February 1945. Probably the Diary was discontinued after this excursion into a literary field (was Jerome's 'Three Men in a Boat' my model?) but as my immature notes capture something of the nature of our 'club', I include these entries in all modesty…

February 5th	A beautiful spring day, with a blue sky, an orange sun and white clouds. Spring is on the move; it's beginning to course in our blood. Later we shall feel the effect. Will we be suddenly lustful, sexy and sensual; or be suddenly struck by the poet's inspiration, or the musician's, or the artist's; or be suddenly cursed by hot choler, spleen and melancholy? I can see all three possibilities appearing in each of us. I see Jimmy, ireful and depressed, rolling his wicked eye and compressing his supercilious mouth, blaming inactivity and senile boredom for what is merely the first red corpuscles of spring in his haemoglobin. I see Lew, oscillating between careless indifference to life and nervous anxiety for his future, under the magical spell of spring. Then there is Pat, concentrating in neurotic spasms upon hard, grinding work, leaving the nightly gatherings before the witches have even met for the nightly dance round the Pelican, ignoring the

subtler pleasures of Oxford life – all because he is bewitched by that seductive meretrix – Spring. And I – well, I remain immune, untouchable by criticism and comment, only mentionable where praise is to be distributed.

And then arrives the first volume of Esquire and all the petty tempers and moods of the inseparables dissipate with one great bellow of joy. Like sopping puddles, our dispositions are dried of wet and dirt before the blazing sun of Esquire, the magazine for man. Deceit is practised, but who cares? Certainly not the culprits. The Varga girls look coyly out of enticing eyes, their lips, and breasts, and hips, and legs just asking for it; and what with Spring, who knows what Pat might have done when he took them to bed with him? But for Lew, Jimmy and myself, this Varga array has artistic influences and in all solemnity we sit around, drawing with varying accuracy the reclining carcase of Lena Horne, and who wouldn't do that against her? Supper is made, onion flip, bread and butter and cocoa; very satisfying, though even that menu cannot keep Pat from bed and his Varga girls. And then to bed, a quiet day, but none the less enjoyable.

February 6th Never was there such a capricious creature as the English weather. Cyclones, winds, valleys, pressure, currents cannot account for the changes. Yesterday, perfect; today, bloody. The rain pours down, the puddles spread, the streets shine, the roofs drip, while we cower inside. Lew and I go to the cake-factory, Pat is at the labs, Jimmy is on parade. Tomorrow night, it is now arranged, the short-course blokes, George, Geoff, Ron, Peter and Butch are coming round for a snack and an earful of the radiogram. And no pin-ups around to attract them! It would seem that we get purer and purer – but no, I can't believe that. Behind all the smug prudery of our faces (I stand down here) lies an absolutely crude mind. Are we repressing our natural feelings, or false feelings? The latter, I hope. But the dirty muck we squeeze out of clean words is surprisingly considerable. Why? Are we sex-starved? I begin to think so in Lew and Pat's case, perhaps in Jimmy's; I am, by the way, sexless. Again, it is suggested we are getting a little tired of each other, that inactivity is getting on our nerves. We want more parties, more crazy behaviour, and more variety in women – all are advocated. Which is best remains to be seen. As for food, Pat needs must scorn our delicacies and hie off to bed, leaving three rather disgruntled beings to eat, drink and be quiet. So ends yet another day.

PRE-ADULTHOOD

February 7th There's nothing like building castles on air and dreaming, so long as they are not saturated. Accordingly Lew and Jimmy form a Habeas Corpus film company, producing improbable films with ingenuity and alacrity. The company is to be very communistic, there being no individual director or producer, and all will play an equal part in the production. Pat (the scientist) and Jimmy (the reconnaissance Brylcreem puff) however, will specialize in photography and lighting, while Lew and I will devote our attention to the literary side of the business. Now which women will suit our desires (no twisting please): Storm, Nina, Hilary or even the phantom-like Jean? As Jimmy would say, "I hae me douts." But of course the idea is perfect, and in four or five years we are going to chuck in our jobs, irrespective of their importance, and divulge (sic) in a holiday of fun, frolic and photography. Habeas Corpus entertained the cadets, in a subdued kind of way, though the strained efforts of Jimmy and Lew to liven the party up by incongruous jiving proved entertaining enough. Pat, the dark horse, said nay to the social evening and galloped off to the Panto by himself. Supper consisted of cakes and buns, tea and State Express 444 – strange diet, but none the less enjoyable. Now we sit round the electric fire, talking of diverse and strange things, and we shall go our way very shortly to bed, that haven of dreams and reveries, of oblivion and peace.

February 8th Under the caption, "familiarity breeds contempt" today we should have attained the antithesis of contempt for one another; for Jimmy and I have been on parade, Pat has been at his medical work, while Lew has scattered his time amongst hours of alternate work, lounging, eating and dreaming. But at the fall of eventide, Lew, Jimmy and myself march out on a visit to the Super to see 'Don't take it to heart' and 'This is the life', two very appropriate titles. Of course we had to pick somebody or two up, and Fate would have it that Nina, Hilary and possibly nice newcomer Joan, were in the queue with obvious results. Arm in arm we escorted them home, arriving back at H.Q. to find Pat hard at it (work, y'know). Baked beans on toast and cocoa provided much needed fodder, and again we sit round in solemn silence, awaiting the sensation of some sudden sharp shock. Ah! And there it is, twelve strokes of the gong, and out marches Jimmy, shortly to be followed by me and the rest.

February 9th With a reputation killed with every word, "The School for Scandal" satirizes all tale-telling, with the obvious result that Lew, Jimmy and myself, lounging on the back row of the circle at the Playhouse, entered upon a long and bitter dissertation about the merits and faults of the gals who receive succour from our gallant and chivalrous services. Fish and chips seemed to be merely hallucinations of the inner stomach, for a bootless search (we had shoes on) for such balmy shops resulted in failure. Anyway, back to H.Q. for a meal of egg omelette and fried bread, and now, digesting the masculated – masculated – remnants, accompanied by bombastic invectives from each about each of our minds, we sit round the electric fire in curious moods. Lew lies on the sofa, troubled in heart and mind, feeling sex-starved and aimless; Pat, back from a tutorial, is in an irritatingly jubilant mood. Jimmy, also on the sofa, feels dull and disillusioned (he has stated that he is still a child, an assertion which has unfortunate repercussions on him). While I sit at the table, above the flight of common men, spending my valuable time writing these bloody notes. Bah! And I fling down my pen in disgust. And then Shakespeare enters the room, and Jimmy and Lew, inspired by the malignant spirits of unmerited playwrights, throw dirt at his ideal figure, calling upon Sophocles, Aristotle, Noel Coward, Shaw and a myriad nonentities to assume the laureateship forcibly taken from poor William. Pat (one of the sheep) and myself (one of the shepherds – ahem) attempt to place the immortal Bard on his pedestal again. Jimmy and Lew debunk his dramatic technique, poetry, characters and thought with the careless indifference of ignorant pups. They both go to the theatre and cinema for their entertainment, yet they like shows having emotional effects; but from both these categories they exclude Old Willie. Bah! I fling down my pen in contempt.

February 10th Receiving the vague words 'arriving at noon', Hab.Corp. prepares for the arrival of one of its esteemed hon. Members, John Procter. Lew dashes off to the station at 11.30, finds no John there, and returns full of indignation; then Pat strolls down at 1.30, to return quite comfortably with the wayward Jonathan. He marches into the room, cries out jubilantly "Hello, you old sods", at once lowering the tone of the highly-strung gathering. He looks well despite his debauch of yesterday; he informs us he was getting a WAAF drunk. Anyway, a party is awaiting preparation and food is laid out, Lew carefully arranging the plates in pseudo-artistic formations, which of course escape the unfeeling eyes of the guests. Jean comes first, looking very pleasant in a new suit, then Nina and Storm, wearing awful capes as a protection from the rain, and then Hilary and Jenny – and the party is fairly complete. And this, note well, is the first real party

PRE-ADULTHOOD

of the term. It is dull in the extreme at first. Storm asks for the "Pavane" and "Clair de Lune" and "the Façade" and Lew, like a fool, gives them to her; the party droops into lazy, depressed attitudes. Then there is a disgustingly serious talk on Olivier's production of 'Henry V', Storm propounding its defects. Ah! and then the party livens up and starts to dance; I could see the twitching muscles and strained faces of the ladies, waiting for it. And at last, the room is cleared, and chivalrous gentlemen proffer their services for the next dance. But there is something lacking, I'm sure; the party missed the first fine careless rapture of last term's efforts. Very good all the same. And when Joan comes, to say she couldn't come, the party is just a little more interesting. Variety is the spice of life. And the visitors are pushed off at 7.0 and we creep surreptitiously (not wishing to pick 'em up again) on a visit to the Scala. There we see "Prison without bars" a reasonably good film and "The virtuous Isadore", an absolutely crude film. I am shocked; the others are delighted – the vital difference. But what with Fernandel's vacant stare, his grin as the fat woman with the low-cut dress bends over him, the caresses the whore gives him, the unfortunate stain on his trousers; and the whole theme and the joking on such a theme – these do not constitute the ideals of life! But to the others, nothing could be better. Then back to food, sausages and omelette, very palatable, to be followed by a lounge round the fire. Enter Gordon and a succession of jet-black jokes. John is dirty, Gordon is filthy, Pat is shady, so is Lew, so is Jimmy, I am faintly tinted. But now we can consider ourselves in the category immediately above. Twelve o'clock strikes and the Recorder stops recording and packs up. Goodnight, you old sods.

February 11th Just as ye Duchess saith to her husband, "You never rains but you pours", so doth ye Goddess of Spring quoth unto ye watery Faun of Water in similar words. Verily, 'tis enough to drown ye curious mammoth of Africa, verily 'tis not fit to send a knight out on a dog like this, verily 'tis bloody awful. And this day doth contains little but monotony for ye companions of ye garter. I play squash, and lose ye game, oh! The gods – the mortification of losing to a comely damsel, a blonde maiden, wearing ye strange slacks of plum hue. May her soul rot in ye hades of hell. I play rugger, and lose ye game, oh! Ye gods and little fishes – when shall I win? Ye dark knights, Lew and Jimmy, armed with raincoats, hie off to ye pictures to see "Ye magnificent Dope", leaving Pat to see Jonah off, he having ye whale of a time, and that feat completed, we work at ye books. Enter to the alarum of imaginary trumpets, ye Lordings, Lew and James, flushed with jocularity, ready to prepare ye feast. Spam and ye real fried hen's eggs provided ye fare, and truly, 'twas as tasty as a boar's head or ye sheep's heart. And thus to bed, to give succour to our weary limbs, as ye Duke saith to ye Duchess. And with our dreams departs the mist of archaism (presumably) and we are back to normal.

Back to normal? The Diary apparently died but HCC continued to enliven our college routine. Although the quartet seems fairly lowbrow in cultural tastes, a learning process was very much in evidence. We started with the limited horizons offered by wartime strictures and relished the chance to celebrate a kind of freedom which owed nothing to alcohol or drugs (we smoked cigarettes 'socially'). We argued a lot and enjoyed ourselves but academic work was not totally neglected. Obviously Pat found the sheer grind of medical studies difficult; he often missed out on HCC excursions but there were times he needed the relaxation to endure further mental pressure. John Procter (the visitor) had been 'up' at Corpus in 1943 – and was now in the RAF; when I returned to St Peter's he became one of the vestigial survivors of my two Corpus terms (still calling me Harry).

As the end of the term approached, my father wrote to ask if he could visit me, as he had no experience of college life and would appreciate looking round Oxford. It was possible for him to stay at Corpus in a guest room, so I booked him in and awaited his arrival with a certain amount of trepidation. No one else's father had sat with him at the dining table in Hall, nor stayed up talking in rooms; and how would he react to my friends, about whom I had spoken so enthusiastically? The visit proceeded smoothly enough and Dad was invited by Lew to have coffee in his room after dinner. Pat, but not Jimmy for some reason, was there. One of the little ironies of life was that Pat's father (knighted) was head of Inland Revenue and therefore Dad's boss, which was an unusual gloss on what might be construed as social climbing but no reference was made to this situation. I think Dad was more concerned about the possible 'bad' influence of two acquaintances who liked swing and jazz, and went to the pictures too often for their own good. I do know that he was not impressed with Esquire magazine with its pin-ups and fashion pages. There was an outcome to this, for under persuasion from Lew I subscribed for six consecutive editions of the magazine, which were to be mailed to my home address. As I was away in the Navy I completely forgot about them. When I came home on leave, I remembered and asked Dad about the monthly deliveries. He replied that he had put them straight in the dustbin as rubbish. Did he think they would contaminate his home? More likely he was frightened of my self-indulgence. I had some sense of guilt, for Esquire was an expensive item and Dad wanted me to stay on the academic rails.

PRE-ADULTHOOD

He was worrying about brother John's slipped discs and varicose veins. He didn't want another son with a slipped integrity. There was little point in making a scene over this though my self-esteem was hurt. At any rate the visit to Oxford passed uneventfully and the time to join the Navy proper had arrived.

But before I hitched up my bell-bottoms full time, there was my first visit to London under the auspices of HCC, or rather Pat Bamford's parents, who had invited us to dine out and go to the theatre to see "Oklahoma!" at Drury Lane. I can't recall the inevitable sightseeing or the restaurant dinner but the brilliance of the musical remains undimmed. My previous experience of musicals had been a weedy wartime production of "No, no, Nanette" at the Grand Theatre, Leeds, but here was dynamic total theatre, just the fillip to launch me into the fray, or spray of nautical adventures.

2. The Navy Lark

My first experience of the RNVR was a night spent on HMS Foudroyant, an old Napoleonic hulk triumphantly captured in Nelson's time. It was anchored permanently in the Portsmouth channels, a brooding presence without any function in modern times save to deliver a sudden sharp shock to effete, pampered youths who had been spoiled by contamination with university life. This was April 1945 and the war had reached a crucial period as the allied invasion of the mainland proceeded inexorably towards the defeat of the Third Reich. Meanwhile we were the latest group of conscripts more or less hand-picked to become naval officers. We wore square rig, which was the seaman's uniform – bell-bottoms and a complicated collar outfit with a fetching round hat on our heads. It wasn't itchy but I didn't like the tight-fitting tunic, which gave no space for accessories. I suppose not having pockets for idle hands was functional. We also carried a long sausage-like hammock wrapped round two regulation blankets, and a large kit bag into which everything we personally possessed or wore was crammed. Every matelot is thus equipped for a life on the ocean wave, and we headed in whalers towards the mudflats where the Foudroyant squatted silently.

The visit was intended to be unsettling and succeeded particularly as we huddled in hammocks slung below on mess-decks with the cannon-ports left open to allow icy blasts of wind from seaward to freeze our bones all night. I suppose by day we were lectured on the hardships of life before the mast and given a taste of naval discipline though no one was sent to climb the mizzenmast or got hose-piped in the scuppers. I briefly re-visited HMS Foudroyant six months later in rather different circumstances but that couldn't expunge the memory of my first night in a hammock. I never took to sleeping in that peculiar manner; it's an art that has to be learned, from the heave-ho of swinging yourself up and curving your backbone to fit the hammock, to the acceptance of one position only (no turning over in the night). Wherever possible I preferred to bunk down on the lockers on board ship.

After that trivial initiation, we reported to our training centre, H.M.S. Raleigh, an isolated camp of Nissen huts and brick buildings situated in a region just outside Devonport and Plymouth called Torpoint. There was a very efficient chain ferry, which took us across the river crossing in five minutes; this was our only lifeline to civilization when on leave. We stayed in this isolated spot for six (or eight?) weeks' basic training, which included the usual square-bashing. There were other groups of recruits undergoing various ordeals but ours was the only 'officer training' section. I have a photograph of the 30 novices who constituted our squad. I assume we had not all been at Oxford for two terms, as I was not acquainted with many of them; perhaps I had spent too many days in company with the HCC enclave.

My memory of these hectic days of instruction and practical tasks is dominated by a double calamity, which set me back after a few weeks. We slept in bunk beds and the bedding was issued more or less at random. There were bed bugs in my thin mattress; I suffered from bites and lack of sleep but such was my naïveté I did not immediately recognize the cause. I then developed impetigo, a facial skin complaint that is most unpleasant. I became definitely 'run-down' and reported to the sickbay. The impetigo gradually disappeared with ointment but the bed bug problem was resolved by a process of de-fumigation of all my belongings. I still had to retain the same mattress, as if I was to blame! The sense of personal humiliation and contamination was far from confidence building. As the training course continued, psychology experts had us responding to intelligence tests, (some no doubt models for the 11 + exams in the new educational system), but one afternoon we had to write an essay on the subject of ourselves. 'How others see us' and 'How we see ourselves' were the two strands of this confessional.

I was ready to indulge my personal feelings and exploded into a denunciation of the contrast between the public persona and the private self, emphasizing the appearance of well-being and self-sufficiency in the presence of my peers and the wretched uncertainty and timidity of the inner man. I downloaded my family bereavement and bewilderment about it. There was an element of self-loathing over the hypocrisy of my extrovert behaviour and the introvert withdrawn self which was the ultimate reality. This was the first time I had been encouraged to express thoughts and feelings on my self-awareness and I welcomed the experience but it never occurred to me that my weaknesses, the self-doubts, repressed feelings, emotional inadequacy and hang-ups were being exposed to 'trick-cyclists' intent on revealing 'unsuitable' traits of character. Within a day of writing my self-analysis, I was interviewed by an officer-psychologist who

PRE-ADULTHOOD

listened with interest as I tried to make light of my unusual confessional. I heard no more from him but the unloading was definitely therapeutic for me. Whether this momentary burst of honesty affected the outcome of my course, I do not know but at the final interview, facing a line of golden hoops on navy blue sleeves, I was advised to go to sea for six months in order to gain experience of marine life.

This was an eminently sensible decision. I had hardly any knowledge of the coastline of Britain, no experience of sea voyages and my seamanship was totally untried. After six months I could resume officer training, they said. The fact is that my attitude was passive and uncommitted to whatever was being planned for me. I was not really interested in qualifying to be an officer. Pride was hurt by this rejection but I had no aptitude for the role. If not adrift, I was floating through my National Service; all interest, hopes and motivation centred on that place at St Peter's and the prospect of studying English Language and Literature for an Honours degree. I lacked self-confidence if you like, but I would have made a totally ignorant and incompetent officer. So here I was, in harness with another 'reject' (who was to sink without trace), reporting to Devonport barracks to await posting to a sea-going ship, two very ordinary sea cadets seeking experience of the sea.

While we were at HMS Raleigh the war in Europe ended but I didn't feel like celebrating because we still had to fight the Japs – and then they capitulated and I didn't feel like celebrating that either as we still had to do National Service. Where was I on VE Day or when the bombs were dropped on Hiroshima and Nagasaki? At which cinema did I see the first pictures from Belsen (though the extent of the holocaust was unknown)? Memory fails and revives only for the events of late autumn in 1945, which is when the two raw recruits were taken by sloop from Devonport to Wilhelmshaven to join HMS Obdurate, one of the 'O' class destroyers of the Royal Navy in Home Waters.

The Obdurate had been on duty for many months without returning to England to give leave. Wilhelmshaven was Germany's HQ for North Sea naval forces and in the aftermath of the total surrender all warships were reporting there for demobilization. Part of the Obdurate's duties was patrolling the coastline and 'showing the flag', but understandably all the crew were itching for extended (and well-earned) leave. I think the sea-going complement for Obdurate was 180, which is quite a lot to cram into this size of warship. Destroyers are neat and feisty, ready to perform any task requiring speed and manoeuvrability, and are built on a human scale. I was glad not to be posted to a cruiser or battleship, which are not unlike inner city tenement blocks in comparison to the destroyer's villa. Submarines are under-water bungalows. Later in my naval career, I was drafted to a minesweeper, which is okay, but like living in a terrace house, limited in range and function.

IRONS IN THE FIRE

My first view of the Obdurate's mess deck was memorable. We must have arrived just before lights-out, for the whole area was covered in hammocks slung in rows upon rows, each pressed against the next hammock like so many fat maggots waiting to hatch out. It was like looking at an extra deck along which you could crawl from one end to the other. Underneath this canopy the matelots were making their final adjustments before swinging up into the body of the hammock, not easy when no space between them exists. The two new recruits slung their hammocks somewhere. This was not my favourite kind of bed; I wanted to turn over, to twist around a bit, to vary the sleeping position for my back's sake. Eventually I opted for the cushioned locker-seats. Mind you, when the storms came the hammock had its advantages as they all swung from side to side in unison. At least you couldn't fall out. I never discovered if Petty Officers used hammocks but officers of course had bunk beds. I think modern conditions allow for an alternative to the hammock, even for the lowest of ratings, but the legacy of Nelson's Victory dies hard.

There was some uncertainty about the novices' learning curve. We were not 'white caps' sent to sea as trainee-officers, a system disbanded, but Ordinary Seamen (O.D.) on the lower deck absorbing 'seamanship' – and therefore to be treated like any other rating, except that we didn't have special jobs. Very often we were scrubbing decks or painting superstructures 'battleship grey'. Each of us was allocated to a separate mess-group (and I was glad about that for my partner was a bore) and we had to integrate with the extraordinary individual diversity of the lower deck. Contact with the officers was remote; in fact the distinct dichotomy between wardroom and lower deck on board Obdurate set me up for life as a left-wing 'man of the people'. Eating (one could hardly call it dining) on the lower deck was pleasantly intimate, for each sub-group (about ten men) sat down at a mess table and, having helped prepare the food, fetched it from the ship's galley and served it. I can't recall whether there was a rota for washing up nor whether we had any say in the menu, but I had no grumbles about the daily fare.

Tied up alongside in Wilhelmshaven, we were well aware of German warships surrounding us, long lines of vessels lying as if abandoned and despondent; but not empty. I hadn't realized their crews were living on board rather than being transferred to the barracks or dockyard, as they would in the RN. Shortly after we joined Obdurate, there was an early morning fo'c'sle parade for the ship's company – most unusual. The First Lieutenant addressed us and solemnly swore us to secrecy. Apparently a mutinous plot to scuttle ships tied up alongside had been exposed; it was to be a mass protest against the surrender of the Third Reich. We had to take immediate action. All the German crews were compelled to leave their ships and march off to the Spartan barracks; our job was to provide small groups of guards to stay on board the ships until the danger of

PRE-ADULTHOOD

scuttling was over. We were particularly commanded not to take anything from the ship we were personally guarding. Alas, the temptation was too great for the half a dozen ratings I was with. We walked through the mess decks of a cruiser remarking the 'cosiness' of their living quarters with personal belongings lying around in contrast to ours with their functional anonymity; before long, souvenirs were sought. Well, nothing valuable was taken as far as I know; in the end I helped myself to a cheap leather belt with swastika badges displayed. I found no use for it and ditched it eventually. Maybe the idea of pilfering had been put into our minds! Apparently the German plot was nipped in the bud. Our First Lieutenant, always a remote figure, was awarded a D.S.O. for his part in the operation, a reward that was greeted cynically on the lower deck. He must have got promotion for he disappeared and was replaced by a curiously accented Scotsman who actually was disliked by the ship's crew for not being remote.

Shortly after this non-event, the Obdurate was posted to Travemunde, in the Baltic. The journey was to provide me with one of the most aesthetic and psychedelic experiences of my drug-free life. As a watch-keeper I had to sit and peer through fixed binoculars on the port side at bridge level, watching the horizon and reporting ships etc on the port bow. We were steaming northeast towards the Kiel Canal and heading into a sharp wind. The sea was choppy and the bows of the ship crashed through waves that deluged over the fo'c'sle and flung spray high on to the bridge. Exposed on the port side, I was drenched with icy seawater from every wave, and my binoculars were pretty useless for observing things on the horizon. I was of course wearing my black 'oilskin and so'wester', so it was only my face that enjoyed this cheek-freezing stimulus. Behind me, though, the sun was fairly blazing and creating dazzling rainbows that shimmered through the approaching cascades. I could watch (spell bound) the vivid rainbow arching over the bows and heading straight for me until I was engulfed in a spectrum of expanding colours that hit the front of the lenses simultaneously with the tingling iciness of spray stabbing my face. I don't know how John Keats could possibly have experienced a similar physical ecstasy of such intensity, but I feel I know what he meant when he wrote in his Ode on Melancholy:

> ... when the melancholy fit shall fall
> then glut thy sorrow on a morning rose
> or on the rainbow of the salt-sand wave
> or on the wealth of globed peonies ...

I certainly glutted my sorrow on the rainbow of the salt-sand wave and was very happy to ignore the horizon for half-an-hour, by which time we were nearing the Kiel Canal and beginning the slow flat crossing into the Baltic.

IRONS IN THE FIRE

Travemunde was little more than a depressed seaside resort with a harbour but the bleak landscape was already in the grip of icy winds from the Steppes. This was to be a very hard winter for German citizens and the chilled dry air froze our marrow as soon as we left the ship for shore leave. We had to walk past pathetic figures (in blue, I think) who hobbled, lame and disfigured, some in wheelchairs, some supported by nurses, all mutilated convalescent inmates of a small military hospital on the sea-front, enduring their afternoon strolls. A naval lorry took us to Lubeck, a fine mediaeval town large enough to afford entertainment and social activity for our matelots. Once dropped in the town centre, our usual ploy was to head for a gabled and timbered old building that housed a vast German restaurant with a cabaret stage; no doubt it had seen better days but now it was managed solely for the benefit of British forces on shore leave, particularly from the ships at Travemunde. Perhaps it was one of the few businesses still operating at a profit for it was swarming with lively ratings boozing beer and eating wurst, but surprisingly well behaved as they listened to the German band and the blonde Dietrich-type singer who sang sad little German songs like "Lili Marlene' to them.

Outside it was bitterly cold, so we were grateful for this genial hospitality – no doubt laid on under the auspices of the NAAFI. My first visit led to my having to face a moral teaser later on. I was with a small bunch of Obdurate ratings and we thoroughly enjoyed the festive atmosphere as the professional German band thumped out its cheerful tunes. The musicians took a short interval and were applauded as they left the stage, for they had earned their break. They left their instruments on stage when they went backstage. My companions and I decided to take a tour of the town centre for about thirty minutes. When we got back to the restaurant there was obviously trouble afoot. The Military Police were interviewing individual sailors and soldiers. No German musicians were on stage but we could see several standing around disconsolately. One of them was openly crying. We asked what was up and gathered that while we were promenading in the cold, a small group of matelots had jumped on the stage and started to fool about with the musical instruments. After they had been cleared off the stage, the German band returned to find one of the piano-accordions was missing. This had belonged to the young player who was weeping in the corner, surrounded by his friends. His livelihood had been taken away and we felt sorry for him but, not wanting to get involved with the Police and with little to say, we left the restaurant.

In fact the theft of the accordion became a local *cause célèbre* and rumours spread that there were search parties, organized by the Naval police, looking for evidence in every ship in the area. An accordion is quite bulky and difficult to conceal. Perhaps someone had tipped the authorities off, but nothing came to light. Now it so happened that I was on watch in the middle of the night some

PRE-ADULTHOOD

weeks later, on my own and for once taking a walk round the upper deck. I surprised two of my least favourite messmates dropping something over the side into the sea; presumably it was weighted for it sank at once, taking the rope with it. I actually caught no glimpse of the object as the two figures bent over the ship's side but when challenged, they swore it was nothing important and told me to forget all about it. I suspected they were getting rid of the accordion – if so, they had certainly succeeded. They vanished below deck, leaving me to ponder on what to do. In the end I did nothing. I had to consider my position on the lower deck over the next six months. It wasn't so much fear of being duffed up by these two characters, though both were capable of skulduggery. It was more a question of being labelled a 'grass', particularly if nothing could be proved, which was likely. The accordion had to lie in its watery grave un-avenged. No further action ensued, but later back in England someone casually mentioned that the ship's butcher had hidden the accordion in his frozen meat store. He was one of my two suspects but by this time the matter had been shelved, though my conscience continues to nag.

Perhaps another episode shows me guilty of moral blame, though in all innocence (I claim). In one of the seedy quarters of Lubeck a black market flourished after nightfall. Needing a wristwatch, I was persuaded by a mess-deck companion to accompany him to this sinister downtown region of Lubeck where wristwatches were in abundance for barter. If I took a tin of tobacco, obtained from the NAAFI store on board, I could easily get what I wanted. It was certainly a black market, being so dark you never saw the faces of people shuffling round looking for business. Torchlights were the only illumination; sometimes a cigarette lighter or match briefly established the nature of the goods being offered. Crowds of muttering townsfolk filled this gloomy wasteland, desperate to exchange goods or money. Tobacco was in high demand and we soon encountered a young man who was willing to barter one of his wristwatches for my tin of cigarette tobacco. On board ship, these sealed tins were standard issue; they contained good loose tobacco to roll in a Rizla paper. You punctured the airtight tin with a special cutting edge on the detached lid and then fitted this over the open top to keep the tobacco fresh. Now it so happened that I was carrying two tins with me on this shore leave, one tin still sealed and ready for the barter, the other already opened and half the tobacco used for my cigarette making. In the murky gloom of this black market I showed the young German my tin and I examined his watches, holding it to my ear to check the ticking. It seemed okay so I handed over the tin of tobacco and we drifted apart, threading our way through the furtive throng while the stars looked down on this underworld scene.

Once we were clear of this hellhole we started to roll our fags. I brought out my tin and tried to open it, but it was totally sealed and lacked the lid by which I could open it. I had bartered the wrong tin! I had double-crossed the German by trading my half-empty tin for his watch. Yet surely I had checked the sealed top during the transaction? The only explanation must be that the missing lid had inadvertently been clipped on to the opened tin and had concealed the half-empty interior. On hearing this, my companion advised a hasty retreat but in fact it was too dark and crowded to find anyone. So I kept my cheap wristwatch, which indeed it proved to be, for it kept poor time and ticked irregularly. A few days later I left it in the 'heads' and when I returned to retrieve it, some snapper-up of ill-considered trifles had relieved me of a moral burden.

Such petty crimes formed a backdrop to our shore leave as we trudged aimlessly round the bars and cafes of Lubeck. It was too cold to take an interest in mediaeval architecture or local culture. There were liaisons and shady deals – Petty Officers spoke openly of keeping a fraulein or frau well supplied in exchange for exclusive favours (they hoped), but on the lower deck getting pissed was the usual resort. One night, while lying on the locker cushions, I watched a sodden matelot manoeuvring himself in his hammock so he could piss on the deck without getting out. I was too far from the flow and it dried out by morning so who was I to complain? Christmas was approaching and still no news of home leave.

And then, on the 22nd December, through the Tannoy system, the Captain of the Obdurate announced that the Admiralty had authorized leave for the Ship's company and he was determined to steam full speed ahead for Devonport, no matter what the weather forecast for the North Sea, in order to give everyone a chance to get home in time for Christmas Day. Enthusiastic cheers resounded through the lower deck! We should be setting sail within hours and everything had to be battened down for the journey as stormy conditions were likely; but nothing was going to stop this dash for home. The First Lieutenant sent for the two raw recruits. He was concerned that we should be kept occupied but out of the way during the voyage so we were to become temporary Wardroom Orderlies. Our main task was to serve the food for the officers. So far neither of us had penetrated the inner sanctum of the quarterdeck (aft), being more or less confined to the 'lower deck' and forecastle. We didn't welcome our new roles.

There followed the most terrifying sea voyage I ever hope to experience. How long did it take from the Baltic to Devonport, across the North Sea and through the English Channel at an attempted steady 25 knots per hour, no matter what nature hurls at you? Was it 24 hours or longer? A storm at sea is usually avoided but this was a destroyer hell-bent on one objective, to get everyone home for Christmas. The two Wardroom Orderlies never got round to serving food, they were both clinging to the poop railings retching over the side, reacting to the greasy stench of beef stew coming from the Officers Galley. All round us, as the stern rose and fell with shattering regularity into the surging swell of green and white, great walls of water towered above us and then shrank to hollows which

PRE-ADULTHOOD

would swallow us up. The sky was covered with a grey-yellow pall, and winds tore round and through us until we were both drenched and frozen. And always the thud and whine of turbine engines driving us through the heaving sea, and crashes and bangs from wind and wave. Retiring to our hammocks, we eventually slept fitfully as the ship bounced and rolled on a course due west, but well aware of waves thudding into the hull and bursting through the hatches to create a permanent swill slopping from side to side on the mess deck. I understood the advantage of hammocks in such conditions. I don't think we crawled out of them until the south coast of England was off the starboard bow and the tempest subsided. The mess-deck was a tip, but on the upper deck the battening-down had held. I did not venture to the Wardroom or officers' quarters, but I guess they were flooded too. I think the Captain of the Obdurate took quite a few risks on this voyage but all went well. The Ship's company was on its way for a fortnight's leave on Christmas Eve and the Obdurate was ready for repairs in the Dockyard while we were away. Looking back, I appreciate this experience of hardship at sea, however slight my involvement in 'seamanship', but I was very sick and miserable at the time.

After the Christmas break, Obdurate was still helping to control the German surrender at sea. We had to rendezvous with a flotilla of German minesweepers off Dogger Bank, where they had been removing their own minefields, and escort them back to Wilhelmshaven. In view of the scare over scuttling ships, it was considered necessary for armed guards to be placed on board these scruffy little, coal-burning boats, though any such patriotic protest would have been ludicrous for who would care if these decrepit fishing boats sank in the North Sea? However, guards had to go on board each of them and it was obviously a useful experience for two green ODs. We were duly taken on board different 'sweepers with a Petty Officer, each being issued with a revolver in a holster and some ammunition to boot. Neither of us had ever loaded a pistol or fired a shot and our presence was cosmetic, not at all intimidatory. It was a pity no one tried to scuttle such decrepit vessels, which were no more than converted trawlers. Living conditions were primitive, especially for the stokers shovelling coal in a black hole amidships. Unexpectedly I talked to a young German conscript who spoke English well and established a brief rapport with him; we swapped family deprivations sympathetically. This little sojourn on a German minesweeper was my only direct contact with 'the enemy'.

In fact the Obdurate was now a destroyer in search of a raison d'être. The war was over so what do you do with redundant warships? We tootled up to Rosyth for a more elaborate re-fit, which allowed me to view the Forth Bridge and visit the Athens of the North. Not that I took a close interest in cultural Edinburgh; I was not exactly a tourist with a guidebook. It was during this period that I was taken for a ride in every sense of the word. I had been allocated to the ship's motorboat in the interests of sea experience, which meant that I was one of a crew of three. A Leading Seaman steered the boat and gave orders about changes of gears to the Stoker who sat by the little engine below deck. And there was a Seaman who stood in the bows of the boat, carrying a long boathook with which to make contact before tying up. During any trip, long or short, the bow man remained standing, holding his boathook upright. That was me and it was actually an enjoyable job, though the crew had to be ready for launching at any time. The trouble was that as bow man I would often get very wet when the sea was choppy or it was raining, even though I wore an oilskin. I suppose I complained about this to the Coxswain Petty Officer and rashly suggested there should be protective clothing for the bow man. He answered that there was a special outfit, which I could wear, and he would see if there was one on board that would fit me. Next day he provided an official chit which I had to present to the Ship's Storeman and I was issued with a hooded jacket and trousers, very white and somewhat soft-textured. When I tried them on, they seemed okay to me and fitted well enough. What I didn't know was that this was an asbestos fire-fighting suit. I looked forward to the next boat outing and shortly after, while we were on our way north to Rosyth, the boat's crew was piped for an exercise launching. I think the Obdurate had stopped moving as I answered the call, stepping out from the mess-deck in a splendid white outfit to take my place in the boat, which was then lowered from its davits into the sea. We circled to starboard, and as we swung round I noticed, from my position in the boat's bow, that the starboard side of the Obdurate was lined with ratings, all watching us and grinning their heads off. I reckon a few of the officers were watching from the bridge too. I began to realize what a spectacle I must present – a motor-boat chugging about with a weird figure in startling white in the bows. I had been hoaxed well and truly but I kept my boathook vertical, stood firmly at the ready and gave no sign that I was embarrassed. The little trip was over, the boat hauled aloft and the Obdurate continued on its way. Once back on board, I had to face smiles and jeers but really I don't think the episode did me any harm as far as my relationship with shipmates was concerned. If anything I was accepted more readily, as if making a fool of myself had broken down barriers. I wasn't humbled by the experience, in fact in a perverse way I enjoyed 'performing' to the ship's company. I admitted my stupidity but was able to laugh at my naïveté and I think the Coxswain approved of the way I reacted – his trick had certainly succeeded and he must have got the First Lieutenant's approval for the whole episode, including stopping engines and launching the boat.

When we returned to Portsmouth Harbour after the visit to Scotland, the Captain put me in charge of the motorboat, which was clearly in aid of my practical seamanship. By this time I was doing the work of a Bosun's Mate, which meant regular watch-keeping, four hours on watch (apart from two-hour

PRE-ADULTHOOD

dog-watches in the evening), and being on duty in the motorboat was a great relief. I don't remember any ratings grumbling about this 'promotion'; in fact I handled the boat fairly efficiently and had no problems with my 'crew'. Portsmouth Harbour is a treacherous playing field for motorboats, with tidal ebbs and flows, mudflats, by-currents and special channels marked by buoys, which you ignore at your peril. It is also full of nautical history in the shape of old hulks, abandoned landing points and submerged relics. Without more than a brief instruction about the need to keep between port and starboard buoys, I took my little boat on shore visits (for the officers), or to ships anchored in the channels or to fetch supplies. It was a bewildering place for, apart from buoys, there were no signposts; the rapidly changing tides changed the appearance and the depths of the waterways.

Twice however I blotted my copybook, first with the Scottish First Lieutenant on board and later with the Captain and his wife. Angus (his name is lost) was squatting and talking to the stoker while I steered a path through the channels of the Harbour. Our destination is lost to memory but the tide was on the turn and I cut a corner close to a buoy. Suddenly the boat's keel was slithering into mud and halting. I tried to reverse without success, and soon we were no longer at sea but on a mudflat that stretched like a cricket field all around us. The tide was rapidly draining through the mud, making sucking noises as water disappeared and left this thick brown gunge. The boat rested on the mud, high but not so dry; we were marooned with little chance of getting off the mud-flat until the next tide refloated us. Angus of course was furious and totally helpless, but to do him justice he blamed himself for not keeping watch. We resigned ourselves to the long wait and gloomily surveyed the sea view. The mud-flat was expanding by the minute, bleak and freezing, for this was winter-time. The nearest vessel was a black-hulled old Nelsonic relic anchored on its own in one of the minor channels. Nothing stirred as the mist gathered and then we heard a voice shouting from a whaler, the kind of large rowing boat that was used to train sea cadets. Our plight had been observed and they were rowing up narrow channels to get as near to us as possible. Then they started to lay down duckboards on the mud until they all but reached us. We had to hop into the pudding for a yard or so, then clamber along the duckboards, abandoning the boat until the tide turned. So Angus and the three-man crew were taken in the whaler to this gloomy black-hulled man o' war like shipwrecked mariners. After a wash and brush up, drinks in the wardroom were offered; we thanked our hosts, Angus was charming and really it was good fun after all. It was my responsibility though. After four hours on a mudflat, attitudes would have changed. What added a piquant flavour to the incident was discovering that this ancient warship was the Foudroyant, the very same ship that gave me my first taste of naval hardship. I had not recognized it (her).

IRONS IN THE FIRE

The calamity with the Captain and his missus was briefer. There had been some kind of courtesy reception while the Obdurate was anchored in the Harbour straits, and after a hospitable welcome in the wardroom the Captain was escorting his wife ashore in the ship's motorboat. I don't think she was very keen on maritime life and sat rather nervously as we made the journey towards the landing point. This was the usual jetty for coming alongside and I assumed my approach to it was like any other. Unfortunately I failed to take into account the high tide which covered a concrete slab normally obtruding a few inches above the water level. Its existence was certainly inexplicable but I ran straight on to it and the keel grated alarmingly as we stopped moving. Obviously I tried reversing but we were stuck and the Captain and his wife were stranded no more than three yards from safety and dry land. There was one moment of bulging eyes and trembling lower lips, and then instant help as another ship's boat hove in sight, threw us a line and dragged us off the treacherous reef backwards. We finished the journey without further mishap, the Captain happy to make a witty comment and his wife thankful to be saved. Now I think about it, she didn't come aboard the Obdurate again.

I reckon I repaid the Captain's magnanimity when we visited Warrington for 'Warships Week', which was a naval fund-raising event celebrating the Royal Navy. The fact that Warrington had to be reached via the Manchester Ship Canal made this the most extraordinary voyage I experienced. At the time I simply accepted the change from Mersey sea water to Canal fresh water as we entered Ellesmere Port and proceeded slowly upstream for 25 miles (though this being a canal perhaps there was no ebb and flow) but it was all rather like Alice in Wonderland. We seemed to be rolling over the waterway, splashing the sides and setting tiny craft jogging, with the Obdurate towering over the houses and town buildings. The surrounding countryside was Lilliputian; we waved to miniature people like Royalty and of course they waved back like loyal subjects. Our spick and span ship, recently painted and polished (I plied a brush over the superstructure and hull like many a good seaman), looked smart alongside the Warrington docks. The only memorable event in Warrington was a rugby union match between a scratch HMS Obdurate team and the local club. This was exciting – I had forgotten how much I missed the smell of leather. I wrote to Dad (or Aunt Ada) for my rugby kit and played centre three-quarter with the Captain of the Obdurate on my wing. For the first time on board I showed animation and enthusiasm, according to one of my mess-mates, and no wonder. We beat the local team and the Captain scored three tries presented on a plate by his inside centre. He was very pleased about that. We left Warrington stern first, but all smiles, engines in reverse for the journey back to the sea.

I don't know what happened to the Obdurate after this. Probably she was heading for moth-balling but I had completed my six months at sea and was

PRE-ADULTHOOD

reporting to HMS King Alfred at Beaulieu in the Solent for further 'officer-training'. I don't remember shaking hands with many shipmates on leaving but I salute them now, Captain and all. I wish I had appreciated the varied experiences provided on that destroyer more fully but the fact is I didn't want them, either because I was still immature and emotionally withdrawn; or because this National Service was delaying my return to University life. There were plenty of good times but I was holding back all the time. I don't doubt the Obdurate months were formative and left indelible impressions on my mind, most importantly an awareness that the lower deck is full of individually talented people, but I didn't *enjoy* myself.

Nor did I when resuming activities at Beaulieu, Lord Montagu's pile, where we lived in Nissen huts and rarely visited the big house. I remained a landlubber at heart and showed no aptitude for naval war or peace. A visit to Whale Island, the arch-gunnery HQ, where we not only saw but actually operated some huge naval guns with fearsome barrels swinging around on turrets, was quite off-putting for this sensitive plant. The various exercises in pursuit of naval excellence did not inspire me. When it was my turn to deliver an impromptu 'speech' during a training session on the parade ground, I was shrewdly given the subject of "Cows" and I held forth somewhat gauchely on the idiosyncrasies of farmyard animals. Afterwards it occurred to me that anyone worth his sea-salt would have talked about "Cowes" and sailing regattas. At the end of this (second) course it was clear that I was inadequate as officer-like material so I was sent to Portsmouth Dockyard barracks to await posting to a ship. I can't remember whether I was given a choice of occupation but I suppose I was designated a seaman, though hardly trained in any thorough way.

Waiting in those Pompey barracks was both boring and idle. One could walk about all day doing nothing but carry a piece of paper with typing on it. I was driven to enrol for a Typing and Shorthand course in the Educational Department, which was interesting but not exactly riveting. I had not progressed far in Pitmans and touch-typing before my draft orders arrived and I had to get ready to leave Portsmouth, but not before filling in a form applying for EVT service. I had to write down my H.S.C. results. Educational and Vocational Training was becoming important as demobbed sailors needed to adjust to Civvy Street and teachers were needed. I completed the form and proceeded to forget all about it because my immediate future had been decided.

Some permutation of clerical logic had drafted me to HMS Myrmidon, a minesweeper at the time stationed in the Orkney Islands. Reaching her involved taking a train journey (in the company of three other matelots heading elsewhere) from Portsmouth to Elgin before crossing to the Orkneys. This was almost Land's End to John o' Groats in one go, and very long, tedious, boring and cold it was. Cooped up in a second-class compartment (or was it third?) with sandwich provisions, we travelled through England's fair land without much interest in the landscape or towns. We arrived in Glasgow, changed trains and continued slowly through the night towards the Highlands. Travellers came and went, and one dapper little Scotswoman sat in our compartment through the night in the company of two sailors and two Wrens. We tried to sleep, without much success until the sweet old lady suggested the two lassies should lean on the shoulders of the two men as that would be much more comfortable for them. Aye, so it was and it led to a wee kiss or two snatched when we thought no one was watching. The old lady had gone when I awoke to a grey morning sky pressing down on interminable snow-covered hills. The steam train was puffing heavily as it crawled northwards and the temperature dropped steadily. The Wrens disembarked anonymously. Gradually the train neared Elgin and clanked into the station. I gathered my belongings, the kitbag and hammock particularly, and stepped on to the platform. And immediately collapsed in a heap.

I awoke in a ward of the Elgin General Hospital, tended by Scots nurses. I had pneumonia, it seemed, and I was in need of a stay in hospital, which was very pleasant while it lasted but after a week's convalescence I was deemed fit to continue my search for the Myrmidon, for by now she had left the Orkneys and was starting to sweep mines off the north coast of Ireland, based on Londonderry. I took the train to Glasgow and the ferry to Belfast; and then the train to Derry, as always lugging my kitbag and hammock. I must have been relieved to find her moored alongside in Derry docks but no one piped me on board. I dumped my kit and looked round this minesweeper.

She was much smaller than the Obdurate, but nonetheless well built for a specific purpose – well, for more than one job, as she also carried depth-charges to attack submarines. The crew was trained for the main work of getting rid of mine-fields and there was a steady application to this post-war task though I seem to remember working a five-day week, with weekends in Derry; but maybe we did over-time to make up for those occasions when it was too rough to sweep mines. All the necessary gear was aft and at sea the Myrmidon worked either alone or with a flotilla of sweepers trawling the sea rather like a line of police seeking the murder weapon on a heath. It was necessary to plough the invisible furrows in straight lines; whoever was at the wheel had to watch the compass needle steadily.

The trawling was effected below the level set for the mines, in order to make contact with the chain that extended from the seabed anchorage to the actual mine. Once hooked, metal-cutting pincers sliced through the chain and the mine bobbed up to the surface. We took pot shots to sink these nasty items when they came in sight, which wasn't as often as might be expected (say, two a day). Occasionally the glass spikes would be severed by shots and the mine exploded on the surface, so we always kept our distance of floating mines. Sometimes the

PRE-ADULTHOOD

apparatus accidentally triggered off a mine under water, which wasn't welcome as this damaged our gear. The shockwaves from the explosion hit the side of the ship and made it shake but I never heard of a minesweeper actually being sunk after hitting a mine. These ships had shallow draughts but there was always a possibility of a maverick mine getting in the way.

I was again a Bosun's Mate keeping watch hours but also taking my turn at the wheel, following instructions from the Duty Officer on the bridge as we ploughed back and forth. Steering the ship was really quite enjoyable and gave one a sense of responsibility which was gratifying but it was a repetitive routine, with the occasional explosion to add interest, as we slowly churned through the Atlantic section by section. If the sea got at all rough, we stopped and retreated to some haven or cove until the weather improved. At least we were usually free of seasickness. When it was really stormy, the Myrmidon headed straight for Derry and the pleasures of draught Guinness.

There was not much to amuse us ashore, Derry being a depressed and dismal dump when viewed from the dockside. The bars, nothing like so comfy as an English pub, were scruffy and utilitarian; I stayed in them as little as possible, but I did like the black stuff, though I never drank to excess. The local inhabitants were reticent and casual, but I knew little about Irish politics and 'the troubles' and sensed no particular hostility. I got educated at the local palais de danse, where I met two attractive colleens who told me about King William and Orangemen and the iniquities of the Pope. They came from poor Catholic families and I have forgotten their names, but I enjoyed dancing with them on Saturday nights. I bought a bespoke tweed jacket (too tight) and flannels through their tailor contacts and turned up in civvies at the palais but everyone knew I was English. One of the girls was keen to nail me but I held back, being terrified of pregnancy – and indeed the 'deed'. They talked hard and bitterly about their prospects; I was a little shocked they were so cynical about 'love', but they were sharp-witted and likeable company.

Prior to this, in Portsmouth and whilst on the Obdurate, I dated an attractive ATS girl friend whom I met regularly in the NAAFI in the centre of town where *thé dansant* afternoon sessions provided a delightful entertainment for enthusiastic young servicemen and women in search of company. Typically, I have forgotten her name though we enjoyed many a passionate session together on the seafront but that relationship collapsed when I rejected her proposal that we rented a room so we could sleep together, as some friends of hers had done. I couldn't take on the responsibility of love making; quite apart from the risk of fatherhood, I had very little experience of the sex act. I was a virgin; she was not. What a pity I was emotionally immature! I had never even seen a 'french letter' and my foreplay was always above the Plimsoll Line. In my defence, I kept the future uncomplicated and played no one false and that went for Irish hearts too.

IRONS IN THE FIRE

After three or four months on the Myrmidon, my duties were slowly wearing me down. The irregular sleep-pattern did not suit my temperament and maybe the basic tedium of minesweeping did not help, despite the pleasures of Irish shore life. The Atlantic Ocean is vast and no doubt exciting when you are going somewhere but we seemed to be nitpicking one tiny patch. However, I was happy to be roused from a deep afternoon sleep by a shipmate when the ship passed through the Outer Hebrides. Still half unconscious, I stumbled out of the gloom of the mess-deck to find the ship silently and slowly (as if reverently) passing an island covered in purple heather, a charismatic apparition floating and shimmering in bright sunshine. It was no more than twenty feet from us. When I crossed to the other side of the ship, a similar and larger island displayed more resplendent heather. Fragrance hung in the air. The channel between these beautiful jewels was dark translucent blue and the Myrmidon seemed to glide effortlessly as if taking part in a hallucination. Do I wake or dream? I went below to continue my 'kip', but the memory of the Hebridean image has not faded like a dream.

I remember a few of my Myrmidon messmates but only vaguely. This puzzles me because the Obdurate memories retain faces and personalities more clearly. Perhaps I was growing more withdrawn from mess deck activities; perhaps the ratings on the Myrmidon were less interesting; perhaps my two Irish girl friends were more distracting. Whatever the causes, I was gloomily forecasting months and months of frustrating and debilitating naval service on this minesweeper when a message was received by the Captain of the Myrmidon. I was summoned to his presence and read the words myself:

> Able Seaman H.M. Morley is to be transferred immediately to the EVT and will proceed to Keele, Staffordshire EVT Headquarters for training. Travel permit supplied.

The Captain of the Myrmidon (faceless, nameless!) was mystified : "What the hell is EVT, Morley?" he grumbled. "And why you?" I could only answer that Educational and Vocational Training was the Navy's response to the problems of mass demobilization from the forces and I had applied for the transfer ages ago. In fact, I had forgotten all about it, having little confidence in my ability to qualify for selection. But I was on my way quickly enough, barely stopping to bid farewell to minesweeping or to question by what strange means I had been lifted out of the Atlantic ocean and plonked down in Keele which was about as far from the sea as you can get.

This Training College was to become Keele University but for the small group of volunteers selected for EVT training it was like going back to school. We met in a classroom and practised basic teaching skills. There were two Sub-

PRE-ADULTHOOD

Lieutenants in our midst, both with degrees, I think, as they seemed to assume a superiority in literary criticism. I had a strong argument with them over Augustan poets like Pope and Dryden whom they both admired greatly but I wouldn't accept that their 'verses' were proper poetry. Romantics like Keats and Wordsworth were my heroes. After perhaps four weeks, we were deemed to be qualified for our tasks in EVT work but I was not at all pleased to be posted to Chatham Dockyard where there was a need for an Economics teacher. Not English at all, but Economics! It was my Sixth-form HSC Pass in Economics that had procured me a role in EVT, though no one had told me. I didn't protest, being anxious to stay in the EVT whatever the cost, and bolstered by a promotion to Leading Seaman status I proceeded to Chatham with a little selection of Economics textbooks and trepidation.

In practice, the Chatham EVT Centre proved a bit of non-event. We were occupying an isolated set of cabins and huts remotely situated in the wastelands of the Dockyard where we operated a five-day week but for some reason the attendance of pupils was desultory and limited in number, no matter which subjects were being offered. I never had more than four 'pupils' in my class each week though classes in English, Maths, French and Current Affairs were better attended. We existed in a relaxed atmosphere and there were few complaints as everyone wanted to maintain the status quo. It was a cushy number by any count. Our CO was a Lieutenant who could have doubled as Captain Mainwaring in 'Dad's Army'; and his right hand was a red-haired ferrety Sub-Lieutenant who claimed allegiance to Marxism. I was rather nervous as he knew far more about Economics than I did but officers apparently did no teaching. They supervised. In my classes, lessons more or less followed the Economics textbook but the teaching was far from inspired. No one told me what to teach and as I knew very little about the subject, I soon got out of my depth. Fortunately we provided 'short courses' only, so the pupils possibly didn't reach the inner limits of my ignorance but I was aware of being a dreadful sham. My co-teachers, all in their early twenties, were waiting to continue university degrees, but unlike me, they were interested in their subjects.

This was a long way from minesweeping and I thoroughly appreciated the contrast. Within the secure isolation of our EVT Centre, the band of youthful teachers enjoyed themselves. At first we were accommodated in dockyard barracks but as controls relaxed, most of us moved nearer Civvy Street, taking lodgings in Chatham where there was an excellent Aggie Weston type of hostel with individual cabins in which we could keep our belongings. In the evenings we changed into mufti, went to the pictures, sat and talked in pubs and cafes, and enjoyed the social life of Chatham and Gillingham.

Once or twice the Navy demanded we participate in service events. We attended a big shooting match at Bisley shooting range, being required to fire rifles at a distant target whilst standing, crouching and lying down, having run a hundred yards between each position. It was quite an enjoyable outing though there was a hold-up when some rating in the butts got hit by a ricochet. At the end of the day I was awarded a modest prize (a few quid, I think) for scoring more points than some of the others, which was rewarding for someone who had never fired a shot in his life.

In contrast, the EVT instructors at Chatham Dockyard organized a trip to a farm where horses could be hired for riding. Most of us had never bestridden a horse previously and made heavy weather of it – matelots in bellbottoms ambling slowly down the lane, including me. But the instigator of this excursion, an Irish Mac, tried to show off his expertise with a furious gallop over the hills. He claimed to be in control but it looked more likely the horse bolted. It was usually placid, so said the farm lady, and Mac must have provoked it; she was angry though not with me as my horse was so bored it eventually gave up moving. It seems like a plot for a comic short story I never wrote.

At this time, the autumn of 1947, the main entertainment for everybody was the cinema. Vast queues formed each evening and after patiently waiting for the next 'house', people could expect two full-length films, a cartoon and the Pathé News showing topical items. Perhaps a cinema organ too, rising from the pit, but not in the Chatham cinemas. You spent three hours in the dusty dark, inhaling cigarette smoke and the fug of human beings packed tight. There were so many good monochrome films (especially British) in this era, no wonder the cinemas were full. This was the period of Carol Reed, David Lean, the Boulting Brothers and a dozen other skilful directors. Trying to keep my critical faculties alive, I started to write my own film reviews in a notebook, but they have not survived, nor deserved to, though I wouldn't mind checking. I had other things on my mind, however. I had met Beryl Hunter.

I called her Bunny because the name Beryl didn't fit. Not that there was anything rabbity about her. I don't know why I called her that; in retrospect it sounds patronizing. She was tall, slim, brown-haired, enthusiastic, sensitive, eighteen and – well, romantic, sensuous and wonderfully natural. I can't recall where we met but early on I discovered she attended a night school class in Literature and loved the Georgian poets like Rupert Brooke. Her mother was a warm, thoughtful person, maybe not unlike my mother in personality. Her father was a Chief Petty Officer stationed somewhere in the vicinity but he never seemed to be around; perhaps he kept me at a distance on purpose. She had a younger sister who looked at Bunny and me in awe, we were so obviously in love. I call it 'love' and yet it was perhaps too naïve to be more than 'calf-love' (whatever that means). It was certainly inhibited. We never 'made love' with unrestrained passion for this was an era when caution was practised. We were not ready for anything like consummation. There was a brother and sister quality

PRE-ADULTHOOD

to our relationship, based on mutual sympathy; but as far as I can remember, I told her nothing about my mother's death. Even Bunny was held back from confidences that I shared with no one.

My inability to share grief and memories was by now engrained in my personality. It made me aloof and withdrawn when other people were openly welcoming and ready to accept intimate exchanges of personal life. I could be enthusiastic and get quite excited about all kinds of activities but I kept my secret to myself. Why should it be a secret? Because I had never come to terms with my emotional response to this trauma. How could I talk to anyone freely when there was a paralysis of communication within myself? 'Never come to terms' is an unhelpful phrase disguised as a cliché but it suggests the need for psychoanalysis, which was certainly not readily available through this period. Ironically I don't know if I could ever have 'submitted' to such therapy. Is it heredity or upbringing that tends to make me favour the stoic tenets, the virtues of self-sufficiency and long-suffering? Maybe my mother's scolding: "don't blub, stand up for yourself" when I was an infant left its mark. I would have been suspicious of any such psychological treatment (and chary of paying for it!) because I was not ill, in fact I was coping in private or public reasonably well, so I thought.

Emotional deficiency meant that I couldn't love Bunny absolutely but I kept in touch with her after I got demobilized and returned to Oxford. Her family by this time had moved to High Wycombe and we both cycled to Marlowe and met on the banks of the Thames. At the end of the first year, we danced happily at a Commem Ball held by Hertford College (none at St Peter's that year) but the dominant interests of my life were now at Oxford. I wrote less and less to Bunny. I began to think of her as too unsophisticated and ceased to see her at all; and yet, after nearly four years, I felt obliged to write a final letter to end the relationship. I really don't know what she thought of me by this time but, looking back, I feel like Othello's base Indian throwing a pearl away richer than all his tribe. How would we have fared if I had been strong enough to trust to young love? Or was it never really like this? Distance lends enchantment to the view and there is nothing like a rose-tinted haze to deceive the eye.

It was a hot summer in 1947 and the EVT instructors sweltered in the Dockyard, stripping to sunbathe in secluded spots whenever 'pupils' were in short supply, which was pretty often. I grew a little careless. On one occasion I skipped off duty and took a bus into the town centre. Just as I was getting off the bus I spotted a Petty Officer glaring at me across the road, and hastily darted up a side-lane, hoping to elude identity. Next day, however, I was called before my C.O. on a charge of unauthorized absence and there was the Petty Officer to prove it. I stood stiffly to attention, not certain what would happen. The C.O. (Captain Mainwaring's look-alike) explained that the Petty Officer had been alone and therefore could not provide corroborative support for his claim that he had seen me getting off a bus in the centre of Chatham. Accordingly, said the C.O., it was the Petty Officer's word against mine. Had I, asked the C.O., been guilty of being on that bus? Whether he had intended to give me an escape-route or not, I took it. "No sir!" I replied. "You are quite sure?" he asks. "Yes sir!" I reply. "Case dismissed!" Exit the Petty Officer sourly. Leading Seaman Morley is exonerated, aware of being a cool-faced liar but free to roam. If I had admitted the offence, I should have been confined to barracks for a period.

I was able to play a few games of rugby during the autumn, eventually being selected for the Nore Command XV on two or three occasions. It was rather low key, without a great deal of regular training, and much though I appreciated the games, it did lead to a shoulder injury which really never went away. Something wrong with my left collar-bone. I spent a week loafing around a hospital ward in Chatham with my arm in a sling, but otherwise no treatment was given. It was the least crowded hospital I ever saw and the Navy doctors the most idle. Eventually I suffered a dislocated shoulder during an important game for Otley Rugby Club, and that put paid to my rugby career. It all started at Chatham. I should have taken more care –or exercise.

It was frustrating to be still on National Service when the University Year for 1947 was starting at Oxford. I was now approaching a three-year stint in the Navy and my presence was hardly essential to post-war conditions, but my demob was not due for several months. Did this mean I would have to waste a whole year waiting to return to my studies? I wrote to 'Huffy' (my tutor) to ask for advice and a book-list; I wanted him to know I was in the offing. He suggested I come up next term (January), meanwhile I should read Chaucer texts. How did it happen so aptly? My demob papers arrived in Chatham just before Christmas and I was on my way home to Yorkshire for a short holiday and then a return to St Peter's Hall in January 1948. I vaguely remember entering some large warehouse, the Demob Centre, trying on a grey suit with a stripe in it and leaving by the exit with something in a large cardboard box but I can't recall whether I was still wearing bell-bottoms or the suit.

One important change had occurred at home. Dad, with Aunt Ada still attached, had decided to move house from Ashwood Villas in Leeds. He had bought a house in Otley, a nearby town, and I was to see it for the first time when I returned to Civvy Street. I was not to visit my old home for many years, nor see some of my personal possessions ever again. Dad, probably in a frenzy to leave, had left or thrown out many of the papers and mementoes that belonged to 'the boys'. I think he was living an isolated life with Brother John at home, still recovering from TB, and Aunt Ada, still housekeeping for him (in fact there was no where else for her to live as she had lost touch with the Edwinstowe Morleys). Brother Neil was not consulted about the move or the dumping of so much of our past though really all I can remember is losing 'Buccaneer' and my school

PRE-ADULTHOOD

magazines (I had been Editor). Anyway, we were both 'at home' for that first Christmas in Otley.

What a dump! However pleasant the house, detached and near to the weir and bridge over the river Wharfe, the town was fit for a scene in 'Wuthering Heights'. It was a market town without much business, a stony succession of buildings converted to chip shops or pubs. Dad, intent on finding some redeeming features, took us into the town centre one evening and we ended up in a seedy snooker club pretending to enjoy a game while eyeing the surly labourers and the run-down furniture. The war had reduced Otley to a depressed backwater and my father had decided to swim in it. This was his choice, and a curious rejection of the middle class aspirations that still clung to Ashwood Villas. Socially he was becoming something of a recluse. He spent many leisure hours playing crown green bowls, at which he was good. He joined a club for snooker and dominoes, staying late at night so he could have the house to himself, sitting by the drawing room fire and warming a saucepan of coffee grounds in milk on the coals. He seemed to seek the company of working-class people (like those he knew in Ashby de la Zouch?) rather than the successful, moneyed 'bourgeoisie'. I use that term warily, realising that it means different things to different people. Aunt Ada, who would tend the fire and his domestic needs, was more or less ignored. She joined the Women's Institute and enjoyed local life.

Remarkably, if we jump forty years, Otley is transformed and redeemed, celebrated now as a market town with character. It is a desirable dormitory town on the outskirts of Leeds admired for its typical Yorkshire granite and grit. Otley Chevin provides spectacular views over Wharfedale and the riverside is picturesque. Way back in December 1946, Otley was just about the pits to a twenty-one year old who was coming 'home' for the first time to a strange house. It was a cold house too, with no central heating. Still, it was the new Morley headquarters and the three boys, John, Harry and Neil, had to adjust to the conditions. At least new beds were installed, my father having realized that the sagging wire frames of the pathetically decrepit beds and the smelly mattresses we had slept on in Ashwood Villas had to be dumped. Later, all three of us suffered from back-aches of one sort or another, probably directly due to those beds. John meanwhile was convalescent; we worried about him. Dad shrugged off the suggestion that he should pay for driving lessons, which might lead John to a sedentary job, and his future remained a problem. Neil was in his final year at the Grammar School and Aunt Glad was giving him comfortable lodgings. I was on my way to Oxford and an unknown new college, so the two younger boys left "Stoneleigh", 7 Prince Henry Road, with temporary relief. There wasn't much home-life there.

IRONS IN THE FIRE

3. The Second Bite

I was a term late at St Peter's Hall. I moved into a small room in an annexe directly opposite the entrance to the college, there being no other accommodation available. Alongside was the residence of Canon Howard, the Master, who sometimes complained about the noise from the students next door. There were about eight of us in this annexe, a mixed bunch in every sense, in age, personality, appearance and study subjects and as far as I could tell, each had established his own *modus vivendi* by the time I moved in. At first I was disappointed with my lodgings (they were very cramped) but I was lucky with the neighbours. Desmond Prince occupied the largest room on the first (my) floor. He was reading English, had served in the R.N.V.R. as a ship's cook and was delightfully hospitable. I took to him immediately and he recognized a fellow-spirit. We shared many coffee-sessions, went to the same lectures and occasionally the same tutors, argued over our essays and thoroughly enjoyed building up a social network that stretched as far as Lady Margaret Hall over the years. Desmond was yet another major influence on me, in many ways the most significant in my life. Brian Barton, Stanley Fisher, Lewis Thomas and now Desmond Prince.

There was more luck on the same floor. Frank Pratt, reading Physics, had fallen under Des's spell, though he maintained his own opinions which were pretty conservative. He had been an Indian Army officer and was somewhat indoctrinated to take a literal view of things. We teased him for being short of imagination and he argued for factual accuracy. He was famed for saying, as he stretched for the last toasted teacake on the plate, "Ah well, think of starving Europe." His logic was not exactly clear but in practical terms he was indispensable when it came to initiating four hitchhiking explorations of Europe, which the two of us undertook together during summer vacations. It is curious that Frank and I did not share many adventures apart from these wonderful trips, when we dovetailed into a close unit. In College Frank played hard and worked hard, ploughing a lonely furrow in the physics labs and enjoying light relief from the two dilettante English students, but he never followed us on the trail to Lady Margaret Hall, where Desmond and I struck up a friendship with a small group of second year undergraduettes.

Desmond Prince bubbled with enthusiasm for simple 'natural' outdoor activities. He had certain similarities to Stanley Fisher, lean and dark with lank hair but more energetically nervous. He was entertaining in company but loved solitude and quiet moments. One of his heroes, known through his book "The Story of San Michele", was Axel Munthe, a Swede who (in the thirties) gave up a lucrative medical practice in Paris to live on the island of Capri, cultivating what came to be called 'the good life'. I was soon also addicted to the San Michele ideal. I guess we were hedonistic in our pursuit of pleasures but there was always a reproving factor – nothing artificial or unnatural (by our standards) and nothing expensive (ditto). This fitted quite well with our reading of the writers of the Romantic period. Desmond was a great outdoor enthusiast, used to pounding barefoot along the sands of the Dee River and bird watching on Hilbre Island. He was brought up in West Kirby in the Wirral and was a product of Caldy Grange Grammar School where his father was Head of English. His sense of humour was infectious. Being half Irish helped, though not with his application to learning Anglo-Saxon. When Des came a cropper in his Finals it was a shock to all our small circle, amongst whom he was rated the outstanding personality.

The three terms in an Oxford year are astonishingly brief – eight weeks officially - and therefore lived intensely. There wasn't time for everything. I turned down acting in a college drama production; I dropped out of the cricket team. Rugby was the game that united most of us during the winter period, and I kept to tennis in the summer, becoming Captain of the college six in the third year. We stayed up after the summer term in order to see open-air college drama productions. Perhaps the most memorable (certainly most lavish) was 'The Tempest' directed by Neville Coghill and staged by the lake in Worcester College. I settled in successfully and relished the life of the undergraduate. We had a friendly, robust circle of fellow-students and the male company at St Peter's, mainly ex-servicemen, was amenable – about 250 in all, I think.

St Peter's Hall was founded in 1927, mainly for ordinands of the Anglican faith and supporting northwest students, but it had gradually expanded since then and by the time war disrupted normal procedures, it was a successful small residential Hall with a wide range of students in residence. In the post-war era, most of these would be on government grants, and that was certainly my situation. This was useful for St Peter's, which was a 'poorly endowed' college. Most of the undergraduates were Commoners, and I can't recall any Scholars and Exhibitioners in our midst. There was an extremely friendly atmosphere about 'Pot Hall' which more than made up for the lack of venerability and annals. The buildings are traditional college design using mellow brick and stone, and if mainly bland in style, the two quadrangles are intimate and well foliated. One of the assets was single occupancy of rooms; in some (older) colleges, post-war overcrowding meant that rooms had to be shared. When I moved into rooms in the middle of the college for the second year, I was delighted to be at the centre of things but, like everybody else, I had to find lodgings in the town for my third year. By that time I had thoroughly enjoyed and benefited from the collegiate system. In 1965 St Peter's Hall was given full university status and became St Peter's College. It has expanded since then, become co-educational, and it now seems to have achieved dignified middle age as a long-established institution.

IRONS IN THE FIRE

Back in 1948, the only student to connect me to Corpus Christi College was John Procter who, with his wife Lesley, has remained a good friend through the years. How did we meet again in this post-war Oxford? He was reading PPE and seemed to burrow regularly into the Bodleian Library, a place I very rarely visited. He sought light relief no doubt and Des Prince and Co could provide it, even if it was just idly punting on the Cherwell with the LMH girls or tea and crumpets in SPH. I started to share digs with John in my third year, renting a room in the home of a mild-mannered Corpus Scout (servant) but I crossed swords with his waspish spouse over an electricity bill and left indignantly. I moved into a large first-floor bed-sit in Iffley Road (£3 a week – standard price) and met a motley crowd of students, including hangers-on of the landlady's inflatable Air Hostess daughter who kept turning up between flights. As this was my Finals year, I kept feet on the ground. It wasn't a bad environment for close study. I remember drinking about eight tins of fruit juice on the first morning of my Examinations and that was a sensible preparation for the ordeal. I survived.

Settling down to reading English Literature and Language had not really been a problem even though I had missed some mediaeval studies in the first term. I had absorbed quite a lot of Chaucer and Langland while in Chatham and enjoyed Middle English texts. Our progress through the centuries of literature was piloted by Huffy but not particularly chronologically. However, we certainly reached the buffers with Byron in the 1830s. Our studies never advanced into Victorian times and as for the twentieth century, it just didn't exist. Instead, we looked back to the origins of English in Anglo-Saxon times, which was necessary when you considered the detail of language studies in our course, but translating Beowulf took an unconscionable chunk out of our time. We were hardly being introduced to anything like a serious study of modern literature and criticism. Since my time at Oxford, the English Faculty has decided to advance more boldly into the twentieth century (via Victorian times); at least I hope it has. Not that I regret the 'looking back' approach. I think the emphasis on Language (technical and social) is well worth sustaining but was there any excuse for not bringing to our notice the existence of F.R. Leavis and the Cambridge School of English? No tutor mentioned him to me – nor other students, I guess. In the larger world of academia and the market-place, that was a big hole to fall through.

During each of the terms, I accepted the field of study mapped out for me by Huffy and wrote one essay a week for him. I had usually a solo tutorial with him, occasionally with another student, and Huffy listened to my 'attempts' patiently and generally approved. I also had to attend tutorials in Anglo-Saxon and language studies. At the end of the first year I had to sit and pass a language examination in Old English. Considering I had less time that most, I coped with this satisfactorily and the prolonged study (and reading) of Beowulf and other

PRE-ADULTHOOD

Old English texts was never an ordeal. In fact I enjoyed translating Anglo-Saxon, which was more than my friend Desmond did, to his ultimate loss.

The second year beckoned without examinations to worry me. It was like visiting the Garden of Delights with books for flowers and no snakes around but first there was the extraordinary hitchhiking trip during that first long vac. Frank Pratt and I shouldered rucksacks, stuffed with sleeping bags and cooking equipment, and set off to hitch-hike our way through France and Italy, not so much in search of starving Europe or the fleshpots of Mediterranean leisure as seeking the cornucopia of culture and history that these foreign shores represented. Frank already had his Baedeker to hand and was counting the number of stars against the listed sights, starting with Paris and reaching as far as Naples. His National Service in India had whetted his appetite for travel and exploration, and given him experience in camping. He led the way and I followed.

This is summer in 1948. Europe is at peace but still nurses its wounds. Refugees have scattered or settled, war-scarred cities have started re-building their urban centres, the vestiges of enemy occupation are gone; the convalescence is going well despite trouble with Russians in Germany (and elsewhere); productivity is favouring ploughshares. The Marshall Plan is in operation but American globalisation a long way off. There is a new spirit around, most clearly evident on the roads and routes where, although there is far less traffic than now, drivers stop to pick up travellers by the roadside, sans peur. L'autostop had become an honourable part of the French highway code and we have no difficulty in getting hitched as we wait at the right side of the routes nationales in our rugby shorts and boots, carrying bulky rucksacks with neat little Union Jacks pinned on the left side, and making pumping movements with our arms. There were short lifts and long lifts, dual or solus, but rarely did we fail to achieve our goals.

We were off to southern climes and the sun hit us in Provence. The combination of that physically crashing heat and the heady freedom of the road was intoxicating. After years of confinement in what seemed a two-dimensional monochrome world, here I was enjoying an intensified, heightened life of sensations. It was all so simple, so natural! The next generation may have got their kicks from drugs and flower power; during that summer of 1948 Frank and I were 'sent' on sunshine and liberty. And there was so much to learn about European civilization!

I shall not attempt any detailed account of our hitchhiking trips over four summer vacations. I am not providing 'travellers' tales', nor trying to analyse the impact of foreign travel on my personal development because it is all a little obvious. I did scribble diary records of the day-by-day events but they have been lost, thank goodness. We undertook these trips in the spirit of 18th century

IRONS IN THE FIRE

Liberal Education more than the Victorian Grand Tour. Both of us were fairly parsimonious in expenditure during the Oxford terms and lived within a budget that financed the vacation trips. Fortunately I was able to stay at home in Otley without paying Dad for lodgings.

The four Itineraries can be briefly summarized as follows:

1. Summer 1948 Via France to Italy. Rome, Naples (including Pompeii and Herculaneum), Florence, Venice. Return via Switzerland and the Alps. France & Benelux.

2. Summer 1949 Via France to Spain. Bilboa, Santander, The Caves of Altamira, Madrid, Toledo. (Frank to Granada & Portugal) I go to Valencia and Barcelona. Return via France separately

3. Summer 1950 Via Holland to Germany. Up the Rhine to Cologne. Coblenz, Black Forest, Heidelberg, Munich and Oberammagau. Austrian Alps. Salzburg. Return via Switzerland and France.

4. Summer 1951 Via France, to Greece. (We separated to rendezvous in Athens). Frank travels to Sicily, crosses to North Africa and through Egypt and Palestine and Turkey to Greece. I traverse northern Italy to Trieste, then through Yugoslavia into northern Greece, Salonika, and south to Athens and the Peloponnese. Frank arrives in Athens late; I am homebound by then.

A few token memories arranged alphabetically for fun:

A.... Acropolis. The ultimate destination, aptly achieved during the final itinerary. The Parthenon incredibly moving; is it more beautiful as a ruin? The temple of Athene Nike exquisite. The whole site seems symbolic of European culture. (Itinerary 4)

B.... Belgrade. After hitching through Slavonia, I arrive in the capital and look for lodgings. This being Titoland, all tourists must report to the bureau for allocation to a suitable hotel, graded A, B, or C. I explain to the clerk I cannot afford a hotel, please may I go to a pensione. "No," he says. I dig my heels in, I refuse to go to hotel C. I want hotel D. I think I win, but only because hotel C lowers its prices for me. I contrast peasant hospitality on the way to Belgrade! (see Z) (Itinerary 4)

C.... The Caves of Altamira – the mysterious caverns, the dark passageways and the subdued lighting on entering the inner chambers, totally overwhelming.

PRE-ADULTHOOD

Beautiful, sophisticated images of animals (bison, deer, horse) painted to fit the rock contours. (Itinerary 2)

D.... Déjà vu. An extraordinary experience of déjà vu stepping out of a Peugeot into the Town Centre in Brussels. I feel I know these ornate public buildings forming an architecturally magnificent square, but this is my first sight of them. I stand for minutes trying to regain reality. I had been cooped up in a long hitchhike from Switzerland – probably the explanation! (Itinerary 3)

E.... Etiquette. With the Boyds (see J) driving through a Yugoslavian village with the rising sun dazzling us. Creeping blindly along the road, we hear a bump and immediately stop. There is an old crone in black lying by the roadside, nursing her leg with her goats beside her. We rush to help. Boldly I lift her skirt to find an injury but she angrily pushes me away, holding her skirt below the knee. Peasant decorum forbids help; we are glad to assume she is okay and drive on nervously, fearing police charges. (Itinerary 4)

F.... Florence. Perhaps the most beautiful town I have visited, both for its cultural and artistic wealth and the superb townscape. Climbed the campanile and basked in the mellow warmth of terra cotta tiles on roofs surrounding the cathedral. The Ponte Vecchio like Tudor London Bridge! Michelangelo's "David" wonderful in the Academia. (Itinerary 1)

G.... Grottos. Ludwig's fairy castles amid the craggy ranges of Bavaria, and amazingly fastidious gardens in the valleys containing romantically Gothic grottos. We float in a gondola through a fantastic series of caves, entertained by singers and flambeaux – all remarkably artificial. (Itinerary 3)

H.... Hi-jack. I walk through a sleepy French village early on a Sunday morning, the sun bright on house shutters still closed as I trudge along the road. I have bivouacked in a meadow without realising this village was just round the corner, unrolling the sleeping bag at sundown contentedly after good progress on the road. Now, rising early, I am on my way again, intending to hitch my first lift of the day. Birdsong accompanies me as I reach woodland, the only other sound a distant church bell more like a toll than a reveille – and my boots clumping as I march along the lane. Perhaps it is too early for local traffic.

Then I hear a car approaching and turn to raise my arm hopefully. It's a small car approaching quite fast but the driver squeals to a halt when he sees me. There are three youths on board, two in the front and one in the back, and they laugh and joke as they make room for me in the rear seat. I sit with rucksack on my lap, politely smiling as the driver slams into gear and zooms off down the lane, but suddenly I am aware that these are adolescent kids out on an early morning razzle. Whooping with excitement, the driver starts to swing the driving wheel from side to side, chortling as the car swerves more and more dangerously. His friends grow alarmed, shouting warnings as we come to a bend in the road. The driver over-compensates, the car slides off the road, turns over in a ditch and comes to an abrupt halt.

There is silence as I open my eyes. All four doors are open, the driver is crawling away from the car and the other two are staggering to their feet and whimpering. They take no notice of me as they start running down the lane, at least one of them hobbling with pain. I am still in the back seat but where is my rucksack? I find it ten yards distant in a bush, unharmed. The woodland seems motionless and self-absorbed in the morning sunshine. I stand still in the clearing and the birds start singing again. What should I do? The car is a wreck, I have miles to travel. I decide to walk on, hoping for another lift. My shortest hitchhike; all over in less than a minute. (Itinerary 3)

I.... Italian Lakes. Hitching north from Milan, we reach Lake Lugano. Lush vegetation and villas surround a picturesque glassy lake where a paddle steamer lazily chugs past. We can't find anywhere to stay, can't relate to the remote self-satisfied detachment of the place, and so hit the trail again towards the Simplon tunnel and Switzerland. (Itinerary 1)

J.... Jalopy. Two young Canadians, Harry Boyd and wife, offer me a lift from Athens to London in their trusty old Ford car. A long way without a break of company! We get on well. Harry is reading English at Cambridge, financing himself by playing ice-hockey with a professional London team. He's a star player; son of a Presbyterian minister in Toronto, a demon on ice. A safe journey. (cf E) (Itinerary 4)

K.... Knots Five, the speed a landing craft travels upstream on the Rhine. Where we met the military officer I can't recall but he offered to take us from Holland to Mainz (where the Moselle flows into the Rhine). Like a luxury cruise up-river, we were thinking, but found not much craft about this floating tin-can. Hitch-hiking is faster. The Rhine is immense but rather industrial. To the east we see a black pall hanging over the Ruhr valley. We head south towards the Black Forest, slowly but surely. (Itinerary 3)

L.... Lourdes by day is a commercial con trick. We visited Bernadette's Grotto, tasted some foul water and viewed the grotesque relics of the cured with scepticism but in the evening we joined the processional stream of pilgrims

PRE-ADULTHOOD

carrying candles slowly wending their way into the church, chanting the traditional hymn. At the porch, we broke ranks. (Itinerary 2)

M.... Marshall Aid in full flow, at least in Yugoslavia. In Trieste, I had found free lodgings in the Sergeants' Mess of the British Army. I trudged across the frontier into Tito's Yugoslavia and unwisely accepted a lift in a lorry which veered along the coast road to Fiume (Rijeka to Slavs), very isolated by mountain ranges. How to get back on course? Fortunately I met this American having a drink in an ethnic bar. He was in charge of Marshall Aid in this region and bored stiff with the job. He was glad to see me, he needed to talk English. "No problem," he assured me. "You can fly to Zagreb tomorrow with me." It was a retired Boeing bomber with no seats. I wasn't hanging around and took his advice. It didn't cost much – my second flight, not unlike the first. (Itinerary 4)

N.... Naples, smart city thoroughfares, slummy side streets. We lodge in a University annexe within tenements. Students take us for a row round the Bay of Naples; romantic and awe-inspiring with Vesuvius in the background. They invite us to accompany them to a brothel (quite palatial). Only when the Signora approaches Frank and me to ask if we are over 18 does the truth dawn. We walk out, refusing to show a British passport in such a place. (cf. Q) (Itinerary 1

O .... Oberammergau Famous for the performance every ten years of their extraordinary Passionspiele. This was 1950 (but I don't think the Nazis approved in 1940). Our main objective in Bavaria. Cheap tickets were available at the local Youth Hostel so we stayed a few days to qualify. I had just sat my Finals and, being out of the country for the results, arranged for a Poste Restante telegram to coincide with our sojourn. Comment on the pretentious play is hardly relevant; my abiding memory of Oberammergau is seeing Frank emerge from the Hostel store holding a piece of paper for me. The telegram from my father had arrived; it simply said: "Congratulations you have got a Two one." (Itinerary 3)

P.... Pompeii. I had not expected such pathos whilst walking the worn streets of the doomed town, revealed by archaeologists below the ground level created by the molten ash from Vesuvius. Excavations revealed not just buildings but a social life suddenly stopped. In the late forties (our visit is 1948), the tourist trade is still sluggish and our guide is incomprehensible. When we get to Herculaneum, the trading port for Pompeii, we are impressed with the neat lay-out of the excavations. And black sand on the beach! (cf V – climbing Vesuvius) (Itinerary 1)

IRONS IN THE FIRE

Q.... Quandary. I am hitching round the Peloponnese with a French-Russian student. A fruit truck picks us up and we head for Corinth. Just past the extraordinary Canal Gorge, the driver diverts down a lane and stops outside a villa. He walks up the driveway, beckons to us to follow and disappears. Puzzled, we approach the main entrance via a delightful garden. Shutters open, girls peer out and jabber excitedly. We sit in a bare room in the company of four or five girls. One of them is definitely superior, beautiful and haughty. I admire her and she accepts my attention but my student companion walks away. I am tempted but I can't take the plunge. I smugly kiss her on the cheek and leave. What a pity, I badly needed to lose my virginity. A session with a Mediterranean beauty was probably just what the doctor ordered. On the other hand, maybe my craven caution saved me from the clap! Would the Madame have provided a condom? (Itinerary 4)

R.... Rome. In Rome, the sun bangs down on me. I need siestas, but the midday sun brings out the mad dog in Frank and he visits the Vatican and the Sistine Chapel alone. St Peter's Cathedral duly impresses materialistically. His statue's foot worn away by idolaters' kisses appals. The Coliseum astounds; you have to imagine the flat arena filled with gladiators fighting and the crowds screaming for blood. (Itinerary 1)

S.... Santander. We meet a bent, paupered old English lady, an ex-nurse left over from the Civil War. In Santander she inhabits a tiny ramshackle apartment on the sea-front but we sleep on her floor well enough. What is she doing here? She hates the Franco regime; I can't remember her ordeals, she rambled and ranted. She seems very bitter and friendless. Frank and I are interviewed by a journalist for the Fascist-controlled local paper. The article says we love Franco, which disgusts our hostess - we have been used! She won't take our money but maybe we can send her a food parcel from England. Back home, neither of us has the grace to send her a parcel. Shame on us, she deserved our support and gratitude. (Itinerary 2)

T.... Toledo. After a short visit to Madrid, which seemed stifling and deserted, we hitch to nearby Toledo - archetypal mediaeval Spain with one or two Don Quixote look-alikes wandering the cobbled streets. Lots of beautiful swords in shop windows, but we search for El Greco's stunning, optically challenged paintings. This is a parting of ways : Frank goes west to Portugal and south Spain, I go east to Valencia and hitch a camion full of oranges to Barcelona and the Costa Brava; then homeward (first time on my own!)(Itinerary 2)

PRE-ADULTHOOD

U.... Upstaged. Salzburg is Mozart's birthplace. I felt the sheer, dominant splendour of its brooding mountain ranges when, after signing on at the Youth Hostel, I wandered about the town, which was surprisingly expensive and sophisticated as far as shops went . I kept being drawn to look up at those towering peaks that made me feel somewhat like an ant crawling over a rock garden. Or perhaps more comfortably, like a member of the audience in a grand theatre captivated by the magnificent backdrop.

It was perhaps the sheer theatricality of the setting that made me want to go to the Opera House. I spoke to another Youth Hosteller, an easy-going Irish lad. He had seen a fantastic performance of an opera by Salieri, a composer I had never heard of. I looked at his ragged anorak and jeans, wondering how he could afford the price of a ticket to the opera. "Ah, you don't think I paid for a ticket, do you?" he said. "I'd be broke for a month if I did that. No, I got in for nothing." He must have won a prize or something, I thought. "Not at all," he said, looking well pleased with himself. "All you have to do is mingle with the crowd, once you're inside you make yourself scarce till the lights go down and then you slide into a seat. No problem."

Could it be that easy? That night there was to be a performance of 'The Magic Flute'. "Well now," said my advisor, "you're in luck. That's one of Mozart's best and it's a very good production, so they say. Why don't you turn up with about ten minutes to go, tag along with the crowd going in and see what happens." So I did. I was smart enough to change my shirt and wear long trousers, though they were a bit creased. Most of the Austrian audience seemed to be wearing evening dress but all went well at first. I successfully mingled with the swarm milling about in the foyer, hundreds of people excitedly chattering, smiling and pushing eagerly towards the narrow entrances to the auditorium. I had decided that my target should be the stalls, not just because this part of the house was most readily accessible but because I would be more conspicuous climbing stairs to the grand circle. I floated past the attendant without so much as a glance at him and found myself in a vast arena, decorated in gold and red, the circles and boxes gleaming in the lights, filling up rapidly with members of the audience. The orchestra began tuning up, and an air of expectancy filled the whole auditorium.

Neither I nor the Irish student had considered the possibility of a full house. I looked around anxiously for empty seats and to my consternation could not find any spaces in the serried ranks. If there was one seat - yes, no one was sitting in that one, I could perhaps sit there – but it was in the middle of a row, I should have to disrupt a long line of up-ended opera-goers to reach it, and I hadn't the nerve. I went to a toilet, and came out quickly because I could hear applause, but it was only the leader of the orchestra joining his colleagues and controlling the mélange of sound as musicians waited impatiently to begin. Then I saw two unoccupied seats at the end of a row in the back stalls and I made a beeline for them. And now the conductor was bowing to the applauding audience. The rituals of classical music.

I tried to look relaxed, sitting in my seat, waiting for the opera to begin. I could see two people entering the auditorium, both clearly agitated by arriving late. An attendant was pointing them to my row of seats as the conductor began the overture. Before they arrived, I knew what to do and graciously rose to offer the two seats to the two apologetic ticket-owners. Casually I strolled to the back of the stalls while the orchestra got into their stride and then an attendant dourly signalled to me and I got the gist – OUT!

But I wasn't caving in easily. My appetite was whetted. I wanted to see the opera, I demanded some corner where I could watch. The attendants, with looks of cold contempt, shook their heads. I had to leave the Opera House, I had no ticket. Obstinately, I said I would not go. One of the attendants, middle-aged and shrewd, beckoned to me. He spoke no English, I spoke no German, but we understood each other. "You come with me," he signalled, "and I will show you where you can watch." "Okay," I replied mutely. So I followed him out of the Opera House, round the corner and to the stage entrance, which was approached via a peculiar tunnel. On the way, he stopped and held out his hand, palm uppermost. This was basic English; he was demanding payment for a favour. "How much?" I semaphored. He held up two fingers, which meant no rude gesture nor victory. He wanted two schillings, not exactly negligible. Reluctantly, I paid him and we proceeded down the tunnel.

I could hear the strains of music wafting unevenly. This is good, I thought, I shall see "The Magic Flute" from back-stage, an interesting view of the opera and I shall be very close to the action. Suddenly I realized the attendant had disappeared; there were twenty people standing in the darkness, all looking towards the end of the tunnel from which emanated music and light. Once or twice, as we stood in the gloom, a grotesque be-feathered creature pushed us aside, waiting for his or her cue to enter the stage and burst into song.

"The Magic Flute" is an enigma to many an opera lover paying his small fortune for a privileged seat in the front stalls. To me, standing in a dark tunnel with no view of the stage and with muffled sounds of voices and music drifting through the cavernous wings, it was a load of codswallop. As the first half of the programme came to a conclusion, with rapturous applause from a very distant audience, I decided I had had enough of Mozart for one night at the opera. I slunk away, leaving the huddling worshippers to their devotions.

I'm afraid I have never taken to "The Magic Flute". I can't help associating it with being taken for a ride. My moral balance tips a little for I don't criticize myself so much for trying to get something for nothing as for being duped by a shrewd, middle-aged attendant. (Itinerary 3)

PRE-ADULTHOOD

V..... **Volcano**. This was Frank's idea! Brilliant! I wrote a description for the college magazine. The editor rejected it but I still think it captures the spirit of the ascent.

Climbing Vesuvius

We left a crowd of youths whispering under the last light in the village. "Arrivederci!" we cried as we tramped by them, rucksacks on our backs. "You are climbing Vesuvio tonight? I will be your guide!" they clamoured. "Nuino manchia!" had soon silenced them.

The village of Boscotrecase lies directly south of the towering cone of Vesuvius. The road led uphill, reaching towards the solemn mass of the volcano. There was no moon, but the stars were magnificent, twinkling furiously in a clear sky; the air was cool, but warm enough to soak our shirts as we marched upward. It was a good road meandering up the lower slopes, one of the legacies of Mussolini's regime, and in the dark night we were thankful for its silver trail.

Two miles south of Boscotrecase, the ghost town of Pompeii had entranced us with its romance and tragedy. Earlier in the day we had stood on the steps of the temple of Zeus and viewed the Forum, once the scene of busy and prosperous life. We had disturbed the basking lizards in the silent streets and examined the casts of bodies buried in the ashes, tragic mementoes of the terror of the eruption in A.D.79. Now we were to pay homage to the stern god Vesuvius, whose wrath had showered death and fertility on the surrounding land. The Neapolitan who had walked with us through the village had been a guide before the war; he sighed for those days of prosperity. Now they were all poor and had to work; there were no tourists, no Americanos, no Inglesi, and Vesuvio? Ah, maledetti Demonio, Vesuvio e finito! We were puzzled. The tourist trade may be languishing but would Vesuvio ever be finished? Our pre-war Baedeker guide-book had described the scene vividly. Even though we had been told vaguely about a minor eruption in 1944, we still expected a huge flat crater over a quarter of a mile wide, accessible to its centre where an eruptive cone was surrounded with weird forms of lava and slag, while scalding steam issued from numerous fissures over which you could boil a kettle. How could the guardian of the Bay be finito!

It was past midnight when we came across the first cinders strewn over the road. It was like treading on coke, and we realized this must be the overflow of the 1944 eruption. Was this similar to the dust that rained down on Pompeii and, mixed with steam, asphyxiated Herculaneum in a thick deluge of suffocating mud? The road was now completely lost, and struggling up over irregular cinders and ash, we felt vulnerable as the summit loomed ominously above us. Below, the Bay of Naples glistened like a mirror, sweeping round in a semicircle of yellow lights. Above, the stars stretched to infinity. So we unrolled our sleeping bags and slept on the cinders.

We awoke with the morning sun on our faces, the sky blue and the sea even more blue. Half-past five, and breakfast warmed by steam awaited us at the crater. The way ahead was over more cinders and slag, climbing upward with the sun beating on our rucksacks. Two hours later we reached the summit unexpectedly, over 3000 feet above the bay. We stood on the vast perimeter of the crater but this was no flat expanse with a pathway winding to central regions and sulphurous exhalations issuing from sculptural lava. We were standing on what seemed a thin wall looking straight down into a yawning cavity with jagged, abrupt sides, perhaps 400 yards in diameter and 100 deep. The immense hollow glowed deep orange in the morning sun. The only movement was steam silently rising from crevices frighteningly distant and mysterious in this empty space.

The entrance to Dante's inferno, or Vesuvio's sepulchre? We stood on the brink of the biggest hole we could ever imagine. Vesuvius had blown its top and lay disembowelled. No breakfast of hot porridge, fried bread and tomatoes and tea for us! But we gazed long and hard at this desolate scene, then faced the Bay of Naples shining in the splendour of a perfect summer's day. What more could we want, with awe on one hand and sublimity on the other?

A vaporous mist swept across the mountainside, momentarily blotting out the view and compelling us to move on. Imagine falling in to that cavity! We set off towards the ruined Observatory glimpsed below, passing the funicular railway which had before the war carried tourists to within 100 feet of the crater. Now it was a mangled mass of twisted girders ripped apart by the eruption of 1944. As we descended to the funicular depot, six lean and dark guides glared at us resentfully. What were we doing coming <u>down</u> the mountain? They gesticulated angrily and pointed to a notice : "It is obligatory to take an official guide to the crater" in Italian, French and English. We shrugged and walked on, pretending not to understand.

We headed due west through fertile fields, vineyards and gardens to Herculaneum, almost a model village excavated from the lava and, sitting on black sand, bathed happily in the sea. "Vesuvio is finito!" the old guide had lamented. The crater no longer allowed visitors to walk across it, the road to the summit was lost, the funicular destroyed, and where were the tourists? But was the volcano finished? Neapolitans say when Vesuvius is silent, it is brewing trouble. Will it end with a bang or a whimper? (Itinerary 1)

W.... Word-hoard. In other words, a loaf of bread, a flask of wine, a book of verse and thou beside me in the wilderness... Palgrave's Golden Treasury (why not?), a regular companion on many a roadside sojourn waiting for a hitch. Lean up against the rucksack, consume your snack and read (and memorize) poems in the compact World Classics series. What is this life if ....(all Itineraries)

X.... Xtravaganza. A fantastic setting for Verdi's Aida : the ancient Roman Baths of Caracalla in Rome. We have tickets for seats half a mile from the stage but the voices travel beautifully. A spectacular production – real elephants, camels and horses though they weren't singing. My first opera. Difficult to live up to, particularly in that spectacular setting. (Itinerary 1)

Y.... Youth Hostels. Staple accommodation, but the further south the scruffier. Most memorable is an Auberge de la Jeunesse at Lyons where I arrived hot, sticky and tired. I need a wash down, but the only shower (cold of course) is in a courtyard overlooked by the femmes' section. I risk it, strip off and stand in the shower. Shutters and blinds fly open, girls of all shapes and sizes lean out, grinning and laughing. I ignore them, turn my back. Too cold to linger. (Itinerary 3)

Z.... Zagreb to Belgrade. Dusk falls as hitches dry up, not that there many anyway. I look for shelter near the main route and approach a farmstead comfortably situated in its own grounds. There is a hayloft and, having knocked at the farm door, I ask for permission to bed down on the hay. The farmer and wife invite me into their house and we wait. And wait. What are we waiting for? The door opens and a priest enters. They speak Serbo-Croat earnestly, then the priest turns to me and asks, "Parlez-vous français?" I reply, "Un peu," and he says, "Vous êtes allemand?" I shake my head and say, "Anglais". He asks more questions, then nods to the farmer. I am approved and the family breathe audibly, shake my hand and bring out the food and drink, and I sleep in a mountainous bed in a sumptuous guest room. Refusing any payment, all smile as I wave goodbye in the morning. Such is peasant hospitality! (Itinerary 4)

These four summer excursions into the heart of Europe were perhaps educationally the most intensive learning experiences I have been able to enjoy. Each was different of course, not just providing insights into other cultures and historical perspectives (Italy, Spain, Germany and Greece) but also throwing up personal and practical challenges. I can't say I made much progress in speaking languages (French my only hope) nor in relating to the fair sex while travelling round Europe. Reaching a destination always seemed to take priority over dilly-dallying, and sometimes over local exploration. We had to stick to a schedule and often dipped lightly or superficially as we moved along, but I have not enjoyed later holidays quite as much as these. Both Frank and I were independent as we hitched our individual ways through countries. Shoe-string budgeting is an asset when you have sunlit health and the freedom of the road. We were lucky to be making our excursions in the summer season of the autostoppeur.

The second year at St Peter's was unfettered by examinations, so it was possible to escape into a mildly lotus-eating existence before the terrifying judgement days of Finals in the third year. I had only a vague notion of the English set syllabus but I dutifully (and enthusiastically) responded to the sequence of literary texts placed before me by 'Huffy'. As far as English lectures were concerned, the great attraction was C.S. Lewis expounding his Prolegomenon to the Mediaeval age; or Lord David Cecil spluttering his ideas on the novel. As the terms passed, we became fairly economical in our attendance at lectures but Des and I had by now met Kit Smith and Maureen Moxon (at a lecture?) and struck up a friendship. Eventually we became daily visitors to LMH for afternoon tea and a leisurely punt on the Cherwell during the summer. As this ladies' college adjoined Oxford's favourite river, there were college punts tied up in an inlet, which offered a constant temptation to the riverless Pot Hall types and their myrmidons.

Kit Smith and I kept company but our relationship remained on a tepid plateau. I don't know if our feelings qualified as 'platonic' but certainly on my side they were not very amorous. We both kept our emotional needs buried and I never openly discussed family deprivations. We were, as the saying goes, just good friends and the friendship did not outlast Oxford. Fifty years on (2000) there was a reunion in Oxford (on the banks of the Cherwell) for a gathering of undergraduates who had taken their Finals in June 1950 and I attended this. Both Kit and Maureen were there and all three of us found the spell was broken; we had nothing in common in 2000 apart from some faded memories of young people whom we hardly recognised as ourselves. We have not met since that strange reunion.

This is a great pity but an indication of the lack of substance in our friendship; yet it was real enough in June 1950 when we all finished our three-year studies. I think there were about seven or eight 'papers' to 'sit', wearing traditional academic garb (a dark suit, a white shirt and bow-tie and scholastic gown), at the Examinations Schools. During that intense fortnight, one was incommunicado but after the final paper we took a punt out to celebrate - Kit, Maureen, Des and myself. I fell in (accidentally), still wearing my demob suit. I never wore it again.

One event I associate with these last months as an undergraduate was the reunion of a few ex-Grammar School students and Stanley 'Flush' Fisher who was now teaching at Magdalen College School and had also been appointed as Chaplain of the College. My contemporaries and I visited his home for afternoon tea and it should have been a really enjoyable occasion but I was disappointed – due partly to my lack of interest in my school contemporaries (except for Geoff Embleton, a good friend), partly to Stanley Fisher seeming rather self-satisfied and patronizing, and partly to my lying to him about a book I had previously borrowed from him. I had kept it as a souvenir of his teaching but thought I had lost it so denied having it. It was a foolish evasion for actually I still have it! Through the years of my teaching I have loaned many books to ex-pupils and students and sometimes they have not returned them. I console myself with the thought that maybe they have wanted to keep them as souvenirs of an admired teacher, like me, but I am well aware how this can sour relations.

After the last farewell party following Finals, Frank and I were preparing for the trip to Oberammergau and I stayed at home in Otley, with no idea how I had fared in the examinations. I was waiting for the additional ordeal of the Viva, when the various dons and professors who had marked the papers grilled the candidates. I had only a hearsay notion of the procedure and travelled up to attend the summons uneasily, aware that one might stand or fall by the spoken word.

There were about twenty students at the Viva roll call. Each of us was to be called at half-hourly intervals and the first name on the list was a Mr H.M. Morley so would he please stay behind. Everyone else suddenly disappeared as I advanced to sit in a chair surrounded by about 10 dons, all looking severely learned. To be the first candidate seemed ominous; I was probably in for a roasting while they were fresh. The Language tutors led the way. I was cross-examined about some of my Anglo-Saxon translation and responded fairly well with a quavering tone of voice. I had missed out a word or two in my Beowulf paper, apparently. I was asked to explain 'Beaw' – I think that was it. I hazarded a few guesses and then was told "Beaw" was short for Beowulf. Oh dear, what a calamity! But I could see one or two Literature dons getting irritated with this Language expert; he was taking more than his share of time and they wanted to consider my literary work. What questions they asked I have long since forgotten except for one – can you name some of the Courtly poets of Stuart times? I trotted out a few fairly confidently, but then I was asked why I had written such a bad essay on a chosen topic – "schools of poetry"? I could only shrug that one off, which was possibly the best tactic. At the end of my 30 minutes I felt drained and despondent. I remember leaning against a pillar at the

IRONS IN THE FIRE

Schools entrance and gloomily thinking : maybe I'm worth only a fourth. What was my future to be if I had done badly in my Finals? Could I return to study for my Educational Diploma after this terrible blow? I knew that I wanted to teach and intended to stay on for another year at the Department of Education.

No matter - soon there was Frank urging me to pack my rucksack and head for the Dover ferry, fixing our sights on Germany and Austria. It was time for our third itinerary and I had to concentrate on passport, paraffin stove and sleeping bag. This was possibly the best response to my fearful self-doubts and being in the Bavarian Alps south of Munich, waiting to see a play in Oberammergau, was probably the best setting for receiving the telegram that signalled success. I must say I could hardly believe the message. We drank a stein of lager in celebration, not champagne.

On my return to England I was to learn of Desmond's disaster – he had failed his finals. Having always deferred to his superior wisdom in literary discussions (and enthusiasm), I was shocked by this result. I still can't grasp what caused the debacle, but a complete paralysis over language questions was probably the problem. By the time I was able to see him, he had already decided not to return to St Peter's for further studies and was working as an assistant chef in a hotel (or hospital?) in North Wales. It was a devastating blow which really fractured our friendship, because the differences between our future goals were difficult to reconcile. Significantly I visited Des but he never came to my home in Otley. I probably never invited him because there was so little to offer by way of entertainment compared with his own life in the Wirral. He was severely chastened by his experience but proved to be admirably resilient. He opted for a career in the kitchens of this world, retained his zest for nature and the countryside, and eventually, after marriage to June (a West Kirby girl), decided to bring up his family in New Zealand. We are still in touch, though a close, warm handshake is not practicable. It was through Des that I met my first wife.

There were developments on the home front. Neil started his National Service in the Army during the autumn of 1949. I was barely in touch and the news that he had been commissioned and appointed to the Education Corps came as a surprise, though that was nothing compared with the news that he was now Captain N.A. Morley, busily involved in training suitable conscripts to become Educational Instructors. Captain! My younger brother was showing the way all right. According to Cousin Muir, Neil had been hand-picked by an aristocratic staff officer who had taken a shine to him. I'm not being snobbish, just conscious that nobles often get their own way. Captain Neil was an impressive figure. In the near future, after two years in the Army (1951), he would start English studies for an Honours degree at Leeds University.

Cousin Muir had also joined the Army for National Service, early in 1948, and was in Austria (Vienna, I think) in the Intelligence Corps, and engaged in

PRE-ADULTHOOD

post-war activities concerning the Four Zones in mid-Europe. I am not sure that he ever met Harry Lime, either on or off the big wheel. Muir had been awarded an Exhibition at St John's College, Cambridge, from Sedbergh School and in 1949 went up to read Modern Languages, having completed his National Service. In January '49 his father, my Uncle Leslie, died – he had been ill since his first coronary thrombosis in '47. Certainly this was unexpected at least by me, for his down-to-earth sense of humour and occasional caustic comments made him a lively and substantial family figure. He always looked after our teeth, not without complaints about the constant sweet decay of the Morley molars.

No doubt some branches of the family met at the wedding of Cousin Jim Forsyth and June Tombs, which took place in 1949 in Doncaster, but I had really lost touch with Cousin Jim who was at the hub of this happy union. After leaving Roundhay School, he had qualified as a dentist at Leeds University , a remarkable achievement if only because I was ignorant of such aspirations and now he was marrying 'Judy', a fellow-dentist, and they were due to move south to Portsmouth after the wedding as Jim, about to start his National Service, had decided to take a commission as a Dental Surgeon in the Royal Navy. Later on, the Forsyths of Old Portsmouth and the Morleys of Eastbourne were to build up quite a friendly relationship, but in 1949 we were ships passing in the night.

The climax of my University days was receiving an Honours degree at the Sheldonian in Oxford, bedecked in gown and mortar board before a packed assembly, at least some of whom would understand the flow of Latin in which the ceremony was conducted. My father came up for the occasion, in the company of Uncle Ro (whose wife was my father's sister). Why him, I don't know; no doubt a proud moment for the family. Perhaps this was late in September 1950, just before I started the new academic year qualifying for a Diploma in Education; I was still part of St Peter's, though not in college, but now a graduate about to study at the University Department of Education for a further year.

I suppose this could be termed the end of pre-adulthood, but whether it heralds the arrival of maturity is a moot point.

CHAPTER FOUR

APPRENTICESHIP

1. Education and the Rugby Field

In the autumn of 1950 I am about to start qualifying to become a schoolteacher, though at this stage I am more likely to refer to myself as a potential schoolmaster, the term 'teacher' being usually applied to (a) females and (b) primary schools. With the erosion of authority (good thing?/bad thing?) through the ensuing decades, schoolmasters and mistresses have dwindled into the generic soup of 'teachers', though 'lecturers' (who remain on a different pay scale from secondary Burnham) still claim a special cachet. Do 'schoolmasters' still exist, outside of a few prep schools, or within some old-fashioned private institutions? They left the classroom with their discarded gowns and now I should look askance at any teacher still wishing to be called 'master' or 'mistress'. In the early fifties, however, many old traditions flourished. It did not occur to me to go against the flow, and I assumed a kind of elevated status, which would lead me along a privileged path to the Public Schools. It is a measure of my ignorance of the new Educational System in England that I was barely aware of the tripartite division of pupils at the age of 11 into Grammar, Technical and Modern grading.

I was continuing at Oxford's Department of Education (after achieving a B.A. (Hons) in English Language and Literature) not because it had any superior educational reputation (it didn't) but because I was at ease in the city of dreaming spires. As far as choosing a career was concerned, I had long since decided that secondary school teaching was the best option for me, partly because I did not relish working in either an office or the market place. Journalism, advertising, commerce, business - these did not appeal to my soft, idealistic sensibilities. I backed away from ambitious, hard-headed 'executives' intent on climbing ladders; I wanted to retain a niche inside the ivory tower and I lacked confidence in whatever skills I possessed ("he who can, does; he who can't, teaches"). However, there were more positive reasons: I liked children and young people (probably more than adults), felt comfortable about living in a learning atmosphere in school buildings, and enjoyed my subject for its own sake. I also felt a need to contribute to society and serve the community, with only a vague notion what that might mean. I wanted to earn a living but rates of pay hardly bothered me.

I had had one short experience of manufacturing industry when, during one of the vacs (Easter/Summer 1950), I took a job for a month in a wool mill owned by an Otley rugby club supporter. This meant a bus ride to Guiseley at some ungodly hour five days a week and I donned overalls to work in the packaging department, preparing and humping large bales of material and woven fabrics for transport all over the world. The packaging department was humdrum and hardly pressurized but at the end of the day I was too tired to want much more than a pint of beer and a bit of gossip in the evening, for you couldn't get way from the racket made by the spinning and weaving machinery next door. There were workers who, having spent a lifetime in the factory, were very hard of hearing if not deaf. Even shouting was inaudible while the machines chattered and rattled; lip reading was essential. I can't imagine what state the brain would be in after years tending those fantastic and intricate machines, though the conditions of work in this wool mill were far in advance of previous ages. This was an up-to-date factory with a comprehensive productivity but there were already worries about competition from newly developed countries. I expect they are no longer in business. It seemed to me the management was pretty enlightened and the workers laboured with good humour. I was given an educational tour of the whole process of turning raw wool into woven cloth. The carding process was very unexpected, disentangling wool fibres so they could be spun into usable condition. I got to know exactly what 'shoddy' was, and 'worsted', and the difference between warp and weft, but it's all a bit woolly now.

For this Education year I remained at the same 'digs' in Iffley Road and looked forward to studying the gentle art of school teaching, though "education" was the subject more readily available. "Teaching" was really left to the second term sojourn at a school, where you were thrown in the deep end of the classroom for one term. I can recall only one lecture on "how to teach English", from which I learned that if discipline flags, one should start dictating suitable passages of literature to the class - not something I ever did; perhaps I should have, for there were many occasions when I really didn't know what I was aiming at. There was time enough for reading, talking and gingerly putting out feelers to explore a larger world than the university. It was a time to pursue personal interests.

I certainly was buoyed up by my degree status, more or less gaining self-confidence overnight; and benefiting from the recent summer's hitchhiking trip to Bavaria and Austria, which revealed a very different world from that of Nazi Germany. The Cold War hardly intruded and (age 24) I was still naively idealistic about the post-war political situation in U.K., believing earnestly that socialism (not communism) would unite people to work for each other as well as themselves. As a beneficiary of the wonderful Welfare State, particularly with regard to health and education, I approved the principles of the Beveridge Plan and, though not politically active, voted Labour. I was content to follow my enjoyable course of studies without much concern for global issues. This

APPRENTICESHIP

educational year, however, was to find me wanting in physical and psychological composure.

Rugby was becoming an exciting activity. During my time at St Peter's the First XV had steadily improved and Desmond, Frank, and myself were three of the stalwarts who had helped our rise up the College League. I had played one game for the Greyhounds (Oxford 2nd XV) but had no ambitions for University Blue honours as there were some very good players from South Africa (Rhodes scholars) claiming the highest positions in those days. Back home, I had decided to relinquish games with the Old Boys (Old Leodiensians) because I was now living in Otley where the local Club was in dire need. The standard of rugby was really not much better but the playing field was bigger and there were spectators watching! I was able to benefit from the move. I was aware of improving ability and reputation with a fellow-Oxonian (Alan Cooper) on my wing. When we were 'down', Otley tended to win their games. A few clips from Sunday Times Sports reports have survived because they refer to me: "Morley star of Otley win" (Sale 8, Otley 16), "Morley, who can beat his man more easily than anyone in Yorkshire ...", " Harry Morley, 6ft. 2in. Otley centre, found yet another gap in the Bradford defence ...", "Morley, 24 years and 13 stone, a deceptive runner, not an easy man to stop, and a stout tackler."

During the autumn of 1950 I was selected to play for Yorkshire as centre three-quarter in the first round of the County Championship. The opponents were Cumberland, and I joined the team who journeyed by coach to a rugby ground at Skipton. In those amateur times, there was no attempt to 'train' as a team; we were a scratch side but we won convincingly. I had a good game. On my return to Oxford, Canon Howard (the Master) asked me if I had read the sports report in The Times. I hadn't, and I was too superstitious to seek it. Apparently I was singled out for high praise, and considering my co-centre in the Yorkshire team was Jeff Butterfield, who went on to enjoy a fine career for England, this was promising indeed. All was not well, however.

I received official notification of my selection for the next game against Durham, this time away, in South Shields. Having read the letter, I realised I had to travel up on the Friday in order to be ready for Saturday morning's departure. The meeting place was the Great Northern Hotel in Leeds, which surely would be the best place to stay the night. It is at this point that my behaviour becomes culpable and inexplicable, though I can analyse my conduct psychologically.

Although a night at the Great Northern was staring me in the face, I decided to ring up Aunt Glad and ask her if I could stay the night at her house in Adel. Was I for some reason reluctant to use a hotel? True, the official letter made no mention of booking in and claiming expenses (being Yorkshire, no doubt they didn't want to encourage local players to have a night out on them). And true, my experience of staying at hotels was, as far as I can remember, nil. Of course

IRONS IN THE FIRE

Aunt Glad agreed to my suggestion, so I proceeded on the Friday to travel up from Oxford by train and took a tram to the outskirts of Leeds where she lived. I had a good night's sleep and next morning trammed to the city centre, arriving at the hotel about 9.15 a.m. to join the team. There was no sign of them; for the meeting-time had been "not later than 8.45 a.m." and the departure time "not later than 9.00 a.m." As I had not been in touch with anyone, my whereabouts was unknown. I had mis-remembered the times and had even left the letter containing the vital instructions in Oxford. I could not even remember where the game was to be played.

Having discovered that this was Whitley Bay in Durham I dashed to the railway station but no train service could get me there in time for the kick-off. Desperately, I asked taxi-drivers to take me, and eventually one volunteered. It was a large taxi; I sat in the back, taut with anxiety as we left Leeds and drove northwards, probably up the A1. We never seemed to be going fast enough and then, nearing some distant town, the taxi man pulled up and said he could go no further, he was low on petrol, the engine was overheating, etc. I would have to take a train or bus to complete the journey. Struck dumb, all I could do was pay what he asked (£8.00) and continue on my way, aware that I had no chance of making the kick-off. Fifteen minutes late, I arrived at the ground. A reserve player had taken my place.

The next few hours were appalling as I tagged on to the successful Yorkshire team, including a fine meal in a fascinating restaurant below sea-level, accessed via an electric lift in a mine shaft. Some sympathy was shown and the taxi fare was actually reimbursed officially, but I deserved little support. My father was waiting up for me when I got home in Otley. He had listened to the game on the radio and was puzzled by my absence. When he heard my lamentable story he bristled at first but when I cried, "How do you think I feel?" he was as docile as a lamb. No words could heal the wound; silence was balm.

This was probably the most traumatic event in my life since the Truro bombing of 1942, beside which of course it peters into insignificance. After all, what's a game of rugby – hardly a matter of life and death? And yet there is a direct connection between the two. What is the basic cause of my missing this match?

I think my decision to stay with my Aunt rather than the hotel where the team assembled can be explained psychologically as a quest for my Mother (to receive praise and love for my endeavours). I had to choose the next best thing – my Mother's sister. Poor Aunt Glad, a substitute for my mother! To this day I cannot understand how I could underestimate the importance of meeting the other players at the hotel. Instead I took the tram miles from the hotel, stayed the night at my Aunt's, and then clanked back to town in the morning. This behaviour was compulsive; I was not thinking straight, I was in the grip of

APPRENTICESHIP

unconscious urges. What compounds the folly was leaving the letter in Oxford, so that I had no access to the vital details. To confuse the coach starting time was pathetic. I was travelling in a state of ignorant bliss beside which the final treachery of the taxi-driver pales into insignificance. It was a day of contributory disasters, a series of waves finally engulfing my aspirations and leaving me drained from nervous exhaustion.

Clearly, judging by such a self-inflicted disaster, I was vulnerable when faced with the challenges of adult living. Like many university students, I had been uprooted and re-planted temporarily in a new environment; nothing wrong with that, in fact it's a matter for gratitude and rejoicing, but somehow I seemed to be floating in a limbo with my feet off the ground. Back in the 'old' world of my father's retreat, which was pretty humdrum and loveless, I wasn't particularly at ease. The house in Otley was never really 'home' – but then the house in Ashwood Villas had ceased to be 'home' either. I had friends at Oxford but merely acquaintances in Otley where there were not many opportunities for socializing or for cultural interests.

For instance, I was invited to be one of the ushers at an ex-grammar schoolboy's wedding. I was out of my shallow depth! Birthday parties, funerals, weddings, births, baptisms – none of these social events occurred in our broken family life. Even a simple event like Shopping was unexplored and, faced with this unexpected summons, I sought advice from Aunt Ada, who was perhaps the only woman available at the time. This was to be a resplendent wedding with all the trimmings, and I had to think of a gift for the happy couple. Aunt Ada suggested that I should buy them a brass bell, an ornament she herself had owned in better days. So I bought a bell (which was probably made of a cheap alloy) and this was considered so bizarre a gift that at the stag party (which I had never experienced and did not attend) this bell was rung many times in jest at the local pub. I felt humiliated. Aunt Ada is not to blame. I should not have been so naïve – or socially inept (as a wedding guest).

Perhaps a trivial social gaffe, but the memory of it embarrasses me. And similarly with a sudden visit from Kit Smith, my Oxford girl friend who telephoned to announce her imminent arrival. I did not want to see her in my home. My immediate reaction was to ring Aunt Glad and ask her to invite Kit and me for tea. Did I think my father's house was too shabby, or was Aunt Ada too frumpy a hostess to present to my visitor? Simply snobbish, perhaps, but I felt inadequate socially and wanted someone like my mother to help me – though in this instance Aunt Glad was far from pleased with my presumptuousness and instantly disliked Kit Smith, so it was a very unproductive move. I was left feeling rueful about my attitude to home life, which seemed reclusive and repressive; though my father was becoming increasingly easy-going and relaxed in his retirement. We still couldn't talk thoughtfully to each other. I remember being unable to respond when, after listening to some wireless programme, he asked me what I thought about Conscience. Where did it originate? I made an excuse to leave the room, feeling flustered and unable to utter words. On another and very different occasion, I grumbled about my father retaining his old three-piece suite in the drawing room (though in this 'new' house maybe it was a 'lounge'). When I muttered cantankerously that he ought to go out and buy some more up-to-date furniture, he surprised me by saying, "All right, you go to an auction, I'll pay."

So I did, taking a bus to a nearby town (I can't remember which) where a house contents were coming under the hammer. I went with a new girl friend called Joan Hampshire to lend moral support, as I had never been to an auction before. I bid for a large, heavy three-piece suite in brown moquette and got it, rather to my astonishment. Maybe that put me off my guard for the auctioneer mistook some of my consequent facial twitches and assumed I was bidding for another item, which was knocked down for me before I realised what was going on. I protested mildly but the chair was quite attractive so I shut up. As for the suite, it was better than the tired old furniture of Dad's Villas days and I kept the chair for services rendered. I enjoyed this introduction to auctioneering, especially when one of the bidders fondly asked Joan if we were setting up home together.

She lived in Bradford though we met at Oxford's Education Department. We enjoyed that Christmas break. We skated on a frozen pond near Saltaire (I wore my father's old skates). On ice she really was as expert as any English Sonja Heine. Once we played tennis in the cold open-air and, being a tennis blue, she beat me hollow. We attended a fancy-dress dance at Leeds University (so Neil must have started his studies there). Speaking fluent French, she was *très attractif* but alas, after that Christmas idyll, we had to go to our respective schools for a term's classroom teaching. Re-united for the final term at Oxford, I should have sealed our union (in the expected manner) when the opportunity arose (and it did) but I was not ready for a serious commitment and not surprisingly she turned from me. There was a former boyfriend in the offing and I couldn't bring myself to match his ardour. Typically, I was not giving myself to any relationship.

Those heart-felt events occurred after the Autumn of rugby games for Yorkshire and the self-inflicted rugby catastrophe at Whitley Bay. I had fully expected to be dropped from the Yorkshire team after that disastrous farce but I was selected for the next County match, which says a lot for the team selectors and their faith in me. I continued enthusiastic training at the Oxford athletics track but it seems the Furies had it in for me; I sprained my ankle so badly on a practice run that I needed physiotherapy and had to phone through to the Yorkshire Secretary (R.F. Oakes) that I must pull out of the game. Surely this rebuff would be fatal but no, a fortnight later, I was selected for the match against

APPRENTICESHIP

Cheshire and, fortified with painkillers, I travelled up for the game. This time, however, I did not play well. I remember dropping a pass that might have led to a vital score. For the final game, against Lancashire, I was a reserve and watched from the stand as Yorkshire lost. It was all very sad! My County season was over; I had actually played only twice and thereby missed being 'capped'.

I might have redeemed myself. At the end of the rugby season (Easter), I was invited to join the Scarborough XV for a Festival match against the Yorkshire President's XV. I had a good game and, watched by County selectors, knew that next season I would not be a forgotten man. This was reassuring because I was recovering from a cartilage injury sustained earlier whilst playing for Northampton, actually against Cambridge University, when I was in the middle of my term at Stowe School. I know I played well, and we won the game but at the final whistle I was hobbling off the field with a torn knee cartilage. The injury didn't help my sojourn at Stowe as I became a lame duck in the classroom (and on the school playing field) but the knee recovered sufficiently for me to play later in the season. The tear in the cartilage began to cause problems later on though. When I took my first job at Sevenoaks (including coaching the 1st XV) the knee periodically gave way and left me on the ground gasping with pain. Eventually I had the offending cartilage removed at Orpington Hospital, remembered particularly for long rows of wartime huts serving as wards.

What put paid to my ambitions to play serious rugby, however, was a totally incapacitating injury to my left upper arm, which was forced out of its shoulder socket by a heavyweight tackle (from a Wakefield forward who played once for England, as if that was any consolation) at the beginning of the next season. No doubt this was related to the injury to the collarbone in the Navy, and not helped by my failure to take pectoral gymnastic exercise. Nursing my dislocated shoulder, I limped off the pitch and in the pavilion someone gave me a cup of tea. Fatal! When taken to Otley Hospital I waited hours in pain and discomfort before the doctor on duty would anaesthetize me (perhaps she needed time to consult the medical textbooks on rotating ball and socket joints). When I 'went south' to start teaching at Sevenoaks School, I nursed my damaged shoulder tenderly but foolishly assumed tendon control was restored. Back home for the Christmas holidays, I decided to play for Otley again. In the first few minutes of the game, the arm dislocated as I attempted a tackle.

There were permanently stretched tendons and sinews in my left shoulder that would give way to pressure and allow dislocation, sometimes in the most inappropriate circumstances. It was always painful and not easy to rotate back in position without an anaesthetic in hospital, yet on two occasions doctors coolly rotated and slid the 'ball' into the socket without anaesthetizing me, which was extremely unnerving and painful though I was grateful for expert attention.

IRONS IN THE FIRE

During the years that followed, my appearances on the rugby field were confined to coaching and refereeing. The shoulder injury persisted and. I was unable to predict when some activity would cause the dislocation. How many dislocations? I can't remember but I think nine is a fair estimate, including some bizarre incidents over six or seven years:

- The original dislocation on the rugby field
- The repeat three months later, after five minutes play
- Whilst pushing a colleague's car that needed a jump-start
- Turning over in bed one morning
- Rock climbing in the Lake District (no anaesthetic – see the account below))
- Playing volley-ball on the beach in Brittany (the only time I had gas, administered by nun-nurses)
- Swimming (the crawl) in a swimming pool near Sevenoaks (no anaesthetic – an experienced doctor was coincidentally at the poolside)
- Bowling overarm on holiday at a farm on Dartmoor.

Each of these dislocations was cause by a different physical situation and there are unpleasant memories to haunt me through the years but the most dangerous (and irresponsible) dislocation occurred at Sevenoaks School (1954). I hope to have recalled the experience accurately and freshly.

Threading the Needle

I was persuaded to accompany a school colleague, Chris Curtis, on an expedition to the Lake District during the Easter holidays. There were about ten in the group, all staying for the week at a Youth Hostel near Wastwater. Most of the time we rambled or plodded over hills and valleys very contentedly but the climax of our stay was always to be a day spent rock-climbing.

Chris, an experienced climber, had worked it out. The main group would relax at the hostel but four of us would climb the Napes Needle and then proceed to scale the granite mass of Great Gable, which loomed behind the Needle. He would 'lead' and I would be what I think was called the 'anchor man", i.e. the tail-ender. In between there would be two pupils, both of whose parents had given approval to the expedition. A rope would link us together at all times.

It was easy to see why this pinnacle of rock was called a Needle; there was no 'eye' but it stuck up independently and tapered slightly at the top. It was considered a 'difficult' climb by the official climbing authorities. At

APPRENTICESHIP

the top there was just room for one, or two, to stand triumphantly after taking a tricky half-hour inching up this solid rock splinter. Chris controlled the ascent by standing at the top and using the rope to help each climber clamber up in turn. I was the last to stand upright on top of the Needle, looking out over a landscape that gradually diminished in clarity as the scree and the distant green slopes descended to the gleaming, flat expanse of Wastwater many feet below.

Having returned to ground level, we faced the sheer wall that Great Gable presented. For this climb we would be roped together in a sequence of moves, rather like a caterpillar. Chris climbed to a position where he could secure the rope linking him to the first boy who now ascended, edging his way upward with the rope kept fairly taut between himself and the leader. This was simpler than climbing the Needle and the first boy fairly quickly reached Chris, who then set off to climb higher, while the second boy started to climb to the first position. I remained at the foot but eventually it was my turn to start climbing.

I found the first footholds and reached up to hook fingers in crevices that would help me rise from the ground. Chris was by now forty feet higher up, with the two boys climbing towards him and I was following the line of ascent, extending arms to reach for a niche or small promontory and finding new positions for my boots. I stretched to find a groove, and adjusted my weight to allow the left arm to take the strain. I hauled myself up – and suddenly the shoulder dislocated. I was standing on the narrow ledge with a useless arm. I was about 20 feet from the ground level.

This was an old rugby injury. I thought I had learned to live with it. The humerus slid out of its socket in the shoulder, as tendons and ligaments slackened. The pain was a sickening kind of ache, very different from natural pains. I had endured probably three or four dislocations before this disaster, and now here I was, helplessly clinging to the side of Great Gable, unable to make any move to climb either up or down. I shouted to Chris and he could hardly believe me. How could I dislocate a shoulder simply shinning up a rock? Fortunately the two boys had reached a safe ledge and were in no immediate danger but it might be rather different if I fell off my perch.

There were some walkers approaching us and I could see them halting to stare at the four climbers half way up the rock-face, all connected by a rope, with the lowest figure hunched on a ledge that allowed only a few inches to shift position. How long could I have stood there? Far above me, Chris suddenly waved and shouted. Providentially help was at hand. A team from the Outward Bound School was exercising just round the corner. As I leaned helplessly against the rock, a climber scaled crab-like

IRONS IN THE FIRE

across the rock-face towards me. He was bearded, wore a woolly hat and was equipped with the clothing and gear any Instructor would wear on a mountain training trip. In remarkably short time two of them were standing by me and removing the rope – I think so, because it was probably a hindrance to my movement as I started the descent. The detail is lost. I do remember that by the time I reached ground level, the Outward Bound team had produced a stretcher and were ready to carry me down the valley.

Ironically this was the most painful part of the whole experience. I was strapped to the stretcher and four stalwarts stumbled and staggered with the laden stretcher along the rocky track, each time jolting me and increasing the pain. After a hundred yards of this kind of shake-up, I cried out that I would rather walk the rest of the way so they stopped and let me loose to make my own way downwards. At least I could keep the arm close to my ribs and avoid sudden lurches. We probably walked (or stumbled) half a mile towards the path leading to Wastwater. There were dry-stone walls now indicating the way down to a five-bar gate at the bottom of this green field and beyond that, a small single-storey house, the only sign of habitation. And, as I approached, a woman opened the gate and came forward to greet me, as if I was expected.

I was never, in all my life, more grateful to fall into the arms of any woman than those of that nurse, for so she turned out to be. This was a doctor's surgery, and he was there, awaiting my arrival. I thanked the Outward Bound rescuers and watched them disappear up the valley to carry on with their mountain training. Chris and the boys had trailed along; now they waited to see what would happen. I assumed I would be taken to the nearest hospital but no, this doctor, dark-featured, calm and confident, sat me in a chair and firmly pulled my arm lengthwise, twisted it and rotated the ball into its socket with one deft swivelling action. It hurt, but at once I knew the arm was back where it belonged. I never knew that doctor's name but I am forever grateful for his skill and nerve.

I was able to walk away with my arm in a sling, feeling whole again. The holiday was over; the excursion to climb the Needle and Great Gable had ended without any tragic incident, but a near thing.

Eventually, years later, after so many casual dislocations, my GP in Eastbourne sent me to New Cross Hospital for expert surgery on the shoulder. I bear a curved scar on my left shoulder; beneath it, divided tendons retain the arm in its socket. I now rotate and stretch my left arm without fear, though I would not like to hang by my left arm in some suspenseful situation.

APPRENTICESHIP

Preceding this series of shoulder dislocations, I had been pursuing my education diploma course at Oxford. There were five sections: History of, and Theory of Education, Psychology, Academic Subject (English) and Special Interest (for me, drama). There were lectures, but mercifully mainly optional. At one point the Education lecturers, aware of falling attendance, tried to operate a signing-in procedure without much success. There were set texts to browse through and one or two essays to write, but little pressure was exerted; we followed our own interests, not all of them (like my rugby) to do with education. The only tedious task towards the end of the year was inventing an English Curriculum for a hypothetical school. Considering we had very little experience of schools it was a rather futile exercise. I decided to base my curriculum on Renaissance Rhetoric, including various Latinate terms. A desperate fellow-student, who should have known better, borrowed my script and recklessly copied chunks wholesale. Plagiarism was not detected, probably because neither was read properly at the end of the year. The only drama activity I remember was attending a workshop on Crowd control on stage. Some wizened old actor from the Old Vic tried to persuade two dozen student-citizens of Rome to swarm on and off stage shouting 'rhubarb!' I did learn a thing or two from him, if only that no one ever said that in a play.

2. A Term at Stowe

Interviewed by an Education tutor, I asked for a posting to a boarding school, as I had no experience of such outlandish institutions. I assumed I was heading for some kind of public school but knew very little about independent schools in general or particular. I was aware of course that many public schools (like Leeds G.S.) were day schools but I felt in need of 'boarding school' experience. I had long outgrown the delusion that midnight feasts made going away to school attractive, and in any case I was now to be a teacher, not a pupil. At this stage, I accepted the general assumption amongst many Oxford graduates that independent (public) schools were necessarily superior, if only because they often paid higher salaries than state (maintained) schools. My only experience of a State school had been a few classroom sessions at Otley Grammar School prior to the start of the Educational year and I had taken little interest in how the school was run. I don't think the lectures at Oxford had made me very aware of the remarkable changes going on in the state system while I was in the Navy and as far as the teaching of English was concerned, I had not discovered any blueprint for success in English lessons. So much for a Diploma in Education at Oxford, or perhaps for one callow student!

IRONS IN THE FIRE

However, I hoped to assuage my ignorance of boarding schools and so, when informed that my teaching experience was to be gained from one term at Stowe School, I was gratified though a little apprehensive to learn that it was one of the top public schools and resident in a Ducal stately home and estate in rural Buckinghamshire. I had never heard of it before.

It was a dark and wintry evening when I arrived at Stowe School by taxi from Buckingham station, with a heady cold in full spate dulling my senses. I stood before this extraordinary stately home in the gloom of a January evening, aware of an imposing frontal edifice, numerous tiers of stone steps, a large pair of entrance doors and long corridors. Back home in Leeds my only experience of a mansion or country house was Temple Newsam, a Tudor pile which, though splendidly ornate, was a mere brick house in comparison to this munificence. I was ushered into living quarters by one of the House Matrons who kindly offered me a cup of tea. I sat in her surgery whilst boys of different sizes drifted in and out, many interested in my presence. This being early 1951, and Attlee's Government nearing its debacle, one of the boys asked how I intended to vote. Unwittingly (and somewhat befuddled by my cold) I replied that I was in favour of 'Labour', and if I had said Marxist or Bolshevik the reaction could have been no more sensational. Gasps of horror, amazement, incredulity from the six or seven boys in the room. Matron's eyes glazed. It was like a Bateman cartoon. I heard someone in the corridor exclaiming, "My God, a Socialist!" and then scores of boys crowded at the doorway to look at the freak. Clogged with cold, tired and thick-witted that evening, I had clumsily put my foot right in it before I appreciated the nature of an establishment that not only served the Tory party but also stocked the House of Lords.

A few days into the term, I chatted to one of the History teachers who gave me some advice. Having heard of my indiscretion, he confided that he repressed his own views in the classroom while teaching, for example, the Industrial Revolution and Victorian laissez-faire. "They just can't understand what was wrong," he said. It was not just the boys but their fee-paying parents who might object to a teacher who displayed a left bent. I was certainly no revolutionary and not even a rebel so I quickly decided to eschew political affiliations and subjects for the time being.

I don't think life for the boys was very stoic at Stowe, though of course it depends what you are used to. I don't remember seeing the living quarters of pupils, but I expect there was plenty of hot water and good food available for all. In the main stately buildings one had to put up with somewhat old-fashioned and inefficient conditions, mainly because the buildings were incredibly venerable and unalterable for, though there had been structural changes through the three centuries of architectural development, mainly with an eye to the grand visual effect looking to and from the north and south fronts, now, with the founding of a

APPRENTICESHIP

school (in the late 1920's), the property had to be taken as preserved. This was not really a handicap as the buildings were so auspicious they silenced any complaints. It was a privilege to be living in the midst of such grandeur. Nevertheless it was a draughty place and the central domed hall where the school assembled for roll-call each morning resembled a wind-tunnel, particularly when the large doors to the south or north fronts were opened. Pupils answered their names at roll-call by shouting "Sto!", which pedagogues knew meant "I stand", a nice touch while one stood shivering in the cross-wind.

The grounds stretched for miles. The effectiveness of the landscape gardening (by Capability Brown amongst others) was remarkable; wherever you looked; the elegance of classically inspired monuments and follies was undeniable and simply to gaze at the south front made one gulp. As a cultured environment, Stowe provided an approximation to Arcadia. Isolated in this expansive walled estate, the school seemed to be providing an environment, which assured the residents that traditional conservative values not only survive but actually flourish. As a school, it was probably well appointed with educational resources and activities, though I wasn't impressed by the art room or the science labs or any theatre workshop (my fault for not searching, no doubt). I do remember one House production of Marlowe's "Jew of Malta" in a small hall and finding it very well performed. I also recall sitting on a settee in the Music room while a distinguished foreign lady played the pianoforte to a mixture of boys and staff. Generally, the pupils seemed content, behaved sensibly in class and appreciated their surroundings, but I was well aware, strolling down the romantically winding path to the lake, that a few stones marked the ruins of villagers' cottages razed to the ground in order to provide a better prospect for the gentry. Hardly a model environment for modern times. On the other hand, how pragmatic to use the stately homes of England as seminaries for private education far removed from contemporary Britain.

The teachers seemed well heeled and well satisfied, though there was quite a divide between those who lived in and those who didn't. Traditionally the School employed bachelor teachers (and the Head too), possibly because the isolation in a country retreat and the nature of the living quarters made conditions unsuitable for married couples; but this somewhat questionable practice was on the wane. Certainly Cousin Muir and his wife Margaret, who joined the Staff about ten years after my time at Stowe, found their marital status the norm. It was something of a coincidence that we both 'went' to Stowe but his experience is so vastly superior to mine that my impressions, based on less than two months' residence, are no more than a flea bite. Muir, transferring from his first post at Liverpool College, found Stowe very much to his liking and capped a long and distinguished teaching career by becoming Deputy Head.

IRONS IN THE FIRE

To me, the Staff Room was like a gentleman's club; with not only a bar and leather armchairs but also a full-size billiard table. The habitués included both hearties and intellectuals, many with strong personalities unlikely to brook much contradiction. Some of these barely noticed me, and the response of the younger teachers to my temporary presence was ambivalent. A few kindly tolerated my presence, which was always superfluous to their requirements, particularly after I developed a knee injury playing rugby. My role was to fit into the English Department, take a few classroom lessons at various levels and more or less get used to the idea of being a schoolteacher (though I suspect the nomenclature was "schoolmaster" at Stowe). There were impressive forebears: the ghosts of G. Wilson Knight and E.H White haunted the corridors of Stowe, for both had found employment at Stowe during the War.

The Head of English was a classicist manqué who thought English needed a Latinate prop. He fulminated about the salary an English tyro like me would get compared with his classical pittance when starting to teach. I never met the English staff as a unit but George Cox, graduate of Cambridge and still at Stowe till he retired forty years later, was the best teacher. He taught history well too. When I attended a couple of his lessons, the middle school class was absorbed in reading an adult history book, a copy of which I still fondly retain. He related well to the boys and was good at rousing discussion. He held regular extra classes for potential university English students in his study and, although I was not invited to attend, I certainly decided this was a good thing to do, though more difficult in a day-school. I taught an occasional lesson. When the tutor from Oxford came to assess my worth, I chose to base the lesson (for a junior class) on Keats' *Ode to Autumn*, but I don't recall his response. I think he was more impressed with my ability to mix and merge in the Staff Common Room. My torn knee cartilage had me hobbling with a stick, a handicap in the classroom and rendering me useless on games afternoons. At the end of term, I gave my thanks to all concerned though I must admit to gaining little insight into the workings of any kind of academic curriculum concerning English. I had no regrets about leaving when my time was up. No doubt I was not Stowe's kind of teacher, but then Stowe was not my kind of school for I had already decided where to start my career in teaching. This was to be at Sevenoaks School in Kent.

3. Teaching at Sevenoaks School

'Where?' queried some Stowe teachers, rather superciliously. Travelling from Stowe for interview, I had visited this school on a bright sunlit afternoon when the cross-country competitive House run was being held in Knole Park, which adjoined the school grounds. The Headmaster, J. Higgs-Walker, was particularly genial and welcoming, strolling with me while the milling schoolboys waited for

APPRENTICESHIP

the start of the race. I was delighted with the woodland and greenery of the Park and the whole occasion seemed relaxed and edifying, showing a school community busily active. I think he deliberately invited me to an interview *en plein air* in Knole Park on the Sports day afternoon for it meant he didn't have to show me round the school very thoroughly. There was no doubting the antiquity of this Grammar School founded by one William Sennocke as far back as the 15th century, but the 'Grammar' had dropped out of use when the boarding side was developed, presumably in Higgs-Walker's time.

There were two rows of alms-houses flanking the gateway entrance. I never saw anyone actually living in these tiny rooms but they were part of the front elevation which was mainly a cubic stone block that housed the school buildings, early Victorian though with a trace of Georgian elegance in the simple conformity of the stone work. It was, of course, by Stowe standards, small and humble, but I felt more at home with these surroundings. I felt in need of a cautious beginning to my first venture into school teaching. It was a minor public school, with a local 'day boy' in-take from the town and environs and three boarding houses (one for juniors), about five hundred pupils in all. This would not be too intimidating for a beginner for whom one term 'in the country' had not provided much self-assurance or guidance and I liked the adjacent Knole Park with its therapeutic copses and vales.

The post offered was Assistant English teacher with residence as House Tutor. I thought the institutional life of a boarding school would suit me – no worries about cooking meals, washing clothes or getting to school on time. Furthermore, I was to 'live in' the main building as House Tutor directly supporting the Headmaster who ran 'School House' with his wife Molly. They were an affable couple, both devoted to running the school according to unwritten but traditional rules derived from public school experience; they exuded confidence and suavity, not unlike minor despots of an emergent state; no, that is unfair – more like landed gentry surrounded by tenant farmers. It took a lot to rattle Jimmy, who was academically a true-blue historian, and Molly clearly long since had drawn a line delineating the entrance to House territory beyond which she would not step. She settled for flower arranging with the assistance of junior boys, an eccentric chain-smoking lady who probably had been a smashing flapper in her day. Jimmy drove an antique Rolls Royce saloon, particularly to rugby and cricket fixtures for he took a keen interest in sports. I imagine Molly was accustomed to being chauffeured around. With her smoker's cough and husky voice, she was as thin as a rake but really quite resilient; Jimmy was plump, an inch shorter than his wife, and clearly devoted to her comfort and welfare.

I was ready to settle into school life, having recently returned from travels in Greece etc. My two rooms were up two flights of stone stairways, where there was a small 'study' squeezed between two dormitories. A little south-facing window gave me a pleasant outlook but the room itself was pokey with only a few basic units of furniture. I remember a desk and a rather severe settee and a gas fire; otherwise all is unmemorable except for a distinct impression of utility. It was like some servant's quarters and I am reminded of the little attic room our maid Eva occupied in Ashwood Villas, though that was far worse! However uninspiring, it was my room and I had to make it habitable, which I tried to do, though I possessed few personal belongings beyond books. Recollecting how conditions have changed over the years, I think this was a rather mean living space for the House Tutor, particularly as I was hemmed in by three dormitories for boys. My bedroom was across the landing, hardly large enough for a single bedstead and a basin by the small window. There was a cold-water tap. For hot water and a bath I had to descend to the basement, indeed the nearest toilet facilities were on the first floor. I can honestly say that I have no recollection of peeing in the bedroom basin, but surely I did; if I didn't, I was a fastidious prude! Altogether my accommodation at Sevenoaks lacked privacy and comfort, yet, in 1951, having accepted the position without more than a glance at these rooms, I was content in my own first 'home'. And of course at the end of each term I would leave and travel to Otley for the holiday periods. Both Dad (and Aunt Ada) welcomed my return, though I can't recall if either John or Neil would also be present.

Whatever the living conditions indoors, there were always pleasant autumn walks through Knole Park (Lord Sackville was Chairman of the Governors). The Park was comfortingly undulating, with woodland and copses of magnificent beeches and oaks. The autumn of 1951 seemed to produce a display and fall of leaves to rival New England's and I wrote a few poems, including this one:

Knole Park

  Autumn shuffles by, veiled in the mists
  Of age and grey experience:
  Browns and golds, rust tints flashing scarlet and yellow,
  Adorn the crone in summer's greenery .
  The embers glow under the shroud
  That mourns the spirit of another passing year.

  Splash your way through the crisp leaves,
  Dry mud encrusted with golden lacery;
  Examine the pallor of ochreous trees
  And wonder at the gaunt elm's tracery.
  The round-backed hillocks huddle in green shawls,

APPRENTICESHIP

Sweeping the leaves into a cheerless hearth,
But the bright acorn drops deep, and falls
Into the moist humus of the earth.

And the silver cord grows strong
Under the sterile embers;
And the wrinkled mist becomes a nurse
Swaddling the newborn babe.

Who cares about small deprivations when such compensation abides outside? In fact, I was too occupied to get worked up about my living quarters. At the end of this first term at Sevenoaks I launched a School House magazine, which we called "Acorn". That's where I aired that poem before shelving it. A modest little publication, "Acorn" ran bi-annually for about four years and I retain a copy of each edition. It was self-supporting financially and involved quite a number of boys. I wonder if others have survived

As House Tutor, I shared with the Headmaster the responsibilities of looking after about sixty boys (age 13 to 18), with two Matrons taking a lot of the strain. Every week-day there was more or less the same routine: rise at seven, attend breakfast, morning school, lunch, afternoon school (or games), prep period, supper and finally to bed (about nine). On Sunday evenings I alternated with HW reading stories to the whole House. My choice of DHL's 'The Rocking-Horse Winner" was well received, I remember. The living conditions for the boys would today be considered inadequate as there was little individual privacy or relaxation, but probably these were no worse than at most boarding establishments or institutions of the time. There was a large cavernous community room where prep was done and this was the leisure centre for the boys' private periods in the evening, with each boy allocated a locker and desk, without screens that would have given some basic privacy. The prefects had their own quarters but these were really no bigger or better. What was extraordinary was the cheerfulness and sociability of these children, who came from all sorts of families and all sorts of backgrounds (but no non-whites). I never saw the Headmaster's confidential files about his charges but I recall no 'problem' children. The boys seemed to accept, if not actually welcome, the cramped impersonal conditions that their parents paid for. Would I have sent my own children there? No, of course not, not to any boarding school if I could avoid it, but I am not unhappy about my three years as House Tutor.

My time at Sevenoaks School conveniently divides into three periods : first, the three years as House Tutor from 1951 to 1954 with H-W as Headmaster; then, the transition year as House Tutor when L.C. Taylor was appointed Headmaster ; and finally my year as a married teacher living 'out'.

IRONS IN THE FIRE

My greatest achievement in those early months was stopping morning cold baths for the boys. H-W kindly accompanied me to my initiation into this barbaric rite, and I was informed that I was expected to keep an eye on procedure thenceforward. At some ungodly hour like seven o'clock each day, before breakfast and in the gloomy basement, house prefects supervised as the row of baths were half-filled with cold water and the shivering boys queued to strip off pyjamas. To martial shouts they then jumped in a bath, immersed themselves totally and leapt out to cover their nakedness with towels. It was absurdly crude (no showers), a long procession of forced ordeals, of questionable value health-wise and with scope for the occasional personal torment of a wretched offender. I stood watching this scene incredulously, then undertook supervision on a few ensuing days before protesting to H-W that I would not participate in prolonging this futile activity, whether the public schools approved or not (no sign of this at Stowe!). H-W quietly pulled the plug out, making no fuss probably because Molly was more humanitarian.

On another disciplinary House matter, I would have liked to curb the power of the prefect body but H-W allowed 'beatings' by senior prefects as long as he was 'informed'. His *modus operandi*, including fags and domestic duties for juniors, was essentially following an outdated tradition and he was only slowly adapting to post-war attitudes. Well, so was I in some respects, but I think I helped to make School House a reasonably well-balanced community which, however Spartan in resources, provided the kids with caring supervision. My relations with the boys were friendly and cooperative. There was a strong house ('family') spirit and the two Matrons looked after emotional and personal activities as substitute 'mothers'. I found contact with the boys at all levels easy and friendly, sometimes more like an elder brother than an authoritative figure, particularly with the little group of 'new' boys who arrived simultaneously with me in September 1951.

Robert Short, a bright-eyed and perky 13 year old, was one of these. Another 6 years later and he would be heading for Cambridge and university teaching, while I was settling into a new job in Eastbourne. We have sustained a fine friendship over the years both in the classroom (he was good at English as well as History) and as regards School House matters he always speaks appreciatively of our shared experiences. For example, he remembers enthusiastically the series of films, which I 'projected' on occasional Saturday evenings for School House pupils, including classics like "The Shape of Things to Come" and Harold Lloyd in "The Clock". However, he will probably murmur quietly that there were 'goings-on' of which I, as House Tutor, knew nothing. I admit my ignorance of human nature as exposed in English boarding schools, for I had been instructed in no basic precautions about sexual repression nor had I experienced anything untoward in my upbringing (even in the Navy!). My house duties always

APPRENTICESHIP

involved a tour of the various dormitories before lights-out and I bade everyone 'good night' blissfully oblivious of the private nocturnal lives of my charges. I certainly did not prowl around looking for trouble in the dormitories but probably I should have done. I still can't bear to ask Robert to provide details of sexual abuse between some senior and junior boys. This hind-sight of my limitations as House Tutor clouds my perception that these three years in School House were successful and rewarding. Nevertheless, there were solid achievements, and when I announced my engagement to be married (in 1955) and sought to retire from being a House Tutor, I think there was genuine lamentation that I was surrendering my position. (Parenthetically, Robert told me that my successor, a Classics teacher already at the school, was compelled to leave for sexual offences against a pupil. I knew nothing of this grim fact until years later).

At the very end of the first term, there was one schoolboy prank that involved me and I have mixed feelings about my reaction. I was asleep in my small bedroom on the last morning and was rudely woken by a shout, which signalled an invasion of boys into my room, some through the door, others through the open window accessed via a balcony. Still half asleep, I found myself seized by hands and feet and though I fought to free myself could not prevent them lifting me off the bed. The boys (a mix of juniors and seniors from one dormitory) were well organised to hold on, and then suddenly a warning cry came from outside the room: "Jimmy's coming up the stairs!" and I was abruptly released and the boys melted away without a sound. I was left to gather my wits and dignity after such a rude awakening. When H-W arrived at my door and politely asked if everything was all right, I decided not to involve him and made no official complaint. Nor did I name the ringleader (Day!), with whom I had a few choice words before we departed for the Christmas holiday. The prank, for so I chose to name it, was thankfully cut short. God knows what Day was intending to do with his captive. There could have been severe reprisals but I made light of it. After all, this was the last morning of term. Did I lose dignity, status or authority? I don't think so. Anyway, on my return from the holiday, I was nursing the second dislocation of the shoulder from my Boxing Day attempt to resume rugby in Otley and the past was forgiven if not forgotten.

At the end of the next term I had to make a dramatic exit to Sevenoaks Hospital with appendicitis ("classic symptoms," said the school's doctor), and then during the summer term I contracted conjunctivitis from swimming in the dubiously cleaned open-air pool. I can still feel the nauseous stickiness that sealed my eyes. During the second year I went to Orpington Hospital for a knee cartilage removal and recurrent shoulder dislocations were beginning to punctuate my physical exertions but the daily round kept me otherwise healthily occupied and I was not in need of entertainment outside the School.

IRONS IN THE FIRE

Sevenoaks town was unexciting in the fifties. Possibly there were dark corners for sinners but it seemed a pretty dull place to me, with one espresso coffee bar in the centre and little sign of community life. It was a small market town with a new status as dormitory for London commuters and apart from playing cricket for a local club and briefly attending an art class run by a talented artist, I recall few social contacts. I can't remember the inside of a local cinema, or pub for that matter. Much more attractive were the small villages where a game of cricket might be played with ale in the nearby inn afterwards and cycling through the Sussex Weald was always a pleasure. Maybe I should have sampled local life more fully. Never mind, I could sit in my little study and gaze out of the window at the Royal Oak (an ancient hostelry I rarely visited) and at St Mary's, the parish church (also ancient and attended on compulsory Sunday services) and then at the roof-tops that led to Johnson's, the other senior boarding House (extraordinarily I was never actually invited there). I think the Korean War was disturbing our tranquillity at this time (1952) and accounts for these poetic thoughts:

Undertones of War

> Cerulean and clear, the sky stands framed
> In the open window; far and near
> The heated moments drift unclaimed
> In the silky afternoon.
> Dreams of the summer house, easy peace
> In the shade of trees, placate the fear
> Of kennelled thoughts kept on a lease
> And cares sink in a swoon.
> Only the threat echoes deeper and lower
> Than summer sounds of rest imply.
> Behind the whirr of the homely mower
> Lies the thud of a gun;
> A car swirls by, but the fierce tank stops
> And rocketing jet-planes rend the sky
> As martins shriek from eaved housetops
> Made heady by the sun.

And so, apart from being a House Tutor, I had to be initiated into the arts and crafts of classroom teaching. I taught classes from First form to Sixth form as might be expected. In charge of what could be called the English Department was the Reverend JMC Parks, a genial personality who was Housemaster of Park Grange, the junior boarding House. I don't think there was actually a curriculum for those teaching English and I was left to follow my own scheme of studies at

APPRENTICESHIP

different levels, but John Parks had invested in a text-book that seemed to me a remarkable support and guide for a tyro teacher. Ronald Ridout made a fortune from his series of carefully organized course books called "English Today", and deserved it. At Oxford I had seen no adequate display of published course books nor had I considered thoughtfully how much grammar and syntax I should teach, or for that matter how little I knew. I was grateful for the help Ridout offered. Later on in this post-war era, in the late sixties, English experts frowned upon course books as a kind of force-feeding too rigidly applied, and of course over-reliance on one source of information or inspiration is counter-productive, but Ridout's course books taught me quite a lot about Language as a complement to Literature which, according to my Honours degree course, stopped in the 1830s. I had a lot to learn about modern literature and language. There were five course books from 1st to 5th year (though we did not use the last one – intended for 'O' level students). You can hardly expect a pupil to appreciate the range of topics and exercises of the books, but as an apprentice teacher I could see the comprehensive scope and detail of "English Today". They may be "English Yesterday" now, but darned useful in the fifties.

John Parks and I took alternate 'A' level English sets, so I started with a Lower Sixth group. The size of English classes (about 6 students) was little different from my day, but now students were expected to study three 'A' level subjects without further Subsidiaries, which was narrowing the range. The English Syllabus had not changed much and I followed the usual texts at Sevenoaks. Paper One was Shakespeare – 2 contrasting plays. Paper Two was Chaucer, and another traditional great writer (Edmund Spenser or John Milton) and for Paper Three there was a variety of periods and my preference was the Romantics. Later on I was able to venture into the Modern Age, which in fact suits most students more obviously, and me for that matter. For 'O' level, with classes of 25 or so, there were two subjects : English Language, which was mainly an Essay and a Précis test, and Literature where three texts were studied. Apart from these Exam subjects, I had to provide General English once a week for upper and lower Sixth formers. Initially I chose one of my favourite books, Samuel Butler's "Erewhon", but as we progressed through the story, the class grew increasingly restive as my choice failed dismally to rouse their interest, except for one bright Oxbridge candidate who thanked me for introducing him to a really interesting book. I had to re-think what goes on in General English but I cling to that one tribute.

The rest of the lessons were five English periods with middle school classes but to my consternation, I was also time-tabled to teach first form Maths and Biology (Nature Study) to the juniors in Park Grange. Nobody had told me about this eventuality. I struggled to do the sums accurately for one term, and then was mercifully relieved; but for two years I continued with the Biology and was given a genuine pat on the back for having given the kids an enthusiasm for the subject.

Each morning the Staff gathered in the Staff Room before Assembly in the Hall. They were friendly and good humoured; if there were any sour personalities I have forgotten them. Gowns were worn in those days, first for Assembly and then in the classroom and even in the street outside the school, for there were scattered school buildings to reach. As the pupils wore boaters (straw hats) seasonally, it must have looked pleasantly old-fashioned as befitted historical Sevenoaks and the traditional English public school, but it was a bit of a façade, for I was soon to learn that academic standards lagged and educational resources were under-financed. Yet the potential was there, as proved when H-W retired and L.C. Taylor was appointed as the new headmaster in September 1954.

Outside the classroom my chief responsibility was coaching the School's 1st rugby XV during the Autumn term (and over the winter months though hockey took priority then). Matches against rival schools were played with tremendous intensity and enthusiasm, and that often included me hectoring the team volubly on the touchline. At times, when teams from other schools visited us, I refereed the matches. In truth it was all a little obsessive and my concern for the success of the team led to at least one miscarriage of justice on my part. It was my turn to referee a game against King's School, Rochester. The previous year (my second) had left us smarting from memories of a narrow defeat and we knew it would be a tough game, for Rochester had not been beaten this season. I refereed the game without mishap or complaint until the final minutes, with the Rochester team leading by a single point and the crowded ranks of Sevenoaks supporters screaming their heads off for a final supreme effort. Then, with time running out, without any conscious deliberation, I prolonged the game until at last our boys forced their way over for a winning try. Apparently, I added at least an extra five minutes to the second half. H-W was in rhapsodies about our wonderful victory, the visiting teacher and coach (a passionate little Welshman) raged about the appalling refereeing and I was left wondering how I could reconcile the passage of time with my wristwatch. That was the last time I actually refereed an important school match at Sevenoaks. I agreed with John Parks that impartial refereeing was essential if peace was to be maintained on the playing fields of Kent. We paid the Society of Referees thenceforward for their services.

Leisure was made more sociable by the arrival of Duncan Townson at the start of my second year. He was two years younger than me, a History graduate of Cambridge who hailed from Keighley, not so very far from Otley, though we never actually visited each other's home during holidays, which is indicative of some kind of reserve between us. Appointed as House Tutor of Park Grange, a rambling dwelling which was the Junior boarding House at the School (boys

APPRENTICESHIP

aged 11 –13), Duncan was provided with living quarters in converted stables that adjoined the Grange, a neat little retreat from the fray. He had been teaching at a Prep school up north for his first job, possibly gingerly dipping a toe in educational waters, and was now transferring to the main stream. We were never bosom pals, but shared plenty of interests. A good all-round cricketer (did he get a Blue?) he coached the school cricket team, and played occasionally for Sevenoaks Vine, one of the oldest cricket clubs in England. The school playing fields were pleasantly situated and during the summer visiting teams came to play. One Saturday afternoon, Duncan sent me a message that one of the visiting team (from London), was asking for me. Who should it be but Brian Barton, instantly recognizable with his round-rimmed glasses, wide grin and pallid complexion. I had not seen him since leaving Leeds six years previously, and now, having 'become' a Wrangler at Cambridge, he was an actuary working for Hugh Gaitskell at the Treasury. No doubt he is a senior Civil Servant (retired) now but on this summer afternoon he was preparing to don a white coat and hat in order to umpire for his team. How did he know I was at Sevenoaks? We chatted but I found no spark igniting our relationship; we both had 'moved on' since those wartime school days. He got on with his umpiring and then returned to London. I went back to my little room in School House.

Duncan and I obviously shared interests, though temperamentally contrasted. He could be critical, sarcastic and methodical whereas I was probably more creative, spontaneous and confused, but we were both transferring from the West Riding moorlands to the pastoral meadows of the south with somewhat scratchy patinas of sophistication. One interest he had nurtured during his Prep School sojourn was Opera and thanks to him I went up to the South Bank's Festival Hall to hear Fischer-Dieskau sing Schubert's Winterreise, and to Covent Garden where Maria Callas performed "Norma". We saw "Siegfried" and "Lucia di Lammermoor", cramped in the gods rather too uncomfortably but these were new experiences for me, for I recall only one opera ("The Bartered Bride") seen in wartime Leeds, none at Oxford, and Handel's "Messiah", which was the nearest approximation to 'opera', attended in church Easter performances with my father for about three years in an effort to create a 'family custom'. I once took the score and libretto in a vain effort to follow the music from the page, but my interest in oratorio (and musical notation) foundered away from 'home'. I preferred the theatre and the spoken word, though there was little evidence of my enthusiasm in Otley. I remember "A Streetcar named Desire", performed at Ilkley's Victorian theatre by a maverick touring company headed by a very young Brian Rix, long before he hit gold with the Whitehall farces, and there were fewer than ten in the audience. The poor performers seemed to be taking solace in off-stage tipples. Tennessee Williams was a bit advanced for Wharfedale but I was surprised by the standard of a likeable production of "The

IRONS IN THE FIRE

Barretts of Wimpole Street" performed by Otley Dramatic Society in the Mechanics Institute. Really my admiration was reserved for those open-air performances in Oxford colleges and the idea of actually producing plays hardly dawned on me during these apprentice years.

The teacher who enticed me back stage was Carol Forder, who was producing the school play for that year, "Clive of India". He taught Geography but his heart was in the theatre. When Jimmy H-W had withdrawn from producing the 'school play', Carol took over, obviously the man for the job. Why, he had played Horatio to a schoolboy Hamlet who was now a star in the West End (though I can't recall exactly whom), and Diana, his supportive wife, had been a dancing trouper courted by Carol as a stage door Johnny. They were a friendly couple and wanted to share their thespian enthusiasm.

The trouble was choosing the right play and "Clive of India" was a rather stolid historical drama which required elaborate scene changes, military uniforms, wigs, exotic costumes and 'native' make-up applied by a typically gay dresser specially hired from Nathan's. I was somewhere back stage but remember very little, apart from the excitement of being in the shadows. The next year's play, "The Inspector-General" by Gogol, was possibly a better choice but the caricature performances were not very convincing. I was in the audience and not back-stage for that one. Then Carol Forder chose "Cry the Beloved Country", a stage adaptation of Alan Paton's novel, full of inflated language, with more 'native' greasepaint and lamentations about apartheid, a worthy subject but heavy going for schoolboys. The fourth play was perhaps an antidote to all this solemn stuff, being derived from a TV play set in a Mexican village and concerned with an American entrepreneur exploiting a peasant potter, but I forget its title. For this feckless play I designed and helped build the set. Carol then enthused about another play he had seen on TV, "The Salt Land" by a new playwright called Peter Shaffer, who came down to Sevenoaks to meet Carol at his home. I was invited to attend. Young Mr. Shaffer, struggling artist at this stage, stood with one arm on the mantelpiece holding forth about the founding of the state of Israel. He was obviously famished and ate all the peanuts and crisps. Was he expecting a meal? I came back to see Carol's production (for this was autumn 1956, the year I moved to Eastbourne). All I remember is bunches of characters in overcoats mournfully waiting on board ship to land in Israel, the Zionist State newly sliced out of Palestine. It was gloomy stuff and not a success. I don't think Shaffer came down from London to see it; he was probably tied up with "Five Finger Exercise" in the West End. I was told later that some parents had protested about the unsuitable plays their children had to perform (and they had to watch) but I don't know anything about Carol's later productions. New plays were bursting into the limelight (spotlights?) and his desire to perform 'new' plays in school was probably spurred on by so much

APPRENTICESHIP

exciting contemporary drama, like "Look back in Anger", "Waiting for Godot", "A Man for all Seasons" and Brecht's 'epic' ensemble plays. I wasn't exactly stirred to emulate him as a 'director', nevertheless his enthusiasm was catching. And I was seeing these new plays in the West End.

Definitely what was to make a valuable contribution to my knowledge of theatre and drama was studying for the L.G.S.M. (Speech and Drama), under the tutelage of John Hodgson, Professor at the Guildhall, who lived in Sevenoaks. This was during my final year before the move to Eastbourne and mainly due to my new wife Vera, who persuaded me to sign up. The course involved all aspects of drama and the theatre, including stage skills like lighting and costumes and design, but there were also the practical techniques of speaking and performance. Regular voice production exercises helped to improve my classroom teaching. My year studying 'education' at Oxford would have benefited from those kinds of discipline. So after about twelve months of private tuition with John Hodgson, I trained for Grade 7 (or 8?) and then sat the final exams at the Guildhall. I was gratified to get high marks in the written papers and scraped through on practical speech skills, but I had absorbed enough 'speech and drama' to give me greater confidence. My first foray into artistic entertainment was organizing a Poetry programme with a junior class in the school hall, choral speaking a selection of poems to an appreciative lunchtime audience. I got my first laugh with one boy speaking his lines like a Sergeant-Major (in "Naming of Parts").

For three years the world revolved round my little study room at the top of School House under the aegis of Jimmy Higgs-Walker and Molly. I think we got on quite well, tolerant of our different political leanings and running a fairly serene establishment. Meanwhile I was teaching English in the classroom and starting some after-school societies, though I have no clear memory of any content. I became adept at rolling off countless A4 sheets (and magazine pages) on the school's Roneo printer, (and sometimes exquisite calligraphic exam papers cut with a stylus). Nostalgically, I recall stained fingers and the smell of the ink – ah, Roneo, Roneo, a rose smells no sweeter. The photocopier banished such mechanical travails later on (versatile but more expensive) but there were still many more years of revolving the drum.

The time approaches when two separate events at Sevenoaks shaped my immediate future. The first of these was the retirement of H-W and the appointment of L.C. Taylor as headmaster. And the second was meeting Vera and marrying her. However, before dealing with these earth-heaving experiences, I need to give some attention to my private and personal life. I wrote the following somewhat whimsical poem one warm summer's evening when I sat in my little room dreamily gazing out of the window and watching the flight of pipistrelling birds (house-martins, if not swifts) that crisscrossed the space between the roof tops.

IRONS IN THE FIRE

Midsummer Eve

The demon swift weaves complex threads
Between the chimney tops.
He screams and loops above our heads
And as the deep magenta spreads
Into the eaves he flops.

Midsummer eve, and all goes well;
The first star winks above.
The church tower sounds a cheerful bell
As curtains meet; ah, who's to tell
I wait alone for love

I admit the school House routine demanded a fairly celibate life-style but actually there was help at hand in the shape of Matrons, who had important roles to play in providing tea and sympathy for the pupils. Mostly they were mother-substitutes as well as medical advisers, laundry-collectors and bed-makers; but also confidantes for House Tutors in need of comfort, verbal or otherwise. Certainly this had been the experience of the previous tenant of the little room upstairs, Tom Mason. He had been incarcerated by the Japanese in Malaya during the war; at Sevenoaks he found solace and love with Beryl, the Senior Matron of two in School House. Carrying on the courtship must have been difficult during term-time and so Tom had opted to 'live out' in preparation for their marriage while Beryl stayed on as Matron. After that event, Denise got the top job and another Matron was appointed. Denise was good with the boys, more sisterly than maternal, being young, and she always welcomed me when I dropped in at the Surgery for a chat. I think it was forbidden, or at least inadvisable, to entertain a Matron in my room but she would have declined anyway, being decorous and religious (strictly Adventist, I think). I was not seriously enamoured, though she was a strapping lass, and it wasn't until the last evening of my second summer term that I realised she was wanting a little more than a chat. Throwing off inhibitions, we ended up in my bed while the boys slumbered in their dormitories. I feel no guilt about this brief encounter but I'm afraid she was remorseful in the morning and inaccessible. I left for the holidays and when back at school in September found she had gone to a boarding school in Essex; a new but rather middle-aged Matron was installed. I have no idea what happened to Lesley, but I hope our passionate moment helped to release the repression and tension from which she undoubtedly suffered. And of course, me too.

APPRENTICESHIP

It was not like that with Valerie, the other Matron in my life, who at that moment in time was appointed to be the Nurse/Matron for the juniors in Park Grange and very good she was at the job. Pleasantly extrovert, she enjoyed the company of bachelors and it wasn't long before she was proving a lively and stimulating companion first of all to both Duncan and myself and then me in particular. I celebrate Valerie as the most naturally sensual woman it has been my experience to respond to. Duncan, being the House Tutor for Park Grange, was perhaps understandably sensitive about her propensity to tease him for being pompous or over-critical and he was a little peeved that I took to her like a tomcat to a bowl of cream. She was firmly robust, dark with a fine brown skin, roguish eyes (how else do I describe her provocative side-glances?) and a warm, comfortable laugh. She was neatly compact though not all that tall, which turned out to be the rub, for although I was under her spell I always sensed that the difference in our heights would deter me from any long-term commitment. Valerie had no inhibitions about her sexuality or indeed about our mutual sensuality; ours was a spontaneous enjoyment of physical love that still stopped short of full penetrative sex. I wonder about that restriction; though it would have been a precautionary measure, I clearly was not ready for condom activity (I had yet to enter a chemist's shop and buy condoms!) but then neither was she.

Our lovemaking was of course carried on discreetly within the confines of school life. We occasionally borrowed Duncan's pad in the old stables but it would not have been sensible to invite her to my quarters. One summer night I crept into Park Grange after everyone had gone to sleep. Removing my shoes, I padded through the dark and silent hall, up the creaking stairs and past the dormitories until I reached Valerie's bedroom. No one was disturbed fortunately, for the repercussions of exposure could have been dire. I felt, surely, not unlike Porphyro creeping through the castle to Madeleine's boudoir on St Agnes' Eve or indeed the poet himself risking scandal in a Hastings boarding house by stealing furtively through the dark to Mrs. Jones's bedroom, an episode which inspired Keats's telling of his evocative poem. Although I was capable of sharing such delicious terror, I certainly am unable to emulate the descriptive power of Keats. And of course, a few hours later, I had to creep out into the night and return to my own single bed. I remember deciding that, however pleasurable, such a madcap outing should not be repeated – if only for Valerie's sake.

By this time I had passed my driving test (at the second attempt) in Sevenoaks and was running a Ford Anglia, which increased the scope of our gallivanting considerably. The chance to take a fairly guileless excursion away from the school occurred when everyone got a holiday for the Coronation of Queen Elizabeth the Second on June 2nd 1953. Having left the school separately, Valerie and I linked up somewhere and celebrated the Coronation at a hotel in Henley-on-Thames. I don't know why we went so far but it was very quiet and

IRONS IN THE FIRE

restful. On returning to school, I met Carol Forder who recounted how he and his wife had wept with the cheering crowds in Westminster as the new Queen passed by in her coach. I couldn't tell him about my own holiday. And then came a further opportunity for our lovemaking when the summer holidays arrived.

That summer remains hazy in my memory. I must have been in contact with brother Neil who had started a graduate trainee scheme with Dolcis and Delta, the up-market shoe company. He had a B.A. (Hons 2 i like me) from Leeds University and had decided to enter the business world, though he toyed with the alternative of teaching. If all had gone well (or badly, who knows?), he may eventually have become a tycoon but unfortunately Dolcis were to take a header in the City later on and ruthlessly discarded all their graduate trainees. However, this was the summer when Neil and I decided to tour Les Chateaux de la Loire. We travelled in my Anglia and camped en route, taking a tiny tent that had survived much childhood maltreatment. It was a stimulating and enjoyable trip which reunited the two brothers after quite a long gap, and involved inspecting at least one chateau per day, as we followed the Loire downstream, including Blois, Chenonceaux, Chinon, Tours and Saumur with the Green Michelin Guide in hand. We camped, cooking on a paraffin stove and zipping ourselves in sleeping bags at the end of each day.

Then I think Neil had to return ahead of me because of business. Perhaps I took him to the ferry but the detail is forgotten. The crucial point is that I was alone for one night before making the final crossing. As I was camping, I asked a farmer if I could pitch my tent near his barn and, permission granted, proceeded to sleep reasonably well. In the morning I tried to show entente cordiale by helping to fork hay or straw in the farmyard before departing. I can remember a back muscle suddenly twanging but, not wishing to appear wimpish, I continued to heave the hay despite the pain until the task was finished. Au revoir et merçi and all that, I just about crawled into my driver's seat, waved goodbye with a rictus and headed for Calais harbour, aware that my back was stiffening and the ache increasing. I survived a calm crossing and then started to drive from Dover towards Sevenoaks, with my spine twisting as the lumbar vertebrae seized up. I should not have been driving, of course, not so much for the pain as for the danger to other motorists. Where was I going, for it was a long way from 'home' in Otley. In my condition I could think only of one destination – the house of Ronnie and Eva Wheeker in Sevenoaks.

It so happened that the Wheeker family was abroad in Bavaria for most of August, having arranged to leave the baby in the loving arms of Valerie who was pleased to have the run of their house. In my desperation I could think of no other haven. Answering the doorbell, Valerie was greeted by a poor corkscrewed man on the point of collapse and what else could she do than take him in, put him to

APPRENTICESHIP

bed and send for the doctor? Who came, prescribed rest as the best cure for the back ailment and then left Valerie to get a prescription or two. Well, all I can say is that it's amazing how quickly a set of pulled muscles can recover and it's fascinating how much lovemaking can occur when you are lying on your back. Valerie found the baby very cooperative during those four or five days. The Wheekers could hardly believe that I hadn't planned this visit to their home but they accepted Valerie's account of events.

I suppose my relationship with Valerie might be considered irresponsible and selfish. Inevitably she was to be disappointed when the crunch came. She wanted me to visit her parents and I declined because I could see what that implied. In the end I had to say that I was not interested in living with her, though there were probably other forces impacting on me at this time, particularly the retirement of Jimmy and Molly H.W and the coming of the new Headmaster, L.C. Taylor. Being School House Tutor, I would be personally involved in the changeover without of course any consultation and I did not feel entirely secure. With Jimmy and Molly, I had established an affectionate respect and familiarity but I was wary of the attitude of the new broom, who was inclined to find fault in the old and to favour the new. In the event, the clean sweep was highly effective and within a few years the School was to achieve remarkable success. L.C. Taylor had actually been a pupil at the School, a Cambridge first in History and a Boxing Blue (heavyweight?). And his wife was New England American. Impeccable credentials. He was also a man with a vision of international standards being applied to this rather complacent little school with one foot in the state system. How it came about I do not know but suddenly the Governors were able to provide access to private savings and funds, encouraging LCT to initiate his ambitious schemes. One of his early demands was the provision of a Headmaster's residence separate from the central School House and I imagine this was provisional to his accepting the post. His wife, who was beginning a family, was not at all taken by the old property and really LCT was not interested in the dual role of Head and Housemaster. Who can blame him? Another early decision was the appointment of a new Head of English, over the heads of both myself and John Parks. The newcomer was Geoffrey Hoare, a Cambridge Leavisite, with all that implies, but by this time I had made two momentous decisions. First, I was marrying; second, I would start applying for posts as Head of English Department in other schools. LCT , it seemed to me at the time, was casually remaindering me. I was actually a little in awe of him and over-sensitive about my status. I remember being offended when he told me that, quite sensibly, he had asked for an Examiner's Report on the standard of the English teaching of our Sixth formers at 'A' level. What annoyed me was the way he seemed surprised that the Report was actually complimentary about my teaching, as if this was not what he expected. On the other hand, I will freely admit that I had not applied my mind to the organization of the English curriculum and I was now being alerted to the need to consider its essentials. I even went so far as to buy "The Teaching of English", a book issued by my Union (the Association of Assistant Masters) and found the verbiage hard-going (and also a little out of date within a year or two).

My announcement to LCT and his wife that I was marrying next Easter (1955) and moving out of School House momentarily disconcerted them but they soon found a member of staff willing to take over. I was sorry to lose contact with many School House students who had shared the three and a half years with me but I was ready for a change in status. Perhaps I was also conscious that my dalliance with Valerie had left me rather exposed. By this time, Valerie had moved on.

read this. Sat 15 April 2006. Easton

4. Meeting Vera McKechnie

It was as a result of a school trip to the Lake District that I met Vera McKechnie who became my wife. This could not have been the occasion when I clung to the side of Great Gable nursing a dislocated shoulder, for I had travelled by school Minibus then. This time I took my Anglia, expecting to stay in the north after the Outing. My intention was to visit Desmond Prince who lived at West Kirby, in the Wirral, Cheshire. Since the debacle of Finals at Oxford, Desmond had become an assistant chef in both hospital and hotel kitchens but I had had few opportunities to meet him. This was the first time for perhaps two years. I don't think he was yet married (though his life's partner would be June Harper, a local girl) and he was living in a flat in West Kirby. When I called more or less unexpectedly, there was another visitor who had dropped in for a coffee. This was Vera McKechnie, a long-standing pal and one of the young 'gang' that tended to socialise in the area. She was a little different from the usual small town girlfriend because her parents ran the "Ring o' Bells" public house and she was on 'the stage'. I knew Vera by reputation while at Oxford, for Desmond had invited her to the college ball and at the last moment she had let him down, apparently forbidden by her parents to travel. What kind of a girl would do that? I asked

And here she was, sitting on Des's sofa, very smart and attractive, smiling and laughing, with her confident voice and manner. She was paying Des a flying visit, it seemed, and she mentioned that next day she was due in Leeds to take part in a Home Service broadcast at the BBC Radio Station. What a coincidence! I was driving over the Pennines to Leeds myself and she could accompany me. Well, if it would cause no inconvenience. Of course not! Hastily my visit to Des's was curtailed in favour of the new arrangement. I was already feeling the strength of her personality, and the journey to Leeds confirmed that I was

APPRENTICESHIP

definitely attracted to her. At one moment I remember being mesmerised by her profile beside me and I narrowly missed bouncing off a car heading in the other direction. On the way I learned that she had been in northern rep doing seasons, from Oldham to Cleethorpes, and also played lead ingénue roles at the Pitlochry Festival Theatre. She had gained an amateur reputation in the Wirral (starring as Alice) and had started Radio work as an outcome of early Elocution lessons and friendship with Christabel Burniston, the E.S.B guru. She had dropped out of a Leicester University Domestic Science course after a year and decided to take the plunge as a professional actress.

I had never met anyone quite like Vera McKechnie. She combined an adventurous character with a charming sophistication and a lively youthful enthusiasm and a vulnerability about her self-esteem. Those four assessments of personality were to be overlaid by more critical evaluations later on, and no doubt I shall have to come to them eventually, but way back in 1954 I was more or less smitten. I had already decided that we should meet again, for I would be in Sevenoaks and she was heading for London, having decided to take the plunge for the second time into a flood of auditions via theatrical agencies in Town. So we would meet perhaps once a week, eating, going to exhibitions, seeing plays though the great renaissance of British drama was yet to come. During the day Vera would be visiting agents, auditioning for repertory tours, competing with a bevy of young pop-starlets all dressed in the polka-dot style in the wake of the Festival of Britain, or maybe it was the tight-fitting roll-on and full skirt of Dior's New Look. Playing bit-parts in B class films was not very rewarding but there was the new phenomenon of closed-circuit television in the offing. Vera showed a certain talent for the full facial appearance before the camera and a mellifluous voice to go with it. By the time we were engaged to be married she was contracted for CCTV presentation announcing at an Ideal Home Exhibition in Manchester.

I can't remember when and where I proposed to her. The marriage was fixed for April 2nd 1955, which gave us about four months to plan ahead. At the end of the autumn term, I headed for Manchester in my little Anglia, aiming to meet Vera at the BBC Radio Station where she was taking part in a religious programme of words and music. The weather was rainy and blustery as I drove north, feeling tired from the school term. At Knutsford, driving in heavy traffic with headlights on, I smashed into the side of an articulated lorry that was negotiating a bend in the road. My car slid down the side of the lorry and hit the rear wheels. I was concussed, pierced with fragments of glass on my face and staggered about the road trying to gather my senses. The road was blocked by the collision but I was led to an adjacent small pub where I sat waiting for the ambulance, unable to think straight. The only thing that seemed to matter was being late for my date with Vera. I was told quite sharply by a helper to stop worrying, I was lucky to be alive. My Anglia was a write-off, and quickly dragged from the road, but the lorry and its driver emerged from this accident more or less unscathed. No charge of dangerous driving was made, the weather conditions being blamed, though I think I had been driving too long. At the hospital my face was cleared of glass shards and the cuts and bruises sprayed with some kind of metallic iodine, making me resemble a Boris Karloff monster when I eventually turned up at the Radio Station.

Concussion can have long-term effects but I think I survived without brain damage or loss of memory. I remember quite sharply my need to rest during the next few days and Vera's determination to continue her plan, which was to show off her fiancé to the neighbours in West Kirby. We walked round the town shaking hands with various dear old biddies and drinking cups of tea, while I floated in a daze, deprived of a rest and a chance to lie down and recover my senses.

We of course stayed at the Ring o' Bells with her mother and father, living above the public saloons and bars in comfortable quarters, though the combination of beer fumes and cigarette smoke lingered everywhere in the building. As far as pubs go, the Ring o' Bells was pretty up-market, standing in its own grounds with a crown bowling green to hand. Although the black and white timbering was not genuinely old, its appearance as an ancient mansion was convincing enough. It was a popular landmark in West Kirby. Vera's father, Bert McKechnie, was Manager of the Ring o' Bells. He had more than once turned down the chance to become Tenant Landlord, on the grounds that he couldn't take on the additional responsibilities of tending the property. It was enough for him to tot up the takings week by week and balance the books for the brewery. In the end the Ring o' Bells did for him, a lifelong smoker, both active and passive, living in the unhealthy atmosphere of the pub. Within a year of his retirement at the age of 60, Bert was dead from lung cancer.

I never warmed to Bert, and he didn't find me easy. He was a Scouser, with a strong Liverpudlian accent, and he couldn't shake off the limitations of his upbringing in the back streets (yet he had a brother who 'rose' to middle-class status in insurance). I couldn't shake off the limitations of my own (middle-class) upbringing either, so he and I found little to talk about. I don't blame him, I was fairly blinkered, as illustrated by the occasion when he asked for a present of the Guinness Book of Records and naively we bought him last year's edition. He must have found one of Vera's previous admirers much more to his taste, a TV drama director called Dennis Vance who had been a naval officer during the war, of whom I became inordinately jealous when I realised he had also been brought home to the Ring o' Bells for inspection. That friendship had petered out apparently. Bert never alluded to this of course. Vera was the apple of his

APPRENTICESHIP

eye and he was ambitious for her to become a star actress, but I suppose I would do if his daughter was so minded to attach herself to a school teacher.

Vera's mother was a definite other cup of tea. She came from a numerous Liverpudlian family, the Costellos, with strong Roman Catholic links. Some basic principles, such as long-suffering, patience, devotion, loving-kindness and loyalty, were deeply engrained in her nature. To some extent she was docile, unresisting, humble, but there was a pretty iron will at work. She never went near the taps, holding herself somewhat aloof from customers. I found her extremely pleasant, indeed lovable. She it was who initiated the speech lessons that had prepared Vera for her career; and who kept an unobtrusive but close watch on her comings and goings.

Naturally, we visited my father (and Aunt Ada) who couldn't make up his mind about my bride-to-be. Perhaps he wasn't convinced by her ability to perform effusive affability when meeting people or perhaps he wondered if she was right for me (or vice versa). On the other hand, he recognized a strong personality when he saw one, and no doubt he was aware that I was ready to take the plunge into matrimony. He gave us a warm welcome, though the house in Otley was freezing (no central heating in those days).

I was not the only Morley to be smitten in 1954. The tide was turning for Brother John. On holiday in Wales he had met Joyce who came from Billingham, near Middlesbrough. It seems they were meant for each other. They were good for each other's self-esteem. He laughed, she laughed. He was 6ft 6in, she was 5ft 10in. He was thin, she was bulky. He was 33, she was about the same. He was impetuous in his courting, she was bowled over by his approaches. They both knew this was their chance. He was willing to travel north to see her, she had a bungalow to share with him. He had a history of physical ailments and no mother, she had brought up two brothers after her mother died (and then her father, who left her the bungalow). In 1956 (Dec 1st) they were to marry in Billington and Vera and I were there; so was Dad but I can't recall who else was there from the family.

Waiting for my own nuptials during the term before Easter '55 was a worrying period, for I was getting nervous about my initiation into full sexual intercourse. A lack of self-confidence about my own cautious achievements, spurred by a somewhat imaginative assessment of Vera's experiences in a wider world, began to trouble me. Her sojourn in Soho, home of theatrical agencies, had paid off. Having auditioned successfully for a repertory company touring South West holiday resorts, there were now rehearsals and performances on tour during the weeks leading up to the end of my term; she was somewhat preoccupied and quite a long way from me. Eventually, to allay my entreaties, and worries, we decided to spend one night at the Imperial Hotel near London's King's Cross, Vera travelling from Torquay and I from Sevenoaks. This was to be our sole pre-marital sexual experience, and it proved to be fairly disastrous. In the first place, the large but seedy hotel seemed full of casually bonking couples and our room was totally devoid of romance. In the second place, all my efforts seemed to end in premature ejaculation. I gained little confidence from the one-night stand. Vera took comfort in saying, "It will be all right on the night…"

5. Wedding Bells

I personally would have been happy with a quiet wedding, with no Catholic complications of course, but I did not expect it to take place at the C. of E. Parish Church down the road from the Ring o' Bells. This was to be a social affair. I remember grumbling about the hiring of a Church Choir as well as bell-ringers, but as Bert McKechnie would be paying I had to shut up. The reception was at a large hotel on the seafront, somewhat cavernous and dark. The event made the front page of a county paper and by sheer coincidence, Carol Forder, up in the Lake District with a school party, purchased a copy glimpsed on a news stand. After the reception, which was pleasantly festive, we took the train from Liverpool and spent our first night in Shrewsbury, where next morning, on impulse, we attended an Easter Sunday Church service but I walked out of the liturgical and (to me) ritualistic ceremonial (never having attended other than Presbyterian nonconformity). Then we journeyed down to Cornwall, to stay for a week in the Lugger Inn at Portloe, a tiny fishing hamlet. The Lugger was very isolated, as befits a place specialising in honeymooners, though that meant the sparse company was withdrawn and self-conscious. Crashing my Anglia proved to be a handicap, for we had to rely on bus services to explore the area, but we got around the coves and inlets contentedly.

Vera and I made slow progress sexually, a little hindered by a nervous periodic hiccup. We moved on for the second week of our honeymoon to stay in Torquay, which is where the Rep Company was performing a short season of plays. Vera had arranged for us to occupy a small flat overlooking an attractive bay. She was now attending last minute rehearsals for Noel Coward's "Private Lives", in which she played a lead part. Astonishing though it may seem, that performance was the only occasion I have ever seen her acting on stage in a full-length play and I wasn't impressed as she seemed to be just being herself. Torquay, elegant with palm trees and cocktail bars, was pleasant enough though the season had hardly started. The weather was unusually hot but we had limited freedom to enjoy it together. I actually painted a few seascapes when I was on my own. We managed to sun-bathe during the day, though Vera had rehearsals to attend, and it was unfortunate that (a) she had to wear a tight gold lamé dress in the Coward play (b) having sunburnt her flesh, it was painful to struggle into this dress, and (c) in bed after the show she couldn't bear being touched.

APPRENTICESHIP

This touring repertory company was a disappointing replica of Priestley's Good Companions. There didn't seem much point to it. The personnel seemed simply to be going through the motions of performing without enthusiasm or inspiration, no doubt affected by poor audience responses but also by the repertory system which had them performing on a treadmill. They were also very poverty-stricken on basic Equity wages probably. For the third week, Vera was playing in a rather insipid romantic drama about the moneyed leisure-class. It was entitled "Sabrina Fair" but apart from the Miltonic allusion of the title, there was little literary merit in it. It was being performed each night during our final week. I went to see it. The stage set was elaborate but Vera's role of little importance, and I found it boring. And note, we were no longer in Torquay. For this third week of our 'honeymoon' we had travelled to Margate, at the other side of England's fair land; and we had spent all day Sunday making the journey by rail. By this time I had had enough of tagging along behind this likeable but uninspired bunch of rep actors. What was I doing there? What were they making of me? Or us, Vera and me? And what were we making of each other? The whole idea of a honeymoon is to provide a time and place where two people can be together, privately and alone. Committed as she was (by contract or inclination?) to this Rep Company, Vera had created a situation where public appearance and team activity prevented both privacy and solitude. Frustrated in every sense, I had no ambitions to become a temporary member of the Company (not that I was asked to do anything). Retrospectively, during that Easter period I consider there was little chance of our relationship being anything but superficial. And not much understanding of each other either.

Once back in Sevenoaks, we rented the first floor of Mrs. Bunce's house in the middle of town (no 8 Holmesdale Road) and settled down to a more stable domestic routine dominated by our jobs, mine as a teacher and hers as an apprentice TV announcer, a new sphere of activity based on the Metropolis. That summer we bought second-hand bikes and started taking trips into the Sussex Weald. They were not very efficient bikes, particularly when freewheeling down steep lanes (once, Vera, with brakes failing, leaped off at high speed and sprawled across the road, fortunately without too much harm) but they gave us freedom to explore. Cousin Muir and Margaret came down (from Liverpool, I guess) to stay with us, with their new baby (Richard) who quite understandably disrupted our tour of Knole House. I remember really hot summer days and we drove around the parched and crowded countryside looking for a river (or pool). I realised what was missing from Sevenoaks, an attractive historical little town but with no river running through it.

Meanwhile Vera's career was beginning to flourish. The week long involvement in Manchester's Ideal Home Exhibition (with Closed Circuit Television) had proved highly successful and she was now preparing to be

IRONS IN THE FIRE

auditioned as a Presenter or Announcer with the BBC in London. One of her exercises was to cut a hole the size of a TV screen in a newspaper and then to sit in a chair speaking through this empty space to the listener (in this instance, me). This was full frontal delivery but only exposing the face and neck (or bust?) and was supposed to help her focus on the unseen viewer (before the invention of the teleprompter). Television was rapidly transforming patterns of entertainment but there was still only one service operated by the BBC and there was a lot of pussy-footing around to refine the new medium. It seemed to be necessary to employ a pretty lady, smartly dressed at least from the bust upwards, to announce the next television programme. Male announcers got a look-in during the evening, wearing (I seem to recall) black bow ties. Presumably this paraphernalia of gracious living made the TV set and its programmes more acceptable in the sitting rooms of middle Britain. Queen of the presenters was Sylvia Peters, who tried to look like the real Queen, while Mary Malcolm looked and appeared to be highly bred. Vera was recruited in company with other pretty faces whose names escape me now (apart from Valerie Pitts, a charming lass who got what she deserved, a happy marriage to (Sir) George Solti).

My own attitude to Vera's ambitions was of course encouraging, though I had no interest in the new medium itself and at times felt that Vera was far more absorbed in the glamour and excitement of television than she was in her husband, who was still hoping for more sexual stimulation. Perhaps the acme of absurdity occurred when the BBC managers chose to parade their Afternoon Hostesses on the little screen, each of them performing whatever personal talent they possessed. Some tried to show off their skills as actress, dancer, singer or comedienne, which really came over as very amateur. Vera, sensibly, opted for a dignified narration of a short story, which I wrote for the occasion, a Christmas ghost story no less, and this paid off, for suddenly the Hostesses were axed and disappeared from the screen but Vera was recruited for Children's television programmes. By the time she and I were moving from Sevenoaks, her name was becoming fairly well known. Apart from the TV appearances, she also was one of the presenters at the prestigious White City Ideal Home Exhibition where she coped with CCTV like a veteran. On the day I attended she was scheduled to interview Peter Sellers and Spike Milligan, very easy actually as these two Goons clowned on a stage in front of the crowd while Vera let them get on with it. It was interesting to compare them – Spike Milligan expending energy strenuously, Peter Sellers simply biding his time to make a laugh. It was not a great hit but these were Radio personalities in the flesh – wow! Vera had the ability to sparkle for the camera and provide a mellifluous voice for speech either recorded or improvised. She was succeeding and thoroughly enjoying herself, which was okay by me as I was absorbed in the classroom. On one of the rare occasions I bothered to visit Broadcasting House, Vera introduced a young Australian

APPRENTICESHIP

making his debut, Rolf Harris, an attractive, confident children's entertainer just over from down-under. He seemed modest and unassuming and very hopeful of his talent being successful in London.

It became clear that now was the time to leave my first teaching job and apply for a more responsible position. I can't remember which pundit said it, but the recommendation was that one moved on after three years in one's first job. I was now doing my fifth year at Sevenoaks and, although well established within the school, I felt ready to take on a Head of English posting. I was very vague about where to go next. I went for an interview to Dulwich College, a large day school of eminence but I was not enthusiastic about the job, as Assistant English Teacher. The Head of English interrogated me at one stage, seeking evidence of my advocacy of F.R. Leavis' stern control of literary tradition. Cambridge graduates suddenly seemed in the ascendant, as in the 'new' Sevenoaks and also at King's College, Wimbledon, where I rented accommodation while Vera was 'performing' in London. I had to endure a diatribe on the evils of English at Oxford from a fanatical and puritanical Leavisite who occupied the rooms next to mine. My rather mild defence that there was room for a wider appreciation of literature than Leavis' great censorship was greeted with snorts of derision.

Anyway, when I went for my next interview there were no such cross-examinations. In fact I felt much more at ease – Eastbourne Grammar School was about the same size as Sevenoaks School, situated in the house and grounds of an Edwardian estate and the staff was pleasantly welcoming. There were six candidates being interviewed. At one point I was asked why I wanted to come to this School and I stated the opinion that the public schools were becoming redundant or obsolescent in modern times, which was not far from my idealistic conviction. There was an amused rustle amid the panel of interviewers, but my simple, artless response probably worked in my favour. The Chairman ({Sir}Sidney Caffyn) offered me the job, Head of English, which I accepted without much reflection. I hardly understood the nature of the State Educational system that I was joining. I knew nothing about the town, having never visited it. I went down to the seafront and stared at the pier and sea on a rather chilly day, wondering if this was the right move. Living in a seaside resort would be a new experience but at least Vera would have direct access to London via Victoria, one and a half hours on the train. As for myself, I was aware that I could choose my own destiny, whether to travel along this path through the wood or try another unknown path. Would all paths lead to the same conclusion? No use beating about the bush – onward!

CHAPTER FIVE

MATURITY IN EASTBOURNE

1. Moving to Eastbourne

All things are relative, saith the preacher, and the title of this chapter is chosen circumspectly. Needless to say, I never regretted the decision to join the state system. One old codger of a colleague told me, "Eastbourne is the graveyard of ambition". Ambition is an ambivalent word, depending on what you aim at. I don't think the urge to 'get on' ever worried me very much and I persevered in school teaching in Eastbourne from 1956 to 1988. And I am still here (2005 at the time of writing this). Some other teaser asks: "Would you rather be a big fish in a little pond or a little fish in a big pond?" My answer has always been the former, not because I wish to emulate a village Hampden, a mute inglorious Milton or a guiltless Cromwell keeping the noiseless tenor of their ways, but because I would get lost in mid-ocean. Furthermore, two personal factors intrude; firstly, the slow deterioration in the state of my marriage, and secondly, the fact that changes in the educational system provided me with fresh challenges without having to move on.

Founded extraordinarily circa 1415, Sevenoaks School was a direct grant grammar school that retained some independence from the local LEA whilst providing a percentage of 'free places' for local boys who passed the 11+ exam. The situation was changing at the time I was leaving to live in Eastbourne. Sevenoaks School, in line with a number of old educational establishments, opted out of the State Education system with extraordinary success, for which no doubt my old friend Duncan Townson could account, as he continued to teach there. In Eastbourne, which was considered a safe Tory stronghold at Westminster, there was a securely established independent ('public') boarding school, founded in late Victorian times that effectively catered for local day boys who for one reason or another did not attend one of the State schools. Relations between teachers at Eastbourne College and the Grammar School varied between indifference and cordiality but there was always a measure of comparative rivalry. It was even on television. There were comic and satiric situations running through the various plots created for "Dad's Army", which is immortally set in wartime coastal locations around Eastbourne. Captain Mainwaring is a product of the local Grammar School while Sergeant le Mesurier went to the local public school, and from this dichotomy a cornucopia of social and personal observations is created for our enjoyment. Perhaps laughing at it helps us to remain resigned to what is a serious national problem in education, the anomaly of private versus state education.

IRONS IN THE FIRE

Eastbourne's County Borough Council at this time (with its own Education Department) was applying the current national policy of a tripartite division of pupils into single-sex Grammar and High School, Technical School and Modern (Neighbourhood) Schools – Cavendish, Ratton, Bishop Bell (Langney) and Hampden Park. When I arrived in town, the Technical College had recently closed down and the Grammar School had a wood and metal technical department in lieu. I was aware of resentment between the "chosen few" at the Grammar (and High) Schools and the non-selected "modern" state schools, both teachers and pupils, which is not surprising as the 20% selected for the Grammar and the High Schools were receiving much more financial support than the others. Until the "comprehensivisation" of State Secondary schooling, there was annual 11+ neurosis in the town. This is another controversial subject and clearly many talented children, who otherwise would not have had the opportunity, were helped to achieve a good educational grounding, including my own. On the other hand, there were even more children who were denied or felt deprived. Of course, the demise of the Grammar-High schools in Eastbourne is regrettable when one thinks of the good work being achieved by those teachers and pupils who were benefiting from the system, but I believe the rejection of the 11+ system and the consequent re-organization of Eastbourne Schools has been a good thing for the majority. If I stop trying to be altruistic, I also know that I myself have benefited. The transformation of the Grammar School into a Sixth Form College in 1978 gave me ten years of not only specialisation with older students but also co-education, both of which I very much appreciated.

From 1956 onwards, until 1988 when, at the age of 62, I retired, I contributed to the rise and fall (or more accurately, the abolition) of the Grammar School and the changing fortunes of the Sixth Form College in Eastbourne, with special attention to English and Drama in all their prolific glory. Apart from my role as a teacher, I was also married and setting up a home, the father of three children, and a dilettante in various performing arts and fine art in the widening circle of Sussex contacts. Faced with the self-imposed task of commenting on 'my life and hard times', I retreat from any attempt to provide a comprehensive survey of these thirty-two years. I can offer random raids on my memory, with moderate concern for chronology and factual accuracy. Maybe I can extract the kind of material that throws light on a search for an understanding of myself – and an assessment of my limited achievements. With this in mind a loose structure will be evident as I plunder the past, sometimes concentrating on public life and sometimes on personal and private matters.

MATURITY IN EASTBOURNE

2. Settling in

In Sevenoaks I had taken hardly any interest in the people living in the community, the local inhabitants who were going about their own particular business, the neighbourhood where people had their homes. I suppose I was too wrapped up in school affairs, especially the three and a half years within School House. When I moved to Eastbourne I became conscious of belonging to the town as one cog in a communal organisation. My teaching, and the school in which I taught, was part of the social fabric covering not only the borough of Eastbourne but also East Sussex. As a married couple my wife and I were meeting many more people in all walks of life.

Eastbourne, noted for elegance, pensioners and a retiring disposition, hit the headlines shortly after I moved into town in 1956. Dr. Bodkin Adams was accused of murdering elderly patients after persuading them to change their wills in his favour. Suddenly Eastbourne was news and the media descended like so many vultures on the town; the trial at the Old Bailey became sensational when, after a series of accusations exposing the doctor, two key witnesses (night nurses) were overheard concocting evidence on the train journey from Eastbourne to Victoria. For one reason or another, Dr. Bodkin Adams (what a name!) was acquitted, though his reputation never recovered and he retired after a few years.

The town sank back into its semi-recumbent posture, cushioned by the Beachy Head promontory and conforming to the usual West-End/ East-End alignment of the south coast towns. Eastbourne, however, had the advantage of land-owner Dukes who could be persuaded to develop parts of the town according to an urban plan and who had the power to control development on the seafront. There have been many changes since 1956, with a huge in-flux of retired people happy to occupy the boxes within the bigger boxes. I am now a long-term resident (near fifty years), having lived in three attractive areas of the town: the Meads sea front, Hampden Park near the Park, and Old Town. The growth in population (92,000+) has been accompanied by distinct improvements though not all the decisions taken by the Planning Department of the Borough contemporaneously have been beneficial to the town. I instance the brutal demolition of the old properties and roadways of Old Town around the Star Brewery in the '60s, and the demolition of part of the town centre in order to make way for an Arndale Centre in the '70s, and the casual decay of buildings in the commercial Seaside area and the neglect of sites like the old Devonshire Baths in the '80s. There was of course Southcliff Tower, subject of a political scandal in the late '60s, and, looking to the future, I hope the scheme to sell the Towner estate to commercial interests and create a new Cultural Centre beside Devonshire Park will not prove equally misguided. But there are positive improvements in Borough Council initiatives arising from a Ten Year Borough

IRONS IN THE FIRE

Plan (though the central park within the circuit linear town has yet to materialise) and the Sea Front Plan in pursuit of coastal defences against erosion has provided some really smart and elegant designs. And the 'new town' rapidly mushrooming at the Marina is an astonishing success, probably.

In the late '50s it was the Towner Art Gallery, with William Gear appointed as Curator, that first enlarged my cultural horizons in Eastbourne. It was inspiring to react to the exciting exhibitions of Abstract Impressionism on show. I responded also to the 'local' artist, Harold Mockford, and not only bought one of his paintings but started mixing my oils with dental powder like him. Cousin Jim, dentist, sent me a jar gratis. I was privileged to become a lay-member of the Art Group – maybe I qualified as a professional when my painting "Skylark and Crows" was bought at the annual exhibition (a snip at £7.00). The art-loving set that gathered for activities at the Towner (nothing like the current patronage of the Friends of the Towner) and elsewhere consisted mainly of lively middle-class professional and public-spirited couples who were particularly interested in the visual arts. They tended to mix parties with cultural activities, though financially we were hardly on a par with most of them. A roll call of names tests my memory. There were the Hoyers, the Harrises, the Watkins, the Chatfields, the Flints, the Taveners, the Joneses, the Quigleys, the Gears, the Riddicks, even June Broadhurst and others in the town. There were plenty of parties in those days and, as far as I recall, no hint of soft or hard drugs. The connection with the 'art-loving' set remained steady, though eventually Gear and Abstract Impressionism moved on.

As I developed more interest and experience in drama productions in and out of school during this period, there was a logical consequence to the social and cultural activity. In 1965, nine years after our arrival in Eastbourne, I was invited to direct an ambitious original production at the newly opened Congress Theatre. This was no less than an inter-schools production of "Noyes Fludde", the opera for children by Benjamin Britten that had recently been performed at the Aldeburgh Festival in Suffolk. Paul Harris (who had seen my school shows) and John Chatfield (musical director) were the brains behind this venture. Of course I accepted the task and set about my double function – raising the cast (there were more than 250 children from 21 schools and colleges involved) and directing the production of this amazing opera (with professional leads Owen Brannigan and Sheila Fell, the original Mr. and Mrs. Noah at Aldeburgh). Despite my inexperience, I was able to assemble a talented production team that was drawn from local circles. A fortunate 'find' was Marguerite Causley, who choreographed the movement and dance. She eventually became a TM guru but at this stage was teaching dance at a girls' school. "Noyes Fludde" at the Congress was a great success both artistically and financially.

MATURITY IN EASTBOURNE

Looking back after all these years, "Noyes Fludde" must be the most prestigious production I have been involved in. It came at a time when Eastbourne was trying to establish its reputation as a leading 'conference town' and this community-based 'thing of beauty' in the new theatre was something to be proud of. For the tyro-director, it was a new experience to be part of, and to be creating, a huge affiliation of creative spirits. The building of the Ark was the crucial moment in the design – with various sections sliding and 'flying' into place to amalgamate Robert Tavener's colourful Ark. Then came the great build-up of animals two-by-two, all of them in fanciful costumes designed by Mary Quigley, until the Ark was ready to sail. And the storm followed, a spectacular visual accompaniment to Britten's music, finally to be resolved in the symbolism of the rainbow. "Noyes Fludde" had been created for performance in churches but we were able to transfer it reverently into a theatrical experience.

Two years later the Headmaster of Eastbourne College, Michael Birley, asked me to do another dramatic presentation at the Congress Theatre as part of the centenary celebrations of the school. Flattered, I met John Walker, the Head of Music at the College, and invited Marguerite Causley (now at Chelsea College) to join us. We agreed to present Bernstein's "West Side Story" with a cast selected from Eastbourne's schools and town societies. This was even more ambitious than "Noyes Fludde" and we rehearsed for over a year, which was too long really and put a strain on me, with other responsibilities at the Grammar School. I think it was Marguerite's dance leadership that ensured that the show was a huge success, not financially (for the College) but certainly artistically (for the town).

I was in danger of losing my foothold with my head in the air. I suggested to the Education Director (and Sir Sidney Caffyn who sat in) that our Education Authority should sponsor a dramatic production of similar dimensions at the Congress, just to show that the state education system could match the private schools. I was disappointed that my proposal bit the dust, which indicates how far I was out of touch with reality. In fact I had been tempted to switch my role in teaching a little earlier on. I went up to Bretton Hall, Wakefield on interview for the post of Head of Drama at this teachers' training college. When I arrived and realised I was the only interviewee, I had to make a decision – if I was offered this job, was I really equipped for it? Furthermore, how would the move affect my wife and family? I withdrew my application before the interview, much to the annoyance of the Principal. Those two marvellous productions at the Congress Theatre were some kind of compensation perhaps.

IRONS IN THE FIRE

3. Seven Years in Westcliff Mansions

In 1956, after staying in digs for two or three weeks of the first term, Vera and I moved into the top flat of an Edwardian property on the seafront called Westcliff Mansions, and set up home in the rooms once occupied by maidservants who would have five flights and ninety stairs to negotiate before reaching the kitchens in the basement (and when they got back upstairs there was probably little time or energy to savour the sea views to the south and the panorama of the town to the north). For us, this was a topping flat. During the summer, after school, I would leap down the stairs and, within a minute reaching the beach, plunge into the sea. There were three bedrooms, a spacious lounge with a fine window area, and a wide hall that acted as our dining room. We installed our own choice of furniture and carpets and were happy to paint the woodwork. I don't think we lived extravagantly (rent was 4 guineas per week, I think) and no doubt guests brought bottles to occasional parties (once more than thirty attending). In the winter, we were a little exposed to the elements but paraffin stoves were all the rage at the time and as long as we trimmed the wicks and re-filled the cans regularly, conditions could be comfortable and not too smelly. With superb views on all sides, this was a comfortable home to come back to after our separate days' work. In the summer, there was always the beach.

I remained rather detached from Vera's television appearances. Obstinately without our own television set, I would regularly cycle four or five miles to a colleague's house to catch a teatime programme presented by Vera. I had little time to watch other programmes, or even the radio, though that led to an embarrassing situation. I had never paid for an annual BBC radio licence during my student days or even at Sevenoaks and I was shocked to receive a summons for neglecting the official reminders about a current licence. A prying agent called one afternoon and asked if he could look round our flat. Of course he was looking for a TV set, which we did not possess, but I was guilty over the radio licence and was fined at the court hearing, which I did not attend. A local journalist leaked the information that this offender was Vera McKechnie's husband, and that merited a front-page picture in the Daily Mirror and a slur about a TV star without a licence. Well, the scandal blew over but my casual neglect of the need for a radio licence seems to me an indication of a psychological reluctance to be responsible for Vera's TV career. Quite illogically, I was asserting that the BBC was in Vera's preserve, not mine, and this petty attitude stemmed from my brooding discontent that she was far more interested in her career than in me personally. I was on the horns of a dilemma as far as marriage to a TV celebrity was concerned. Her success in the new medium was remarkable and in no way was I discouraging or obstructive. I admired her skill and nerve in front of the camera. But the absorption in these activities

MATURITY IN EASTBOURNE

seemed to obstruct her concern for what to me seemed the incomplete emotional relationship of our home life.

This had little or nothing to do with having to play 'second fiddle' or being a camp follower, though I did not enjoy such outings. Attending school Speech Days, where Vera was giving out prizes and delivering corny speeches (I can say that because I contributed most of them); or church fetes or garden parties, or speech and drama events where she adjudicated, were tedious activities for me. I would have preferred a quiet home life but Vera seemed to revel in the acclaim, or at least to assume that she ought to be fulfilling this 'celebrity' role in society both in Eastbourne and further afield. She took these 'personal appearances' seriously, which I could not do and so opted out.

There was one odd booking made by her agent - to open a particularly grand fund-raising event organized by, of all schools, Leeds Grammar School, and of course I had to take note of this. I soon realized that this could not be considered a gratuitous event, for to Vera it was essentially a financial deal and the organisers had no idea that an Old Leodiensian was coincidentally involved. I had to play my part by accompanying the crowd-pleaser, staying overnight in a luxury suite at the Grand Hotel in Leeds, taking my place in the opening parade of notables and going round all the stalls and shops and exhibitions installed in classrooms in which fifteen years previously I had received my education. Feeling strangely detached from that former pupil, I certainly was playing a part as I paid this quaint last visit to my alter mater. We contributed a cheque extracted from Vera's fat fee in aid of this well-supported enterprise. Her presence seemed to contribute to the success. She performed brightly and circulated like royalty for a few hours, with me giving the occasion a fillip. Incidentally this was the only occasion I claimed any control over Vera's earnings. Generally, as a matter of principle, I took no interest (!) in her profits and emoluments. As long as she settled her own income tax demands she could spend her 'pocket money' how she liked, which was often to the family's benefit. Meanwhile I remained fairly sceptical about some of the side effects of being a television personality. I said very little at school, avoided local involvement in her appearances, and on the rare occasions I visited Lime-Grove studios, kept what is often called a 'low profile'. There was an intriguing moment when the newly appointed Head of TV Educational Drama productions invited me to apply for a TV drama director's post in his department, but I genuinely wasn't interested, neither in the job nor in the prospect of commuting to or living in London.

Vera of course was absolutely in her element and for perhaps five years she was appearing in BBC Children's programmes such as "Studio E", a very well directed magazine programme involving interviews and documentary presentations, and then "Watch with Mother", which made her a bit of a maternal icon associated with Andy Pandy, the Flowerpot Men and other such creations. Changes in the administration and personnel at the BBC eventually took effect, and new programmes brought in other faces and 'personalities', but while it lasted these were good times for Vera. Yet it wasn't roses all the way, and there were psychological side effects. She could rise to the self-preening challenge of assuming her persona for the camera but for every high-spirited performance there was a consequent low. She had moments of doubt about herself; her self-esteem was vulnerable, her need for encouragement constant. It is perhaps a familiar story. The most critical aspect of these five or so years, when the spotlight was being directed at her, was her inability to give equal attention to private and public life. No doubt her upbringing had been somewhat confined, and she sought regard and love in the public domain. A novel by Muriel Spark, written about this time, created a somewhat tragic portrait of a woman like Vera. The story was set in Italy but the difficulties facing anyone who has to play the role of a 'celebrity' were sharply analysed. This perceptive novel was entitled "The Private and Public Image". Even Vera could see the likeness.

At home there were two factors beginning to cause trouble for the security of a long-term marriage. One was the comparative failure of our sex life in terms of frequency and intensity. Of course intercourse took place but there was little enthusiasm for repetition. And foreplay became more like afterplay. There is not much point in apportioning blame. The fact is that our marriage lasted twenty years, by which time what started as a relatively tiny niggle about the dissatisfactions of union had grown into a fairly unbreachable blockage compounded of frustration and resentment. The breakdown was gradual, though friends could see it coming in the constant bickering between husband and wife. The other destructive factor was the discrepancy between the public 'persona' of Vera's screen image and the actual private 'personality' at home.

And what of my own responsibility for the flawed relationship? One of the problems was the lack of preparedness for the 'instant' success of Vera's career that followed our engagement and marriage. I had expected a conventional domestic partnership, or if not exactly that, then at least a concentration of two minds and hearts working in unison. I felt unable to compete with the heady glamour of Vera's rise to prominence, which took her away from me, and I began to doubt my own ability to provide the sexual fulfilment which I had imagined would be ours. This lack of confidence did not help me to withstand the more dominant leadership shown by Vera. And so, as the years went by, I allowed this deficiency in our relationship to continue, instead of seeking some kind of solution through confrontation or therapy. Which is a pity, for in many ways we were well equipped to form a constructive partnership. Nevertheless, I found it rewarding to get involved in cultural and educational activities that formed a kind of compensation. And most of all, there were three children to take our minds off personal failings.

4. Children at home

After Vera and I had lived three years in Westcliff Mansions, Simon Patrick arrived. The year was 1959 and fathers were not yet expected to participate in the labour throes, so I was quietly reading at home when the phone rang to inform me that I was a father and the baby a fine bouncing boy. Vera, fortified by Grantley Dick Reid and his 'natural birth technique', had triumphed. It was time for our two other bedrooms to become occupied – first, Simon's nursery and second, a room for the au pair girl, Françoise from France, for Vera after concentrating on maternal services for a short spell, was returning to BBC television programmes. Franny was about nineteen, not particularly experienced but trustworthy with the baby though after a year she returned home (her English still a little basic). Thanks to her contacts in the coffee bars of Eastbourne we were able to replace her with a German girl, Sabina (Beany), who was unhappy with her au pair duties as she was employed as a cleaner in a dance academy and not a child-minder. I scolded the dance lady for exploitation and, much to Beany's relief, took her into our custody. She was cheerful and always friendly. After her year with us, she kept in touch and indeed was very hospitable when we visited her (now a Frau) in Limburg twelve years later. Three years after Simon's arrival, Catherine Rose was born. Again I was not present at the birth but I remember this time it was an excited Vera who was phoning to announce a safe and smooth passage for the baby. We advertised for a 'nanny' and were very fortunate to get a response from a warm-hearted middle-aged woman called Mrs. Eggerton, who quickly became Mrs. Egg. Looking back, I marvel at the devoted care and love she gave to the two infants, over a period of perhaps three years. I have no memory of what we paid her (probably because Vera would almost certainly be doing the paying), but we certainly owed her a debt of gratitude while we lived in this eyrie of a home.

Then, after seven years in residency, we were informed by the estate agents that the owners had decided to knock it down and re-build a block of flats five times as accommodating as our Edwardian original. We were given notice to quit and, after some uncertainty about what we could afford, moved to a four-bedroomed detached house in Brassey Avenue, Hampden Park. Simon was perhaps four years old, and Kate (never Catherine) a one-year old toddler, which raises the question, who helped to look after them in the new environment? And the answer must be Vera's mother, who was now a widow. Poor Bert McKechnie, having retired from the Ring o' Bells, had succumbed to lung cancer in less than a year. Smoking, active and passive, in that pub atmosphere, had done for him. We attended the funeral in West Kirby and arranged for Rose to join us. For a time she lived with us and eventually Nanny (as she was called) moved into rented accommodation but she could always be relied upon to look after the children.

Finally, some time after we had moved into the house in Hampden Park, our third baby was born. Emma Clare was five years younger than Kate, and completed the family. One interesting statistic: all three children have birthdays during the month of February. Coincidence? Family planning? Or a kind of seasonal frugality? At least the babies got the best of summertime warmth during their first few months and all three have been blest with good health, brains and looks. In this house they had separate bedrooms for most of the time and the garden was large, with a sturdy oak, a few fruit trees, enough grass to keep me tinkering with a lawn-mower and a revolving summer house. The cul-de-sac of Brassey Avenue culminated in a Primary School, which was no more than a stone's throw from our house. Simon, Kate and Emma attended in succession and received a good education there up to the age of eleven. The shopping mall may not have been up to much but Hampden Park was just round the corner, providing lake-side walks, paths through the wood and play areas. It was an attractive place in which to grow up.

I am reluctant to recount nostalgic reminiscences of their childhood. I love my children more than anyone else in this world (except myself, on the evidence, I suppose) and my recollections of their various activities would occupy much time and many pages. As for describing their characteristics and idiosyncrasies, that would take ages. I could easily get sidetracked and somehow I have to steer my narrative to the bitter end (that's just a cliché, why should the end be bitter?). I know the three children (Simon 19, Kate 16 and Emma 11) were deeply shocked (but not traumatized) by the breakdown of the family life in 1976. Despite their awareness of and sensitivity to the empty spaces that existed between their parents, they had no foreknowledge of a total collapse of the superstructure. For the time being, I draw a dark veil over these sad, though inevitable events.

5. Teaching at the Grammar School

All this time I have been teaching at the Grammar School. Three terms each year, a repetitive pattern with infinite variations on a theme. It starts in 1956 when I was appointed by Rex Shaw, the Headmaster. He had been a science teacher at Lancaster RGS before his appointment three years previously, following a run of three new headmasters in rapid succession. The school needed a steady hand in control, which RWS provided, though it was not finely manicured. He was a square-headed, grim-mouthed man who tried not to beat

MATURITY IN EASTBOURNE

about the bush in his dealings with the boys. He didn't give them love but at least he provided a fair run up to School Certificate and he definitely enlarged the way to University entrances, particularly Cambridge (his alter mater). His manner was brusque but this was mainly due to shyness and not aggression. And in the case of Morning Assembly, when the Headmaster led the prayers as if he was giving God his orders for the day (so we used to say), his private disbelief prevented dissembling. Despite the hard front, he was not entirely confident in his handling of staff, not many of whom were appointed by him and who were unimpressed by his manner. In fact RWS, with a first-class degree in Chemistry, was not equipped to run a balanced educational establishment, in which creative sensitivity finds a place next to intellectual knowledge. Such Headmasters are hard to find (LC Taylor was one). Or perhaps it would be better to argue that RWS was chiefly interested in academic achievement and university entrants. As this meant he favoured at the most 20% of the 20% in-take of pupils selected by the 11+ exam for the Grammar School, he clearly would have been better employed as Head of a school for Mensa high-achievers. That does not mean he totally neglected the rest of the pupils, for he was always appreciative and helpful when efforts were made to introduce and develop schemes that involved them, as for example when I started my speech, drama and other activities. But it was always clear where his heart was.

The year after I joined his staff, RWS created his Alpha policy, which separated 20-25 boys from the rest of their year and caused them to be taught in one group or stream. The remaining 80% in that year were set according to their ability in particular subjects. Boys in the Alpha stream took 'O' level after four, not five, years and were expected to stay on in the Sixth Form to prepare for Advanced and University success. The idea was that the accelerated pace gave the bright boys an extra year at the top end. It did work to some extent. Successes at Cambridge, Oxford and elsewhere increased, but there were drop-outs who suffered from the process; the extra work-load caused stress to some; many would have got there anyway and the class sizes for remaining pupils were increased. Most of all, however, I think the effect of the Alpha stream policy was to create sub-divisions in the school. Marking my disapproval, I decided to concentrate on the other sets and eventually appointed a regular English teacher (Chris Mason) to stick with the Alpha stream.

RWS was plagued with dissension from some members of staff. Mainly I was on his side because obviously he was aiming to improve standards at the school and a few teachers were deliberately obstructive and selfish, behaving as if the school existed for their own comfort, for example where duties were involved. But he wasn't helped by appointing a new Deputy Head who was neither popular nor dynamic. And there were quite a few elderly teachers who wanted a quiet life before retiring. Fortunately over the next three or four years they were replaced but there were two individuals staying on who had a deep grudge against RWS. Both were fanatical 'soccer' football practitioners and RWS, when he arrived at the school, had instituted rugby football. Boys could opt for rugby as well as football, which made these two soccer types seethe with resentment. You could argue that this caused a split as large as the Alpha stream innovation, but you can't expect me to disapprove of the plan to play rugby.

The two 'mavericks' were both strong personalities with a personal interest in school sport. Although having different temperaments, they shared an arrogance and self-assertiveness in the staff room. J G was Scottish, a former Rangers footballer and now Physical Education instructor. He spent most of his teaching time in a poorly resourced gym where physically weak pupils dreaded his lessons. Perhaps it was his independent means that caused him to seem bored with physical education. He was disliked by many though most people preferred to keep on the right side of him because he could be vindictive and violent. At times he was charming and courteous, but he had quarrelled with most of the staff, including me. He took time off to suit his interests, including horseracing and football matches. On one occasion, I noticed one fifth-year boy was missing from my English class and when I enquired where he was, was told that J G had detained him after the preceding gym lesson. I decided to investigate and went in search of the boy. Sure enough, J G was casually talking to the boy in the staff cloakroom. Not very politely I demanded that the boy should attend my lesson at once. He glowered and then suddenly thumped me on the chest. And just as suddenly apologised, asking me to help him defeat his short temper. He knew the boy had witnessed his attack and I could report him. I clashed with him on a number of occasions over fairly innocuous matters but never shopped him.

His crony was R M, a boisterous Woodwork teacher who, after four years as a prisoner of war (RAF), trained in one year to teach. He was the goalkeeper for Eastbourne Town and eventually became their trainer. To some people, he was a jovial fellow with a loud voice, but he carried around with him a set of ersatz 'BNP' prejudices ranging from racist to anti-art. The rough side was his assumption that he could hector people into accepting his point of view about the British way of life. I crossed swords with him a few times. The most absurd occasion was when he objected to my production of "Othello" because I was using High School girls in the cast and one of them had to play the part of a courtesan (Bianca). He too asserted his own version of discipline on the boys. Once I opened the woodwork room door after school hours (seeking stage materials) and saw him about to strike a 15-year-old boy bending down to receive punishment. I regret that I closed the door and retreated. I should have interfered, for only the Headmaster was authorised to administer physical punishment. But I walked away from that responsibility.

MATURITY IN EASTBOURNE

Shortly before RWS retired, J G decided to retreat from teaching and live in one of the Channel Islands, where among other things he played golf and died about fifteen years later. R M succumbed to cancer after two traumatic experiences. He sliced off the top of one of his fingers on the circular saw, and had it sewn on again by a black doctor at the Hospital. And a few years later he protested foolishly about edicts installed by the new Headmaster (J.S. Morris) and complained to the Governors. At the hearing he was treated with polite indifference. I seriously think he was mortally humiliated.

Focussing on these two blots on the landscape may seem an admission that Eastbourne Grammar School was a disappointing move for me. That is definitely not so, for two main reasons. First, as already implied, my horizons were widened and my objectives clarified by the change from Sevenoaks to Eastbourne. And second, most of my colleagues cooperated willingly, and worked and played hard to get good results, not just in examinations but also in cultural and social activities. And a third reason was – I was Head of English. 1956 was the year we moved to Eastbourne. It was also the autumn of the Hungarian uprising, which was put down with brutality by the Soviets. In the West we huffed and puffed but all we could do was raise funds to aid the deprived Hungarians. I was persuaded to stage a Revue in aid of the Mayor's Appeal and this worked well for there was plenty of talent and enthusiasm around. We managed to put together a series of sketches, songs and comedy on the theme "Down with Skule", climaxing with an inspired rendering of Tchaikovsky's Swan Lake danced by a totally inexperienced corps de ballet in tutus (one junior boy attended dance classes). It was not a bad start for my succession of play productions. Twenty-six years elapsed before I devised another (more sophisticated) Revue to mark the coming of the Sixth Form College, staged at the Tivoli theatre in Seaside in 1982.

At first the teaching of English at the Grammar School was impeded by lax classroom skills, particularly by one teacher who was torn between willingness to cooperate and resentment that I was taking over. He had blotted his copybook with RWS by demanding payment for staging a school production of "Julius Caesar" (rather badly, apparently) and of course I did not sympathise with his attitude. After a couple of years he moved on and that paved the way for the arrival of Chris Mason, fresh from Cambridge. He had heard through friends that life in the English Department at Eastbourne Grammar was both good fun and meaningful; he applied for the main Assistant English post when the vacancy occurred. Summertime, with lively and cooperative 'new' teachers and a few 'older' staff members, was pleasantly embellished with light-hearted outings (hardly parties, sans alcohol, music or shouting) on the beach or at home (we played intriguing games of Lie Dice). Some of the participants were Walter Tillyard (German), Morris Romans (Art), Reg Bertin (Music), George Dixon

IRONS IN THE FIRE

(Geography), Neville Hortop (Maths), Frank Collett (Maths), Vernon Davies (Geography), John Mallion (German and CCF), Bert Harpum (Economics) and a few more who haven't made a lasting impression on me. One who did of course was Chris Mason, and his wife Margot. Friendship continued after Chris moved on to Reigate Grammar School as Head of English where he stayed until he became Deputy Headmaster. He was the best supporting English teacher and I never found a comparable replacement through the next phases of my years at the Grammar School. There was a string of teachers through the years (second in the English Department) but I can't even remember all their names, let alone their idiosyncrasies.

Another stroke of luck was the run of successful entries at universities, particularly with some English students. Senior Grammar boys seemed more mature than their Sevenoaks counterparts. At the end of my first year, Christopher Ravilious (nephew of Eric) was offered a State Scholarship in English at Cambridge and he was followed by David Willoughby and Michael Gilsenan two years later (both returning from college entrance exams to learn gigantic parts in 'The Alchemist' within a week) and then two years later, three outstanding English students, Stuart Olesker and Nicholas Nye (they played Othello and Iago) and John Constable. The English Department moved forward confidently not just in exam successes but also various ancillaries like speech and drama, magazine writing and a Sixth Form literary society. RWS backed my proposal to turn an attic room into a Sixth Form Clubroom, which helped to give Sixth formers a privileged identity, with a tea bar and seating for about 40. It served its purpose well until the School moved to a brand new site in King's Drive.

I introduced the English Speaking Board examinations in the lower school for any boys wanting to improve their speech skills. Vera had close connections to the founders of this independent organisation, Christabel (Coidy) Burniston and Jocelyn Bell, and much good work came from its stimulus, but I found less time to spare after a decade and I was aware that the fees inhibited some entrants. Instead we started our own Class Talks in the classroom as part of the over-all English exams in the middle and lower school. Exams of course were built into the system. And we always arranged annual speech 'competitions' at year levels, not looking for elocution or acting ability (or exam marks) so much as simply clear and confident speech. There was a regular Speech Festival in the town and for a period we entered. A group of upper schoolboys bowled the adjudicators over with a choral rendition of "Bats" by D.H Lawrence. Gradually however I lost interest in competitive speech and drama – too divisive!

One of my first tasks had been to choose texts for English classes through the four years before "O" level. Perhaps I should have been bold enough to select a more recent course book, but I played safe by introducing Ridout's "English

MATURITY IN EASTBOURNE

Today". For an English Curriculum I simply picked out the most important topics that had been threaded through his carefully deployed programme and wrote them down as essential items for class work over four or five years. Some of these would be factual – items like Syntax, Synonyms and Antonyms, Parts of Speech, Figures of Speech, Spelling, Punctuation, Prefixes and Suffixes and so on. Others would be exercises to stimulate comprehension and composition. Obviously all English staff were expected to bide by this directive, though I applied little pressure and actually preferred each teacher to follow his own course (within reason). Some teachers were opposed to formal grammar exercises - I compromised over 'informal' treatment. In the Curriculum it was laid down that each term a class should be using not just the course book but also two literary readers - a novel and a poetry anthology (at one point we tried specifying particular poems but some teachers disliked that). In the interest of variety and stimulation, we swapped teachers for each class year by year. A lot depended on the skills of individual teachers; sometimes we shared activities like Speech competitions. On the other hand, some attempts to 'diversify' failed: we tried projecting short films to combined classes at each year level but dropped the idea when lack of preparation time was leading to weak output (discussion and written responses).

Of course there were plenty of other English activities (such as creative writing, reading aloud and discussion, newspaper reading, précis, analysis of advertisements, history of language, drama etc), all of which should be accommodated in English lessons. Perhaps we never resolved some basic questions: is English a 'subject' at all, or simply a medium? What is the place of grammar? How do language studies relate to literature studies? Should there be two examination subjects? In speech is dialect or accent acceptable? At first (in the '50s) there were plenty of preconceived ideas, indeed prejudices, to hold on to (such as not ending a sentence with a preposition – or two).

6. The Uses of English

This English Curriculum was reasonably workable but judged by modern standards it was too regimented and there was a lack of diversity with all in the same class usually reading the same textbooks. Throughout my three decades of teaching, the contents of the English curriculum remained a major issue, with controversy dogging the way and finding many lampposts en route. The '60s and '70s were particularly disturbing – not just for English teachers but everybody! There was the knock-on effect of upheaval in the USA (Civil Rights Movement, Free Speech, Student Protest and Sit-ins, Elvis and flower people, rock'n'roll and drugs, the anti-Vietnam War campaign, assassinations and space probes). Nearer home in '69, the ferocious French university rebellions, and for us teachers in the

'60s the Beatles and Philip Larkin, comprehensive schools and new doctrines about 'progressive' education issuing from teacher training colleges, and then a whiplash from Black Paper reactionaries in the '70s. At our Teaching of English Association, which held meetings regularly, some teachers expressed anxiety about how far Grammar School academic standards should change to accommodate new concepts. Opinions differed. At secondary level there was confusion as well as lack of cohesion.

English and Mathematics (literacy and numeracy) are generally accepted as the root subjects in any school curriculum. I can remember in the '60s leafing through a New Mathematics textbook based on binary number system and (without much comprehension) realising its relevance to the computer. In contrast, there was no such clear direction in which English teaching had to travel. Conventional attitudes placed Grammar and Literature at the head of any list of essential subjects within English. Traditional grammar had a special prestigious role, imposing rules and usage based on Latin, but the absurdity of that had already been spotted and even during the war years grammar teaching was in decline. It may not be boring but it was inconsistent and often inapplicable to an analytic, positional language (Anglo-Germanic) like English.

There was an academic stir about Linguistics in the early '60s. This offered an alternative to what was generally accepted as 'grammar'. Traditionally teachers tended to treat 'correct' language as if it were based on a set of facts and rules more or less separable from experience. Linguistics considered language to be 'patterned social behaviour' operating meaningfully in social situations and taking different forms in the process. This is obvious really: you change your English to suit the situation, but conventional grammar, influenced as it was by deference to class, snobbery and classical education, failed to distinguish these many kinds of English or the varied 'references'. However, the linguistic school textbooks seemed stodgy and there was a lot more to linguistics than 'grammar'. By the time I was benefiting from this appreciation of language as manifold in usage and adaptable to many changes through time, I had decided Linguistics led to the semantically boggy terrain of 'structuralism', and to anthropological theories about the origins of language, neither of which would be of practical use in the classroom. In the '80s, there was a 'new' approach to literary criticism called "Stylistics" based on Linguistic tenets. I know of no English teacher who enthused about that clumsy name but in Sixth Form studies the concern for matching appropriate language to particular situations (the register) was useful in critical appreciation. Linguistics provides a realistic grammar of the vernacular as actually spoken and written; it replaces bogus Latin-oriented grammar, but I am still in favour of pupils leaving secondary school with some understanding of the grammatical structure of sentences and words, both in terms of syntax and parts of speech, just as they should have some acquaintance with our heritage of great literature (inc. Shakespeare). But the devil is in the detail and it is a question of timing.

I am on firmer ground with regard to Literature, traditionally the other essential pillar in English studies. In fact English is often considered to be synonymous with Literature, which is as wrong as calling the junk mail on your doormat literature. Certainly I spent three years more or less reading/studying literary works without considering what might be called 'transactional language' in all its manifold variations. I might add that my degree course also excluded, or ignored, participation in active, creative and personally artistic responses to literature (we wrote essays but were not expected to write poems or fiction) but I don't wish to bite the hand that fed me with the means to teach English. Although no preparation for teaching English to Third Formers, at least the joint study of Language **and** Literature at Oxford (and some other universities) was encouraging a potentially balanced view of English as a subject to be taught. At Cambridge, Old and Middle English were options often declined by students and at this time the admonitory finger of Dr. Leavis wagged over literary texts with strictures about certain moral and cultural traditions which should be acknowledged as superior. Quite apart from this extreme partiality for selective Great Art, the prestige and exalted status which Literature texts enjoy can be harmful if they lead (as sometimes they do) to depreciation of other language uses - as if there was a division between 'literary works', which are in the premier division, and transactional communication, which is in a different (and lower) league. Yet no one kind of language is intrinsically 'better' than another. All depends on the suitability for the context. Literature, though, has huge resources to be drawn on within the classroom. Stories, poems and plays display language at its most expressive and aesthetic level and the vital appeal is through the imagination. I have always thought (naively) that English has a specially important role to play in the school curriculum because through Literature the teacher can stir the pupils' imagination and stimulate their sensitivity to feelings and the senses. Literary texts, mainly through the guise of narrative and characterisation, can posit moral dilemmas and situations that help pupils to develop their understanding of personal responsibilities and social obligations. No wonder the teaching of English is so rewarding, and so absorbing! But yet again, in the sober light of experience, it is rather pretentious to think that English teachers have a special responsibility for the spiritual health of our charges. Isn't it?

In 1967 the Plowden Report on Primary Education (commissioned by the Labour Government) supported many of the current 'progressive' views. One of the basic tenets was the assertion that research had *proved* that the traditional 'formal methods' used by most teachers were wrong and the new child-centred learning (via discovery) would raise standards – 'wrong' because not only were these old-fashioned methods inefficient in advancing literacy in our schools but also education should be based morally on the individual child who will develop successfully at his or her own pace. The teacher as 'authority' was out of date, his or her role should be as 'facilitator', encouraging children to explore and discover for themselves. The class was no longer to be taught as a unit. Each child must learn for his or her self.

Many teachers (not only primary) approved the new ideas, though clearly they were at variance with the selective principle of the 11+ exam. As a father, I was impressed by the relaxed atmosphere at my children's Primary Schools and the enthusiasm of the teachers who were putting Plowden into practice. But George Brown (H.M) wasn't going to extremes – 'discovery methods' did not rule out 'being told'. Some enthusiasts allowed children far too much freedom to explore, or to do nothing, and harassed teachers sometimes failed to provide an adequate structure or framework that would make use of the 'discoveries'. And this went for secondary school teachers too. I was influenced to consider changes to the Grammar School curriculum.

The Course book was now frowned upon. True, we had introduced some variation in the choice of texts in the classroom and by mid-'60s, Ridout was more or less tattered and shelved, but perhaps we should be ousting all course books, for surely they were encouraging English teaching that might impede individual pupils from exploring on their own 'learning journeys' and benefiting from their findings. These were boom years for educational publications and the solution seemed to be to stock up a vast array of books. Unfortunately our English budget could not expand much in response. Geoffrey Summerfield compiled "Topics in English" in '65 but I read it a decade too late.

> The day of the textbook dominated by the examination and of the pupil dominated by the textbook, are mercifully numbered. This volume, a new kind of aid for teachers of English, appears at a time when new possibilities are being explored by the more enterprising and adventurous amongst them.

There followed in the book a selection of more than 30 Topics, from 'Predators' to 'Fights', with suggestions under three headings: Teacher's Reading, Extended Reading for Pupils, and Assignments for Pupils. Without sufficient enterprise or adventure, it seems, the Grammar School teachers tried to launch the 'explore and discover' method. The two buzzwords were 'topic' and 'project', but the trouble was that pupils had already done plenty of 'topic-work' in their primary schools. "

MATURITY IN EASTBOURNE

About one child in ten finds a topic in which he is genuinely interested ... the other nine children choose a topic at random in an attempt to oblige teacher. (Sybil Marshall '64)

The pitch had been queered.

Attempting a compromise, we decided to combine the reading of literature texts with personal projects on related topics. The teachers prepared brochures on themes, containing notes and suggestions for topics and ways of presenting findings. For example, in the middle school:

Project Theme	**Class Reading**
A Study of Power and Government	Macbeth, Animal Farm and St. Joan
Education	Hard Times, Pygmalion and The Rainbow (section)
Group Pressures and Prejudice	The Chrysalids, The Insect Play and Lord of the Flies
The Social Misfit	Brighton Rock, Catcher in the Rye, Death of a Salesman
A Study of Conflict	Brave New World, 1984 and The Tempest

The scheme fell between two stools, neither allowing enough freedom to explore nor providing enough guidance. There were few successfully completed Projects (one in ten?). We resumed using short-term activities and exercises, relying on Roneo prints and then photocopies. I note that teachers' resource material is now conveniently filed and readily available for class work, some of it specifically for National Curriculum topics and looking remarkably like leaves from a course book.

Meanwhile, as far as Sixth Form English was concerned in the '60s/'70s, there was little to stir controversy at first. The 'A' level syllabus ruled supreme and a growing number of students opted for English, particularly after we switched from the Romantic period to the Modern Age. Popular were the regular trips to Stratford-on-Avon, staying overnight and sometimes seeing three plays in two days, and occasionally outings to London theatres. I attended a NATE Conference and became aware of hotbed agitation between leading 'progressive' and 'reactionary' representatives. I also attended two enjoyable literary Conferences organised by the Editors of the Critical Quarterly magazine, and was surprised when they published their Black Papers on the state of education, and particularly the teaching of English, in England and Wales. At issue was the progressive rejection of examinations and competitive listing as a major agent in education. What was called 'continuous assessment' was gaining ground. I have read C.B. Cox's memoir on the ensuing furore – it was more than that, it was a major confrontation between educational and political heavyweights, indeed Labour and Conservative policies. The Press whipped up a frenzy of vituperative hostility against Cox, who was pilloried as a stick-in-the-mud opponent of all the innovative changes taking place in schools. True, Cox had old-fashioned faith in the grammar school tradition at a time when comprehensive schools were going through an uneasy initiation but he was not against all changes within the system. The five Black Papers exuded much hot air, and so did the Press but despite "the Great Betrayal" (Prof. Cox's dramatic book title) the outcome was surely victory for him – he headed the official Working Group that established the National English Curriculum in 1989.

> The English Working Group was asked to make pronouncements about all the major controversies in the teaching of English: how to teach reading (phonic methods or look and say), how to teach spelling, handwriting and punctuation, how to promote enjoyment of reading, how to teach grammar and Standard English (spoken and written), how to cope with bilingual pupils, how to introduce drama, media studies and information technology into the curriculum, how to encourage speaking and listening, how to promote both imaginative writing and the ability to communicate in clear, vigorous English, how to devise a core curriculum for literature, how to assess all these things, how to advise on arrangements for children with special needs, and, last but not least, how to teach English in Wales. (C.B. Cox)

There must be many teachers of English who dislike the imposition of a National Curriculum during the '90s (one criticism cites 'the Nanny State') but I would have welcomed it.

A decade after the Plowden Report came the Bullock Report. I preferred Professor Alan Bullock's splendid speech at a Grammar School Prize-giving ceremony in the early '60s. His 1975 Report urged English teachers to seek "language across the curriculum" in our schools and to activate a language policy with other departments. As English is the medium through which all learning is achieved (except perhaps 'direct method' teaching), every teacher is a teacher of English. The English specialist should establish a shared policy in their schools for (say) correcting spelling, punctuation and grammar mistakes, and setting standards in compositions. Intentions were honourable but some Heads of

MATURITY IN EASTBOURNE

Department muttered darkly about empire building. I doubt if there was any intent to indulge in 'social engineering' in the recommendations of the Bullock Report but as a conscientious teacher of English I have absorbed the views of Noam Chomsky on the political manipulation of language – it always favours the interests and concerns of the established leaders in society and is exploited as propaganda ("actual language use tends to maintain structures of authority and domination"- N. Chomsky).

7. Changing Sites and Heads

I have wandered in a time-space continuum and need to backtrack in order to recover some sense of perspective. For the first seven years of our married life Vera and I lived in the top flat of Westcliff Mansions. At first we were concentrating on making our separate career moves successful, particularly Vera with her TV appearances and me coping with school matters. When we move towards phase two with the arrival of our children (over eight years), we bury personal problems and try to focus on the family though both continue to pursue interests outside the home. Vera is still in demand at the BBC and gradually I have established an adequately motivated English Department while getting more involved with drama productions in the town and of course at the Grammar School. Now, however, (in 1962) the School had outgrown its previous lodgings and is quickly establishing itself on the brand-new, expansive campus along King's Drive.

The 'new' Grammar School's architectural design was so bland and uninspired that it was obviously the work of a bureaucratic member of the Borough Planning Department, following instructions without inspiration. I suppose the powers-that-be wanted to ensure a contrast to the town's most recent 'modern school' (Ratton), which copied the standard flat-roofed and modular style of the early sixties, so they put up plain brick rectangles with ridge roofs to affirm the town's solidarity with regard to traditional academic design. It was no doubt cheaper than hiring a proper architect to design something exciting but it couldn't avoid the soubriquet of 'sausage factory'. One of its better features was the assembly hall, conventionally with proscenium arch but with a spacious stage no more than 3 feet above floor level (thus providing an easier link with the auditorium) and a cyclorama wall across the back of the stage (thus facilitating the lighting of sky effects). Sound and lighting were technically far superior to the cramped quarters at Eversley Court, though the intimate 'cottage hospital' ambience there had encouraged us to design and construct ingenious stage sets for those early play productions. On the new stage I still reached forward towards the audience with enlarged 'apron' and got hold of rostra to improve audience sightlines.

IRONS IN THE FIRE

Having established the Grammar School on the new site and consolidated its reputation, Rex Shaw retired in 1971. He had certainly made his mark over 21 years as Headmaster. I have indistinct memories of muted salutes being given to Rex when handing over the reins to J.S. Morris. His lasting memorial was always going to be the extraordinary links with Cambridge (and to a lesser extent Oxford) made by Grammar School boys. I don't know the statistics, but for a state school of moderate size Eastbourne GS held a remarkable record of academic successes for over a decade. And no doubt he would swell with pride to recount how John Novak became the first EGS rugby player to play for England. But he couldn't inspire a school community to work in unison, either pupils or staff. Walter Tillyard found words to express the deficiency after one assembly – "no love, he gives them no love!" Probably he was getting too hardened to care, knowing the alpha selective scheme was likely to be superseded with the decision to go comprehensive. Incidentally Eastbourne had lost its Education Department and was now part of East Sussex LEA.

The new Headmaster, John Morris, was chalk to Rex's cheese. He was a six-footer, thin, balding and rather gawkily structured but he did more laughing in a day than Rex did in a term. He was looking forward to the double transformation act (from Grammar to Grammar-High to Sixth Form College) for he was ambitious for power, and perhaps a little personal esteem, but he showed a much more balanced concern for the running of the boys' school. One of JSM's first decisions was to abandon the alpha stream. My son Simon was a participating observer of events under each Headmaster. I think he was aware of an improvement in the morale of the school under JSM, but he no doubt remained critical of the establishment (partly due to his having a father on the staff). I did not always like JSM's authority as he took control but I recognized the sound qualities in his approach and I was aware these were difficult times with educational changes afoot.

An unexpected responsibility was dumped on me by JSM when facing the problem of a viable alternative to Latin in the middle school. Integrated Studies was a new and experimental educational concept, involving subjects like History, Geography, Current Affairs and Drama under one heading, though it was expediency and not educational policy that ruled in this instance. I don't know how a decision was taken (did I volunteer?) but I was put in charge of planning a course of studies that fitted our requirements. Perhaps rather arbitrarily, (for I neglected to ask for the cooperation of Heads of relevant Departments), I worked out a syllabus that dealt with four topics: the Vikings, the Aztecs and Incas, the Voyages of Captain Cook and the world of the Future. These would be educationally useful and interesting, and were outside the normal syllabuses of other subjects. Obviously the teaching was integrated between the teachers and the scheme worked reasonably well though I was hard-pressed to devote time to

MATURITY IN EASTBOURNE

it. After five years I was glad to hand over to Kevin Anderson, who had worked enthusiastically on the scheme (Ecology his special interest) and Integrated Studies continued till the amalgamation with the High School.

Back in the mid-seventies, the arrival of a number of lively young teachers coincided with the change in headmasters. Not only were they young, they were talented and wanted to participate in the schools' musical and dramatic performances. I was lucky to have John Purcell, Kevin Anderson, Tony Morse, Rod Watts, Roger Press, Ken Reed, John Gregson, Martin Jeanneret, Godfrey Forder, and others wanting to help on stage. A measure of the increased cooperation of staff members was the response when I asked for volunteers to support a school production of "Rosencrantz and Guildenstern are Dead". Fifteen members of staff took part as courtiers and dramatis personae. For me it was a rare appearance in a major role (the Player-King appropriately).

The amalgamation of the Grammar and the High Schools (in '77) in preparation for the full comprehensivisation of Eastbourne's state schools produced an extraordinary situation. Suddenly we became an unwieldy two-Headed monster trying to function between two sites, with overcrowding of staff rooms and a shortage of ladies' toilets. It took four years to lose the annual intake of juniors, with a pupil depletion each year up to O level. During this time the swollen Grammar-High School flourished, mainly because there was double the number of selected 11+ pupils and partly because of co-education, though classes continued to be boys or girl only. But there was plenty of mixing out-of-school hours (and certainly increased liaison between bachelor teachers and some of the more precocious High School pupils – two marriages at least). The full impact of co-education came later when the Sixth Form College was confined to the King's Drive site. English lessons then really did become much more enjoyable and instructive. To celebrate the imminent amalgamation, I staged Jean Anouilh's "Thieves' Carnival" in the grammar school hall with a cast drawn from both sites at the end of the summer term. It was a memorably enjoyable production, but it was to be the last play in this hall, for in the autumn nemesis struck.

I had hired a set of Elizabethan costumes from EODS and they were laid out on stage overnight. We were in the process of building the set for "Twelfth Night". During the night, a young arsonist broke into the school and, sprinkling paraffin on the costumes, the scenery and the stage, set light to the hall. It must have burned like a furnace. The whole building was razed to the ground. The spectacle when I arrived for work that morning was totally stunning. Smoke was still smouldering within the shattered shell of the hall, but nothing survived amidst the ashes. Small groups of boys and girls, and shocked teachers too, simply stood at the school gates hardly able to comprehend what had happened. We knew it must be the work of an arsonist and indeed by midday his classmates were shopping the culprit to the police. This difficult fifth year boy had even boasted that he would burn the school down and got up in the middle of the night to do the deed. He chose the right time for this was the month of the Firemen's Strike. Army Green Goddesses were in attendance but everyone was helpless when confronted by this conflagration. One consolation was that the hall was virtually a separate building and the blaze hardly touched the rest of the school. My involvement with a play production in the hall meant that I was directly affected but I don't think I was personally targeted (he had not been in any class I taught). Were we insured? Yes, but our little criminal was treated as a damaged youth and offered penitential accommodation within the Bishop of Lewes's monastic Retreat. Morris Romans was appointed to make regular trips to Lewes in order to provide schoolwork for the boy's O level exams six months later. I don't recall any contribution from me.

Actually, we bounced back. The production of "Twelfth Night" was transferred to the High School hall successfully and was much appreciated as a show to celebrate the union of Grammar and High. Although lessons were undisturbed at the Grammar School site, we had lost our normal 'theatre' so I had to use the less well equipped High School stage for three more annual shows (Three Plays by W.B. Yeats, Robertson's "Caste", and my original musical adaptation of "The Insect Play" by the Capek Bros) without loss to our dramatic standards. Then, with the new hall built on the foundations of the old, we resumed normal activity. The powers-that-be had decreed that this replacement hall should be multi-purpose in design so it possessed no stage and there was an odd pair of vast velvet curtains to contend with, but at least it was an open-plan space that we could use dramatically. The effect of the arson attack on the school was disturbing although, as shown by the quick recovery of "Twelfth Night", the amalgamation hardly suffered, except that JSM succumbed to angina and needed to rest. Technically the provisional name (the Grammar-High School) meant that no longer could 'new boys' qualify as Grammarians. It seemed as if the old institution (ninety years service to the town) would be put to rest but extraordinarily the Old Boys Association has risen from the ashes and, fanned by the late George Dixon on the staff, flourishes by holding annual lunches, sporting occasions and social events with an ardour never previously encountered. It also provides funds for needy students in the new order. Significantly, Rex Shaw has become a kind of patron saint (he died after quite a short retirement). There are now well over 700 Old Boys who retain allegiance to a school that no longer exists and it is always a bizarre pleasure to attend the autumn gathering.

Over this period of comparative change, with new buildings, new headmaster and new educational alignment, my main preoccupation was running the English Department but clearly I was getting more and more concerned with the role of drama and theatrical productions. Nothing in my contract specified that

MATURITY IN EASTBOURNE

producing drama was expected but I soon discovered that not only was I enjoying the 'freedom' of voluntary engagement in activities outside the classroom but also putting into effect my conviction that English was the one subject that allowed creative activity to flourish. There were reactionary teachers who, for whatever reason, grumbled at my endeavours to involve young people in various out-of-class activities. I should stick to my job teaching English grammar in the classroom, perhaps. One significant occasion I recall was the result of discussing modern art with a class in an English lesson and I decided to set the homework for that evening. "Make your own mobile," I said. No writing, no reading, but making something, if possible original. The class responded and the mobiles were displayed during the next lesson with such success that I decided to ask the Canteen manageress if we could hang some of them decoratively from the light pendants in the canteen. She agreed but, unfortunately in my absence during the lunch break, the teacher who was on dinner duty removed them, claiming they were unsuitable adornments while he was in charge. Guess who that was. I didn't bother to complain.

The "school play", traditionally presented at the end of each autumn term (but sometimes elsewhen) had become a regular activity at the Grammar School. The consistency of such productions is worth stressing and I am extremely grateful to other members of staff who helped during these years. Some came and went but I could always rely on certain key supporters (e.g. John Purcell, Kevin Anderson, Ken Reed). Outstanding was Geoffrey Newman (Physics) who through many years at the school skilfully and patiently organised the lighting plots for these performances. His contribution was immense. My only regret about my reliance on him is that I never had to learn enough about lighting techniques.

There was also another kind of school drama that I had became interested in after staging five 'home-made' plays to mark the end of the Grammar School at Eversley Court, using the floor of the old hall with the audience on three sides. Why not try something like this in the new King's Drive hall? I asked for more plays by students and found them good enough to be acted and staged 'in the round' with an audience, sitting on raised seating on four sides with the stage used as one of the sides. I called this event 'Five in One Arena Theatre' and it became a regular feature of the school's cultural life, which was continued at the Sixth Form College even more successfully. The Staff Thespians began to appear annually too. Vital to the scheme was the construction of an arena with the audience on four sides. Each time we borrowed rostrums from the Borough and, looking back, I marvel at the support given by students, who volunteered to fetch and carry these heavy items in order to make tiered seating, always out of school hours. Later, we actually purchased our own folding rostra. I simply mention three elements: the high quality of the writing and acting of these one-act plays, the large number of student and teachers involved and the enthusiastic support of audiences.

8. Extra-Mural Activities

Quite apart from educational and creative activities within the school, I decided to launch a local English educational association that catered for all teachers who were interested in English in schools (and our slogan was: "every teacher is a teacher of English"). This was intended for both Secondary and Primary teachers. I think our Teaching of English Association (TEA) was founded out of impatience with the vagaries of NATE (the national organisation). For over a decade (1968–80) I was Secretary of the TEA, to which many Sussex teachers at all levels subscribed (there were about 40 members). It was of course a social as well as an educational assembly. There were talks, lectures and discussions on a variety of topics relating to English and the arts, with many distinguished guest speakers. There were Conferences and Outings. I recall two outstanding events – a party (with academic lecture included) at Batemans in honour of Kipling and a visit (with academic lecture too) to Charleston Farmhouse to celebrate the so-called Bloomsbury set. Both were attended by 80-100 members and guests. Why, we even presented our own Son et Lumière shows at summer venues. Perhaps the TEA's most ambitious project was to organise Sixth Form Conferences at the Congress Theatre on Shakespeare's plays, with more than 200 students from Sussex schools attending. All this took a great deal of organising and, considering I had no educational axe to grind, I wonder now why I was so devoted to its multifarious activities. Perhaps I enjoyed being a control freak, but if that's true I can only congratulate myself on being responsible for so many thoughtful and entertaining events supported by many local English teachers. I was grateful for support particularly from two Chairmen serving over this period - Arthur Callow and Bernard Hurn. The fact is the TEA folded when my marriage hit the buffers.

The English Speaking Board (ESB) employed me as an Examiner during the summer months in the '60's when hosts of foreign students visited England. Some pioneer pre-TEFL organizers used the ESB to provide a final test and assessment of students who could proudly flourish a 'Certificate' on their return. It was very subjective examining and I was always aware that my grasp of their native tongue was far weaker than theirs of mine. Few of the examiners practised phonetics or recognized mutually agreed terms, and assessing students in ten-minute interviews was hardly thorough. Eventually ESB withdrew from this work, but these short visits to south coast holiday resorts provided pleasant breaks and brought in pocket money for family holidays caravanning abroad.

MATURITY IN EASTBOURNE

ESB re-entered my diary of events later on (1969). I was asked to attend a meeting of interested parties in order to discuss a proposal put forward by Robert Maxwell, this being to publish an expansive 'library' of texts encouraging speech and language amongst the very young, aimed largely at young mothers. There was an explosion of educational publications at this time, a response to 'progressive' policies. Could the ESB provide a host of 'text' books, theme books and colourful picture books to catch the eye of supermarket shoppers? Maxwell's sudden interest in ESB had somewhat flustered Coidy Burniston, and she was anxious to create a team that could contribute ideas or scripts. Out of these meetings came a proposal that I should 'edit' a series of secondary school theme books and I immediately started research on one of these: "Planning a Town". This was a subject in vogue, with plans to create New Towns, with vast schemes to elaborate the urban roadways, motorways and internets, and with the erection of concrete blocks and high towers which were to replace slum and condemned suburban dwellings. In contrast to this concept of total control of the urban environment (le Corbusier) I would place the concept of organic growth in a town (Lewis Mumford). I approached the subject by taking aspects of town life (e.g. City centre, Neighbourhoods, Transport, Work etc). In fact, the further I went into the subject, the more complex it became. Despite signs that the grand scheme being hatched by ESB and Pergamon Press (Maxwell's Publishing Co) was disintegrating, I continued my research and started to amass a lot of material. Eventually I seemed to be the only survivor, urged on to continue this "Planning a Town" idea by the Pergamon Editor. When I showed my script to John Innerdale, an Eastbourne architect with an enthusiasm for education and design projects, he was extremely supportive. In fact, he demanded to be put in charge of the illustrations in the book and the two of us spent hours accumulating photographs and drawings.

I had met Robert Maxwell at an ESB conference, and actually chaired the meeting where he spoke on the future of the Press. In introducing him, I referred to SuperMac (the nickname for Macmillan the P.M.) and then called Maxwell SuperMax. He liked that, of course. He was a flamboyant figure and at this time full of bonhomie to the ESB, though maybe we should have seen the future of Maxwell in his choice of subject. The Pergamon Press had proved his chief investment to date but the temptations of owning a popular tabloid were already succeeding. When I finally submitted my MS and illustrations to Pergamon, John Innerdale and I travelled to Oxford for a meeting with the Editors of the Pergamon English Library. Maxwell greeted us, sherried us, introduced his wife and then disappeared. This hospitality took place in an elegantly fitted room in Headington Hall, which Maxwell rented as HQ for Pergamon. I was very struck by the splendid curved bookcase along one wall, gleaming with leather-bound books. To produce the sherry, Maxwell had to press a button, which caused the bookcase (and dummy books) to swing open to display a cocktail bar. Did this reveal the man? John and I then visited the main offices of the Press, a recently erected specimen of the open-plan design that provided a vast, cavernous space into which were fitted identical business furniture units arranged to form an interlocking series of work places for the staff. We sat in one of these areas feeling very exposed while a secretary explained how she was editing my script (quite ruthlessly, I thought).

Suddenly Maxwell was selling Pergamon and my MS was put on hold. John, more streetwise than me, immediately demanded payment for his work on the illustrations and received £200, while I had to wait until final decisions about 'work in progress' came to light. As expected, publication of my "Planning a Town" book was finally cancelled. I was compensated to the melancholy tune of £250, which was hardly a fair estimate of the time and travel and outlay I had been involved in. Of course I don't blame Robert Maxwell or his minions but my book was left stranded. No other publisher liked its format and so I shelved it. Now, on opening the file containing my MS and the illustrations, I wonder how I had the nerve to try coping with such a specialist subject. For two or three years I was busily engaged in planning this project book, and it is a pity it failed.

Ironically, in 1972 (in the wake of this publishing disappointment) I discovered there was a simpler way of becoming a published 'author' without having to research and slave at a typewriter. The Arena Theatre and the Five-in-One Plays had blossomed into a real success with performances not just in the school hall but also at festivals (such as the Gardner Arts Centre). I could see this was original drama suitable for young players and the right material for 'theatre in the round' so I decided to submit a set of six scripts to Heinemann Educational. The Editor, Edward Thompson, immediately responded by agreeing to publish "Five Arena Plays", which sold quite well to schools for a decade and was reprinted in 1976. I chose the kind of plays that used the 'arena' with large casts, flowing action and suitable themes for teenage performers at school. Three of the plays were mine: "The Children's Crusade", "The Tale of the Four Winds" and "Under Beachy Head". A fourth play, "Colombo", was written mainly by a boy's father and the fifth, "The Chimney Sweeps", was by a seventeen-year-old Sixth former. I provided production notes on each of the plays. Getting published by a reputable educational firm was prestigious and there were also modest royalties, something like 10% of each 60p paperback sold, part of which I doled out dutifully to the writers where apt. Orders came from many parts of the world, and a South African anthology of drama included my "Tale of the Four Winds". With such an unexpected windfall, I learned that achievement best comes naturally like leaves on a tree (to use Keats's image). Enjoy the creative experience for its own sake.

MATURITY IN EASTBOURNE

During these years I did not consider myself an actor and only twice actually performed in someone else's amateur dramatics in the town. On both occasions I stepped into roles at short notice, in 'Henry V' and 'Romeo and Juliet'. I think I was initiated into the heart of the cast when, during the final performance, playing the part of the Duke of Messina, I received the vital letter that revealed all to the characters on stage. I had decided not to learn this speech by heart but to rely on a written 'crib', which was to be handed to me by the Messenger. Imagine my consternation on the last night, dear reader, when I opened the letter and read the words "Good luck, Mike." Not one word of Shakespeare's lines. I improvised doggerel desperately and did not 'dry'. It was a poor joke; I deserved it actually but the producer was furious with his cast. I went on to direct three productions for the Shakespeare Society: "Under Milk Wood", "A Midsummer Night's Dream" and "The Importance of being Earnest".

The Shakespeare Society was in decline. At the final meeting I proposed that we should create a TIE (Theatre in Education) touring group, which could use the equipment and services of the Shakespeare Society, and the motion was carried. Michael Brewer as Stage Manager was vital. We agreed to call ourselves 'The Travellers' and began touring worthwhile plays in schools with myself directing and sometimes acting. We mainly performed in the evenings. The first production was the avant-garde play by James Saunders "Next Time I'll Sing to You", which was very well received. For the next three years I was involved with directing 'The Travellers', visiting schools and colleges in Sussex and thoroughly enjoying 'an actor's life' on the side. Perhaps the best dramatic achievement was "Othello" but the acme undoubtedly was performing "Frankenstein" to a packed audience of schoolboys in the superb theatre of the Bluecoat School in Horsham. It was a romantic enterprise, always operated on a shoestring and really going nowhere, and certainly an activity that occupied too much time. "The Travellers" continued for nearly a decade though I dropped out as my marriage disintegrated.

In the early '80s, I ventured into serious examining of 'A' level English students. I can't recall what drove me to apply for this kind of extra-curricular work but if it was to earn money all I can say is that it improved my teaching at 'A' and 'O' level (or GCSE). Appointed by the Associated Examining Board (AEB), which operated from Guildford and London, my brief was to mark Paper One of the English Language and Literature 'A' level syllabus, which comprised an Essay and a Précis or Comprehension exercise. I quite enjoyed methodically ploughing through the succession of bulky packets sent through the post, trying to maintain a cool and collected judgement as I read hundreds of essays and précis. After about seven years, I was more than a little bucked to be promoted to become a group leader in charge of a set of examiners, which involved a tricky process of checking their assessments and trying to explain to them where they might be failing. I continued examining whilst being retired for a further four years, after which I was replaced rather abruptly. I think my comments to fellow examiners were becoming finicky and longwinded - perhaps retirement gave me too much time to fuss.

9. Family Relations – Marriages, Births, Funerals

In racing through this list of various commitments, responsibilities and voluntary activities over two decades, I have isolated myself from family matters, not just those relating to my married life but also the Morley/ Forsyth extended family. I need to go back to a kind of starting point when we settled into domestic stability at 66 Brassey Avenue during the early sixties. We were enjoying a fairly standard middle-class life, I suppose, with a car proving essential, but it was not easy to save much. My salary seemed to disappear into the mortgage (I paid £5,500 for this four-bedroomed house) and endowment policy. Vera, finding TV opportunities diminishing, was contributing less, but really we were in a very privileged position with a comforting circle of friends. And there were three splendid children as the focus of our joint efforts.

It was during the mid-sixties that my father suddenly decided to sell his house in Otley and move to Eastbourne. He had been living alone, for Aunt Ada had seized the opportunity to occupy an apartment in a residential home in Burley-in-Wharfedale, where she lived for a further five years. I visited her twice while she was there, happily installed and glad to be away from Dad, and I have to admit that the family's concern and gratitude for Aunt Ada's loving care were somewhat lacklustre. But then, visits to Dad were also infrequent as I settled into a working life in Eastbourne. Eventually we mourned Ada's passing and attended her funeral, realizing how much she had enjoyed her 'freedom' in old age. Dad, aware that he had shown little interest in Aunt Ada's retirement, continued to live on his own, tending his cabbages, he would say. Until this sudden change of heart. He could choose to retreat to Redcar, where John and Joyce lived, or Leicester, to Neil and Marion, or to Eastbourne, which perhaps was an inevitable haven for a tall, stooping old man who was playing his final games of bowls. He asked me to buy for him a small flat at short notice, which I did. He enjoyed a year and a half in Eastbourne, converted to flat green bowling very successfully, and that summertime he accompanied us on holiday to Dorset very affably, but then once back home he collapsed. I think he must have known he had cancer of the lower bowel but I never suspected until told by the locum deputizing for our GP who was on holiday. He lay in bed at Brassey Avenue, visibly shrinking and jaundiced, incontinent and weak. Downstairs Vera was coping with the new baby, upstairs I was changing sheets. After a couple of weeks under the feeble aegis of the locum, the GP returned and immediately

MATURITY IN EASTBOURNE

transferred Dad to hospital. Brother Neil visited just in time (I can't remember if John made the long journey) and we paid one short visit to the ward. The next day the autumn term began and I received at school the news that he had died that morning. At the hospital the Matron asked whether I wished to see the body. Perhaps, she said, I would prefer to remember him as he was rather than the shrivelled corpse he had become. I chose not to see him. I have never seen a dead body, neither my mother nor my father and so far, no one else.

My father's death was inevitable, though it came so suddenly. He endured till he was 84, which is longer than most of the family lived. As he grew older he became less irascible and he mellowed philosophically, somewhat surprised that his three sons had somehow shaken off dependency on their father and now all three were married and producing offspring, though rather far from Otley. He had settled for a self-absorbed obscurity, a familiar black-bereted figure on the local bowling green, and playing dominoes or snooker with working-class companions at the club. His was a lonely old age, though he may not have seen it that way; he loved his daily routine, his crossword puzzles, his chess problems, his pottering about the garden, his music. There were not many letters from his boys, and fewer visits, yet I don't remember him complaining. Life had knocked him about but he continued to look on it with bemused appreciation. He was no sentimentalist but he had a caring, sympathetic concern for ordinary people as well as a critical attitude. He certainly influenced me through the years.

Dad had seven grandchildren. Margaret, daughter of John and Joyce. Simon, Kate and Emma, children of Harry and Vera. Gillian, Philip and Nicholas, children of Neil and Marion. During the time Vera and I were settling into 66 Brassey Avenue, and I was wrapped in "Noyes Fludde", Neil, whilst working (for British Shoe Manufacturing Co Ltd) in Accrington, had courted and married Marion, a nurse. We all attended the wedding (in 1966). I felt it was a significant moment in our Morley saga, drank deeply and impromptu rose to address the assembled guests, roundly scolding Dad for calling his sons 'bloody fools' when they were young, for here was the last of the 'bloody fools' getting married, something to be proud of. Neil and Marion moved to Leicester, what might be called a definitive move, for they certainly put down roots there. Both were devoted Thespians and trod the boards of the Little Theatre, as actors and directors successfully joining the team; in contrast, I joined few societies or clubs and preferred to work independently and be in control. The Leicester Morleys became five in number over the next decade: first born was Gillian, then Philip and finally Nicholas. Meanwhile John and Joyce Morley, living near the somewhat bleak ICI industrial landscape (a thing of beauty by moonlight) that fringes Redcar, were rejoicing in their daughter Margaret. Contact with my brothers was infrequent. I used to think this was because the wives did not get on but probably the truth is that in Eastbourne we were too busy to keep in regular touch.

The needs of three children, with a tendency to pursue their separate interests, were not neglected, though the parents bickered. In the summer holidays the family made a concerted effort to live in unity and harmony, particularly when we ventured over the Channel to spend three or four weeks abroad. A second-hand caravan was bought with cash made available by my father's death; it was a small 12 ft. Fisher with no luxury contents but delightfully challenging for a family of five with an awning attached. Perhaps we missed out on Eastbourne's summer attractions by heading for the cross-channel ferry for five years in succession, travelling through different regions of France, and once to Germany but these fairly Spartan holidays were something the children (and I) remember gratefully. I always enjoyed them, despite the cramped single berth sleeping and I clung on to that caravan long after cross-channel trips lost their savour. There were attractive places to visit in England and Wales. Eventually, while I lived with Dorrie, the caravan was put out to graze in an obscure corner of a Paul Harris field until vandals set it ablaze. It merited no more than a mention in the Police records.

The one relation Vera and I were in touch with was Jim Forsyth, who (with Judy) now lived and practised dentistry in the Portsmouth area. We began to make the occasional exchange visits, though I can't remember the children mingling, perhaps because their two boys, Charles and William, were away at school. I had a great admiration of Jim, which stretched back to childhood days when he seemed streets ahead of me. He had 'risen' from the ranks to become a dentist and naval officer while I was trying to cope with my lot and here he was sensibly installed in Old Pompey with Judy, who had her own dentistry patch. They were very much a professional couple, perhaps more sophisticated than us, though vulnerable on the arts side. I remember (when we went to the theatre) wondering why they couldn't understand what Pinter's play "The Caretaker" was all about. At this point in time I was rehearsing "West Side Story" for Eastbourne's Congress Theatre and Jim, responding to an enquiry from me, borrowed two stylised cane mannequins from the Portsmouth Art Gallery and brought them over, which was very thoughtful. Judy and Jim seemed well-balanced, Jim's affability matching Judy's occasional asperity. I don't think either Vera or I had any inkling that an estrangement was going to occur, for there were long gaps between our meetings.

We were certainly not prepared for the telephone message in March 1970 that told us Jim had ended his life, using his dental equipment very deliberately. To this day I do not know the full story of what drove Jim to suicide. It is true that there was mental instability on his mother's side but that adds up to little in this context. For Judy and his sons, Charles and William both teenagers, his death was a shocking blow which hurt them cruelly because the manner of his passing signified their isolation from him. I myself felt guilty of neglect but there had been no signal of distress and the few enquiries I made after the event led nowhere. I felt very sorry for Judy and I was glad she and Vera were able to become close friends until her untimely death in 1994. In recent years, Charles (now a doctor, married with a family) and William (a language teacher, married with a family) have asked me about their father's life and death but I really have very little to say. He was always cheerful, generous and caring (for his mother, for example) with an extrovert manner that obviously concealed deep emotional fissures.

10. Marital Breakdown

The decade of the '70s started with the deaths of my father and my cousin. It ended with the breakdown of my marriage. Whatever was going on in school life, and of course mighty changes were afoot, there was a concomitant private life which was reaching a logical outcome with or without connection to school matters. That's nonsense of course. My school activities were all affected by the deterioration of my relations with Vera. Perhaps the breakdown was a long time coming, but there were always obvious signs of our differences of opinion, indeed of separate interests, and discord had been part of the Morley family for years. The children accepted the situation as 'normal' as we went through the motions of running a family household, bringing up three children and indeed, during this decade, welcoming Vera's mother as part of the family. In some ways we seemed to be pretty stable as a family. We took summer holidays abroad and the children were growing up fast. Simon experienced life on an Israeli kibbutz and in 1977, the crucial year, won a place at Mansfield College, Oxford, to read History. Kate was at the High School and approaching GCE. Emma was in her last Primary year at Parkland's. Vera worked occasionally at Radio Brighton and helped a friend in a fashion shop. I was busy with many irons in the fire, of which The Travellers was the hottest at that time. I don't think Vera would have minded a continuation of this status quo, and I don't think she had any idea I was heading for a crisis.

I had developed a back problem, which no doubt started as pulled muscles years ago, but now I was beginning to get spasmodic pains and a twisted spine. Trying to rise from my bed one morning I experienced two incredible spasms that racked my vertebrae and left me gasping with pain. Dr. Barkworth arrived, examined me, listened to my account of chest pains and said, "You have had a heart attack, Mr. Morley. I had one six months ago and this is very similar." I was whisked into intensive care at once. A specialist took one look at me and said, "This isn't a heart attack, you're not the type!" And so it was. They decided, after tests, that I had pulled intercostal muscles in countering the nervous spasms in the spine. All I needed was rest, three weeks of it. Meanwhile Vera had spread the news like wildfire – I was a heart victim. Well, maybe that was right. I convalesced at home, resting in the garden and brooding on my condition. I remembered that Vera, as I was being stretchered from the house, had leaned over me to murmur, "I'm sorry for everything!" What she meant I don't know, but to me it signified a truth – everything was wrong. Perhaps it was the male menopause influencing me but it seemed that I had lived through twenty years of married life without experiencing true sexual fulfilment. Our lovemaking lacked passion, and basically my sex life was a washout. Whatever protest I made to myself or to Vera ended in resigned tolerance of the situation, for I felt that I must take my share of the blame. I thought I was a poor lover. Ours might have seemed a marriage of true minds but the impediment of a limp honeymoon had continued to affect progress for twenty years.

Perhaps one solution (or at least one compensation) might have been to seek solace elsewhere during this time but I was not after a quick fix and I was too much in the public eye to cover my tracks. Attending English holiday Conferences (ESB/NATE) gave me freedom away from home, but only one flirtation ended with us both in bed together, which was enjoyable but clearly going nowhere as she lived a thousand miles away. Pondering during my convalescent three weeks, I faced the fact that a slow but steady process of emasculation had occurred in my life. I had resigned myself to accept the marital situation through all these years while the children were growing up. Vera would always rule the roost at home and compared with her, I trailed behind in strength of character. Without resorting to bullying tactics, I was unable to match her sharp verbal dexterity. What was the solution? I simply made a deliberate and desperate decision that I must seek a sexual relationship elsewhere, not some kind of one-night-stand but a more lasting affair, before it was too late.

Ironically it was Vera who provided the opportunity. Friends from West Kirby came to stay and then introduced us to local relations, in particular Dorrie who lived with her three sons on the outskirts of Eastbourne. The feelings were mutual when we met, felt after exchanging a few words and glances on a busy street corner. That evening I phoned to ask casually if we could meet for a chat over a cup of coffee. She took the wind out of my sails by replying, after a short pause, "You mean you'd like an affair with me." I harrumphed a bit, not wishing to expose my intentions quite so quickly, but after we had gone through the coffee preliminaries, we followed the direct line of approach. We responded instinctively to each other, for both were in need. Dorrie's personal history is complicated, and really stranger than fiction – at least worthy of a fascinating narrative but, although I would like to celebrate her as a heroine of my time, I don't think she would appreciate the intrusions into her privacy. When I met her,

MATURITY IN EASTBOURNE

she was in the process of emerging from a period of grieving for her second husband, who had died five years previously. Before this, she had been unhappily married and now had five children from two husbands, though in physique she showed remarkably little wear and tear. It is certainly true that the mother-substitute was part of the appeal that she had for me but there was no doubting the sexual union between us. This was the best sex I have ever had.

It was addictive enough for me to decide that I could not continue without it. For almost a year Dorrie was my secret love, and I span a crafty web of deception to conceal the real reason for my irregular hours at home. Significantly, Vera was shocked when someone broke the news to her; she had no idea. She demanded my return and abstinence. I tried to comply but failed. To go on living the lie, propping up the empty relationship between husband and wife, was impossible. Even if it meant giving up the house and the comfortable status of middle-class respectability, I had to leave this false world and accept another, more honest reality. Even if it meant breaking the natural bond between myself and my three children, I had to live away from them. These were not easy decisions but, having left Brassey Avenue, taking my personal possessions with me, I knew there was no turning back. Only one regret troubles me now, and that was my failure to gather my three children together in order to tell them that I was leaving home but not deserting them. For one reason or another, I could speak to them only separately, and each was bewildered. I spoke to Simon, 18 years old, who was perhaps the least disturbed, but to Kate (at 16 the same age that I had lost my mother) I never properly explained anything and, although I talked to Emma (age 10) she has no memory of the occasion. I can see traces of a travesty of how the three Morley boys received the news of their deprivation separately forty years ago but of course that was far from my mind. In the end, the fracturing of relations with my children proved a barrier between Dorrie and myself, particularly when it became clear that her sons were also adversely affected by my presence.

My defection from the family caused major alterations. The economic implications were legally controlled through Separation and then Divorce with a Final Settlement. Having made the decision to live with Dorrie and her family, there was no going back for me. I deeply regret the emotional stress and domestic unhappiness that resulted, which may seem a hypocritical remark when I myself was benefiting from another home but there had to be no alternative, given my course of action. And I believe that in retrospect my children accept that it was better to end the prolonged and repressed situation and try to re-create something more truly loving and understanding. But there was bitterness and anger on many occasions. And jealousy as the pulls of the two 'rival' families created tensions. Vera's response was partly to welcome the break and partly to rally support for her cause. Reconciliation via marriage guidance proved impossible.

IRONS IN THE FIRE

Not wanting to stay in Brassey Avenue, she decided to move to a smaller house near Berwick Station, which was not as traumatic as it might have been, for the children were all on the move educationally. Simon was about to embark on his University years away from home. Kate could leave the High School and start her 'A' levels at Priory School in Lewes and Emma, who had been in the last year of the 11+ exams, moved from Parklands Junior to secondary school level at Ringmer School.

The house had to be sold immediately. Not difficult, though it was not a seller's market. I agreed to an instant offer from a neighbour, which cut out the estate agent's fee but was still below market value. Vera's life changed considerably, particularly as she chose to reside in a clutch of houses, which was no more than an isolated sub-hamlet really. The children adapted, more or less. I tried to keep in touch but the girls' trust in me was severely tested. It must have been gruelling to see me in the company of Dorrie's boys, as if I had swapped them for good. As time went on, it was becoming difficult to see what the future was to be. There was an impasse over children. I wanted to see more of my children; Dorrie wanted me to see less of them and to be a father to her boys. The issue came to a head during the summer of 1981, shortly after the Grammar-High School became the Sixth Form College. Dorrie's son Richard apparently was failing to make progress at Bexhill Grammar School and this was blamed on my presence at home. He did not like me. Dorrie suggested that for a year I should 'live out' while Richard had a chance to concentrate on his 'A' level studies. I decided, with misgivings, to look for a flat and ended up visiting an empty house in Bradford Street, Old Town, which was in a fairly decrepit condition (no bathroom, an outside toilet) but, as my architect friend John Innerdale said, it was "as sweet as a nut". My offer was accepted by the estate agent and I made plans to renovate the property.

That summer I was determined to take Emma on a week's holiday in the caravan, which still served me well, but Dorrie opposed the idea, as it would mean leaving her at home. For once I ignored her wishes, and off I went to Dorset and Lyme Regis with Emma and her very pleasant boy friend. It was a very enjoyable holiday. On my return, there was Brian, Dorrie's son, barring the entrance to her house politely and firmly. I was being punished for my disregard! It was almost laughable but I took the re-buff at face value and set off with my caravan to find a camping site, being reasonably happy to continue my open-air life-style with the weather so balmy. I found a very pleasant field on a farm near Hailsham and there I stayed, and stayed, and stayed until the College term was halfway over, and it was getting too chilly and damp for comfortable living. Dorrie's plan had misfired badly, though Richard no doubt would benefit. The fact is the spell was broken. I loved Dorrie and she loved me, but both of us loved our own children more than that. Maybe the first fine rapture of our passionate affair was on the wane but the realization that children came first altered our perception of the relationship. Buying this little cottage in Old Town had put me in a strong position to gain independence. By the time the fogs and rheums of November were upon me, I was determining to live on my own. Dorrie, of course repenting of her rash scolding tactic, visited me at the caravan but I was already reacting to an impulse that gained conviction the longer I was away from her. I loved Dorrie but not her children. Dorrie loved me, but her children more. I would have to break the connection. I am sure that she was feeling the same pressures. The years I spent with Dorrie were recuperative and emotionally healing. We were very much in love and didn't mind expressing it in public but both of us recognized the power of atavistic allegiances. I don't think I broke her heart by leaving her; I think we still treasure those loving years as something precious and unique.

In the meantime, family relationships were taking new shapes, sometimes beyond my control (deservedly). Having spent two years at Priory School, Lewes, Kate decided to leave home and marry Jim, and their first child, Rose, was born shortly after this. Despite difficulties, this marriage started happily and certainly bloomed, for there were two more children in fairly quick succession (Erin and Finnegan) – the Irish names marking the Irish connection. They were a delightful family when the children were young, and still are but now, as I write, they are all growing up and facing independent lives. Two sadnesses were deeply felt when the grandmothers died, first Jim's mother, Peggy, which caused Jim to call forth an Irish wake long remembered for the Irish jig band before which little Rose danced continually in the Irish manner, learnt at Peggy's knee. A few years after her death, Rose McKechnie died peacefully, aged 94, having devoted so much loving care to her grandchildren. She was kind to me, forgiving and patient. Unusually these days, she was laid to rest in her grave. I have not attended many burials and found this part of the mourning very moving.

Grandma-in-law's Funeral

> Her burial seemed perfunctory,
> no prelate's pomp though circumstantially
> a regular Catholic service.
> Family gathering round a sombre hole
> under a stunted yew tree
> in Ocklynge cemetery.
> The wind gusting along rows of tombs,
> graves and crosses; autumn leaves
> caught in crevices, clouds scudding overhead,
> bowed heads muttering the responses.

IRONS IN THE FIRE

The coffin dipped from sight,
roses dropped silently, and that was that.
Quiet hugs, hands held, lips pressed,
eyes glancing at wreaths and flowers,
red roses, remembering her name.
And then the parting of ways.

The Church Ceremony had lasted thrice as long,
splendid in robes and ritual:
the coffin reverent before the priest
hymns, prayers, blessings and passing bell
punctuating the flow of tributes.

At the graveside I sensed
the handmaid returning to her Lord
who promised Salvation.
If anyone deserved it
my Grandmother did.

Vera had decided to return to Eastbourne, finding Berwick too isolated for comfort, and was now living in a terrace house in the town centre. By a twist of fate she was very near Mrs. Eggerton's abode (Mrs. Egg to the children). During the next decade she found employment and indeed job satisfaction in a series of teaching and supervising posts at Girls' Schools, including Roedean and St Margaret's, Bushey. Emma, who had been a pupil at Ringmer, now continued her education at the neighbourhood school, Cavendish, and thence to Croydon Technical College to qualify in Ceramics. Simon, completing three years at Mansfield College with a two one hons degree in Modern History (1979), set out for Milan in search of an alternative to the office and soon found it in painting and art. He moved on to Paris, studied there, and headed for New York where he met Kaethe, married her and eventually returned to home waters in the mid-eighties, intent on a career as an artist. Kate, with Jim helping to look after the three children at home, began her studies at Brighton University, a degree course in Art, aiming to start secondary school teaching. The children were more often 'out of town' during this period, but at least we could be 'in touch'. I was now living in my small house in Bradford Street in Old Town, comfortably enough on my own. I had accepted that my relationship with Dorrie must end, for there was no way back to a sustained relationship with so many hang-ups over children. I knew we had to separate though I was totally grateful for the loving security that she had given me. The memory of our love survives and enlightens my life.

MATURITY IN EASTBOURNE

11. The Sixth Form College emerges

While my private life was undergoing these fits and starts, events at school had entered a critical new phase. The Grammar-High School was becoming a Sixth Form College to which secondary schools would send their pupils after GCSE for 'A' level studies. There are two unpleasant personal experiences that few teachers welcome: firstly, a School Assessment by Ofsted Inspectors, and secondly, the threat of redundancy and compulsory deployment. The former I have escaped through no grace of my own but I was threatened by the latter during the months leading up to the founding of the Sixth Form College in 1980. The two teaching staffs, amalgamated for the gross Grammar-High, had somehow to be thinned down to suit the new slimline College. There were bound to be redundancies and some teachers had to face deployment to other jobs and schools. And another delicate problem: who would be appointed as the Heads of the various Departments and Faculties?

As far as English was concerned, it was clear that there were two contenders – myself and Barbara Wilson, who was the Head of English at the High School. There were many more girls studying English than boys, and Barbara's record was sound and, as most of the other responsible appointments were going to the male Grammar teachers, perhaps it was necessary to redress the balance a little by appointing Barbara. Could JSM be prejudiced against me? Although he admired The Travellers and their touring productions, he considered this was a distraction from my teaching – and indeed, he had told me so. I had taken the hint and started to withdraw from active participation in their TIE tours. Now, at my interview, he was suggesting that perhaps I could become Head of Drama and Barbara Wilson Head of English. I rejected this notion firmly; after all, there was no such thing as a Drama Department. Producing plays was an after-school-hours activity; I was essentially a teacher of English in the classroom. It was not a question of salaries for we retained these anyway, but of responsibility and control. In the end JSM made a compromise: there would be two Heads of English sharing the responsibilities of the Department – with Barbara concerned for Exams; and me for Drama. Both Barbara and I accepted this situation, knowing that we could share duties and planning; once or twice we disagreed about policy but our decisions were always based on mutual approval. Neither of us was bigoted; we worked reasonably well together with a large English Department. I was grateful that JSM had not sold me down river. In fact, it was the best compromise he ever made. In the new Sixth Form College, English classes were able to grow in popularity and size, and my drama productions were to become a vibrant part of the cultural life of the College.

With my future teaching career more or less resolved peacefully, I celebrated with two experimental drama productions in one term. First, to initiate the new multi-purpose assembly hall I gathered a group of talented middle school actors and presented Thornton Wilder's "Our Town", which proved an excellent subject for the new setting (no stage, no scenery, plenty of lighting). Then, a couple of months later, I experimented with an 'in the round' production of "The Italian Straw Hat", quite complex and zany though farce is best played on stage. I was certainly trying to adjust to the absence of a proscenium arch. The following summer I had to make my personal decision to leave Dorrie and was living somewhat *al fresco* in my caravan in the Hailsham farm field as the second year of the Sixth Form College began. On balmy autumn evenings in my caravan, alone, I started to visualize how to stage the next production, which I decided should be "The Coventry Mystery Plays". This was a different kind of drama and I don't know why it should come to mind but presumably I felt liberated and ready for a large-scale celebration. My version of these mediaeval religious plays would make full use of the flat hall space as a total acting arena, with clusters of audience raised in sections round the walls. There would be a large cast flowing in and out, very much in the tradition of community drama. Some scenes would occupy the whole hall, like the village market or the Morris dancing or the river baptism or the final spectacular celebration of the risen Christ. Other scenes would be localized. Geoff Newman obliged with some comprehensive lighting effects. In the event the production was a startling success with local clergy unusually in evidence, and although "The Coventry Mystery Plays" wasn't "an act of worship" (as headlined in the Gazette), well, with Christ on the Cross and all that, we did it proud.

It pointed the way to the kind of drama that I was able to develop in the Sixth Form College, an attempt at 'total theatre', with music, song, dance, projected images, and large casts prominent in the presentations. No matter how amateur my shows may have been, this kind of 'total' concept was successfully evident in my next productions: "David Copperfield" adapted with music and songs, and then "The Threepenny Opera" which became a cause célèbre for special effects. Next, my own musical "the Wooden Horse" (music by Roger Malley) in tandem with Euripides' "The Trojan Women" (J-P Sartre's version). And then "A Midsummer Night's Dream" which was so successful, we re-staged it at the Hippodrome Theatre for two charity performances before full houses of school children. And Peter Ustinov's "Romanoff and Juliet", which I think I improved by introducing a troupe of touring dancers to the plot and dividing the scenes into two parts, not three.

During this period, the Eastbourne Gazette gave awards for amateur dramatic achievements. Four out of five years running, I received a trophy for 'the Best Youth Drama Director', which I modestly would share with my production team if it were possible. Without belittling the achievement of College productions during these years, what was genuinely more personally satisfying for me was

MATURITY IN EASTBOURNE

the success of our annual experimental and entertaining College Arena Plays, written by students and enthusiastically performed in the round. The Sixth Form College flourished as the dramatic productions established a reputation. Two outstanding students actors were Su Corbett and Miltos Yerolimou, beside whom I would place predecessors such as Mervyn Cumming, Stuart Olesker, Nick Nye, Pip Simmonds, John Cummings, Peter Talbot, David Burrows, John Huddart, David Balcombe, Malcolm Hayes, David Scutt and many others who have not just contributed to the school and college performances during three decades but have also preserved their enthusiasm and talent for drama and the theatre. That tribute I extend to members of the School and College Staff Thespians - Chris Mason, Geoff Newman, Kevin Anderson, Tony Morse, Chris Clarke and Peter Sharples in particular.

10. Marriage à la Second Mode

I was now devoting a great deal of my time to drama, always out of school hours. I could be found back-stage during most lunchtimes and rehearsing after afternoon lessons. I was set designer, and stage-managed the construction of the stage area, often using scaffolding. I could rely on the Art department to look after décor, but I had no staff stage manager. I worked on the reel-to-reel sound track at home. Costumes I personally obtained from Lewes Little Theatre. Oddly, I was neglectful of makeup requirements, which seemed less important. There was no shortage of back-stage help from Sixth Formers and we established a timetable of (1) major college play in the first term; (2) one-act plays Arena Theatre in the second term and (3) a free wheeling home-made entertainment at the end of the summer term. Looking after the drama was becoming obsessive, though I did not neglect my English teaching assignments. Classroom work was always essential and I think my teaching of students at this level was successful, mainly 'A' level work but also GCSE groups, with a continual flow of student essays to read, mark and comment on.

The split with Dorrie had led to my living a single life in 63 Bradford Street during the first year of the Sixth Form College, but there was an unexpected change when I renewed acquaintance with a former friend who was now living in Brighton. It was something like twenty-five years since I had known June, who in the '60s had owned an unusual (for Eastbourne) shop, specializing in modern designs in home furnishings and materials. Art School trained (Scarborough), she had been recruited for Heal's furniture emporium in London, and then married an Eastbourne estate agent. Now, following a move to Cornwall and the breakdown of her marriage, she was installed in central Brighton with her daughter Anna, having qualified as a social worker. Actually, by the time we met again, she was studying psychotherapy and the gentle art of self-analysis. It seemed we were well matched, with many interests in common, and it wasn't long before we were sharing beds, meals and holidays. Our initiation into camping en vacance in western France proved rather primitive as we failed to take a soft mattress, but our holiday organisation improved. We visited Majorca and Bulgaria in successive years, sampling through hotel package deals the luxuries of capitalist global consumerism and then the utilitarian strictures of the communist satellite state.

Meeting 'the family' meant journeys to north Yorkshire, which not only revived acquaintance with Saltburn, our holiday venue in the thirties, but also introduced me to the Yorkshire moors and to Whitby and Staithes. I got on well with June's mother (now at the time of writing, 102 years old) and also her daughter Anna who was a student at the time. My own children liked June too, which was certainly not the case with Dorrie who got the blame unjustly for causing the breakdown of my marriage. All seemed to augur well for a long-term relationship and when the notion of a wedding was mooted, I did not oppose it. Marriage was mainly a way of placating her mother, who maintained old-fashioned standards about us sleeping together. At the back of my mind also was the thought that I had to put Dorrie 'behind me'. I had enjoyed a blissful sexual union with her and I did not expect to find anything to rival that. No doubt I was being calculatingly selfish. I thought that married life with June would be comforting and reassuring, not just for me but June too.

All went well at first. In 1987, the wedding ceremony (at Brighton Register Office) and feast (at Il Duomo restaurant) was much enjoyed by sixty guests. I moved from Eastbourne to live in June's house but I did not adapt easily to life in Brighton, a town/city which I found rather schizoid as it exudes an air of raffish foppery on the one (the right) hand and slovenly decrepitude on the other. I was restless and did not adjust easily to June's acquaintances and routines. Nevertheless, I commuted to College and continued teaching happily enough, very conscious of educational storm signals being hoisted at staff meetings. It was obvious that directives from educational sources were attempting to control the output and input of teachers. Accountability was a key concept as managerial policies began to shift power and responsibility in the college. Suddenly I decided this was a good time to opt out, sensing that I should leave before the more rigorous, bureaucratic attitudes took over.

I decided to retire from the Sixth Form College at the end of term. The retirement procedure was enjoyable. Aged 62, I felt I was 'going out on a high', even representing a golden age that was being put to rest, for my dedication to school/college drama and English had been a personal commitment that was appreciated by students – and a few teachers too. Celebrating my imminent departure, I recall a fancy dress retirement party held at my house, attended by many friends and colleagues; elsewhere there were speeches (JSM paying tribute nicely, see Appendix) and presentations; the Governors treated me right nobly and I enjoyed a bibulous ceremony in Lewes for teachers 'serving' for 30 years and more.

But *retirement* was not really on the cards. I didn't feel that old. I was still able to teach, to examine, to direct, to write, to paint, and I seemed to be busier than ever. Brighton was not the centre of all this activity, however. I needed more positive exigencies there, for there were so many things to do in Eastbourne. My house in Bradford Street was both a retreat and an activity centre. My Amstrad PC was there for a start, and I could set up an easel in my study room and paint too. All my books, scripts, papers were there – whereas I had no niche in June's house, where I felt more of a visitor than a resident. Nevertheless, I joined the Sussex Playwrights Club in Brighton and made quite a good first impression with the playscripts I wrote. Some of these won competitions and/ or got published but I craved more involvement with a theatrical group. Not very far from June's house was the Brighthelm Community Centre where the Prospect Players performed. I joined them, designed and built a rather good set for their next play production and directed two of my own plays at Brighthelm. For a time I attempted to enlarge the dramatic activities there by encouraging local people to get involved in a kind of community play. This was Thornton Wilder's "The Skin of Our Teeth" with a cast of 30, but though this was quite successful I began to realise my ideas were not supported by some members of the drama group, for this was basically a Church foundation. That was something of a setback. At home June was now fully qualified as a psychotherapist and was absorbed in her patients' problems. We started re-structuring her house in St Nicholas Road with a view to putting it up for sale though I had little to say about this. Knocking down walls became some kind of therapy or protest. Increasingly I was aware of losing touch with my children, who were now facing growing-up problems, and I was feeling restless about my comfortable, selfish life. I did not want personal prosperity which took me further from them. My guilt could not be ignored, even though I knew my children had accepted the fracture of my bond to them.

I think it was after the second Christmas of our married life that I proposed to return to Eastbourne for a 'rest'. June agreed, of course, for our relationship was always tolerant and caring, but I don't think she thought this would lead to a permanent move. Nor did I, but the freedom I discovered living on my own made me increasingly reluctant to return to the 'bonds' of marriage in Brighton. My little house, which I altered, designed, decorated, furnished and claimed as 'all my own work' was an important part of my personal life. I could no more give it up than fly. I was accustomed to my routines there and deliberately stayed on, keeping contact with those people I knew well and establishing the 'life-style' of a retired schoolteacher, whatever that means. I think it implies that I had multiple interests (irons in the fire) and now had the opportunity to test some of them out. June accepted my plea for freedom and I am grateful for her cooperation. I think we both feel that marriage was inappropriate in our case, at least as far as living together is concerned. We could have survived as 'partners', each retaining a firm measure of independence while sharing activities regularly, but the close communion of man and wife put too much pressure on our personal commitment. Although we rarely see each other nowadays, our marriage remains existent and June, as my wife, receives the widow's enhanced pension when I die, but I have not been able to honour the marital vows. I shall go on loving her, admiring her, wanting to keep in touch but stalling when faced with the responsibility that goes with living with her. This may seem the ultimate selfish action, and perhaps I should not be presuming June's tacit acceptance of the situation. Without this decision, however, I don't think I could have achieved the reasonably contented position I now occupy, with a balance between my family, my children, my personal happiness and my public involvement. I think I am doing more good in the world this way.

11. Coming through Retirement

In 1988, still living with June in Brighton, I retired from teaching – ending the 'happiest days of my life'. I was sad to leave students who were still studying for 'A' levels and talented staff colleagues who had shared activities with me. I was reasonably content to hand over total control of the English Department to Barbara (though the fact that she retired early at the end of the next year perhaps signifies something) and I was pleased to have worked in unison with her during the excellent College decade. I was less sanguine about JSM's decision to appoint the successor to my Drama empire from the current staff, more or less on the grounds that Nigel (Music & English) wanted the job and his appointment would save on a salary. The outcome was soon evident in the drop in audience support as Drama became subject to the new controls. Nigel, to justify his position, decided to introduce 'A' level Drama, thus limiting the scope and significance of play production in the College. What had been a major expression of community life at the College dwindled into a minor exam subject for a narrow band of students. I still kept in touch, helped to prolong Arena Theatre for another year and took an interest in the creation of the small Drama Workshop that was to be carved out of the multi-purpose hall, which itself was soon to be transformed into a Computer Resources Centre. There was no room for an assembly hall, auditorium or a stage in the new set-up. This was throwing out the baby with the bath water. But more was to come, for the Sixth Form College was assuming the status of a Tertiary College, in direct competition with the near neighbour ECAT. Renaming was all part of the transformation: Park

MATURITY IN EASTBOURNE

College and South Downs College respectively, and now these two proud institutions (each with histories of high repute) have been amalgamated and merged with Lewes Tertiary College. A new baby is being born and may be flourishing, though many of the teachers (and my former colleagues) have lost out in the process. There seems to be a general consensus that teaching is not what it used to be (worse!).

There have been sad personal losses since retirement, the most devastating being the deaths of my brothers John and Neil. That Neil should be struck down by cancer, and should die after a hard-fought fight, was a shock. The fact that he was three years younger than me seemed to invalidate his death. He was dying before his time doubly. Apart from Marion, I felt I was closest to Neil in terms of upbringing and shared experiences and yet I am well aware those deep-seated bonds kept us silent, unable or unwilling to talk about the family trauma. We didn't open our hearts to each other, we didn't communicate about the things that really mattered. I admired the way he coped with his later years, finding a happy kind of compensation and fulfilment in directing and acting on stage, always shared with Marion, the two of them being key players for Leicester Little Theatre. Neil was a devoted thespian but also a genuine family man with a loving concern for his wife and children. It's good to know Gillian, Philip and Nicholas are all 'doing well'.

When John died, I rejoiced in his life. Despite what had seemed like all the odds, he had succeeded. Nearly 80, frail and dependent on dialysis he had still retained his enthusiasm for life, much helped by Margaret and Steve (and the grand-children) with whom he was living at the end. John had recovered from the death of his wife Joyce ten years previously but really the two of them made a remarkable love-match of their life together. Joyce was the perfect partner for my brother. It was difficult to reconcile the nervous, introverted John I knew as a boy with the cheerful, confident adult who was so proud of his wife and daughter and who was greeted with affection by friends and neighbours alike.

A further untimely death (in late-nineties) was that of Chris Mason, who had retired from Reigate GS owing to ill health. Our heyday together was the five-year period 1958-64 when we were running the Grammar School English Department, and also trying our hand at writing plays. His affable, unflappable good humour and wisdom were always evident, even when disapproving the breakdown of my marriage. Margot Mason remains a good friend. When I retrospectively consider the individual friends who have influenced me both at school and at home, Chris is the most recent and the first to depart. Lewis and Betty Thomas still offer hospitality in Haverfordwest, John and Lesley Procter in Somerset, Desmond Prince (alas without June) lives in New Zealand. I give them thanks in retirement.

IRONS IN THE FIRE

Not that I have been entirely content to be on my own permanently. I can cope with the chores of domestic cleanliness or cuisine, enjoy creating a personal ambience in my home and keep the front and back gardens reasonably tidy, including pruning two apple trees and roses bushes (though weeds prosper and grass seed fails to take root in my light soil), but I do like a little company. After six months of re-adjusting to bachelor solitude, two occurrences re-structured my life. The first and most important of these was the chance meeting in Gildredge Park with someone I had not met since Dorrie and I attended a party in her home in the Goffs about five years previously. This was Alexandra, who, showing true motherly devotion, had offered to help back-stage when her daughter was acting in a Victorian comedy ("Caste") at the Sixth Form College. Alexandra was also running a successful Youth Drama Group in the town, though by the time we were bumping into each other in the Park, that enterprise had folded. In fact, she had suffered a succession of disasters over the years, including divorce. Embracing when we greeted each other was mutually gratifying. At the time of our reunion, her daughter's marriage in Holland was failing but in fact the return of Tania (with two young daughters) to Eastbourne helped Alexandra to recover. The Dutch connection had been breached twice, for her ex-husband was a Nederlander. Tania, Skyla and Imogen are now Sussex bred and very supportive and the Brown family, with Scottish roots, has gained strength from renewed bonding.

Through ten years Alexandra and I have maintained a loving 'partnership'. Maybe we have the advantage of possessing our own homes, which allows us the freedom to retreat from each other when desired. We have our personal interests. Alexandra is a Reiki Master Practitioner who treats friends and patients in her flat; I am often wrapped in my own compulsive PC tapping. Domestically we cope with our own 'pads' but share evening meals, alternating with the cooking. Generally we keep to our own beds these days, but that is because I think sleep comes more easily by myself. We shall continue to plait our colourful threads until (fancifully) the tapestry is complete.

The other occurrence that helps me to enjoy my days as a 'senior citizen' is the U3A (University of the Third Age). It was Ted Mcfadyen, a friend and member of the Playwrights' Club, who advised me to seek membership of the Eastbourne branch in 1991. This was really just the kind of educational activity that I needed and Eastbourne Central U3A affairs occupy quite a lot of my time and energy. The U3A movement provides educational as well as social and cultural stimulus for elderly people and I have contributed in many ways since joining. Being elected Chairman for a two-year stint in the mid-nineties was important, firstly because I steered the branch out of troubled waters successfully and secondly because I proved to myself that I could manage an unusual

MATURITY IN EASTBOURNE

responsibility diligently. I remain a co-opted member of the Committee and edit the Newsletter.

One of the chief ingredients in the U3A cornucopia is the provision of Study Groups, which meet in members' homes regularly (monthly). Here I do shine.

1. For over a decade I have run a devoted study group of eleven 'third agers' that studies and discusses Drama and Literature texts;
2. I lead a personal writing group of ten that writes, reads and discusses 'essays' on chosen themes, and from time to time we publish some of these in our own magazine;
3. I have adapted 'Desert Island Discs' for monthly record programmes, chiefly for 'castaway' U3A members selecting their eight pieces of music;
4. Each year I organize a "Study Group Miscellany" on a chosen theme. This allows quite a few of our Subject Study Groups to participate in the presentation;
5. Perhaps most significantly I lead a U3A Thespian group that stages 'live' entertainments and on five occasions have taken them on tour to other U3A branches; and
6. I produce regular Newsletters, which are highly regarded for their style and content.

I get a kick out of all this activity. When I retired from teaching (and producing college plays) I never expected to be so much involved. Am I a control freak at work? Even if so, I derive enormous pleasure from these 'achievements', and so have many (mainly elderly) people. Just recalling the career of the Thespians makes me rejoice. We were always a scratch side and the award of a Millennium grant in 2000 (£1000) was quite unexpected. Most of this was spent on stage equipment and touring a show with a cast of 20 (too many!). East Sussex CC honoured the Thespians with an Award for our contribution to Adult Learning in 2001. More recently, in 2004 the Thespians (with our U3A Dance Group) successfully celebrated the 21st birthday of this U3A branch with a Variety Show at the Underground Theatre. Maybe it is time to relax. Running the Thespians requires much energy and it has been quite stressful, mainly due to the unpredictable condition and support of elderly performers. In personnel, the Thespians dwindle.

Another retirement interest has been the Sussex Playwrights Club in Brighton. The aim is to write plays and to get them published, but despite achieving this with six or seven one-act plays, I have been disappointed that on the open market my wares have not attracted attention. I have written four or five full-length plays but without success in terms of performance by drama groups. They don't even satisfy myself, let alone theatrical buffs. Nor have I persevered with radio or television scripts. One reject and I give up! I became quite intensely involved with two full-length bio-documentary plays which needed considerable research: "Monsters of the Weald" is about the life (and hard times) of Dr. Gideon Mantell, a Lewes doctor and pioneer of dinosaur discovery, and "Dodo at the Seaside" is a fanciful extrapolation about Charles Dodgson (Lewis Carroll) and his supposed involvement with an actual Eastbourne murder. My practical involvement with the U3A has led to a slackening of concern for playwriting.

A further retirement interest continues. Ken Reed, Walter Tillyard and myself, three teachers sharing pedagogic memories in retirement, many years ago began meeting regularly to discuss 'life' and gradually this trio expanded into a sestet of male contemporary Senior Citizens who meet for discussions in each other's homes. I call this 'select' group "the Bonders", but other titles ("The Old Devils, The Wise Ones") are more ironic. We share an Eastbournean background and a fairly sceptical respect for each other's points of view, but sometimes I wonder what we are doing. I am happy to continue the perpetual motion of our meetings, thanks to Ken Reed, Hugh Riddick, John Boyle, Frank Glyn Jones and Peter Pickett. And thanks also to Bryan Clough, writer, publisher and friend.

12. Conclusion

The end of this chapter sees me eighteen years into retirement. It was never part of my plan to write about the current affairs and events of these years, though clearly my pensionable status begins to establish a considerable 'period' of my life. In writing these reminiscences, I wanted to make contact with the past, particularly those early years of childhood and adolescence which somehow seem to concern someone else, a youngster who is related to me rather than being 'me'. I have tried to piece together the stages and phases of growing up and I hope the later years involving maturity have been described honestly and sincerely. I could quite dispassionately round off the manuscript now and keep it just for my own reading in really old age.

> When you are old and grey and full of sleep
> And nodding by the fire, take down this book,
> And slowly read, and dream of the soft look
> Your eyes had once, and of their shadows deep ...

I hope I shall be able to do that but there is always a legitimate desire to share what has been written and thus, while completing this record of 'a life' for my own benefit and enjoyment, I have been aware of a readership out there consisting of members of the family, kith and kin who relate to the Morleys and Forsyths, and of friends and acquaintances whom I have been fortunate enough

MATURITY IN EASTBOURNE

to know. I hope they find enough within these pages to keep them reading till the last chapter.

One further thought: I have refrained from making detailed reference to my children despite the fact that, all through the text, they have their own recollections of events and have been severely affected by my behaviour. How they view these 'memoirs', which I claim to be writing for my own benefit, I can't be certain. They may well look askance at this account of their father's life. It's an alarming fact that they now approach middle age and mature adulthood, but I hope they will accept that this chapter should not close without a brief reference to their present 'condition' both as individuals and members of society.

Simon married Lindy, happily and creatively in the nineties. He is an artist (exhibiting internationally), a writer (he published a big book on modern art in 2004), a curator and a lecturer and tutor at the Sotheby's Institute. Lindy has published two novels (both well received) and will soon finish writing her third, a major work.

Kate has recently separated from Jim. She teaches art, studies play therapy, and happily is qualifying for educational specialization in Sussex. Her three children are now grown-up: Rose with her son Sol, her partner Danny and a ladies' dress shop in the town centre. Erin, with a good Fine Arts degree, is currently backpacking round the world, at the time of writing in South America. Finn has moved to Brighton, partners Nadia and her daughter Tallulah, and creates music CDs.

Emma lives with her son George and her partner Martin in Sheffield. She has diplomas in Ceramics and has recently qualified for a B.Sc. degree (Design and Technology) at Hallam University.

All the signs are that my offspring, having been through their rites of passage, are maturing happily. My four grandchildren and one great grandson (Rose, Erin, Finn, George and Sol) are in their different ways 'developing well'. To round off this valedictory note, the women in my life (Vera, Dorrie, June, Alexandra) remain in touch, however tenuous.

I have reached The Present, and I shall wait here for the present. How much time The Future will provide remains unknowable but I do believe my health is reasonably sound. Whether I have strung together the five phases of my life so that there is an adequate causative sequence over nearly eighty years remains to be read. Those earlier chapters seem to be about different times, not quite a figment of an old man's imagination but a narrative taking place in one of Philip Pullman's parallel universes. I know two fractures changed the direction and content of my life; whether I go sufficiently deep to reveal a broken heart is doubtful. I would like to think there is evidence of a golden thread such as could guide me through the labyrinth but I haven't kept a grip on it. In any case, I am no Theseus, though various women played Ariadne for me.

IRONS IN THE FIRE

When a Sixth Former at school, I read Bernard Shaw's Preface to "Back to Methuselah" and enjoyed it (more than the expressionistic play). His theme was Evolution and he provided an absorbing account of Darwin's theories based on "The Origin of Species" and "The Descent of Man" but Shaw deplored his contention that Man has had little or no control over his evolution and argued that the theories of Lamarck are much more acceptable – man can through will power or *élan vital* cause hereditary changes. I never quite believed that, learning from 'Flush' at school that "there is a divinity that shapes our ends rough-hew them how we will," though this was à propos circumcision and the nature of the divinity was not in question at the time. Darwin's theories have been quite clearly validated through discoveries during the 20th century and my retirement reading has taught me not only to accept Darwinian evolutionism but also to follow Richard Dawkins' lead in rejecting religious dogmas and institutions, and to doubt that there is a Creator (anthropomorphically). I rejoice in the wonderful achievements of Homo Sapiens. It is almost incredible how this extraordinary creature has evolved in relation to Gaia, the living planet, and to his own burgeoning consciousness. I quote Shakespeare, or rather Hamlet (again)

> What a piece of work is a man! How noble in reason, how infinite in faculties, in form and moving how express and admirable, in action how like an angel, in apprehension how like a god! The beauty of the world, the paragon of animals – and how yet to me, what is this quintessence of dust

All is dust to dust. And all his endeavours and achievements have no meaning beyond the world in which Man has evolved. Science provides a partial understanding of the workings of the cosmos; Art provides an opportunity to create and express an enthusiastic response to being alive. And all this within the universe where we spend our lifetimes. Isn't that wonderful? I don't want to believe in 'Luck' as a decisive factor in evolution. It is a funny word with etymology unknown, and it runs either way – good or bad. I don't believe in it as a reality and I am not a gambler but it's sometimes possible to seize the opportunity, enjoy the day, *Carpe diem*. Should I equate the bad luck of losing my mother when I was sixteen with the good luck of gaining a place at Oxford? If I believed in some kind of eternal providence that would be not luck, but poetic justice. But I don't accept the premise. Life is so much more complicated than that. Is it luck that the tsunami happened in the Indian Ocean rather than the North Sea? Nor was it caused by the wrath of God. I do not believe that my life will continue in any individual form after I die. *Requiescat in pace.* Perhaps I want to be remembered affectionately by 'loved ones' for a little while longer, and this account of my life will help to make that possible, but I won't bet on it.

APPENDIX

A PLETHORA OF PLAY PRODUCTIONS

The following pages record a chronological sequence of plays, which I have variously produced and/or directed. Most of these are full-length plays or one-act play programmes performed at Eastbourne Grammar School, the Grammar and High School or the Sixth Form College, but I was able to get involved with other dramatic and musical productions in the town particularly when Reg Bertin (Head of Music) was presenting some enterprising operatic and musical productions and orchestral concerts in the school hall.

I possess a large folio containing mounted photographs of most of the school and college play productions, though the Arena one-act plays and my 'extra-mural' productions regretfully are not included. What is the point of compiling a comprehensive list? Well, it affords a panoramic view of dramatic activity over fifty years. It allows me to make a subjective assessment of the challenge and the achievement, the public presentation and the private aspiration. And I can register some debts of gratitude to those participating. And salute some good friends, both students and teachers. If nothing else, I can count them one by one.

I want also to pay tribute to the achievement of the Grammar School "Five in One Arena Theatre" and the Sixth Form College "Arena Theatre Plays". These original plays, written and produced and performed by pupils/students and sometimes teachers, were staged 'in the round' and, in my opinion; they contributed greatly to the celebration of drama at school and college. It is worth noting that audience attendance at the Arena plays was consistently high.

There is a random element about some of the comments on the play productions, my concern being to register a personal remembrance of each production, and to record memorable fact or anecdote. This inventory is confined to amateur theatre, particularly school plays but including occasional adult productions. Nothing is perfect, especially with *amateurs,* but standards can be high and the achievement relatively worthy. I think I have the chronology right anyway.

A. Period 1956-63, when the Grammar School was at Eversley Court

1. **Down With Skule** (Dec 1956)
   In my first term I organised a Revue in aid of Hungarian Relief Fund, with an obvious subversive theme, using original sketches and including musicians etc. This was a surprise success and an effective starting point for getting support for my first full-length play production.

IRONS IN THE FIRE

2. **The Shoemaker's Holiday** by Thomas Dekker (Dec 1957)
   A School production. An Elizabethan comedy that I had studied for 'A' level at Sevenoaks. It centres on London citizens and trades-people. All the female roles were played by junior boys (and one senior). The tiny stage (with proscenium arch) was fronted with rostrums borrowed from Devonshire Park tennis store and we built scaffold side units. Joe Harrop constructed the set. Morris Romans painted a delightful Tudor townscape. A reviewer from the Times Educational Supplement was invited and amazingly he came and gave a glowing report of our production.

3. **The Alchemist** by Ben Jonson (Dec 1958)
   A School production. Doublet and hose again, this time complicated with much technical jargon, not easy to learn. Was this a set text? Another scaffold design (of house interior) effective. Some of the contemporary satire lost, comedy became a bit knockabout but caricatures sustained. Still using boys as girls. The same Times Ed. critic gave a luke-warm review, a brave effort but thought it too farcical.

4. **Four One Act Plays** (May 1959).
   An experimental school presentation inspired by the achievement of Sixth Former Peter Clarke and his Youth Club actors in winning the County Drama Award with their production of Eliot's "Sweeney Agonistes" at Glyndebourne. Four plays were performed, with casts drawn from different age levels. Juniors presented a St Francis play; the middle school production was "St Simeon Stylites", both trailblazers for the award-winning "Sweeney Agonistes". The finale was a light-hearted Staff production of "The Nightingale and the Emperor". First 'staff' performance.

5. **St Joan** by Bernard Shaw (Dec 1959)
   A School production. My first real success. Started ominously with protest from older boys that I am choosing a play about a girl. I cast a middle school boy as Joan – Chris Ashdown is brilliant. The cast begins to understand the plot. Excellent interplay between Olesker and Nye, also Peter Clarke and Howard Kirby (as the Inquisitor). The court scene is mesmeric with Joan condemned. Young members of audience weep - music emotionally powerful. Perhaps the epilogue prolonged the climax but I blame GBS for that!

A PLETHORA OF PLAY PRODUCTIONS

6. Mr Bolfry by James Bridie (April 1960)
A Presbyterian by upbringing and sympathy, I was pleased to produce this witty comedy set in a Scottish Manse with St Andrew's Church players. Tom Jeffreys remembered as a dynamic Minister but I forget who played the Devil (Mr Bolfry). Warm reception by audience but one or two Wee Free doubters and one sour lemon in the cast (a would-be directrice). Happy memories of a small-scale success.

7. Othello by William Shakespeare (Dec 1960)
A School production. Ambitious attempt at mature tragedy but Stuart Olesker and Nick Nye are well matched in lead roles. For the first time, High School girls invited to participate, obviously much more 'real' with them. Largest cast of extras so far, but space limited. A disgruntled Times Ed Reviewer attends our first night performance – reports stage-setting problems slowing action. Going off the Times Ed. (a Carol Forder idea anyway).

8. The Love of Four Colonels by Peter Ustinov (Oct 1961)
EODS invites me to direct their autumn production at the Devonshire Park Theatre. I had hardly been backstage at any professional theatre so it was quite initiating. The play needed a stronger director but the cast was supportive and experienced. The production was well received. I could not resist attending most of the performances; apparently good directors walk away. No further invitations from EODS, but I was too busy at school anyway. I never took to EODS actually.

9. Five in One Arena Plays: No. 1 (April 1962)
Compiled to mark the end of an era – the school moving to new buildings. A play-writing competition produces 9 scripts, from which "Bags of Fun" (M. Palmer), "The Prison" (A. Chester), "Colombo"(C. Astridge[1]), "Worship" (P. Enser), "The Red Hand and the Green Ring" (M. Cumming) are selected for performance in a 3-sided arena – a successful salute to the old hall 'theatre' but also planting the seed of 'arena theatre in the round'.

---

[1] "Colombo", actually written by a parent, was one of the Arena Plays published in the 70s.

IRONS IN THE FIRE

B. Period 1962–77, After the Grammar School moved to King's Drive

10. **The Insect Play** by the Capek Bros (Nov 1962)

    A School production. Expressionist German style – where did I find this? Ideal for ensemble playing and special effects. This was the first production on the new stage at King's Drive. Scope for large cast, climaxing with a spectacular Ant War scene, using Civil Defence equipment. Butterflies played as flappers, Creepers and Crawlers as City money-grubbers, the Ants as totalitarian dictatorship – satire on human conduct. N.B. Still using boys for female roles. Play very well received. Good set (Morris Romans) with cyclorama backing. Probably the play, which made me evoke imaginative responses most clearly, with firm cast control necessary.

11. **Five in One Arena Plays: No 2** (April 63)

    Encouraged by the success of the first set of original plays, we chose six plays (one too many!). The creation of a well-lit arena in the round was a major achievement of Geoff Newman and Sixth former H. Eysenck. "Complexity" (K. Sherlock), "A Stroll in the Park" (J Hylands), "The Monument" (CJ Mason & M Morley), "Be Bloody, Bold and Resolute" (C. Astridge), "Sea Mist"(J Martin), "At the Going Down of the Sun" (M. Cumming). N.B. "The Monument" was performed by members of the staff. This show confirms the potential of Arena theatre in the school.

12. **The Winter's Tale** by William Shakespeare (Dec 63)

    A School production. 'A' level set text. A better production than previous attempts at WS. The new stage, with extensions, provides much more acting space and the lighting effects help. Good costumes (Sheila Collett creates costume team). Confident performances, esp. John Norman as Leontes. High School girls involved very successfully. Quote from the review: "This was a production for which I would have been proud to be responsible. Agreeable to the eye, beautifully lit, attractively dressed, intelligently spoken, it had pace, above all the production kept a firm grip on the story"(Lionel Green)

13. **Five in One Arena Plays: No 3** (April 64)

    "A yet higher standard, even as 1963 excelled 1962, with more confident use of theatre in the round" – retired professional critic Richard Gilbert offers regular reviews of the plays. "Pictures at an Exhibition" (Chris Payne), "Hot Sound from Hell" (Roger Harrison-Jones), "The Return of the Beagle" (HMM with Gen Eng set), "The Café" (P. and J. Harber), "Charade" (Chris Mason), this being performed by members of Staff -

A PLETHORA OF PLAY PRODUCTIONS

Chris's swan song, as he moves on to Reigate GS. The Beagle play was about Charles Darwin, whose autobiography I had been reading with a Sixth Form group: "a play on a higher level, both in content and execution ..." (R.G.)

14. Images of The Tempest (Nov 64)

This was our contribution to the inaugural drama presentation at the Congress Theatre organised by EODS with other town amateur groups. I create a sequence of scenes/images, with Moira House girls (under M. Causley) and GS boys performing. Spectacular staging with lighting, music and special effects. Officially we are allocated 8 minutes, I plan for 15. Timekeepers furious but comment from audience picks out our Images as the item with the most professional brio. No regrets – especially as Eastbourne College has been allocated 20 minutes to enact a crummy crowd scene from Julius Caesar.

15. Henry IV Part One by William Shakespeare. (Dec 1965)

A School production. Ambitious perhaps, though I can't cast Falstaff at school level so I invite Lionel Cooper (Primary School teacher and amateur actor) to play the part – successfully but an 'unpardonable error' to some reactionaries. The rest of cast was entirely GS and highly competent – including Laurence Downey, John Huddart, John Cummings, Alan Bennell, Peter Talbot. Set design works well. Battle scenes very effective, using home-forged swords. Ironically, spotted talented extra who *might* have coped as Sir John. Very much my favourite WS play, thanks to all for keeping it that way.

16. Noyes Fludde The Chester Miracle Play, Music by Benjamin Britten (Jan 1965)

A special 'town' performance at the Congress Theatre. Daniel in the lions' den for me. Thanks to the network of enthusiastic and talented supporters I could call upon to form a production team, this was an outstanding success that was noted beyond the bounds of Eastbourne. The initiators were Paul Harris (impresario) and John Chatfield (music). To these I added Marguerite Causley (movement), Robert Tavener (design), Geoffrey Flint (stage décor), Mary Quigley (costumes), Alun Jones (sets) and a few more too. In the event, more than 300 children from 21 schools and colleges took part. A few years later (1971) I turned down an invitation to direct a second "Noyes Fludde" at the Congress (why repeat?) – and Philip le Brocq took over. No comparison!

IRONS IN THE FIRE

17. Five in One Arena Plays: No 4 (March 65)
Standard improving each time. "Welcome Home, Robert" (B. Rayner & A. Ludby), "See You in my Dreams" (R. Harrison-Jones), "The Lads " (Peter Henderson), "The Tale of the Four Winds"[2] (HMM), "Waiting for Goddard" (P Harber). This year there is more sophistication in the writing, the "Four Winds" fantasy brings Marguerite Causley and dancing Moira House girls into orbit.

18. The Rivals by Richard Sheridan (Nov 65)
A School production. A cast of enthusiastic young actors, and girls from the High School included – but Mrs Malaprop played well by Stephen Brown, with strong support from David Burrows, John Cummings, John Novak, Chris Burden and Anthony Delves. A successful attempt at Restoration comedy style. Good pace, set changes adroitly made by servants, excellent costumes hired, live music group including a harpsichord for John York. Morris Romans continues stage design skill.

19. Five in One Arena Plays: No 5 (April 66)
This was probably the best quintet so far, with two of the plays eventually published in 'Five Arena Plays' and the finale providing one of the funniest and best-acted comedies, directed by Tony Morse. The 'in the round' setting well exploited. "Under Beachy Head" (HMM)[3], "Reunion" (David Cant), "Highly Favoured Island" (Anthony Moore), "The Chimney Sweeps" (Anthony Delves)[4] and "Terminus" (B. Rayner and A. Ludby).

20. The Fire Raisers by Max Frisch and **The Public Eye** by Peter Shaffer
(Nov 66)
A School production, experimenting with a double bill and two directors, with Tony Morse choosing to direct the Shaffer, a choice disapproved on moral grounds by some critics. Itself part of a double bill, this play was verbal and witty but dramatically thin. 'The Fire Raisers' made a good

---

[2] Inspired by Chinese style (and seeing "The Royal Hunt of the Sun" at Chichester with its music and mime), this is one of the "Five Arena Plays" published by Heinemann in the 70's and it was chosen for a School Anthology of short plays by a South African editor.

[3] "Under Beachy Head" picked out as a very good arena play.

[4] "The Chimney Sweeps" picked out as a very good arena play.

A PLETHORA OF PLAY PRODUCTIONS

contrast in content and style, it was well performed, and built up tension successfully and it climaxed with a fine conflagration via lighting and a gauze wall (Geoff Newman's skill). A comic firemen's Chorus adds to the fun, but effective tension created by the lead performers. No problems but perhaps a double bill gets a bit competitive or divisive for the performers (and directors?).

21. Five in One Arena Plays: No 6 *(April 67)*
Competent set of one act plays, but less exciting that the previous year. "Too Many Hands" (Simon Burr) a lively north country comedy, "Tomorrow Will Never Come" (J. Aukett) plot not registered, "The Old Man" (Stephen Burrows), an existential study with Chris Joyce excelling, "A Spade in the Works" (improvised by a Middle School Group with Nick Nye now back teaching English) rich comic situation but paced too slowly, "Michelangelo" (John Cummings) a creditable effort to dramatise heroic sculpting.

22. West Side Story by Leonard Bernstein, Laurens and Sondheim (May 67)
A large-scale 'town' occasion, performed at the Congress Theatre, sponsored by Eastbourne College centenary, involving both some adults and pupils from private and state schools (mainly Eastbourne College). The professional Congress stage is not intimidating for the inspired cast, with clever mobile scaffold towers, excellent dancing and firm musical accompaniment. It was an artistic success by any standards, the audiences raved – a perverse review by local paper caused a backlash protest from townsfolk. The production was masterminded by Marguerite Causley (choreography), John Walker (Music) and HMM (Director). We rehearsed at Eastbourne College for over a year, too long for me but MC never faltered. Nicholas Hills's setting was effective, David Blake's lighting excellent. Widely reviewed as outstanding youth theatre.

23. The Life of Galileo by Berthold Brecht (Dec 1968)
Probably a difficult play for a school production, with many scenes, ensemble playing and many characters. I included anyone who wanted to take part (more than 40), some loose performances consequently - better to have doubled up parts amongst fewer (but more skilled) players. John Huddart rose to the challenge of playing Galileo very intelligently. High School support good. I think we kept the action moving rapidly but perhaps 'the plot' got rather complex. Although it impressed audiences ("interesting subject" etc), it was beyond our powers in practice.

24. The Italian Straw Hat by Eugene Labiche (Dec 1969)
Perhaps an antidote to previous year's weighty drama, this was enjoyable to rehearse and perform. The High School girls (with Jill Watkins choreographing) were invaluable, lifting the boys' dance and movement. We set the play in the twenties and introduced the Charleston, played by a little jazz band, led by Kevin Chapman. Lots of colourful characterisation. Quoting RG: "If the undertaking represented a daring venture by the cast into a field in which the school's dramatic history had given them no experience, the result tended to prove that an acting tradition is a good equipment for any style." An acting tradition eh? High praise. This could also apply to Stage Management. My policy has been to give Sixth formers responsibility for stage crew management and several 'specialists' have done well. None more than Geoff Moore, who became a regular National Youth Theatre Stage Manager in the summer of 1969.

25. Five in One Arena Plays: No 7 (Nov 70)
A postponement of this quintet from 1969, when performed it became one of the outstanding presentations. "Ransoms at Agincourt" (Peter Lambert) concerned 'Henry V' seen through the eyes of minor characters – ingenious, "Strike while the Tea's Hot" (L. Burton and A. Prout) a work-place comedy, "A Place in the Country" (Roma Hayes) a family drama, by a High School contributor, "A Stag for Breakfast" (Nigel Broome) a rollicking farce, and "The Children's Crusade" (HMM)[5], a mediaeval 'community' drama with a cast of 100 middle school pupils, and also some staff performers. This arena play was performed at the Gardner Arts Centre in March 1971 as part of a County Schools festival and received accolades.

26. The Tempest by William Shakespeare (Jan 1971)
A School production with a fairly inexperienced cast, including Simon (cabin boy). Eventually worked satisfactorily, though probably rather a slow pace. Nigel Broome (fresh from touring EOC opera of Britten's Dream) does well as Prospero but support a bit rigid from courtiers. Caliban and Ariel, Trinculo and Stephano well characterised. Effective costumes and scenery, though I should have employed more special effects, despite the Herald critic's comment: "So sophisticated are the stage design and lighting techniques that they introduce a fresh imagery to the play". Lots of background music (but whose I forget).

---

[5] It was this play that stimulated the idea of publishing some of our Arena plays (by Heinemann Educational).

A PLETHORA OF PLAY PRODUCTIONS

27. **Widower's Houses** by Bernard Shaw (Dec 1972)
An unusual choice for a School play but well worth it, despite the small cast. Topical theme (Rachmanism). Very enjoyable rehearsing intense scenes, with girls unusually from Coll. of F.E. (more mature). The male leads very well characterised. The three-scene stage design good – first scene has garden setting with a proliferation of pot plants remarkably loaned by the Borough Dept, other two interiors scenes suitably Victorian. Colin Brook as S.M. very capable.

28. **Five in One Arena Plays: No 8** (April 1973)
Versatile experimental work evident, with a Mime improvisation duo, middle school Improvisation exercises round a Black Box, a farce set in a railway carriage, a domestic family drama, and rock group drama. Mirror Image (H. Cosham and M. Read), The Black Box (Middle school group), The Fleeing Scotsman (N Robson), The Holiday (HMM & Ian Thomas), Spin us another one, do (N. Chapman). Performed and highly praised at Gardner Arts Centre as part of Schools drama festival. Son Simon in evidence in The Black Box.

29. **Under Milk Wood** by Dylan Thomas (May 73)
Having joined the Shakespeare Society, I produced this 'experimental' endeavour at the Library Theatre. Michael Brewer and Alan Edlund are key stage management. Pleasant adult company for a change! Production works well, enjoyably rehearsed and played with real vigour and insight by the large cast. Appreciative audience but whatever happened to follow-up policy?

30. **Macbeth** by William Shakespeare (Dec 73)
A School production. The plan to perform this tragedy nearly ditched as the lead actor leaves unexpectedly. David Balcombe (age 14) remarkably offers to play Macbeth and succeeds brilliantly. He will eventually become a National Youth Theatre actor. Lady Macbeth from Lewes, Witches are Sixth formers, enthusiastic support from large cast. Kilts etc well made from canvas. An effective set devised, trying to make space enough for plenty of movement.

25. **A Midsummer Night's Dream** by William Shakespeare (May 74)
A Shakespeare Society production. Performed at The Hippodrome Theatre after visiting Mayfield College. I set the play in the twenties, no doubt with memories of "The Italian Straw Hat" – and Sidney Bechet Jazz numbers. Mixed cast, some very good performers. My set was quite elaborate and the

transformation scene was judged 'professional' by Hippodrome stage hands. Audiences rather thin.

26. **Rosencrantz and Guildenstern are Dead** by Tom Stoppard (Dec 74)
    An ambitious School production that included at least 15 members of staff, most of them courtiers. The leads brilliantly played by David Balcombe and Graham Long, both Sixth formers. For once I have important role to play, the Player-King, as well as directing. Chris Mason visits and provides gratifying praise in review – "His voice was somewhat Robert Donat gone to seed." Altogether a very enjoyable production with two star performances.

27. **The Importance of being Earnest** by Oscar Wilde (March 75)
    This was my third production for the Shakespeare Society. Again, touring to Mayfield College and then performing at the Hippodrome Theatre. Disaster in auditorium, 'new' seats (from Stratford RSC) found to be flea-ridden. Temporary seating uncomfortable, audience even thinner. Yet the actual show was well played by an experienced cast, a pity it bombed. The writing is on the wall for the Shakespeare Society.

28. **Next Time I'll Sing to You** by James Saunders (Oct 75)
    The Travellers Touring Group is created from the demise of the Shakespeare Society, based on Theatre in Education principles. I decide to direct avant-garde contemporary play. A strong cast includes myself, Kevin Anderson and David Balcombe from school. Also Brian Ayres and Judith Allen. We tour to five venues, ending at Teacher's Centre, Eastbourne.

29. **Five in One Arena Plays: No 9** (Dec 75)
    Another interesting experimental quintet, after a respite. Kevin Anderson (staff) contributes play. Repeat Harlequin (Chris Walter & Jas Pyman), Wish You Were Here (Kate Morley), Occupying Power (Kevin Anderson), The Wooden Horse (large Middle school ensemble), Esprit de Communicor (HMM). Daughter Kate contributes from High School, writes one play, acts in another. The Wooden Horse sets Troy in a prep school – adapted as a musical later. Four of the plays were performed at the Gardner Arts Centre (East Sussex Drama Festival) and highly praised. Later in year, Colin Brook, 'boy' stage manager leaves – one of the succession of handpicked boffins who organise back stage. David Balcombe joins the NYT in London.

A PLETHORA OF PLAY PRODUCTIONS

30. **Frankenstein** by David Campton (Feb 76)
    The Travellers on a major tour of Sussex Schools, culminating at Bluecoats Horsham Arts Centre to a packed house. According to official report, our production was voted the 'best play' of the year. Very exciting venue. The production entirely in the round, an excellent cast, sound effects, and Michael Brewer stage-managing. We hire diesel van from Charles Vance to aid touring. I edit a booklet of essays contributed by various teachers and experts on 'Frankenstein' themes, which I still retain and admire. This is TIE in action.

31. **Under Milk Wood** by Dylan Thomas (Dec 76)
    A School production, though somewhat based on the concept for the Shakespeare Society in 1973. A mixed younger team of performers, with some problems over casting. No High School girls, but two lively damsels from Ratton and also Cavendish, plus Primary children, but transvestite gossips from Sixth form. The Narrator (Ian Brady) and Captain Cat (Michael Seeram) do well but the performance never quite reaches a convincing climax.

32. **Othello** by William Shakespeare (Feb 77)
    The Travellers on another successful tour, with David Morley (no relation) as Othello and Brian Ayres as Iago. Strong performers both, particularly in the intense scenes. Good support from Kevin Anderson as Cassio, Christine Carter as Desdemona (they marry later on!). Costumes well selected. Wintry conditions for touring and a power cut to boot. Rikki Warburton reviews: "The best amateur "Othello" we can expect!"

33. **Two Plays for Children** by Michael Morley (April 77)
    A Travellers production touring Primary Schools in East Sussex. "The Tale of the Four Winds" and "The Monument" (co-author C.J. Mason), both originating in Arena Theatre. Although successful, the number of performers made this an elaborate mobile show and performance times were sometimes inconvenient. Travellers' tours continue for a further five years but I begin to pull out of committed involvement. My private life goes awry.

34. **Thieves' Carnival** by Jean Anouilh (July 77)
    A School production in the King's Drive hall celebrating the amalgamation of the two schools, with a lively Grammar-High cast. This is fated to be the last production in this hall, and it was extremely popular as entertainment. Some good improvised (musical) comedy. An excellent set with foliage and

shrubs etc borrowed from the Borough. Malcolm Hayes and Nick Harrison shine.

The Hall is burned to the ground in the middle of the Autumn term (during the Firemen's strike). This act of arson by a Fifth Former destroys the planned production of "Twelfth Night" at King's Drive as the entire set on stage and a range of Elizabethan costumes hired from EODS are obliterated. Productions of plays and "Five in One Arena Plays at King's Drive no longer possible.

C. Period 1977–1980. The Grammar and High Schools amalgamate. The King's Drive Hall burned down in October 77. School Productions restricted to High School Hall, Eldon Road, for three years.

35. **Twelfth Night** by William Shakespeare (Nov 77)
    A School production (Eldon Road). Given the emergency, the stage set and costumes improvised successfully with help from sympathizers. The cast rise to the occasion – production conventional but praised! The lead performances catch the mood of the play. The girls in the ascendant for once. Despite the rehearsing handicap, this turns into quite a lavish, stylish show.

36. **I am of Irelonde** A Miscellany for the Towner Arts Festival (Oct 78)
    A school presentation with items from High and Grammar pupils, a multi-media show presenting aspects of Ireland ancient and modern. Well supported and highly praised.

37. **Caste** by T.W. Robertson (Dec 78)
    A School production (Eldon Road). An 'A' level text, but interesting enough to provide a topical and melodramatic appeal. The play's three sets were successfully Victorian. A small but talented cast of eight (a music group in costume under the baton of Reg Bertin provides entr'acte Victoriana). First sight of Alexandra backstage, with daughter Tania playing comedy rôle ably. Enjoyably rehearsed with intelligent characterization but not quite capturing the over-the-top melodrama.

38. **And So Ad Infinitum, A Musical Insect Play** by K & J Capek (Feb 79)
    A School production. (Eldon Road) An additional presentation encouraged by County Hall adviser who wants a suitable festive show. Plastic/rubber mask-making equipment provided, and we organise large scale insect cast with costumes etc. This time (compare previous production) the play transformed into a musical version, which exploits changing popular music,

A PLETHORA OF PLAY PRODUCTIONS

styles through decades. Elaborate set built. Transferred to the Winter Garden stage for one final performance to mark the retirement of Chief Education Officer. Some good acting, dancing, singing from the leads and chorus line, involving over fifty in insect roles. There have been three productions of my Insect script at secondary schools (by ex-pupils now teaching).

39. Three Plays by W.B. Yeats (Dec 79)
A School production (Eldon Road) "The Words upon the Window-pane", "A Full Moon in March" and "On Baile's Strand". This was certainly 'experimental' drama and possibly rather over the heads of most of the audience. Still, most interesting to produce. Three styles of drama – naturalistic, poetic and epic. Performed very well, I think. An extremely successful stage design for three very different settings. This was the last presentation at Eldon Road before the transfer back to King's Drive site.

D. Period 1980–1990. Grammar-High School becomes the Sixth Form College. New Hall on King's Drive site opened.

40. Our Town by Thornton Wilder (Sept 80)
A College production. Experimental, in the new hall without a stage. With talented middle school pupils this was testing the open space and the lighting (the play demands no scenic backing). Extremely well performed by young actors. Unexpectedly moving.

41. The Italian Straw Hat by Eugene Labiche (Dec 80)
A College production. Experimental version 'in the round' with Art Nouveau features (thanks to Rosemary and Martin Jeanneret). Music and movement, robust knockabout and caricature. Enjoyable though farce is not really suitable for such close exposure to the audience. The previous version I directed years ago worked better on the proscenium stage. Geoff Newman good on lighting effects.

42. Coventry Mystery Plays (Dec 81)
A College production. A further experiment with space and movement. The audience placed in blocks against the walls. The central area variously used for scenes with a trolley helping scenic movement. Effective overhead 'stained glass' panel and stunning collapsible Cross made by Borough Dept. Christ on the Cross highly dramatic. Effective costumes, many hired from Lewes LT. Play builds to a splendid climax. Many lauds. "Excellent use of resources" (GWMK). Certainly a highly convincing presentation. A kind of freewheeling production on a very big scale (50 in cast), inspired perhaps by

my 'caravan' experience, embracing the concept of 'total' theatre. Received the Gazette Award for Best Director of Youth Drama (a new inception).

43. **David Copperfield** from Charles Dickens' novel (Dec 82)
    A College production. Another big test for this open stage, with a roll-up cyclorama cloth now installed – superb storm cloud images in motion for climax. Two trolleys provide set scenes brought on and off stage, plenty of movement, singing, colourful sets. Characterisation well sustained. Costumes good (Jane Seymour). Folk songs, some dancing, with many extras (fishermen, village women, urchins). Ingenious reversible Peggoty's boathouse. Stirring stuff as the cast take over! Also received best Youth Drama Director Award.

44. **College Arena Plays: No. 1** (March 83)
    The challenge to write plays accepted by Sixth formers. The Arena is re-structured with our own folding rostra. A new era in 'theatre in the round' starts. "Maratek" (Tim Paterson) heroic comedy which spawns its own offspring later, "Best Friends" (Michael Morley) lively fifth formers respond, "The Great Mime" (Improvisation Group) imaginative creative activity, "At Greenham Common" (Cheryl Brady), a topical feminist situation drama, "The Bus Stop" (Ken Reed) a symbolic drama for the Staff players, "Do you Know Why You are Here?" (Tim Bale & Jacqui Cowdy).

45. **The Seaside by Side Show** staged at the Tivoli Club Theatre (July 83)
    A College production, an End of Term Revue that honoured the four Music teachers who were due to leave the College, being 'redundant'. Reg Bertin, Head of Music, after many years of impressive achievements, retires early. John Purcell, Classics and Jazz, composer and performer, transferred to Top School. Kevin Anderson, Languages, director, musician, moving to Cavendish School, Rod Watts, Mathematics and key-board exponent going freelance. After a host of well-performed items, the entertainment ends with a mock Governors' meeting and eventually custard pie tributes to the quartet. A sharp-edged satirical show performed with skill and confidence by 'students' (no longer pupils).

46. **The Threepenny Opera** Berthold Brecht and Kurt Weill (Dec 83)
    A College production. Ironically, bereft of Music teachers, I bring in Roger Malley, Music Lecturer at the Coll of Educ., to help the students, particularly to form a music group and to teach the songs. Characterisation excellent, singing surprisingly good. Difficult multi-purpose set built with scaffolding, with startling images projected on suspended screens. Student

A PLETHORA OF PLAY PRODUCTIONS

response very committed to the sardonic satire. Weill's music well played by scratch music group. A coup de théâtre but shocking to one Governor and one newspaper editor. JSM calls round to express sympathy. Impeachment avoided. This was a good show by any standards.

47. **College Arena Plays: No. 2** (March 84)
 The standard of playwriting and performance is developing well. "Son of Maratek" (David Scutt), a sequel to the heroic comedy, "Five Faces of Eve" (Improvisation Group) again using mime and movement, "The Brief Case" (Tim Bale and Jacqui Cowdy) a tense confrontation at law, "Living on the Contrary" (Eva Kannouris) concerning immigration, "Aerobics are Good for You" (Louise Lynch) a family comedy, "Bright Sol is Shining" (Michael Morley) a mediaeval farce performed by the Staff Thespians.

48. **The Wooden Horse** and **The Trojan Women** A Double Bill (Dec 84)
 A College production of two plays about Greeks and Trojans: "The Wooden Horse" started as an Arena cavort for middle school pupils but I revised it as a musical and asked Roger Malley to return and provide the musical backing. The Wooden Horse is a Gym apparatus in a Prep school. Lyrics set to music very well. A kind of violent St Trinian's scene excitedly enjoyed. "The Trojan Women": by Euripides, version by J-P Sartre, is a big contrast: Greek tragedy. A fine bloodied set designed and improvised by John Gregson (Head of Art). The heroic stature not quite achieved, but characterization and dramatic situation well conveyed. Awarded the Gazette trophy again.

49. **College Arena Plays: No. 3** (March 85)
 Again the students provide interesting material. "Under Observation" (Julian Rivett) a monologue for a hospital patient, "Hide and Seek" (Louise Lynch), a family comedy, "The Dry Rock" (Eva Kannouris) adapting a short story, "Daughter of Maratek" (Kate Helyer and Carol-Ann Reddy), aptly providing a feminist slant to the heroic comedy, "Hexagons" (Improvisation Group), another strange mime for the team, "The Nautilus Shell" (Michael Morley), about Daedalus and Icarus, a Staff Thespians play. The tradition appears to be well planted and nurtured.

50. **A Midsummer Night's Dream** by William Shakespeare Dec 85 and March 86
 A College Production. Two outstanding performers are Sue Corbett (Puck) and Miltos Yerolemou (Bottom), but all three categories – lovers, fairies and mechanics – are well served. The Stage crew entirely sixth formers (no

IRONS IN THE FIRE

Staff i/c). The forest set is excellent and the lighting (still Geoff Newman thankfully) is effective. Speaking of lines intelligent and clear. One of the most satisfying productions I can recall. Invited to revive the show at the Royal Hippodrome, we perform twice to full houses, school children at matinee, adults in evening, and make a lot of money for charity. Awarded the Gazette Trophy again.

51. College Arena Theatre: No. 4 (March 86)
All goes well. Metamorphosis II (Sue Corbett) using the scaffold tower gymnastically, Da-da and Ma-ma (Improvisation Group) enigmatic mime and movement, New World (David Prevatt) young men with problems, Halfway to Paradise (Glen Richardson) a symbolic drama, Knight-at-Arms (Michael Morley), a study of Don Quixote and Sancho Panza, a Staff play (plus Miltos).

52. Romanoff and Juliet by Peter Ustinov (Dec 86)
A College production. I think I improved the play by changing Ustinov's three-act structure to two. To provide extra parts, I introduced a travelling troupe of dancers, which fitted nicely into the plot. Also took charge of the set design, using units hung from scaffolding, efficiently opening up on either wing to form USA and USSR households. The up-stage Town Hall with clock was well made too. The political satire mainly registered and the characterization was effective. Awarded another Gazette trophy.

53. College Arena Theatre: No 5 (March 87)
This was the best of the annual Arena presentations and received an accolade from Rikki Warburton – "superior to many professional dramatic performances this year." "What the Dickens!" (Sophia Kyprianou), a comedy set in a café, "Family Circle" (Michael Morley) a tense family confrontation for the Staff Thespians, "Commedia" (Improvisation Group) a stroll in the park, "A Sort of Battery" (Siobhan Downes), a witty legal two-hander, "Excuses" (Nigel Kenyon), a study in solitariness, Lords, "Ladies and Gentlemen" (Darren Shepherd), a hilarious farce. Altogether a varied and sophisticated set of original plays.

54. The Caucasian Chalk Circle by Berthold Brecht (Dec 87)
A College Production. Once again, a battle to tame Brecht's 'epic' people's drama. I think the first Act was well dramatised with pace and movement. Some well integrated songs and music from Nigel Kenyon, plenty of interest in the action, pathos for Grisha. The second half flagged a little in scenes

A PLETHORA OF PLAY PRODUCTIONS

requiring a faster pace and energy before the famous climax of the chalk circle.

I retired from the Sixth Form College in July 88. There were two further presentations of College Arena Theatre Plays produced by Nigel Kenyon, to one of which I contributed a play for the Staff.

I cannot resist recording verbatim this eulogy written by John Morris, Principal of the Sixth Form College, at the time of my retirement in the Sixth Form Review 1988.

> Mr Michael Morley joined the Staff of Eastbourne Grammar School for Boys in 1956, after five years teaching at Sevenoaks School, four years at Oxford, where he studied English as St Peter's Hall and took a Diploma of Education, and three years in the Royal Navy.
>
> Mr Morley was a very good rugby player, having represented Oxford in the University Greyhounds XV and Yorkshire County XV, but it is as a gifted teacher and outstanding producer that most past and present students of Eastbourne Grammar School, Eastbourne Grammar and High School and Eastbourne Sixth Form College will remember him.
>
> Mr Morley is one of those extremely rare people who set no limits to the development of their Art, their personality and the contributions which they make to the Community to which they belong. He was already well known for his mastery of Drama, both inside and outside school, when he was still of an age when youthful exuberance might be expected. The annual Drama productions at the Grammar School and the regular "Five in One" plays involving staff and students, and sometimes girls and children from other schools, were all highly successful. Many former pupils look back with gratitude and enthusiasm, because of their experiences in the dramatic productions being performed at that time. For Mr Morley, however, that was only a foretaste of what was to come. The advent of the mixed Grammar and High School, despite all the disadvantages of losing the College Hall in the 'Great Fire' in 1977, provided theatrical resources beyond those in a single sex school, and Mr Morley put on a brilliant production of "Twelfth Night" less than a month after the Grammar School Hall was burned down, transferring the whole production to the stage at Eldon Road, which was the other site for the Grammar and High School. This was followed in the succeeding year by a production of "The Insect

Play", which was then transferred to the stage at the Winter Garden as part of an East Sussex Schools Festival.

There may have been some who thought that this must be the apotheosis. However, this was not to be. Theatrical productions, which have become an essential and vital part of Eastbourne Sixth Form College life, soared even further in quantity and quality. Every year there are now three magnificent drama events. The annual major theatrical production in the Autumn term, which constantly receives the highest accolades from the critics, and which is shown to parties of children from neighbouring schools at a special pre-first night matinee, is followed in the Spring Term by the Arena Plays, at which five or six completely new plays are produced by staff and students, the plays being written and directed as well as acted by the students themselves or a member of the teaching staff, while in the past few years there has been an annual dramatic romp at the end of the Summer Term, involving staff and students in a Revue written and produced by the maestro himself.

Among the outstanding successes during this epoch, "The Coventry Mystery Plays", "A Midsummer Night's Dream", "David Copperfield" and "Romanoff and Juliet" come to mind, but all productions have been extremely good, and in addition to their intrinsic dramatic value have had the great advantage of involving well over half the students in the College in one way or another.

Alongside these highlights, Mr Morley has also shown himself to be a dedicated English teacher. His own writing is always entertaining, lucid and informative, and he has shown himself capable of inspiring his students with his own enthusiasm and energy. As Head of English at Eastbourne Grammar School for Boys and Joint Head of English with Miss B.A.E. Wilson since September 1977, he has kept fully abreast of the many changes in the curriculum during his long period of service.

Mr Morley is leaving the Sixth Form College at the end of August 1988 and will be greatly missed. He has stood firmly in the fine tradition of those teachers whose dedication to their subject and wide cultural interests have brought additional excitement and buoyancy to every member of the community. We wish him great happiness and still plenty of excitement and drama in his retirement.

J.S. Morris
July 1988

A PLETHORA OF PLAY PRODUCTIONS

Thanks for all that.

Since retirement, membership of the Sussex Playwrights Club, which meets in Brighton, has encouraged me to attempt to write plays. Well, I have written a few but I don't think I have done particularly well in this field of dramatic artistry though I have completed about twelve scripts, half of which (one-acters) have been published, but I spent perhaps too much time and study on what turned out to be "bio-dramas", which are not often popular despite the local connections. I became quite absorbed in Dr Gideon Mantell of Lewes for a period (he of Iguanodon fame) but could not turn his life into effective drama though it was given a rehearsed reading during the Brighton festival of 1995. And I pursued an interesting conjecture that involved an infamous schoolteacher in Eastbourne and Lewis Carroll (Dodgson) without success, though it was short-listed for the Warehouse Croydon International Competition. Through the nineties I wrote one-act plays, some of which have won prizes and awards - most memorably in Clonmel (Eire) where my two entries were awarded first and second prizes. Seven of my one-act plays have been published by New Playwrights Cooperative (though royalties have been more or less non-existent). "And This Was Christmas Eve!", *"The Holiday"*, *"The Enchanted Flight"*, *"Britannia Circus"*, *"Twenty Forty"*, "Chrysalis" and "Best Friends" (Player Playwrights). Those italicised were competition prizewinners.

I have written a few full-length plays: school plays include "A musical Insect Play" and "The Wooden Horse" (libretto available, but music incomplete). Also "Monsters of the Weald" (bio-drama on Dr Gideon Mantell) and "Dodo at the Seaside" (bio-drama on Lewis Carroll) and "The Spirit is Willing" (comedy thriller).

During my three years in Brighton, I directed some plays for Prospect Players at the Brighthelm Community Centre.

55. The Skin of our Teeth Thornton Wilder's expressionist extravaganza.

56. Body and Spirit - My own prototype for "The Spirit is Willing"

57. And This Was Christmas Eve! - My own one-act play

Later, back in Eastbourne, I directed my own adaptation of

58. Maria Marten, Murder in the Red Barn for Eastbourne Central U3A Thespians.
An extraordinary postponement of this production at the eleventh hour was precipitated by the breakdown of our leading lady, but The Thespians (inc. cast changes) eventually triumphed with the production a year later, taking

the play on tour to U3A branches before performing to a full house at the Underground Theatre in Eastbourne.

59. **Congratulations!** A variety show celebrating 21 years of the U3A in Eastbourne at the Underground Theatre.

I have become a Trustee of the Rude Mechanical Theatre Company. Pete Talbot (ex-EGS), creator and director of this brilliant professional touring company, received his initiation into drama at the Grammar School (he acted Owen Glendower splendidly). I am an enthusiastic supporter of his productions.

No doubt by dedicating myself to so much 'drama' in my teaching career I have inadvertently provided a nest from which a number of talented fledglings have flown into the wider world of the professional and amateur theatre. I salute thespians like Mervyn Cumming, Pip Simmonds, John Cummings and David Balcombe and more recently Susannah Corbett and Miltos Yerolimou. I have never actively encouraged young 'actors' to enter the profession (for obvious reasons, I think), and my chief concern has always been to create an environment in which my own creative aspirations can stimulate young people to stretch their capabilities as actors, writers, musicians, designers, technicians, set builders, directors and so on. And of course, I myself have benefited immensely from contact with them.